Enhancing Steganography Through Deep Learning Approaches

Vijay Kumar
NIT Jalandhar, India

Srinath Doss
Botho University, Botswana

Chiranji Lal Chowdhary
*Vellore Institute of
Technology, Vellore, India*

Sandeep Singh Sengar
*Cardiff Metropolitan
University, UK*

Shakila Basheer
*Princess Nourah bint
Abdulrahman University,
Riyadh, Saudi Arabia*

IGI Global
Publishing Tomorrow's Research Today

Published in the United States of America by
   IGI Global
   701 E. Chocolate Avenue
   Hershey PA, USA 17033
   Tel: 717-533-8845
   Fax: 717-533-8661
   E-mail: cust@igi-global.com
   Web site: https://www.igi-global.com

Library of Congress Cataloging-in-Publication Data

CIP PENDING

ISBN13: 979-8-3693-2223-9
Isbn13Softcover: 979-8-3693-4940-3
EISBN13: 979-8-3693-2224-6

Vice President of Editorial: Melissa Wagner
Managing Editor of Acquisitions: Mikaela Felty
Managing Editor of Book Development: Jocelynn Hessler
Production Manager: Mike Brehm
Cover Design: Phillip Shickler

British Cataloguing in Publication Data
A Cataloguing in Publication record for this book is available from the British Library.

All work contributed to this book is new, previously-unpublished material.
The views expressed in this book are those of the authors, but not necessarily of the publisher.

Table of Contents

Detailed Table of Contents

Chapter 1
Silent Guardians: Exploring the Vital Role of Steganography in Cyber Security. 1
    Mohit Kumar Kakkar, Chitkara University Institute of Engineering and
        Technology, Chitkara University, India

Steganography, as used in digital communication and information technology, usually refers to the process of concealing data inside other files, including text, photos, audio, and video. The idea is to embed the concealed information so that, to those who are not expressly searching for it, they cannot discern it. Cybercriminals are still using the internet as a platform to spread malware, avoid detection, communicate, and exchange information. This work provides a thorough examination of the crucial role of steganography in cyber security by fusing historical context, technical details, and forward-looking viewpoints to give readers a comprehensive understanding of this quiet but potent defender of digital environments. In this chapter, the authors propose a steganography concept that is based on a genetic algorithm. This chapter examines ways to embed and extract concealed information in the digital domain, with a focus on the technological aspects of steganography.

Chapter 2

R. Rathi, Vellore Institute of Technology, India
P. Visvanathan, Vel Tech Rangarajan Dr. Sagunthala R&D Institute of
    Science and Technology, India
R. Kanchana, Vel Tech Rangarajan Dr. Sagunthala R&D Institute of
    Science and Technology, India
E. Deepakraj, Vellore Institute of Technology, India
P. Abinash, Vellore Institute of Technology, India

Steganography, a covert communication technique, is important in ensuring secure data transmission over the internet. Traditional steganography methods face challenges in terms of robustness and security. In recent years, the integration of deep learning has revolutionized steganography, enabling advances in hiding information in digital media. This chapter highlights the synergy between deep learning and steganography for enhancing internet security. This chapter starts with the basic concepts of steganography and deep learning, explores new applications of deep learning in steganography, and evaluates its effectiveness using real-world case studies. Additionally, the authors discuss adversarial attacks and defences, metrics, and performance analysis. Finally, this chapter reviews current challenges, future directions, and ethical considerations in deep learning-driven steganography. This comprehensive study highlights the transformative potential of deep learning to enhance cybersecurity through innovative steganography techniques.

Chapter 3

M. Angulakshmi, Vellore Institute of Technology, India
M. Deepa, Vellore Institute of Technology, India

The process of securely, imperceptibly, and recoverably embedding information under a cover image is known as digital image steganography. The application of deep convolutional neural networks (CNNs) to digital image steganography is investigated in this study. The preparation, concealment, and extraction stages of the steganography process were carried out using a two-dimensional CNN. However, the research's technique applied CNN's structure and employed a gain function based on multiple image similarity criteria to increase the imperceptibility of a cover picture and stenographic image. Several commonly used image metrics, including peak signal to noise ratio (PSNR), mean square error (MSE), and structural similarity index measurement (SSIM), were used to evaluate the effectiveness of the suggested approach. The outcomes demonstrated that, while still offering high recoverability, the steganography images generated by the suggested technology are undetectable to the human eye.

    Harpreet Kaur, Chandigarh University, India
    Chiranji Lal Chowdhary, Vellore Institute of Technology, Vellore, India

Steganography, the practice of concealing information within other non-secret data, has evolved significantly with the advent of digital technologies. Traditional methods often struggle with maintaining a balance between capacity, imperceptibility, and robustness. Recent advancements in deep learning offer promising enhancements to steganographic techniques, addressing these challenges more effectively. This chapter explores how deep learning approaches can enhance steganography, focusing on the utilization of neural networks for embedding and extracting hidden information. Deep learning models, particularly convolutional neural networks (CNNs) and generative adversarial networks (GANs), have shown superior capability in learning intricate patterns and representations. CNNs can be employed to optimize the feature selection process, ensuring that hidden information is embedded in less noticeable regions of the cover media, thereby improving imperceptibility.

    Nidhi Chakravarty, National Institute of Technology, Kurukshetra, India
    Mohit Dua, National Institute of Technology, Kurukshetra, India

Spoofing attacks are a major risk for automatic speaker verification systems, which are becoming more widespread. Adequate countermeasures are necessary since attacks like replay, synthetic, and deepfake attacks, are difficult to identify. Technologies that can identify audio-level attacks must be developed in order to address this issue. In this chapter, the authors have proposed combination of different spectrogram-based techniques with Residual Networks34 (ResNet34) for securing the automatic speaker verification (ASV) systems. The methodology uses Mel frequency scale-based Mel-spectrogram (MS), gamma scale-based gammatone spectrogram (GS), Mel filter bank-based Mel frequency cepstral spectrograms (MCS), acoustic pattern-based acoustic pattern spectrogram (APS), gammatone filter bank-based gammatone cepstral spectrogram (GCS), and short-time Fourier transform-based short Fourier spectrogram (SFS) methods, one by one, at front of the proposed audio spoof detection system. These spectrograms are individually fed to ResNet34 for classification at the backend.

This chapter explores how machine learning transforms health information security. Based on a thorough literature review, it examines the detailed patterns of encrypted internet visits using steganography to protect sensitive health data. A thorough literature review on information security machine learning methods and advances was prepared in this chapter. Synthesizing multiple perspectives created a solid basis. Data analysis, examining encrypted network traffic and picture data trends, was crucial. A rigorous study revealed complex methods that detected encrypted internet visits and created practical steganographic algorithms. The chapter uses thorough data analysis to show machine learning's potential in detection and concealment and weaknesses, suggesting a balanced approach. This study shows how pattern recognition, data analysis, and security secure health information.

Chapter 7

This chapter explores integrating deep learning-based steganography with machine learning to enhance crop disease detection and secure data transmission in smart agriculture. It examines advanced deep learning techniques that improve the security and robustness of steganography by embedding data imperceptibly in images. The chapter also highlights machine learning algorithms' effectiveness in accurately identifying and classifying crop diseases through image analysis. It proposes methods to securely transmit agricultural data, including vital crop disease information, using deep learning-based steganography. This ensures sensitive agricultural data is protected during transmission, enhancing smart agriculture systems' overall security. Several case studies illustrate practical benefits, showing how this integration can lead to more resilient and secure agricultural practices. Ultimately, the chapter underscores the potential of these technologies to revolutionize smart agriculture by safeguarding data integrity and improving disease management.

Chapter 8

    Narendra Kumar Chahar, Manipal University Jaipur, India
    Arvind Dhaka, Manipal University Jaipur, India
    Amita Nandal, Manipal University Jaipur, India
    Vijay Kumar, Dr. B.R. Ambedkar National Institute of Technology,
       Jalandhar, India

The technique of hiding confidential information in digital photos, or image steganography, is becoming more and more important in the field of digital communication. In order to improve security and robustness, this chapter investigates the combination of image steganography and artificial intelligence (AI) approaches. Developing AI-driven steganographic methods, improving security, and investigating practical applications are among the goals. The process includes gathering data, creating models, evaluating them, and applying them to actual situations. The importance is found in better data capacity, stronger security, the creation of countermeasures, and practical applications in a variety of industries. This work supports privacy and data security in the digital age by furthering AI-driven image steganography approaches.

Chapter 9

    S. Rajeshkumar, Vellore Institute of Technology, Vellore, India
    Chiranji Lal Chowdhary, Vellore Institute of Technology, Vellore, India

Machine learning has revolutionized fields like medicine and information security, enabling advances in brain tumor classification, diabetes detection, and cancer diagnosis. This study emphasizes progress in dermatology, specifically in the detection and classification of skin diseases such as skin cancer using machine learning and deep learning techniques. Additionally, the chapter explores how these methods can benefit steganography. Malignant melanoma, with high mortality rates according to the World Health Organization, is a key focus. The researcher developed a model that integrates deep learning algorithms, machine learning methods, image analysis, and various feature extraction techniques to investigate skin cancer using different datasets. Evaluation metrics like recall, precision, F1-score, sensitivity, specificity, and accuracy are employed to measure the model's effectiveness. These technologies not only improve early detection and treatment of skin diseases but also offer new approaches to enhancing secure communication

This chapter examines how steganography can enhance security in cloud-based environmental pollution monitoring systems using IoT sensors. It covers various steganographic methods for different media and their potential use in protecting environmental data. The study explores advanced techniques like DNA-based and deep learning approaches, particularly in cloud settings. The research addresses challenges and ethical issues, including legal and privacy concerns, associated with applying steganography to environmental monitoring. It presents case studies on air and water quality monitoring to illustrate the practical benefits and limitations of integrating these technologies. The review concludes by looking at emerging trends such as quantum steganography and AI-driven methods, stressing the need to balance data security with transparency in environmental research.

Over the past few years, the deep learning technique as it pertains to steganography, the art of hiding a message in public information, has progressed significantly. This chapter compares the different techniques of deep learning-based steganography and conventional steganography. The emphasis in traditional methods of embedding information like the LSB substitution rests on the number of messages that can possibly be embedded and the level of resistance towards statistical detection. In contrast, the deep learning-based steganography approaches incorporate artificial neural networks which enhance the embedding process to optimize the data capacity, security, and functionality of many different types of media. Deep learning methods are, however, innovative and provide more security and robustness, although their disadvantage is the high processing power. For that deep learning steganography is an advancement. This is an emerging trend in the field where deep learning is likely to be incorporated in the coming days as an important enhancement of other sketched vision system.

Chapter 12

Blockchain and Steganography: A Deep Learning Approach for Enhanced

Hemlata Parmar, Manipal University Jaipur, India

Vijay Shankar Sharma, Manipal University Jaipur, India

Siddhanta Kumar Singh, Manipal University Jaipur, India

The rapid expansion of quantum computing presents a substantial obstacle to the available encryption methods, especially those employed in blockchain technology. Because of the impending dangers posed by quantum computing, there is an urgent requirement for more secure systems for the encryption and transport of data. The quantum-resistant blockchain steganography (QRBS) framework is a revolutionary concept presented in this study. Steganography and blockchain technology are both included in this framework, which is further strengthened by quantum-resistant cryptography and deep learning. Furthermore, the authors present an adaptive deep-learning model for steganography that can evolve to deal with attacks that are becoming increasingly complex. Experiments have been conducted to validate the proposed system, demonstrating considerable gains in security and robustness. As a result, this system is an appropriate option for secure data management in future quantum computing settings.

    R. Geetha, S.A. Engineering College, India
    Umarani Srikanth, Panimalar Engineering College, India
    Srinath Doss, Botho University, Botswana
    E. Kamalaban, Vel Tech High Tech Dr. Rangarajan Dr. Sakunthala
        Engineering College, India
    R. Shobana, S.A. Engineering College, India

Cloud is the primary platform that enables the users to upload their documents and allows searching and updating the documents on demand. It is vulnerable in providing security to the stored documents. Cloud service providers are the major contributors of data storage and query services that are maintained in cloud platforms. Searching and efficiently updating the document collection is possible by applying dynamic searchable symmetric encryption schemes. Existing schemes partially address on-demand information retrieval. This work focuses on a scheme which enables the user to search from a collection of dynamic documents in a cloud environment. It also integrates steganography to enhance the protection of sensitive information, adding an extra layer of security while concealing its presence from potential attackers. Furthermore, to insert the verifiable document into the top-k searches, a verifiable matrix and ranked inverted index have been constructed. This shows promising results by incorporating a cost-effective communication mechanism for the deletion of documents.

Chapter 14

IoT-Enabled Steganography-Based Smart Agriculture Using Machine
Learning Models in Industry 5.0

R. Geetha, S.A. Engineering College, India

T. Veena, S.A. Engineering College, India

*E. Kamalaban, Vel Tech High Tech Dr. Rangarajan Dr. Sakunthala
    Engineering College, India*

Srinath Doss, Botho University, Botswana

Prashant Nair, Amrita Vishwa Vidyapeetham, India

*Turgay Ibrikci, Adana Alparslan Science and Technology University,
    Turkey*

Farmers are facing a lot of hurdles in cultivation and earning profit out of it. The advancements in technology are growing rapidly and can be used by the farmers to increase their yield. This work enables the use of artificial intelligence-enabled Industry 5.0 in the field of agriculture. The farmers can manage their farms by using smart IoT-enabled technologies in three phases. The first stage is farm management where they can manage planting time and harvest. The second stage is internet of things (IoT)-enabled monitoring in which IoT devices such as node MCU, soil moisture sensor, and DHT11 sensor are used to monitor soil moisture, air humidity, and temperature. These data are collected and transferred to the user in a secure manner using stenographic techniques. The third stage is the detection of crop diseases which helps the farmers to upload pictures of infected leaves using cell phones. The machine learning models are used to analyze steganographic data which is uploaded by the farmers and suggest treatments for plant illnesses with high precision.

Chapter 15
Real-Time Applications of Deep Learning-Based Steganography in IoT

Harpreet Kaur Channi, Chandigarh University, India

The growing amount of resource-constrained IoT networks makes data security and privacy major concerns. In many cases, the most widely used traditional cryptographic techniques fail to be optimal for secure real-time communication in an IoT environment. This work investigates deep learning-based steganography, which aims to covertly send confidential information hidden along with seemingly innocuous data. Here, the authors examine whether neural networks can support better hiding as well as extraction processes at low overhead, targeting constrained IoT devices. They have analyzed diverse deep learning architectures—the convolutional neural networks, autoencoders—improving payload capacitance and adding robustness against detection attacks. The simulations and case studies emphasize the diverse applicability of these advanced security features in a wide spectrum of real-time applications: smart homes, industrial IoT, health monitoring. Finally, the proposed deep-learning-based steganography offers scalable and efficient aspects of communication within secure aspects of evolving IoT landscape.

Preface

In an era defined by digital connectivity, securing sensitive information against cyber threats is a pressing concern. As digital transmission systems advance, so do the methods of intrusion and data theft. Traditional security measures often need to catch up in safeguarding against sophisticated cyber-attacks. This book presents a timely solution by integrating steganography, the ancient art of concealing information, with cutting-edge deep learning techniques. By blending these two technologies, the book offers a comprehensive approach to fortifying the security of digital communication channels.

Enhancing Steganography Through Deep Learning Approaches addresses critical issues in national information security, business and personal privacy, property security, counterterrorism, and internet security. It thoroughly explores steganography's application in bolstering security across various domains. Readers will gain insights into the fusion of deep learning and steganography for advanced encryption and data protection, along with innovative steganographic techniques for securing physical and intellectual property. The book also delves into real-world examples of thwarting malicious activities using deep learning-enhanced steganography.

This book is tailored for academics and researchers in Artificial Intelligence, postgraduate students seeking in-depth knowledge in AI and deep learning, smart computing practitioners, data analysis professionals, and security sector professionals. It is a valuable resource for those looking to incorporate advanced security measures into their products and services. With a focus on practical insights and real-world applications, this book is an essential guide for understanding and implementing steganography and deep learning techniques to enhance security in digital transmission systems.

We hope this book will inspire and equip readers to explore the potential of deep learning in transforming steganography, contributing to more secure and resilient digital environments.

ORGANIZATION OF THE BOOK

Chapter 1: Silent Guardians: Exploring the Vital Role of Steganography in Cyber Security

This opening chapter introduces steganography as a vital yet often overlooked tool in cyber security. By embedding information in digital files such as text, photos, and audio, steganography ensures that data remains concealed to those not actively searching for it. In today's digital landscape, where cybercriminals continuously exploit the internet for malicious purposes, this chapter emphasizes the historical and technical importance of steganography as a silent defender. Additionally, it proposes innovative steganographic concepts based on genetic algorithms, while offering insights into embedding and extracting hidden information securely.

Chapter 2: Enhancing Internet Security with Deep Learning and Steganography

In this chapter, we delve into how the combination of deep learning and steganography offers new avenues for securing data transmission over the internet. As traditional steganographic methods face increasing challenges, deep learning emerges as a transformative force, improving the robustness and imperceptibility of hidden information. This chapter outlines the foundational principles of both fields and presents real-world case studies that demonstrate their effectiveness. Moreover, it discusses adversarial attacks and defenses, performance metrics, and ethical considerations, making the case for the integration of deep learning as a key tool in enhancing cybersecurity.

Chapter 3: Image Steganography Using Deep Learning Techniques

Focusing on image steganography, this chapter explores the secure embedding of information in digital images using deep convolutional neural networks (CNNs). It highlights a two-dimensional CNN-based methodology designed to improve the imperceptibility of hidden images while maintaining their recoverability. A comprehensive analysis of image metrics such as PSNR, MSE, and SSIM underscores the effectiveness of this approach, demonstrating that the proposed steganographic images remain undetectable to the human eye. The chapter provides a deep dive into the technical processes of concealing and extracting data within image-based media.

Chapter 4: The Role of Deep Learning Innovations With CNNs and GANs in Steganography

This chapter investigates how deep learning innovations, particularly CNNs and GANs, are revolutionizing steganography. Traditional techniques often struggle to maintain a balance between capacity, imperceptibility, and robustness, but deep learning models address these challenges more effectively. By using neural networks, the chapter explores enhanced methods for embedding and extracting hidden information in less noticeable regions of digital media. The chapter positions CNNs and GANs as powerful tools for optimizing steganographic processes, improving imperceptibility, and achieving more secure communications.

Chapter 5: Securing Automatic Speaker Verification Systems Using Residual Networks

The rise of spoofing attacks in Automatic Speaker Verification (ASV) systems presents significant security challenges, particularly against threats like replay, synthetic, and deepfake attacks. This chapter introduces a novel approach that combines various spectrogram-based techniques with Residual Networks (ResNet34) to bolster the security of ASV systems. The use of multiple spectrogram techniques enhances the detection of audio-level attacks, providing a detailed classification and securing the system from malicious attempts. The chapter offers valuable insights into defending ASV systems with advanced deep learning techniques.

Chapter 6: Machine Learning for Health Information Security

Chapter 6 focuses on how machine learning is transforming the security of sensitive health information. Through a combination of steganography and encrypted network traffic analysis, the chapter offers a thorough investigation into how these technologies can safeguard health data. By examining complex data patterns and encrypted visits, the chapter provides practical algorithms for ensuring the confidentiality and security of sensitive health information. The findings reveal both strengths and vulnerabilities in machine learning-driven steganography, offering a balanced approach to health information security.

Chapter 7: Deep Learning-Based Steganography for Smart Agriculture

In this chapter, deep learning-based steganography is explored as a solution for securing data transmission in smart agriculture, particularly for crop disease detection. By embedding critical agricultural information within images, steganography ensures the security of vital data while transmitting it through IoT networks. Case studies demonstrate how these techniques not only enhance data integrity but also improve disease management in agriculture. The chapter highlights the potential of these technologies to revolutionize smart farming by offering both enhanced security and better data analysis for crop disease detection.

Chapter 8: Image Steganography Using Responsible Artificial Intelligence Techniques

This chapter addresses the growing importance of responsible AI-driven image steganography in enhancing digital communication security. By integrating advanced AI techniques, the chapter explores how steganographic methods can be optimized for greater data capacity and robustness. The application of AI allows for the development of countermeasures and practical security solutions across various industries. This exploration highlights how responsible AI enhances both security and privacy in digital communication, supporting the evolving landscape of steganography.

Chapter 9: Deep Learning for Skin Cancer Detection: Insights and Applications

Chapter 9 bridges the fields of dermatology and steganography, focusing on the use of deep learning for skin cancer detection. The chapter highlights how advanced algorithms are transforming the detection of diseases like melanoma, emphasizing their potential in both medical diagnostics and secure communication. The integration of deep learning, image analysis, and feature extraction offers promising results for early diagnosis and effective treatment. Additionally, the chapter provides insights into how these methods can be applied to steganography, advancing secure data transmission in healthcare.

Chapter 10: Steganography in Cloud Computing Environments: Leveraging Data Security for Environmental Pollution Monitoring

In this chapter, steganography is applied to secure cloud-based environmental pollution monitoring systems. By combining steganographic techniques with IoT sensors, the chapter explores methods to protect sensitive environmental data in cloud computing environments. The study focuses on advanced methods such as DNA-based steganography and deep learning to address legal, ethical, and privacy concerns. Practical case studies in air and water quality monitoring illustrate the potential of steganography to enhance data security in environmental research.

Chapter 11: Comparative Analysis of Traditional vs. Deep Learning-Based Steganography Techniques

Chapter 11 provides a comparative analysis of traditional steganography methods and their deep learning-based counterparts. Traditional techniques, such as LSB substitution, are evaluated against more modern, deep learning-enhanced methods, which optimize data capacity, security, and functionality. Although deep learning offers significant advantages in robustness and imperceptibility, the chapter also discusses the high computational costs associated with these methods. This comparison highlights the future of steganography as it evolves alongside deep learning technologies.

Chapter 12: Blockchain and Steganography: A Deep Learning Approach for Enhanced Security

This chapter presents a Quantum-Resistant Blockchain Steganography (QRBS) framework that combines steganography, blockchain, and quantum-resistant cryptography to address the growing threats posed by quantum computing. The chapter introduces an adaptive deep learning model designed to counter increasingly complex attacks, making it suitable for secure data management in future quantum environments. Experimental results validate the proposed system, underscoring its potential as a robust solution for ensuring secure data transmission in blockchain systems.

Chapter 13: An Efficient Keyword-Based Search Mechanism in Encrypted Cloud Storage Using Symmetric Key Methods with Steganography

Chapter 13 explores a novel scheme for efficiently searching and updating documents in cloud storage environments using dynamic searchable symmetric encryption schemes. By integrating steganography, the chapter enhances data protection, ensuring that sensitive information is concealed from potential attackers. A verifiable matrix and ranked inverted index are used to improve communication efficiency and document deletion. The chapter presents a promising method for securing cloud storage while maintaining optimal functionality and cost efficiency.

Chapter 14: IoT-Enabled Steganography-Based Smart Agriculture Using Machine Learning Models in Industry 5.0

In this chapter, IoT-enabled smart agriculture is advanced through the integration of machine learning and steganography in Industry 5.0. IoT sensors and steganographic techniques allow farmers to securely transmit critical data, such as soil moisture and air temperature, while machine learning models analyze crop disease information. The chapter demonstrates how these technologies enhance yield management and disease detection, providing farmers with precise solutions to agricultural challenges while safeguarding data.

Chapter 15: Real-Time Applications of Deep Learning-Based Steganography in IoT Networks

The final chapter explores the real-time applications of deep learning-based steganography within IoT networks, emphasizing the importance of secure communication in resource-constrained environments. By leveraging neural networks, the chapter demonstrates how confidential information can be covertly transmitted alongside innocuous data, offering enhanced security in areas such as smart homes and industrial IoT systems. Case studies and simulations highlight the scalability and efficiency of deep learning-based steganography in securing IoT networks.

Vijay Kumar

NIT Jalandhar, India

Chiranji Lal Chowdhary

Vellore Institute of Technology, Vellore, India

Shakila Basheer

Princess Nourah bint Abdulrahman University, Riyadh, Saudi Arabia

Srinath Doss

Botho University, Botswana

Sandeep Singh Sengar

Cardiff Metropolitan University, UK

Introduction

In the rapidly evolving digital age, cybersecurity has emerged as a critical area of focus, driven by the increasing complexity and frequency of cyber threats. As organizations and individuals rely more heavily on digital infrastructures, the need to safeguard sensitive information and maintain the integrity of digital communications has become paramount. This book delves into the multifaceted domain of cybersecurity, offering insights into various advanced techniques and methodologies aimed at enhancing digital security.

This volume explores a range of topics, from traditional and deep learning-based steganography to machine learning applications in health information security and the safeguarding of automatic speaker verification systems. Each section contributes to a comprehensive understanding of the current landscape of cybersecurity, highlighting innovative approaches and emerging trends that are shaping the future of this field.

The role of steganography in cybersecurity is extensively examined, providing a historical overview and discussing its evolution from ancient practices to modern-day applications. The integration of deep learning with steganography is a focal point, emphasizing how neural networks and generative adversarial networks (GANs) can be leveraged to enhance the imperceptibility, capacity, and robustness of embedded data.

Further, the book delves into the use of deep learning to secure automatic speaker verification systems, exploring techniques for detecting and mitigating replay attacks. It also highlights the critical application of machine learning in health information security, addressing the challenges posed by the digitization of medical records and the rising incidence of cyberattacks on healthcare organizations.

In the realm of smart agriculture, the use of deep learning-based steganography is explored, showcasing how these methods can protect agricultural data and ensure the confidentiality and integrity of information in smart farming systems. Additionally, the book discusses responsible AI techniques in steganography, underscoring the importance of ethical considerations in the development of secure communication methods.

The insights presented in this book have far-reaching implications for practitioners, researchers, and policymakers in the field of cybersecurity. By combining theoretical insights with practical applications, this volume provides a holistic understanding of how advanced techniques can be employed to safeguard digital communications and protect sensitive information.

As cyber threats continue to evolve, the research and innovations discussed in this book will serve as a foundation for future advancements in cybersecurity. The collaborative efforts of experts from various domains underscore the importance of interdisciplinary approaches in addressing the complex challenges of the digital age.

This book offers valuable insights and innovative solutions that will undoubtedly shape the future of digital security, ensuring a safer and more secure digital environment for all.

Chiranji Lal Chowdhary

School of Computer Science Engineering and Information Systems, Vellore Institute of Technology, Vellore, India

Chapter 1
Silent Guardians:
Exploring the Vital Role of Steganography in Cyber Security

Mohit Kumar Kakkar

*Chitkara University Institute of Engineering and Technology, Chitkara
University, India*

ABSTRACT

*Steganography, as used in digital communication and information technology,
usually refers to the process of concealing data inside other files, including text,
photos, audio, and video. The idea is to embed the concealed information so that, to
those who are not expressly searching for it, they cannot discern it. Cybercriminals
are still using the internet as a platform to spread malware, avoid detection, communicate, and exchange information. This work provides a thorough examination
of the crucial role of steganography in cyber security by fusing historical context,
technical details, and forward-looking viewpoints to give readers a comprehensive
understanding of this quiet but potent defender of digital environments. In this
chapter, the authors propose a steganography concept that is based on a genetic
algorithm. This chapter examines ways to embed and extract concealed information
in the digital domain, with a focus on the technological aspects of steganography.*

1. INTRODUCTION

Since organizations began to employ computers for business, the complexity and
financial implications of cyber crime have been steadily rising(Anderson et al., 2013).
Criminals have discovered a cost-effective way to generate money as technology
between countries involved in international business improves. Cyber assaults from
outside sources are becoming more common and devastating to businesses and other

DOI: 10.4018/979-8-3693-2223-9.ch001

organizations(Agrafiotis et al., 2018). Additionally, cybercriminals have banded together to inflict harm in the name of a challenge, payment, extortion, blackmail, etc. To get over a government or corporation's lax security measures, external attackers often use the Internet to launch their attacks(Jean Camp & Wolfram, 2004). An organization is particularly vulnerable to an internal cyber-attack because of the insider information that source possesses about the agency or enterprise. Given the pervasiveness of technology in modern life, cybersecurity has assumed paramount importance. Digital asset, personal information, and critical infrastructure security has emerged as a top priority in the face of ever-increasing cyber threats(Clark & Hakim, 2017). An enormous attack surface has been created for malevolent actors to exploit vulnerabilities due to the interconnection of devices and the ubiquitous usage of the internet. Ensuring the security of sensitive data and the systems that support vital services, such as healthcare and financial transactions, is of the utmost importance in the digital age(Sun et al., 2019). Cybersecurity is becoming more important in reducing risks, protecting privacy, and preserving the faith that people, organizations, and governments have in the internet as our dependence on it grows(Michael et al., 2019). In order to promote innovation, economic stability, and societal well-being in the face of ever-changing and ever-present cyber dangers, a strong cybersecurity framework is essential(Azmi et al., 2018). Reputation of any organization is at stake when unapproved online access to a client's data threatens their security. It is possible for clients to work with untrusted parties when using more secure and powerful methods(Mittal et al., 2021).Mathematical methods pertaining to data integrity, secrecy, entity authentication, and data origin authentication are the focus of cryptography, a branch of information security. There is another name for cryptography: the science of secret writing. Making data unintelligible to a third party is the main objective of cryptography(Smith, 1955). The two main categories of cryptographic methods used for network security are symmetric (with a secret key) and asymmetric (with a public key). When encrypting and decrypting communications, symmetric algorithms employ the same key for both processes(Yassein et al., 2017). To protect the privacy of stream data, asymmetric algorithms use a public-key cryptosystem for key exchange and subsequently employ quicker secret key algorithms. One key is made public in public-key encryption methods; this key is utilized to encrypt data before it is transmitted to the recipient, who has the private key. It is necessary to trade both the private and public keys, which are distinct(Bellare et al., 2001). The first section of the chapter explores the historical foundations of steganography, following its development from prehistoric customs to its current applications in the field of cyber security. Readers are given a more nuanced view of the lasting relevance of steganography as a covert mode of data security and transmission by way of this historical perspective. Further we have discussed different methods for implementation of steganography and then we have used a nature inspired algorithm to improve LSB based steganography. We have also used regular singularity method (RS method) as a statistical analyser for identifying steganographically concealed messages.

2. STEGANOGRAPHY

Steganography (from the Greek στεγανός - hidden + γράφω - I write; literally "secret writing") is a science that allows us to hide transmitted data in some container, thus hiding the very fact of transmitting information.

Unlike cryptography, which hides the contents of a secret message, steganography hides the very fact of its existence. The concept of steganography was first introduced in 1499, but the method itself has been around for a very long time. Legends have brought to us a method that was used in the Roman Empire: a slave was chosen to deliver a message, whose head was shaved, and then the text was applied using a tattoo. After the hair grew back, the slave was sent on his way. The recipient of the message shaved the slave's head again and read the message(O'Toole, 1991).

Since the beginning of recorded history, there has been steganography. For secret communication, the ancient Greeks would scrape the wax from tablets, inscribe on the wood, and then reapply the wax(Kahn, 1996). Because of this, the message was concealed from plain sight. Intelligence organizations have utilized microdots as one of their methods for concealing signals in the contemporary era(Conway, 2017). Stego has been fine-tuned to an even higher degree with the rise of digital technologies. With today's computers, us can "hide" one file within another, whether it a document, photo, or audio file. The secret data can be sent by email, saved on portable media, or kept on a computer.Steganography, the practice of hiding data within apparently harmless carriers, has a long and illustrious history that stretches back to antiquity(Kannadhasan & Nagarajan, 2021). The ancient Greeks employed a method known as "scytale" to encrypt messages on a rod and subsequently decipher them, making their usage of steganography one among the first documented cases of the practice(Blake, 2010). For clandestine communication throughout the Middle Ages, people used invisible inks and concealed messages within sacred texts(Macrakis, 2014). In order to conceal important information in seemingly innocuous documents, such as photographs or music sheets, steganography was widely employed by both the Allied and Axis governments throughout WWII(Rathidevi et al., 2017). With the development of new technologies, steganography adapted to take use of the internet. Researchers in the 1980s and 1990s, when personal computers were becoming more common, developed digital steganography techniques to conceal data inside digital photographs(Dalal & Juneja, 2021). Steganography is still used in cybersecurity today, for both good and bad reasons. Though it has many uses in secure communication and digital watermarking, it also makes it difficult to identify and prohibit covert actions. This makes it a dynamic and ever-changing part of the information security field's cat-and-mouse game.

Figure 1. Conceptual description of steganography

2.1 How Does This Steganography Concept Work?

Steganography allows us to hide information without arousing suspicion. One of the most common steganography techniques is LSB (least significant bit): secret data is embedded in the least significant bits of the media file.

Each pixel in an image consists of 3 bytes of data corresponding to the colors red, green and blue. Some image formats contain an additional fourth byte for transparency, called an "alpha channel".

LSB steganography allows us to change the last bit of each of these bytes so as to hide one bit of information. Thus, to hide 1 MB of data using this technique, us will need an 8 MB graphic file.

Changing the last bits of a pixel does not affect the visual perception of the image, so when comparing the main and modified files, the difference is invisible.

The same technique can be applied to other media files, such as audio or video, where the information is embedded into the file with little or no change to the audio or video.

Another steganography technique involves replacing letters or words. In this case, the text of the secret message is embedded in another text, much larger in size, and the words are placed at certain intervals. Although the replacement method is easy to use, the final text may look strange and unnatural, since the secret words may not be meaningful in the sentences.

Other steganography techniques can hide entire sections of hard drives or embed data in the headers of files and network packets. The usefulness of these techniques is determined by how much information we can hide and how easy it is to find this information.

2.2 Detecting Steganography

Not many technologies exist that can give investigators definitive information about the presence of steganography, and detecting it is not easy either(Kadhim et al., 2019). Comparing file sizes is one approach. Files with concealed data, or "suspect" files, "MAY" be bigger than the original. From time to time, investigators are able to "SEE" little alterations made to a picture that conceal information.

- In both instances, the comparison can't be made without the original and the "suspect" file.
- It is important for investigators to be knowledgeable about the tools that may be used to conceal information while analyzing a suspect's system.
- If the suspect is in possession of these tools, it suggests that they are utilizing stego to hide data.

2.3 Some Examples of Steganography in Today's World

Steganography is useful in ensuring privacy and security of cryptocurrency transactions and watermarking. Cryptocurrency transactions employ steganography to hide transaction details through blockchain data. By concealing transaction information like recipient addresses or amounts within unrelated blockchain transactions, this technology makes it much harder for third parties to follow or examine such transactions thus making it more difficult for outside observers to trace or analyze transactions thereby boosting a user's privacy. This technique enhances anonymity of cryptocurrency transactions, which is extremely important when users value their confidentiality.

In this regard, steganography plays an integral part in embedding identifying information or copyright details into multimedia files like images, videos, or audio recordings. These are invisible watermarks that authenticate and prove ownership of intellectual property rights as deterrents against unauthorized use or distribution of digital content. The watermark must be hidden; otherwise, the media will be spoilt but by using steganography reliable identification and tracking can be made back to specific origins or owners of the content while preserving its integrity. In the field of cybersecurity, steganography can veil harmful activity inside network traffic. Hackers may hide commands or data in what would appear to be normal packets transmitted across a network so as to avoid being detected by an IDS. Social media platforms are ripe for cyber criminals to use steganography for covert communication. For instance, users could hide information within the colors or pixel arrangements of a picture, which the intended recipients will then extract via specialized software tools. Steganography is not limited to digital media alone. It is applicable to physical objects. For example, invisible ink and microdots can conceal messages on paper documents and stamps.

These instances are simply a few examples of how steganography is practiced in today's digital and analogue world. As technology progresses, new and more advanced ways of doing steganography continue to come up, thus posing challenges for security officers who need effective countermeasures against them.

2.4 Steganogaphy Software

With the help of steganography software, one may insert concealed data—like a picture or video—into a carrier file and then retrieve it. The message does not need to be hidden at all in the original file. As a result, nothing has to be changed in the original file, making detection challenging(Cheng et al., 2017).

- S-Tools-Encrypts audio and video files (such as BMP, GIF, and WAV) using Stego Software's S-Tools.
- BMP Secrets - Encrypt information within BMP images.
- Gif It Up -Messages may be concealed in GIF files using Gif It Up.
- StegoHide -Messages in BMP files can be concealed with StegoHide.
- MP3Stego-Another way to encrypt audio files.

3. ROLE OF STEGANOGRAPHY IN CYBER SECURITY

Cybersecurity relies heavily on steganography, which allows for the concealment of information inside other, more benign data types like text, audio files, or photographs. In contrast to encryption, which seeks to safeguard message content, steganography seeks to conceal the communication's very existence(Sharma & Kawatra, 2022). Some important functions and uses of steganography in cyberspace are as follows:

Covert Communication: With the use of steganography, which involves hiding hidden messages within apparently harmless carrier files, clandestine communication is made possible. In cases when encryption on its own could draw suspicion, this might be vital for safe communication.

Counter-Forensics: In forensic investigations, steganography can be employed to alter digital evidence or conceal signs of malevolent activity. Because of this, it becomes more difficult for cybersecurity experts to piece together what happened and identify responsible parties.

Data Hiding: Steganography makes it likely to encrypt digital media, making it impossible task for unsanctioned people to decipher or access the encrypted data. When dealing with crucial information, this is of very importance(Nunna & Marapareddy, 2020).

Digital Watermarking: This method uses steganography to covertly insert data into digital documents like photos or movies. Uses for this data include confirmation, copyright protection, and intellectual property tracking(Cox et al., 2002).

Enhanced Anonymity: By embedding information in seemingly unrelated files, steganography can enhance the anonymity of communication. This is particularly relevant in situations where maintaining the confidentiality of the sender or recipient is crucial (Kamau, 2014).

Security in Hostile Environments: In the situations where hostile objects may actively monitor communication, steganography delivers an extra layer of security by making it problematic for adversaries to even recognize the existence of hidden data(Ogiela & Koptyra, 2015).

For the end user, detecting a stego container (any object used to secretly embed a message) can be a difficult task. As an example, we have used two containers: empty and filled, for which we have used a standard image for graphic research Lenna .

Look carefully at these two pictures in Figure 2. We are not able to find any difference in these two images of lenna. They are the same in size and appearance. However, one of them is a container with an embedded message. Both images are of same weights in bytes, but the one on the right contains messages.

Figure 2. Comparison between two images left one is empty but right image contains the messages

So how can we determine whether an image is a filled container or not? There are different ways, but the simplest of them is a visual attack. Its essence lies in the formation of new images based on the original one, consisting of the least significant bits of various color planes. This looks simple because the analyst and researcher can easily see the embedded data. And it's difficult because such analysis is quite difficult to automate. Fortunately, scientists and researchers had developed several methods for identifying filled containers based on statistical characteristics of the image. But they all rely on the assumption that the embedded message has high entropy. Most often this is true: since the container's capacity is limited, the message is compressed and/or encrypted before injection, i.e. its entropy increases.

4. CYBER SECURITY ENHANCEMENT USING STEGANOGRAPHY

An organization's cybersecurity strategy may be enhanced by including steganography, which allows for discrete communication and data protection. To reduce the likelihood of interception, steganography provides a stealthy way to transfer sensitive data inside apparently harmless digital files(Sahu & Gutub, 2022). Groups can set up covert communication channels that are harder for would-be attackers to find by hiding messages or data inside photos, audio files, or papers. Digital watermarking is one way steganography may help protect sensitive information, and the technology can also authenticate users and guarantee the security of important assets. When we used this steganography concept with encryption, this method creates a powerful security system by hiding the identity of sender and the contents of the communication. (Mishra & Ahuja, 2022). In addition to other cybersecurity practices like frequent security audits, access limitations, and staff awareness training, it is important to use steganography responsibly, considering the implications for both ethics and law. Steganography is one of the main concepts in a well-executed cybersecurity policy for safeguarding important data and digital assets. The successful integration of steganography into cybersecurity strategy of an organization necessitates targeted training for key personnel. IT and cybersecurity professionals should receive specialized training to understand the nuances of steganography, including its applications, detection methods, and potential risks(Moura, 2022). Network managers and security experts are mainly crucial in recognizing cyber threats. Additionally, employees responsible for handling sensitive information, such as data custodians and privacy officers, should be trained to recognize and securely manage steganographic data(Rout & Mishra, 2014). Training programs should emphasize ethical considerations, legal compliance, and responsible use of steganography to prevent misuse. Furthermore, user awareness training is essential for all employees to recognize signs of potential steganographic activities and to adhere to organizational policies regarding the use of encryption and steganography. A well-informed and trained workforce is crucial for implementing steganography effectively and securely within the organization's cybersecurity framework.

5. METHODS FOR STEGANOGRAPHY

Throughout the twentieth century, both steganography and the science of determining the fact of embedded information in a container - steganalysis (essentially an attack on the stegosystem) - were actively developing. But today we are seeing a new and dangerous trend: more and more malware and cyber espionage developers are resorting to the use of steganography. Most antivirus solutions today do not protect against steganography or protect poorly, however, us need to understand that every filled container is dangerous. It may contain hidden data that is exfiltrated by spyware, or communication of malware with the command center, or new malware modules. Steganography makes use of a wide variety of techniques to encrypt data within various carriers. Some typical techniques used in steganography are as follows:

LSB Substitution (Least Significant Bit)

One such technique is LSB Substitution, which stands for "least significant bit." In this approach, the secret data is substituted for the pixels with the least significant bits in digital assets such as photos, sounds, or videos. Because the least important portions don't add much to how the information is seen as a whole, changes aren't often easy for humans to notice. Eight bits are used to represent each pixel in a grayscale picture. Since its value will only change the pixel value by "1," the final bit in a pixel is termed the Least Significant bit. Therefore, the data in the image may be concealed using this attribute. Since the last two bits only change the pixel value by a factor of "3," it is reasonable to assume that they are LSB bits.Many methods that conceal messages within multimedia carrier data have evolved from the LSB embedding approach. LSB embedding may be used in certain data domains as well; for instance, a concealed message can be embedded within the RGB bitmap data's color values.Each pixel in an RGB image uses 24 bits of information, but in a greyscale image it only uses 8.

For example, a grayscale picture may have the following bits:

The possible values are: 11110011, 11011011, 10110110, 11011100, 11011111, 11010111, 00100110, 01000011.

Suppose we want to conceal the letter "A" within it. In ASCII, the letter "A" has the value 10000001.

Simply by swapping out the final byte with a string of "A" bits, the technique gives us 1111001**1**, 1101101**0**, 1011011**0**, 1101110**0**, 1101111**0**, 1101011**0**, 0010011**0**, 0100001**1**: consecutive numbers.

LSB techniques provide large data capacities(Celik et al., 2005). The experimental findings of a stego image made by swapping out every pixel in the cover image are displayed in Figure 3. The LSB of the cover picture is increased to produce the stego images. N is the number of LSB bits that are substituted for the secret bits. The outcome demonstrates that using more LSB bits reduces image quality.

Figure 3. Demonstration of image quality using different LSB

Cover image	Secret image

Image-1 Hidden Bits-1	Image-2 Hidden Bits-3	Image-3 Hidden Bits-5	Image-4 Hidden Bits-7

The selection of cover pictures holds great significance as it has a substantial impact on the security and design of the stego system. The design of a secure steganographic system is also greatly influenced by the selection of the picture format.

Spread Spectrum Technique: Using the full spectrum of the carrier signal—whether it's an audio or picture file—spread spectrum steganography disseminates the secret information. Because the changes are spread out over several frequencies, detection becomes more difficult.

Whitespace Steganography: A method of encoding secret information in text documents by manipulating whitespace characters (spaces, tabs, line breaks) is called whitespace steganography(Budiman & Novamizanti, 2015). Since adding or removing whitespace from plain text files is less likely to raise suspicion, this strategy works especially well with those files.

Image-based steganography: Data can be embedded into digital pictures using image-based steganography techniques such as palette-based image concealing or information can be hidden in the frequency domain (using Fourier transformations). Most of the time, people can't even tell that anything has changed.

Audio steganography: In audio steganography, data is concealed by manipulating the amplitude of specific frequencies or by employing low-amplitude noise. The goal of audio steganography is to hide data with little audible distortion.

Video steganography: Like image steganography, video steganography encrypts video files to conceal data. To do this, us may either edit the frames or insert data into certain video properties like motion vectors(Chandel & Jain, 2016).

Network steganography: The practice of network steganography entails hiding information in network protocols and data transmissions(Mazurczyk et al., 2016). Methods may involve using low-order bits in IP addresses, changing packet timing, or taking use of unused fields in network headers.

6. PROPOSED METHODOLOGY

The image files contain data areas that are not crucial for the corresponding image's visualisation(Plant & Schaefer, 2011). If these areas are changed or altered, the image will not visually change noticeably, so it is possible to conceal information from view with near-certainty. Genetic algorithm is used to facilitate research into the impossible task of choosing from a large number of combinations. The genetic algorithm is a versatile optimization technique that converts an optimization or search problem into the gradual evolution of chromosomes. After multiple generations, the best individual is chosen, resulting in an optimal or near-optimal solution.

The genetic algorithm consists of three key operations: reproduction, crossover, and mutation. The selection process is influenced by the fitness values of each individual. Typically, individuals with higher fitness values are more likely to be chosen for breeding in the subsequent generation(Shopova & Vaklieva-Bancheva, 2006).

A detailed depiction of the proposed algorithm based on genetics is presented below,

Steps in Genetic Algorithm

```
1.[Starting step] Generate random population of n chromo-
somes (suitable solutions for the problem)


2.[Fitness evaluation] Evaluate the fitness f(x) of each
chromosome x in the population


3.[Generation of new population] generation of a new popula-
tion by repeating below mentioned steps until the end of gener-
ation of new population


- [Selection process] Select two parent chromosomes on the
basis of their fitness based on their


  PSNR and MSE values


- [Crossover process] cross over the parents with some prob-
ability to form a new child.


- [Mutation process] mutate new children with some probabil-
ity at each positioned.
```

```
     - [Accepting process] new children should be placed in a new
population
```

```
     4.[swapping] Use the newly created population to continue
the algorithm.
```

```
     5.[verification] If the final condition is met, exit and re-
turn the best solution for the current population.
```

```
     6. Go to step 2
```

In this article, the carrier photograph is selected such that the least significant bits of the hiding data(image) and the carrier photograph match with higher compatibility, and a genetic algorithm-based concealing process allows the changes in the resulting stego-image to be becomes negligible.

The proposed method achieved some improvement compared to other existing methods. Choosing the right cover photo to hide sensitive data and increase visibility can be a daunting task.

The process typically has five phases, in a genetic algorithm.

- Initial population(IP)
- Fitness function(FTF)
- Selection(SL)
- Crossover
- Mutation
- Initial Population

This process begins with a group of individuals called the population. Bring everyone together to solve problems. People are characterized by a set of traits known as genes. These variables are assigned to strings to develop a solution called a chromosome. Genes are embedded in chromosomes. As shown in Figure 4, the binary digits 1 and 0 are used to represent an individual's gene set and are represented by an alphabet.

Figure 4. Basic elements of genetic algorithm

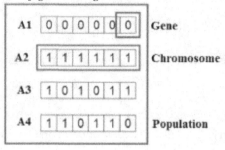

PSNR

Peak signal-to-noise ratio (PSNR) is the ratio of an image's highest potential power to corrupting noise's ability to degrade the image's representation quality. A picture's PSNR must be estimated by comparing it to the best feasible clean image with the highest power. The higher the PSNR, the better the quality of the compressed, or reconstructed image(Sarkar & Samanta, 2023).

As a performance metric for evaluating the results of hiding, PSNR was utilised to assess the quality level of the outcomes from our suggested strategy and the other aforementioned ways. The decibel (dB) value of the PSNR is as follows:

$$PSNR = 10\log_{10}\left(\frac{R^2}{MSE}\right)$$

Following is the python code for finding out the MSE and PSNR value.

```
def psnr(imx, imy):
if imx.dtype != (np.float32 or np.float64):
imx = imx.astype(np.float32)
if imy.dtype != (np.float32 or np.float64):
imy = imy.astype(np.float32)
mse = np.mean((imx - imy)**2)
if mse == 0:
return 100
return 10 * math.log10(255 / mse)
```

We have used Genetic algorithm and PSNR, MSE concepts for embedding the secret image (data) in to host image as described in the Figure 5. Process of extraction of secret image from stego image is also described in the Figure 6.

Figure 5. Proposed method for embedding

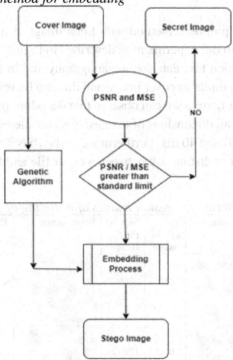

Figure 6. Proposed method for extraction

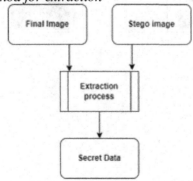

7. RESULT ANALYSIS

We have used our proposed method with Lena Image as a host image of three different dimensions in our experiment as described in Figure 7., and we have used text message as a hidden text data for steganography and in Figure 6 we can see that stego images are similar to cover image and this can be verified by their PSNR values as well and in Figure 8 we can observe that decoding time is quite less than the encoding time for all dimensions of images. It is considered standard for PSNR value to be between 20 and 40 dB. Furthermore, if the PSNR value exceeds 37dB, the human visual cannot distinguish between a cover file and Stego file.

Figure 7. PSNR of different dimension images after hiding of text message

Cover Image	Type of the image	Size of the Image	Stego image	PSNR
	BMP	64 *64		29.19
	BMP	128*128		29.05
	BMP	512*512		29.057

Figure 8. Encoding and decoding time of different dimensions images

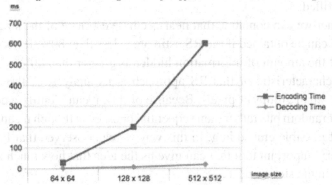

7.1 Statistical Analysis

The RS approach, A different statistical technique for identifying complete stego-containers was put out in 2001 by Andreas Pfitzmann, Jessica Friedrich, and Miroslav Golyan. The approach is referred to as the regular-singular method, or RS method (Grachev & Sidorenko, 2001).

The entire image is split up into many pixel groups, and each group is then subjected to a unique flipping process. All groups are separated into normal, single, and unused categories based on the discriminant function's value both before and after flipping was applied. The technique is predicated on the idea that there should be roughly equal numbers of regular and singular groupings of pixels in the original image and the one after flipping. If there is a considerable change in the number of these groups when flipping is applied, then the picture being studied is a filled container.

The algorithm operates in this step-by-step manner:

- Groups of n pixels $(x_1,..., x_n)$ make up the picture.
- Explains the so-called discriminant function, which gives the value $G = (x_1,..., x_n)$ to every group of pixels, real value of $f(x_1,..., x_n)$.
- We can define a discriminant function for a group of pixels $(x_1,, x_n)$.
- We also define a flipping function that has the following properties:

$$F(F(x)) = x,$$

- Based on the values of the discriminant function before and after flipping, all groups of pixels are divided into regular, singular and unused.

After applying this RS method on Figure 7 we have observed that 34% of the container is filled.

And further we can conclude that near-accurate estimate of the size of the hidden message can be obtained if the RS estimate is less than 80%. If not, it is safe to presume that the amount of information hidden is greater than 80%.

Primary characteristic of this RS approach is its analysis of the quantitative traits of very small groups of pixels. Because of this, it can identify a concealment comprised of random bits rather than sequential ones, even though it cannot identify the region of possible embedding. In this way we can observed that RS statistical method is very important tool that can give us the idea that how much information is concealed in the stego image.

8. PROPOSED PROTECTION AGAINST STEGANOGRAPHY ATTACKS

Using steganography for attacks is relatively easy. It is much more difficult to protect against such attacks, since their organizers are becoming more sophisticated and inventive. Here are some ways for protection.

- Cybersecurity training can help increase the knowledge of the risks associated with downloading media from untrusted sources. These trainings will also teach how to recognize phishing emails containing malicious files and understand the severity of the threat posed by steganography. Individual users first need to pay attention to unusually large graphics files. This could be a sign that they have been stegano graphed.
- For greater security, organizations should implement traffic filtering, as well as monitor regular software updates and the emergence of new patches.
- Enterprises should also leverage modern endpoint security technologies that go beyond static analysis, signature signatures, and other legacy security elements. Malicious code and other types of obfuscation hidden in images are much easier to detect using dynamic behavioral analysis. Enterprises need to focus their threat hunting efforts directly on the endpoints, where obfuscation and encryption are easier to detect.
- Businesses should also use threat intelligence from a variety of sources to stay on top of the latest trends, including steganography attacks in their own industry.
- A comprehensive antivirus solution can detect, quarantine, and remove malicious code from user devices. Modern antivirus products update automatically to provide protection against the latest viruses and other types of malware.

9. CONCLUSION

Steganography is a silent guardian in the world of cybersecurity, offering a unique and powerful defence against malevolent agents. The growing popularity of steganography highlights the importance of having a solid understanding of this covert field as our digital environments continue to evolve. By incorporating technological knowledge, historical background, and prospective perspectives, this work contributes to a broader comprehension of the crucial function that steganography fulfils in safeguarding digital assets. The chapter presents a proposed steganography concept based on genetic algorithms, illustrating the industry's continuous innovation and the need for shifting defensive strategies to fend off cyberthreats that are always changing. Defensive strategies need to change in order to combat the ever-changing nature of cyber-attacks. The proposed steganography concept based on genetic algorithms, which is presented in this chapter and serves as an illustration of the field's continuous innovation, serves to illustrate this. With the growth of the Internet and communication channels, data security has become a major area of study. In the topic of security, cryptography and steganography are two essential areas. During cyberattacks, steganography can be used to hide malware, steal data, or enable covert communication. This means that creating both offensive and defensive security procedures is necessary for the usage of steganography in the digital sphere. Image files play a dual role in cybersecurity as potential threat vectors as well as objects of protection. Steganography is a helpful technique in the world of cyber security that verifies that a user has successfully used confidential data by encrypting it with a unique key. We presented a genetic algorithm-based steganography method in this chapter to improve security. The least significant bit (LSB) of cover image contains the hidden message. To preserve the statistical characteristics of the stego-image, the genetic algorithm is employed to alter the pixel values. We have also seen that LSB substitution decrease the quality of the final stego image as the number of bits increased for embedding. In the last section of result analysis, results demonstrate the necessity of using RS method in order to draw conclusive conclusions about the existence of embedded information within an image's least important pixels. Steganography, which enables information to be hidden inside other, more data formats like text, audio files, or photos, is crucial to cybersecurity. In order to successfully mitigate various risks, establishments must have a different-layered security tactic.

REFERENCES

Agrafiotis, I., Nurse, J. R. C., Goldsmith, M., Creese, S., & Upton, D. (2018). A taxonomy of cyber-harms: Defining the impacts of cyber-attacks and understanding how they propagate. *Journal of Cybersecurity*, 4(1), tyy006. DOI: 10.1093/cybsec/tyy006

Anderson, R., Barton, C., Böhme, R., Clayton, R., Van Eeten, M. J. G., Levi, M., Moore, T., & Savage, S. (2013). Measuring the cost of cybercrime. *The Economics of Information Security and Privacy*, 265–300.

Azmi, R., Tibben, W., & Win, K. T. (2018). Review of cybersecurity frameworks: Context and shared concepts. *Journal of Cyber Policy*, 3(2), 258–283. DOI: 10.1080/23738871.2018.1520271

Bellare, M., Boldyreva, A., Desai, A., & Pointcheval, D. (2001). Key-privacy in public-key encryption. *International Conference on the Theory and Application of Cryptology and Information Security*, 566–582.

Blake, B. J. (2010). *Secret language: Codes, tricks, spies, thieves, and symbols.* OUP Oxford.

Budiman, G., & Novamizanti, L. (2015). White space steganography on text by using lzw-huffman double compression. *International Journal of Computer Networks & Communications*, 7(2), 136A. DOI: 10.5121/ijcnc.2015.7210

Celik, M. U., Sharma, G., Tekalp, A. M., & Saber, E. (2005). Lossless generalized-LSB data embedding. *IEEE Transactions on Image Processing*, 14(2), 253–266. DOI: 10.1109/TIP.2004.840686 PMID: 15700530

Chandel, B., & Jain, S. (2016). Gurumukhi Text Hiding using Steganography in Video. *International Journal of Computer Applications*, 975(6), 8887. DOI: 10.5120/ijca2016909843

Cheng, L., Liu, F., & Yao, D. (2017). Enterprise data breach: Causes, challenges, prevention, and future directions. *Wiley Interdisciplinary Reviews. Data Mining and Knowledge Discovery*, 7(5), e1211. DOI: 10.1002/widm.1211

Clark, R. M., & Hakim, S. (2017). Protecting critical infrastructure at the state, provincial, and local level: issues in cyber-physical security. *Cyber-Physical Security: Protecting Critical Infrastructure at the State and Local Level*, 1–17.

Conway, M. (2017). Code wars: steganography, signals intelligence, and terrorism. In *Technology and Terrorism* (pp. 171–191). Routledge. DOI: 10.4324/9781315130712-12

Cox, I., Miller, M., Bloom, J., & Honsinger, C. (2002). Digital watermarking. *Journal of Electronic Imaging*, 11(3), 414. DOI: 10.1117/1.1494075

Dalal, M., & Juneja, M. (2021). A survey on information hiding using video steganography. *Artificial Intelligence Review*, 54(8), 1–65. DOI: 10.1007/s10462-021-09968-0

Grachev, Y. L., & Sidorenko, V. G. (2001). Steganalysis of the methods of concealing information in graphic containers. *Method of Estimating the Size*, 39.

Jean Camp, L., & Wolfram, C. (2004). Pricing security: A market in vulnerabilities. In *Economics of information security* (pp. 17–34). Springer. DOI: 10.1007/1-4020-8090-5_2

Kadhim, I. J., Premaratne, P., Vial, P. J., & Halloran, B. (2019). Comprehensive survey of image steganography: Techniques, Evaluations, and trends in future research. *Neurocomputing*, 335, 299–326. DOI: 10.1016/j.neucom.2018.06.075

Kahn, D. (1996). The history of steganography. *International Workshop on Information Hiding*, 1–5.

Kamau, G. M. (2014). *An enhanced least significant bit steganographic method for information hiding*.

Kannadhasan, S., & Nagarajan, R. (2021). Secure Framework Data Security Using Cryptography and Steganography in Internet of Things. In *Multidisciplinary Approach to Modern Digital Steganography* (pp. 258–278). IGI Global.

Macrakis, K. (2014). *Prisoners, Lovers, & Spies: The Story of Invisible Ink from Herodotus to Al-Qaeda*. Yale University Press. DOI: 10.2307/j.ctt5vkzst

Mazurczyk, W., Wendzel, S., Zander, S., Houmansadr, A., & Szczypiorski, K. (2016). *Information hiding in communication networks: fundamentals, mechanisms, applications, and countermeasures*. John Wiley & Sons.

Michael, K., Kobran, S., Abbas, R., & Hamdoun, S. (2019). Privacy, data rights and cybersecurity: Technology for good in the achievement of sustainable development goals. *2019 IEEE International Symposium on Technology and Society (ISTAS)*, 1–13. DOI: 10.1109/ISTAS48451.2019.8937956

Mishra, P., & Ahuja, R. (2022). A Novel Image Watermarking Method Against Crop Attack Using Two-Step Sudoku Puzzle. *ECS Transactions*, 107(1), 8351–8360. DOI: 10.1149/10701.8351ecst

Mittal, S., Kaur, P., & Ramkumar, K. R. (2021). Achieving Privacy and Security Using QR-Code through Homomorphic Encryption and Steganography. *2021 9th International Conference on Reliability, Infocom Technologies and Optimization (Trends and Future Directions)(ICRITO)*, 1–6.

Moura, J. C. Z. da S. (2022). *Smart techniques and tools to detect Steganography-a viable practice to Security Office Department.*

Nunna, K. C., & Marapareddy, R. (2020). Secure data transfer through internet using cryptography and image steganography. *2020 SoutheastCon, 2*, 1–5.

O'Toole, J. M. (1991). Herodotus and the Written Record. *Archivaria.*

Ogiela, M. R., & Koptyra, K. (2015). False and multi-secret steganography in digital images. *Soft Computing, 19*(11), 3331–3339. DOI: 10.1007/s00500-015-1728-z

Plant, W., & Schaefer, G. (2011). Visualisation and browsing of image databases. In *Multimedia Analysis, Processing and Communications* (pp. 3–57). Springer. DOI: 10.1007/978-3-642-19551-8_1

Rathidevi, M., Yaminipriya, R., & Sudha, S. V. (2017). Trends of cryptography stepping from ancient to modern. *2017 International Conference on Innovations in Green Energy and Healthcare Technologies (IGEHT)*, 1–9. DOI: 10.1109/IGE-HT.2017.8094107

Rout, H., & Mishra, B. K. (2014). Pros and cons of cryptography, steganography and perturbation techniques. *IOSR Journal of Electronics and Communication Engineering, 76*, 81.

Sahu, A. K., & Gutub, A. (2022). Improving grayscale steganography to protect personal information disclosure within hotel services. *Multimedia Tools and Applications, 81*(21), 30663–30683. DOI: 10.1007/s11042-022-13015-7

Sarkar, A., & Samanta, S. (2023). A Radical Image Steganography Method Predicated on Intensity and Edge Detection. In *Novel Research and Development Approaches in Heterogeneous Systems and Algorithms* (pp. 173–190). IGI Global. DOI: 10.4018/978-1-6684-7524-9.ch010

Sharma, D., & Kawatra, R. (2022). Security Techniques Implementation on Big Data Using Steganography and Cryptography. In *ICT Analysis and Applications: Proceedings of ICT4SD 2022* (pp. 279–302). Springer.

Shopova, E. G., & Vaklieva-Bancheva, N. G. (2006). BASIC—A genetic algorithm for engineering problems solution. *Computers & Chemical Engineering, 30*(8), 1293–1309. DOI: 10.1016/j.compchemeng.2006.03.003

Smith, L. D. (1955). *Cryptography: The science of secret writing*. Courier Corporation.

Sun, Y., Lo, F. P.-W., & Lo, B. (2019). Security and privacy for the internet of medical things enabled healthcare systems: A survey. *IEEE Access : Practical Innovations, Open Solutions*, 7, 183339–183355. DOI: 10.1109/ACCESS.2019.2960617

Yassein, M. B., Aljawarneh, S., Qawasmeh, E., Mardini, W., & Khamayseh, Y. (2017). Comprehensive study of symmetric key and asymmetric key encryption algorithms. *2017 International Conference on Engineering and Technology (ICET)*, 1–7. DOI: 10.1109/ICEngTechnol.2017.8308215

Chapter 2
Enhancing Internet Security With Deep Learning and Steganography

R. Rathi
https://orcid.org/0000-0002-3903-2099
Vellore Institute of Technology, India

P. Visvanathan
Vel Tech Rangarajan Dr. Sagunthala R&D Institute of Science and Technology, India

R. Kanchana
Vel Tech Rangarajan Dr. Sagunthala R&D Institute of Science and Technology, India

E. Deepakraj
Vellore Institute of Technology, India

P. Abinash
Vellore Institute of Technology, India

ABSTRACT

Steganography, a covert communication technique, is important in ensuring secure data transmission over the internet. Traditional steganography methods face challenges in terms of robustness and security. In recent years, the integration of deep learning has revolutionized steganography, enabling advances in hiding information in digital media. This chapter highlights the synergy between deep learning and

DOI: 10.4018/979-8-3693-2223-9.ch002

steganography for enhancing internet security. This chapter starts with the basic concepts of steganography and deep learning, explores new applications of deep learning in steganography, and evaluates its effectiveness using real-world case studies. Additionally, the authors discuss adversarial attacks and defences, metrics, and performance analysis. Finally, this chapter reviews current challenges, future directions, and ethical considerations in deep learning-driven steganography. This comprehensive study highlights the transformative potential of deep learning to enhance cybersecurity through innovative steganography techniques.

INTRODUCTION TO STEGANOGRAPHY AND INTERNET SECURITY

Steganography, derived from the Greek words "steganos" (meaning hidden) and "graphia" (meaning writing), is the practice of concealing secret information within seemingly innocuous carrier media such as images, audio files, or text (Jamil, 1999). Unlike cryptography, which focuses on encrypting messages to render them unintelligible to unauthorized parties, steganography aims to hide the existence of the message itself, making it imperceptible to anyone unaware of its presence. The history of steganography can be traced back to ancient times, where techniques such as invisible ink and hidden messages within wax tablets were used to covertly communicate sensitive information.

In the context of internet security, steganography plays a crucial role in ensuring the confidentiality and integrity of digital communications. With the widespread use of the internet for transmitting sensitive data, the need for robust methods of secure communication has become more pressing than ever. Traditional encryption techniques, while effective at protecting the contents of messages from eavesdroppers, often leave traces that can arouse suspicion and attract unwanted attention. Steganography offers a complementary approach by allowing users to embed secret messages within innocuous cover objects, thereby avoiding detection and preserving the privacy of communications. However, traditional steganography methods are not without their limitations and challenges. One of the primary challenges faced by traditional steganography techniques is the trade-off between robustness and imperceptibility. In order to ensure that the hidden message remains undetectable to unintended recipients, steganographic algorithms must manipulate the carrier media in such a way that the changes introduced are imperceptible to the human eye or ear. This often necessitates subtle modifications to the cover object, which may compromise the robustness of the hidden message in the face of potential attacks or transmission errors.

Figure 1. Methods of steganography

Steganography can be categorized into three types, traditional, hybrid, and deep learning-based methods as shown in Figure 1 (Płachta et al., 2022) (Chaumont, 2020). Traditional steganography methods typically involve directly manipulating the carrier media, such as altering the least significant bits of image pixels or modifying the frequency components of audio signals. These techniques have been widely studied and implemented, offering a balance between imperceptibility and robustness. However, they often rely on predefined embedding algorithms, which may become vulnerable to detection as steganalysis techniques advance. Hybrid steganography approaches combine traditional methods with other cryptographic or obfuscation techniques to enhance security and imperceptibility (Jamil, 1999). For example, a hybrid method may encrypt the message before embedding it into the carrier media, adding an extra layer of protection against unauthorized access. By leveraging multiple techniques, hybrid steganography aims to mitigate the weaknesses of individual methods while capitalizing on their strengths, providing a more resilient solution for secure communication. Deep learning-based steganography represents a more recent development in the field, leveraging neural networks to automatically learn and optimize embedding strategies Kheddar et al., 2023). These models are trained on large datasets of cover media and corresponding secret messages, learning to encode information in a way that minimizes perceptible changes to the carrier. Deep learning approaches offer the potential for increased imperceptibility and robustness compared to traditional methods, as they can adapt to the intricacies of different types of media and potentially outperform handcrafted algorithms. However, they also introduce new challenges related to training data availability, model interpretability, and potential vulnerabilities to adversarial attacks.

Moreover, traditional steganography methods are susceptible to detection and attacks by adversaries with access to sophisticated analysis tools. Steganalysis, the process of detecting the presence of hidden messages within carrier media, poses a significant threat to the security of steganographic systems (Hussain et al., 2020) (Boroumand et al., 2018). Adversaries can employ various statistical and machine learning techniques to analyse the properties of the carrier media and identify anomalies that may indicate the presence of hidden information. As a result, there is a constant arms race between stenographers and steganalysis, with each side striving to develop more effective methods for concealing and detecting hidden messages, respectively. To address these challenges and enhance the security of steganographic systems, researchers have begun to explore the use of deep learning techniques Kheddar et al., 2023). Deep learning, a subfield of machine learning inspired by the structure and function of the human brain, has shown remarkable success in a wide range of applications, including computer vision, natural language processing, and speech recognition. By leveraging the power of deep neural networks to learn complex patterns and representations from data, researchers aim to develop more robust and secure steganographic algorithms that are resistant to detection and attacks by adversaries. The use of deep learning in steganography offers several potential advantages over traditional techniques. Deep neural networks have the ability to automatically learn features and representations from raw data, eliminating the need for manual feature engineering and potentially improving the robustness of steganographic algorithms Kheddar et al., 2023) (Boroumand et al., 2018).

Moreover, deep learning models can be trained on large datasets of cover objects and corresponding hidden messages, enabling them to capture subtle patterns and correlations that may not be apparent to human observers. This could potentially lead to more imperceptible and secure steganographic systems that are less susceptible to detection and attacks by adversaries. In this chapter, we will explore the fundamentals of deep learning and its applications in enhancing steganographic techniques for robust internet security. We will discuss the various deep learning architectures and algorithms that have been proposed for steganography, as well as their advantages and limitations. Additionally, we will examine the challenges and opportunities associated with the use of deep learning in steganography, and discuss potential directions for future research in this exciting and rapidly evolving field.

RELATED WORK

This survey examines the application of deep convolutional neural networks (CNNs) in image steganography and steganalysis. It explores how CNNs are utilized to hide secret information within images and to detect such hidden content. The study provides insights into the recent advancements, challenges, and future directions in this field. By leveraging the power of CNNs, researchers aim to enhance the security and robustness of steganographic techniques while also developing more effective steganalysis methods to detect hidden information (Hussain et al., 2020). Deep learning has significantly advanced steganography, the art of hiding secret messages within innocuous cover data, and steganalysis, the detection of such hidden messages. Through convolutional neural networks (CNNs) and generative adversarial networks (GANs), researchers have developed sophisticated techniques to embed information imperceptibly into images, audio, or video files. Conversely, deep learning models can accurately detect hidden content by learning complex patterns and irregularities in data. This synergy between deep learning and steganography/steganalysis presents both challenges and opportunities in cybersecurity, privacy protection, and digital forensics (Chaumont, 2020). This review explores the application of deep learning techniques in steganalysis across diverse data types. It investigates how deep learning models are utilized to detect hidden information within various media formats such as images, audio, and text. The review covers recent advancements, challenges, and future directions in the field. By leveraging deep learning, researchers aim to enhance the effectiveness of steganalysis algorithms in uncovering covert communication channels. Understanding these developments is crucial for addressing emerging threats and ensuring the security of digital information across multiple domains (Kheddar et al., 2023). A comparative performance assessment of deep learning-based image steganography techniques was conducted to evaluate their effectiveness in hiding information within images. Various deep learning models and methods were examined, including convolutional neural networks (CNNs) and generative adversarial networks (GANs). Performance metrics such as imperceptibility, robustness, and capacity were analysed to assess the quality of the hidden information and the resilience against detection. Results indicate that certain deep learning-based approaches demonstrate promising results in terms of both hiding capacity and maintaining image quality, highlighting their potential for secure and efficient steganographic applications (Himthani et al., 2022). A study explores the use of deep learning and ensemble classifiers to detect image steganography. Steganography hides secret information within an image to evade detection. The research focuses on leveraging the capabilities of deep learning models alongside ensemble classifiers to accurately identify such hidden content. By training these algorithms on a diverse dataset of both normal and steganographic images, the study aims to develop robust detection methods capable of recognizing subtle alterations indicative of steganographic techniques. This approach shows promise in enhancing image security by effectively uncovering hidden information (Płachta et al., 2022). The application of deep learning in steganalysis involves utilizing a spatially rich model to detect hidden information within digital media. This approach leverages advanced neural networks to analyse intricate patterns and features in spatial data, enabling the identification of potential steganographic content. By training deep learning models on spatially diverse datasets, the system becomes adept at recognizing subtle alterations indicative of hidden information. This fusion of deep learning and spatial analysis enhances steganalysis capabilities, providing a robust method for detecting concealed content in digital images and other media (Xu et al., 2017), Shynu et al., 2020, Bebortta et al., 2023).

Xu-Net is a sophisticated deep learning framework designed for steganalysis, particularly focused on images. It utilizes a multi-scale approach, allowing it to analyse images at various levels of detail simultaneously. By leveraging deep learning techniques, Xu-Net can effectively detect the presence of hidden information or steganographic alterations within images. Its ability to operate across multiple scales enhances its sensitivity and robustness in identifying concealed data, making it a valuable tool in digital forensics and security applications (Zeng et al., 2023), Padinjappurathu et al., 2022), Chowdhary et al., 2019). Yedrouudj-Net is a powerful deep learning framework designed specifically for the steganalysis of images. It employs advanced techniques to detect hidden information within images, particularly focusing on uncovering steganographic content. By leveraging deep learning algorithms, Yedrouudj-Net can efficiently analyse large volumes of image data, accurately identifying any concealed data or alterations. This framework is invaluable for ensuring the security and integrity of digital imagery in various applications, from forensic investigations to cybersecurity measures (Hussain et al., 2020). This proposes a novel approach utilizing deep residual networks for steganalysis, particularly focusing on JPEG images. By leveraging the residual learning framework, the model can effectively distinguish between cover and stego images, even when the payload is subtle. Through extensive experimentation, it demonstrates superior performance compared to existing methods, showcasing its potential for practical steganalysis tasks. This method offers a promising avenue for detecting hidden information within JPEG images, thereby contributing to advancements in digital forensics and cybersecurity (Boroumand et al., 2018). Generative Adversarial Networks (GANs) have shown promising applications in both steganography and steganalysis. In steganography, GANs can be utilized to embed secret information into cover images while maintaining perceptual quality. Meanwhile, in steganalysis, GANs are employed to detect the presence of hidden data by discerning alterations made by steganographic techniques. These adversarial models have advanced the field by enhancing the robustness of hiding techniques and improving detection accuracy, thereby contributing significantly to the development of secure communication systems and countermeasures against covert information transmission (Shi et al., 2018).

FUNDAMENTALS OF DEEP LEARNING

Deep learning, a subset of machine learning, has revolutionized various fields including computer vision, natural language processing, speech recognition, and robotics. At its core, deep learning encompasses a set of algorithms that attempt to model high-level abstractions in data using architectures composed of multiple layers of nonlinear processing units. In this section, we will delve into the basic concepts of deep learning, provide an overview of neural networks and their variants such as convolutional neural networks (CNNs) and recurrent neural networks (RNNs), and elucidate how deep learning models learn features from data.

Basic Concepts of Deep Learning

At its essence, deep learning involves the use of neural networks, which are computational models inspired by the structure and function of the human brain. These networks consist of interconnected nodes, or neurons, organized into layers: an input layer, one or more hidden layers, and an output layer. Each neuron receives input signals, performs a computation, and produces an output signal that is passed on to the next layer. The strength of deep learning lies in its ability to automatically learn hierarchical representations of data. This means that instead of manually designing features to be extracted from raw data, deep learning models can learn these features directly from the data itself. This is achieved through the process of training, where the model is presented with a large dataset consisting of input-output pairs. By iteratively adjusting the parameters of the network (such as weights and biases) using optimization algorithms like gradient descent, the model learns to map inputs to outputs, capturing complex patterns and relationships in the data. Table 1 provides an overview of various deep learning algorithms commonly used in steganographic techniques. It highlights the key characteristics, advantages, and disadvantages of each algorithm, offering insights into their suitability for different tasks and contexts within the realm of deep learning.

Table 1. Comparison of neural network architectures for steganography

Algorithm	Description	Advantages	Disadvantages
Generative Adversarial Networks (GANs)	Utilizes two neural networks: a generator (creates cover images) and a discriminator (distinguishes real from stego-images).	- High embedding capacity	- Complex training process
Convolutional Neural Networks (CNNs)	Efficiently extract features from images, suitable for embedding and steganalysis.	- Good balance between embedding capacity and imperceptibility	- Vulnerable to targeted attacks
Autoencoders	Learn a compressed representation of the cover image to embed the secret message.	- High imperceptibility	- Lower embedding capacity compared to other methods
Deep Residual Networks (ResNets)	Utilize residual connections to capture complex dependencies in images, enhancing steganalysis performance.	- Improved steganalysis accuracy	- Require large datasets for training
Capsule Networks (CapsNets)	Focus on capturing spatial relationships between object parts, potentially improving steganography robustness.	- Potentially superior robustness	- Limited research and implementation compared to other methods

The provided table offers a comprehensive overview of cutting-edge neural network architectures utilized in steganography; a field critical for bolstering internet security. Steganography, the art and science of concealing secret information within innocuous cover media, plays a pivotal role in safeguarding sensitive data from unauthorized access and detection. At the forefront of steganographic advancements are Generative Adversarial Networks (GANs), a revolutionary approach that pits two neural networks—generator and discriminator—against each other in a fierce competition. GANs excel in achieving high embedding capacities, allowing for the concealment of extensive information within cover images. However, this prowess comes at the expense of a complex training process, necessitating careful optimization and tuning to attain optimal performance. Despite these challenges, GANs represent a formidable tool in the stenographer's arsenal, offering unparalleled embedding capabilities. Supplementing GANs are Convolutional Neural Networks (CNNs), renowned for their proficiency in extracting intricate features from images. Leveraging hierarchical layers of convolutional filters, CNNs can discern subtle patterns and textures, making them indispensable for both embedding secret data and detecting steganographic alterations. Despite their efficacy, CNNs are vulnerable to targeted attacks aimed at exploiting weaknesses in their architecture, underscoring the importance of robust defence mechanisms in adversarial environments.

Further diversifying the stenographer's toolkit are Autoencoders, neural networks specialized in learning compact representations of input data. By compressing cover images into latent codes, autoencoders facilitate seamless embedding of secret messages while preserving visual fidelity. However, compared to GANs and CNNs, autoencoders typically exhibit lower embedding capacities, limiting their applicability in scenarios demanding extensive data concealment. Deep Residual Networks (ResNets) represent another formidable contender in the realm of steganalysis, the process of detecting hidden messages within digital content. Employing residual connections to capture intricate dependencies within images, ResNets excel in discerning subtle alterations induced by steganographic techniques. Nonetheless, the efficacy of ResNets hinges on the availability of large-scale datasets for training, underscoring the importance of robust data acquisition and curation practices. Rounding out the ensemble of steganographic innovations are Capsule Networks (CapsNets), a nascent paradigm focused on capturing spatial relationships between object parts. Although relatively less explored compared to their counterparts, CapsNets hold immense promise in enhancing steganography robustness, offering a novel approach to concealing and detecting secret information within digital media. In essence, the table encapsulates the state-of-the-art deep learning techniques in steganography, elucidating their pivotal role in fortifying internet security against emerging threats. By harnessing the collective power of GANs, CNNs, autoencoders, ResNets, and CapsNets, researchers and practitioners can advance the frontiers of steganography, ushering in a new era of robust data protection and confidentiality in the digital age.

OVERVIEW OF NEURAL NETWORKS, CNNS, AND RNNS

1. Neural Networks (NNs)

Neural networks consist of layers of interconnected neurons, with each neuron performing a weighted sum of its inputs followed by the application of an activation function.

The input layer receives raw data, which is then passed through one or more hidden layers before producing an output. Training a neural network involves feeding it with input data, computing the output, comparing it with the desired output, and updating the model parameters to minimize the error.

2. Convolutional Neural Networks (CNNs)

CNNs are a specialized type of neural network designed for processing structured grid-like data, such as images. They are characterized by the use of convolutional layers, which apply filters to the input image to extract features such as edges, textures, and shapes. CNNs also typically include pooling layers, which down sample the feature maps obtained from the convolutional layers to reduce the spatial dimensionality of the data. CNNs have been highly successful in tasks such as image classification, object detection, and image segmentation. The workflow of CNN model in steganography is shown in below Figure 2,

Figure 2. CNN in steganography

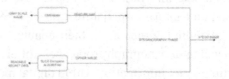

Figure 2 elucidates how CNNs process structured grid-like data, like images, in steganography. By leveraging convolutional layers, they extract features such as edges and textures crucial for concealing or detecting hidden information. CNNs have been pivotal in tasks like image classification and object detection, making their role in steganography vital for ensuring robust security measures in digital communication.

3. Recurrent Neural Networks (RNNs)

RNNs are designed for processing sequential data, such as time series or natural language. Unlike feedforward neural networks, RNNs have connections that form directed cycles, allowing them to maintain a memory of past inputs. This recurrent connectivity enables RNNs to model sequences of data and capture long-range dependencies, making them well-suited for tasks such as language modelling, machine translation, and speech recognition. However, traditional RNNs suffer from the vanishing gradient problem, which limits their ability to capture long-range dependencies. The workflow of RNN model in steganography is shown in below Figure 3.

Figure 3. RNN in steganography

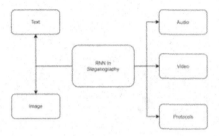

Figure 3 showcases how RNNs handle sequential data, like encoded messages, in steganography. Their recurrent connections enable them to capture long-range dependencies, essential for understanding context and extracting meaningful features from text or time-series data. Despite challenges like the vanishing gradient problem, RNNs play a crucial role in steganography tasks, especially in scenarios where maintaining sequential context is paramount for effective data concealment or extraction.

EXPLANATION OF HOW DEEP LEARNING MODELS LEARN FEATURES FROM DATA

Deep learning models learn features from data through a process known as representation learning, Figure 4 shows the working of deep learning in steganography. The goal of representation learning is to transform raw input data into a more abstract and meaningful representation that captures relevant information for the task at hand. This is achieved by learning hierarchical representations of the data, where each layer of the network learns to extract increasingly complex features from the raw input. During the training process, the parameters of the deep learning model are adjusted to minimize the discrepancy between the model's predictions and the true targets. This is typically done using an optimization algorithm such as stochastic gradient descent (SGD), which iteratively updates the model parameters based on the gradient of the loss function with respect to the parameters.

Figure 4. Deep learning steganography

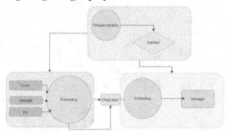

Figure 4 illustrates the essence of deep learning in steganography, depicting how neural networks learn complex representations from data. Deep learning models, including CNNs and RNNs, automatically extract hierarchical features from raw input, enabling them to excel in tasks like image and text processing. By learning abstract representations, deep learning models enhance the security and robustness of steganographic systems, ensuring the covert transmission of sensitive information across digital channels while thwarting adversaries' attempts at detection or interception.

As the model is trained on more data, it gradually learns to generalize from the training examples to unseen examples, capturing the underlying patterns and regularities in the data. This process of feature learning enables deep learning models to achieve state-of-the-art performance on a wide range of tasks, from image classification and speech recognition to natural language understanding and reinforcement learning. Deep learning represents a powerful paradigm for learning representations from data, with neural networks serving as the foundational building blocks of this approach. Through the use of architectures such as CNNs and RNNs, deep learning models can automatically learn complex patterns and representations from raw data, enabling them to excel in a wide range of tasks across various domains.

STEGANOGRAPHY TECHNIQUES

Steganography, the art of concealing secret information within seemingly innocuous carrier media, has a rich history dating back to ancient times. Over the years, various techniques have been developed to hide messages within different types of cover objects, including images, audio files, and text documents. In this section, we will provide an overview of traditional steganography methods, focusing on the widely used technique known as LSB (Least Significant Bit) embedding, and discuss the challenges and limitations associated with these techniques in terms of robustness and security.

OVERVIEW OF TRADITIONAL STEGANOGRAPHY METHODS

One of the most common and simplest steganography techniques is LSB embedding, which involves replacing the least significant bit of each pixel in an image or audio sample with a bit of the secret message. Since the least significant bit is the least likely to affect the perceptual quality of the cover object, this modification is often imperceptible to human observers. By repeating this process for each pixel or sample in the cover object, the secret message can be embedded without significantly altering its visual or auditory appearance. Another popular steganography technique is known as hiding data in the frequency domain. This involves transforming the cover object into the frequency domain using techniques such as the discrete cosine transform (DCT) or the discrete wavelet transform (DWT), and then embedding the secret message in the transformed coefficients. By carefully selecting the coefficients to modify, it is possible to hide the message in such a way that it is difficult to detect using statistical analysis techniques. Other traditional steganography methods include hiding data in the spatial domain, such as modifying the colour values of individual pixels in an image, or in the temporal domain, such as altering the timing of individual samples in an audio signal. These techniques rely on exploiting the imperceptibility of the modifications introduced to the cover object to conceal the presence of the hidden message.

CHALLENGES AND LIMITATIONS OF TRADITIONAL TECHNIQUES

While traditional steganography techniques such as LSB embedding have been widely used for concealing messages in digital media, they are not without their limitations. One of the primary challenges faced by traditional steganography methods is the trade-off between robustness and security. In order to ensure that the modifications introduced to the cover object are imperceptible to human observers, steganographic algorithms must make only subtle changes to the carrier media. However, this can also make the hidden message more vulnerable to detection by adversaries with access to sophisticated analysis tools. Moreover, traditional steganography methods are often susceptible to attacks aimed at detecting the presence of hidden messages within the cover object. Steganalysis, the process of detecting and extracting hidden information from steganographic media, poses a significant threat to the security of steganographic systems. Adversaries can employ various statistical analysis techniques, machine learning algorithms, or visual/audio inspection methods to identify anomalies or patterns that may indicate the presence of a hidden message.

Additionally, traditional steganography techniques may suffer from issues related to capacity and robustness. The capacity of a steganographic algorithm refers to the amount of secret information that can be embedded within the cover object without causing noticeable degradation in quality. While LSB embedding has a high capacity due to its simplicity, it may not be robust against certain types of attacks or transformations applied to the cover object, such as compression or resizing.

Furthermore, the security of traditional steganography methods relies heavily on the secrecy of the embedding algorithm and the key used to encode and decode the hidden message. If an adversary gains access to the embedding algorithm or the key, they may be able to extract the hidden message or modify the cover object to reveal its presence. As a result, ensuring the security of steganographic systems requires robust encryption techniques and secure key management practices. While traditional steganography techniques such as LSB embedding have been widely used for concealing messages in digital media, they are not without their challenges and limitations. Addressing these limitations requires developing more robust and secure steganographic algorithms that can withstand attacks by adversaries and ensure the confidentiality and integrity of hidden information. This has led to the exploration of new approaches, including the use of deep learning techniques, to enhance the security and effectiveness of steganography in the digital age.

ANALYSIS OF PERFORMANCE BASED ON CASE STUDY RESULTS

Case studies provide valuable insights into the real-world performance of deep learning-driven steganographic systems. By evaluating these systems on diverse datasets and under various conditions, researchers can assess their effectiveness in practical scenarios. For example, a case study evaluating the performance of a deep learning-driven steganographic system for image transmission in healthcare systems might focus on metrics such as imperceptibility, capacity, and security. Researchers could measure the PSNR and SSIM values of the stego images to assess imperceptibility, calculate the embedding capacity achieved by the system, and evaluate its resistance against steganalysis attacks. Similarly, a case study examining the use of deep learning-driven steganography for confidential document sharing in financial institutions might focus on metrics such as security and robustness. Researchers could assess the detection rate and false positive rate of the system under different steganalysis techniques, and analyse its performance in the presence of common transformations such as compression and resizing. By analysing the results of these case studies, researchers can gain insights into the strengths and weaknesses of deep learning-driven steganographic systems, identify areas for improvement, and guide the development of more effective and robust techniques in the future. Overall, the combination of evaluation metrics, comparative analysis, and case study results provides a comprehensive understanding of the performance of deep learning-driven steganography in real-world applications.

CASE STUDIES: REAL-WORLD APPLICATIONS

Case Study 1

Deep Learning-based Steganography for Secure Image Transmission in Healthcare Systems (Ding et al., 2023): In healthcare systems, preserving patient privacy and confidentiality is paramount. Deep learning-based steganography offers a promising solution for securely transmitting medical images while ensuring patient data remains confidential. In this case study, a deep learning model is trained to embed patient information, such as medical history or diagnosis, into medical images using imperceptible modifications. These modified images are then transmitted over insecure networks, such as the internet, without arousing suspicion. At the receiving end, another deep learning model is employed to extract the hidden patient information from the received images. By leveraging deep neural networks, this approach provides a secure and efficient means of sharing sensitive medical data among healthcare professionals while protecting patient privacy.

Case Study 2

Application of Deep Learning-driven Steganography for Confidential Document Sharing in Financial Institutions: Financial institutions handle vast amounts of sensitive information, including financial reports, customer data, and transaction records. Deep learning-driven steganography can be employed to securely share confidential documents among employees and stakeholders within these institutions. In this case study, deep learning models are trained to embed confidential text documents into cover objects such as images or audio files using imperceptible modifications. The resulting stego objects appear unchanged to the human eye or ear, allowing for seamless transmission over communication channels. At the recipient's end, another deep learning model is utilized to extract the hidden documents from the received cover objects. By integrating deep learning-powered steganography into their workflows, financial institutions can safeguard sensitive information from unauthorized access and maintain compliance with data privacy regulations.

Case Study 3

Enhancing Data Privacy in Communication Networks Using Deep Learning-powered Steganographic Techniques Communication networks are susceptible to various security threats, including eavesdropping and data interception. Deep learning-powered steganographic techniques can enhance data privacy in communication networks by concealing sensitive information within seemingly innocuous data packets. In this case study, deep learning models are trained to embed plaintext messages into network traffic using imperceptible modifications. These modified data packets are then transmitted over the network, making it difficult for adversaries to detect the hidden messages. At the recipient's end, another deep learning model is employed to extract the concealed messages from the received data packets. By integrating deep learning-driven steganography into communication protocols, organizations can enhance the privacy and security of their data transmissions, mitigating the risk of unauthorized access and interception.

In each of these case studies, deep learning-driven steganography demonstrates its effectiveness in addressing real-world security and privacy challenges across different domains. By leveraging the power of deep neural networks, organizations can securely transmit sensitive information while preserving confidentiality and integrity. As deep learning continues to advance, the potential applications of deep learning-driven steganography are likely to expand, offering innovative solutions for protecting data in an increasingly interconnected world.

Adversarial Attacks and Defence Mechanisms

Adversarial attacks pose a significant threat to the security and robustness of steganographic systems, as adversaries seek to exploit vulnerabilities in the embedding process to detect or manipulate hidden messages. In the context of steganography, adversarial attacks can take various forms, including steganalysis attacks aimed at detecting the presence of hidden messages, and adversarial perturbations designed to distort the cover object in a way that reveals the embedded message. In response to these attacks, researchers have explored how deep learning models can be used both for attacks and defences in steganography, leading to the development of techniques such as adversarial training and robust optimization.

Adversarial Attacks on Steganographic Systems

In Figure 5 the stego image in Adversarial attacks on steganographic systems aim to compromise the confidentiality and integrity of hidden messages by exploiting vulnerabilities in the embedding process. One common type of attack is steganalysis, where adversaries analyse the statistical properties of the cover object to detect anomalies or patterns that may indicate the presence of hidden information. Adversaries can also launch targeted attacks by deliberately manipulating the cover object to reveal the embedded message, either by introducing perturbations that disrupt the embedding process or by exploiting weaknesses in the steganographic algorithm.

Figure 5. Adversarial in stego image

Deep Learning Models for Attacks and Defenses

Deep learning models have been leveraged for both attacks and defenses in steganography, offering powerful tools for both adversaries and defenders. Adversaries can use deep learning techniques to develop more sophisticated steganalysis algorithms capable of detecting hidden messages with high accuracy. By training deep neural networks on large datasets of cover objects and corresponding stego objects, adversaries can learn to identify subtle patterns or artifacts introduced by the embedding process, leading to more effective steganalysis attacks. On the other hand, defenders can employ deep learning models to develop robust steganographic systems that are resilient to adversarial attacks. One approach is adversarial training, where the steganographic system is trained on adversarially perturbed examples to improve its robustness against steganalysis attacks. By incorporating adversarial examples into the training process, the system learns to defend against potential attacks and becomes more resistant to detection by adversaries.

Recent Trends in Deep Learning-Based Steganography, Applications Beyond Traditional Domains, and Evaluation Metrics

In recent years, deep learning-based steganography has witnessed significant advancements and emerging trends. One notable trend is the development of novel architectures and algorithms that leverage deep neural networks to enhance the security and robustness of hidden communication systems (Herodotus et al., 2007). Researchers are exploring sophisticated deep learning models, including Generative Adversarial Networks (GANs), Convolutional Neural Networks (CNNs), Autoencoders, and Capsule Networks (CapsNets), to improve the imperceptibility and capacity of steganographic systems (Herodotus et al., 2007). These models not only excel in concealing secret information within cover media but also demonstrate resilience against adversarial attacks and steganalysis techniques. Moreover, the applications of deep learning-driven steganography are expanding beyond traditional domains such as healthcare and finance. Industries like telecommunications, defence, cybersecurity, and media/entertainment are increasingly adopting steganographic techniques to secure communications, protect sensitive data, and enhance privacy. For instance, in telecommunications, deep learning-based steganography is used to conceal messages in network traffic, thwarting eavesdropping and interception attempts. Similarly, in cybersecurity, steganography helps in hiding sensitive information within digital assets, making it challenging for malicious actors to access or manipulate the data.

When evaluating the performance of deep learning-driven steganographic systems, several key metrics are used to assess imperceptibility, capacity, security, and robustness (Ognjanovski, 2019). These metrics include Peak Signal-to-Noise Ratio (PSNR) (Jamil, 1999) is given equation.1 and Structural Similarity Index Measure (SSIM) (Kingma & Ba, 2014, Fei-Fei et al., 2020, Hardesty, 2017) is given in equation.2. Researchers employ rigorous testing methodologies and benchmarking procedures to analyse the effectiveness and reliability of steganographic algorithms under diverse conditions and scenarios (Ognjanovski, 2019).

The formula for PSNR is given by:

$$PSNR = 10 \cdot \log_{10}\left(\frac{MAX^2}{MSE}\right) \tag{1}$$

where:

- MAX is the maximum possible pixel value of the image (e.g., 255 for an 8-bit grayscale image or 1 for a normalized image).
- MSE (Mean Squared Error) is the average squared difference between corresponding pixels of the cover and stego images.

The formula for SSIM is given by:

$$SSIM(x,y) = \frac{(2\mu_x\mu_y + C_1)(2\sigma_{xy} + C_2)}{(\mu_x^2 + \mu_y^2 + C_1) + (\sigma_x^2 + \sigma_y^2 + C_2)} \tag{2}$$

where:

- x and y are the cover and stego images, respectively.
- μ_x and μ_y are the mean values of x and y.
- σ_x^2 and σ_y^2 are the variance of x and y.
- σ_{xy} is the Covariance of x and y.
- C_1 and C_2 are Constants to stabilize the division with weak denominator.

Overall, the recent trends in deep learning-based steganography showcase the evolving landscape of covert communication techniques, with applications spanning across various industries and domains (Herodotus et al., 2007). The emphasis on advanced architectures, broadening application areas, and robust evaluation methodologies underscores the growing significance of deep learning-driven steganography in addressing modern security and privacy challenges.

TECHNIQUES SUCH AS ADVERSARIAL TRAINING AND ROBUST OPTIMIZATION

Adversarial training is a popular technique for defending against adversarial attacks in steganography. During adversarial training, the steganographic system is exposed to adversarially perturbed examples generated by an adversary, and the parameters of the system are adjusted to minimize the likelihood of detection by the adversary. This process effectively "hardens" the system against potential attacks, making it more robust and resilient to adversarial manipulation. Another technique for defending against adversarial attacks is robust optimization, where the objective function of the steganographic system is modified to explicitly account for potential adversarial perturbations. By optimizing the system parameters with respect to a worst-case scenario, robust optimization ensures that the system remains secure and effective even in the presence of adversaries attempting to compromise its integrity.

In conclusion, adversarial attacks pose a significant challenge to the security and robustness of steganographic systems, but deep learning offers powerful tools for both attackers and defenders. By leveraging techniques such as adversarial training and robust optimization, researchers can develop more resilient steganographic systems that are capable of withstanding sophisticated attacks and maintaining the confidentiality and integrity of hidden messages. As adversarial techniques continue to evolve, ongoing research in this area will be essential for advancing the state-of-the-art in steganography and enhancing internet security.

COMPARATIVE ANALYSIS WITH TRADITIONAL STEGANOGRAPHY METHODS

In comparison to traditional steganography methods, deep learning-driven steganographic systems offer several advantages, including improved imperceptibility, higher capacity, and enhanced security. Traditional methods such as LSB embedding often suffer from limitations in terms of robustness and perceptual quality, as they rely on simple heuristics and do not optimize for imperceptibility or security. Deep learning-driven steganography, on the other hand, leverages advanced neural network architectures and optimization techniques to learn complex patterns and representations from data, enabling it to achieve better performance in terms of imperceptibility and security. By training on large datasets of cover objects and corresponding hidden messages, deep learning models can capture subtle features and correlations that may not be apparent to human observers, resulting in more imperceptible embeddings. Moreover, deep learning-driven steganographic systems can adapt to different types of cover objects and steganographic payloads, making them more robust against steganalysis attacks. They can also be optimized for specific performance objectives, such as maximizing capacity while maintaining imperceptibility, or enhancing security against specific types of attacks.

ANALYSIS OF PERFORMANCE BASED ON CASE STUDY RESULTS

Case studies provide valuable insights into the real-world performance of deep learning-driven steganographic systems. By evaluating these systems on diverse datasets and under various conditions, researchers can assess their effectiveness in practical scenarios.

For example, a case study evaluating the performance of a deep learning-driven steganographic system for image transmission in healthcare systems might focus on metrics such as imperceptibility, capacity, and security. Researchers could measure the PSNR and SSIM values of the stego images to assess imperceptibility, calculate the embedding capacity achieved by the system, and evaluate its resistance against steganalysis attacks. Similarly, a case study examining the use of deep learning-driven steganography for confidential document sharing in financial institutions might focus on metrics such as security and robustness. Researchers could assess the detection rate and false positive rate of the system under different steganalysis techniques, and analyse its performance in the presence of common transformations such as compression and resizing.

CHALLENGES AND FUTURE DIRECTIONS

Deep learning-driven steganography represents a promising approach for enhancing the security and robustness of hidden communication systems. However, it also faces several challenges and limitations that must be addressed to realize its full potential. In this section, we will discuss the current challenges and limitations in deep learning-driven steganography, explore potential future research directions, and examine the ethical considerations and implications of using deep learning in steganography for internet security.

CURRENT CHALLENGES AND LIMITATIONS

Imperceptibility vs. Security Trade-Off

One of the primary challenges in deep learning-driven steganography is the trade-off between imperceptibility and security. While increasing imperceptibility helps conceal the presence of hidden messages from human observers, it may also make the steganographic system more vulnerable to detection by sophisticated steganalysis techniques. Balancing these competing objectives remains a key challenge in designing effective steganographic algorithms.

Generalization to Different Domains

Deep learning-driven steganography models are often trained on specific datasets and may struggle to generalize to unseen data or different domains. This limits their applicability in real-world scenarios where cover objects may vary widely in content, format, and characteristics. Developing techniques that can generalize across diverse datasets and domains is essential for the widespread adoption of deep learning-driven steganography. Robustness to Adversarial Attacks: Deep learning models used in steganography are susceptible to adversarial attacks, where an adversary deliberately manipulates the cover object to reveal the presence of hidden messages. Adversarial attacks can exploit vulnerabilities in the steganographic algorithm or the neural network architecture, leading to the failure of the steganographic system. Enhancing the robustness of deep learning-driven steganography against such attacks is a critical challenge.

Interpretability and Explainability

Deep learning models are often considered black boxes, making it difficult to interpret and understand their decisions. This lack of interpretability and explainability poses challenges in steganography, where it is important to ensure that the embedding process is transparent and predictable. Developing methods for interpreting and explaining the behaviour of deep learning-driven steganography models is essential for building trust and confidence in their use.

POTENTIAL FUTURE RESEARCH DIRECTIONS

Adversarial Defence Mechanisms

Future research in deep learning-driven steganography could focus on developing robust defense mechanisms against adversarial attacks. This may involve incorporating techniques such as adversarial training, where the model is trained on adversarially perturbed examples, or robust optimization, where the model is optimized to be resilient to small perturbations in the input (Rathi & Acharjya, 2018).

Multi-Domain Generalization

To improve the generalization capabilities of deep learning-driven steganography models, future research could explore techniques for training models across multiple domains or datasets. This may involve domain adaptation methods, where the model learns to transfer knowledge from one domain to another, or meta-learning approaches, where the model learns to quickly adapt to new domains with limited training data.

Privacy-Preserving Steganography

With growing concerns about data privacy and surveillance, future research could focus on developing privacy-preserving steganography techniques that protect sensitive information from unauthorized access. This may involve incorporating cryptographic primitives such as homomorphic encryption or secure multiparty computation into the steganographic process to ensure end-to-end confidentiality and integrity.

Interpretable Steganography Models

To address the lack of interpretability in deep learning-driven steganography, future research could explore methods for making steganography models more interpretable and explainable. This may involve designing architectures that produce human-readable explanations of the embedding process or developing visualization techniques that illustrate how the hidden message is encoded within the cover object.

ETHICAL CONSIDERATIONS AND IMPLICATIONS

The use of deep learning in steganography raises several ethical considerations and implications, particularly in the context of internet security and privacy. One concern is the potential misuse of steganography for illegal or malicious purposes, such as concealing illicit activities or spreading disinformation. As such, researchers and practitioners have a responsibility to ensure that deep learning-driven steganography is used ethically and responsibly, with proper safeguards in place to prevent abuse. Another ethical consideration is the impact of steganography on privacy and surveillance. While steganography can be used to protect sensitive information from unauthorized access, it can also be exploited by governments and other entities for surveillance purposes. This raises questions about the balance between security and privacy in the digital age and the need for robust legal and regulatory frameworks to safeguard individual rights and freedoms. There are ethical implications associated with the development and deployment of deep learning-driven steganography models, particularly with regard to bias and fairness. Deep learning models are trained on large datasets that may reflect societal biases and inequalities, leading to biased or discriminatory outcomes. It is important for researchers to address these biases and ensure that steganography models are fair and equitable for all users. Deep learning-driven steganography holds great promise for enhancing internet security and privacy, but it also poses several challenges and ethical considerations that must be carefully addressed. By addressing these challenges and conducting research in areas such as adversarial defense, multi-domain generalization, privacy-preserving techniques, and interpretable models, we can unlock the full potential of deep learning-driven steganography while ensuring its responsible and ethical use.

CONCLUSION

In conclusion, this chapter has provided a comprehensive overview of deep learning-driven advancements in steganography for internet security. We explored the basic concepts of deep learning, including neural networks, convolutional neural networks (CNNs), and recurrent neural networks (RNNs), and discussed how these techniques are applied to conceal secret information within digital media. Through the examination of traditional steganography methods and their limitations, we highlighted the potential of deep learning to overcome challenges such as imperceptibility, security, and robustness.

The importance of deep learning-driven advancements in steganography for enhancing internet security cannot be overstated. By leveraging the power of deep neural networks, we can develop more robust and secure steganographic systems that are resistant to detection and attacks by adversaries. These advancements have the potential to significantly enhance the confidentiality and integrity of digital communications, protecting sensitive information from unauthorized access and surveillance. Looking ahead, the future impact and potential of this technology are vast. Continued research and innovation in deep learning-driven steganography will lead to more sophisticated and effective techniques for concealing hidden messages, ultimately contributing to a safer and more secure digital environment for users worldwide.

REFERENCES

Bebortta, S., Tripathy, S. S., Basheer, S., & Chowdhary, C. L. (2023). Deepmist: Towards deep learning assisted mist computing framework for managing healthcare big data. *IEEE Access : Practical Innovations, Open Solutions*, 11, 42485–42496. DOI: 10.1109/ACCESS.2023.3266374

Boroumand, M., Chen, M., & Fridrich, J. (2018). Deep residual network for steganalysis of digital images. *IEEE Transactions on Information Forensics and Security*, 14(5), 1181–1193. DOI: 10.1109/TIFS.2018.2871749

Chaumont, M. (2020). Deep learning in steganography and steganalysis. In *Digital media steganography* (pp. 321–349). Academic Press. DOI: 10.1016/B978-0-12-819438-6.00022-0

Chowdhary, C. L., Goyal, A., & Vasnani, B. K. (2019). Experimental assessment of beam search algorithm for improvement in image caption generation. *Journal of Applied Science and Engineering*, 22(4), 691–698.

Ding, Y., Wang, Z., Qin, Z., Zhou, E., Zhu, G., Qin, Z., & Choo, K. K. R. (2023). Backdoor Attack on Deep Learning-Based Medical Image Encryption and Decryption Network. *IEEE Transactions on Information Forensics and Security*.

Fei-Fei, L., Deng, J., Russakovsky, O., Berg, A., & Li, K. (2020). *ImageNet*. Stanford University.

Hardesty, L. (2017). *Explained: Neural Networks*. Massachusetts Institute of Technology.

Herodotus, S., Robert, B., & Purvis, A. (2007). *The landmark Herodotus: the histories*. No Title.

Himthani, V., Dhaka, V. S., Kaur, M., Rani, G., Oza, M., & Lee, H. N. (2022). Comparative performance assessment of deep learning based image steganography techniques. *Scientific Reports*, 12(1), 16895. DOI: 10.1038/s41598-022-17362-1 PMID: 36207314

Hussain, I., Zeng, J., Qin, X., & Tan, S. (2020). A survey on deep convolutional neural networks for image steganography and steganalysis. *KSII Transactions on Internet and Information Systems*, 14(3), 1228–1248.

Jamil, T. (1999). Steganography: The art of hiding information in plain sight. *IEEE Potentials*, 18(1), 10–12. DOI: 10.1109/45.747237

Kheddar, H., Hemis, M., Himeur, Y., Megías, D., & Amira, A. (2023). Deep learning for diverse data types steganalysis: A review. *arXiv preprint arXiv:2308.04522*.

Kingma, D. P., & Ba, J. (2014). Adam: A method for stochastic optimization. *arXiv preprint arXiv:1412.6980*.

Ognjanovski, G. (2019). Everything you need to know about neural networks and backpropagation—machine learning easy and fun. *Towards Data Science*.backpropagation-machine-learning-made-easy-e5285bc2be3a.

Padinjappurathu Gopalan, S., Chowdhary, C. L., Iwendi, C., Farid, M. A., & Ramasamy, L. K. (2022). An efficient and privacy-preserving scheme for disease prediction in modern healthcare systems. *Sensors (Basel)*, 22(15), 5574. DOI: 10.3390/s22155574 PMID: 35898077

Płachta, M., Krzemień, M., Szczypiorski, K., & Janicki, A. (2022). Detection of image steganography using deep learning and ensemble classifiers. *Electronics (Basel)*, 11(10), 1565. DOI: 10.3390/electronics11101565

Rathi, R., & Acharjya, D. P. (2018). A rule based classification for vegetable production using rough set and genetic algorithm. *International Journal of Fuzzy System Applications*, 7(1), 74–100. DOI: 10.4018/IJFSA.2018010106

Sharma, G., & Garg, U. (2024). Unveiling vulnerabilities: Evading YOLOv5 object detection through adversarial perturbations and steganography. *Multimedia Tools and Applications*, 83(30), 1–20. DOI: 10.1007/s11042-024-18563-8

Shi, H., Dong, J., Wang, W., Qian, Y., & Zhang, X. (2018). SSGAN: Secure steganography based on generative adversarial networks. In *Advances in Multimedia Information Processing–PCM 2017:18th Pacific-Rim Conference on Multimedia,Harbin, China,September 28-29, 2017, Revised Selected Papers, Part I 18* (pp. 534-544). Springer International Publishing.

Shynu, P. G., Shayan, H. M., & Chowdhary, C. L. (2020, February). A fuzzy based data perturbation technique for privacy preserved data mining. In 2020 International Conference on Emerging Trends in Information Technology and Engineering (ic-ETITE) (pp. 1-4). IEEE. DOI: 10.1109/ic-ETITE47903.2020.244

Xu, X., Sun, Y., Tang, G., Chen, S., & Zhao, J. (2017). Deep learning on spatial rich model for steganalysis. In *Digital Forensics and Watermarking:15th International Workshop, IWDW 2016,Beijing, China,September 17-19, 2016, Revised Selected Papers 15* (pp. 564-577). Springer International Publishing. DOI: 10.1007/978-3-319-53465-7_42

Zeng, L., Yang, N., Li, X., Chen, A., Jing, H., & Zhang, J. (2023). Advanced Image Steganography Using a U-Net-Based Architecture with Multi-Scale Fusion and Perceptual Loss. *Electronics (Basel)*, 12(18), 3808. DOI: 10.3390/electronics12183808

Chapter 3
Image Stenography Using Deep Learning Techniques

M. Angulakshmi

Vellore Institute of Technology, India

M. Deepa

https://orcid.org/0000-0002-4794-7096

Vellore Institute of Technology, India

ABSTRACT

The process of securely, imperceptibly, and recoverably embedding information under a cover image is known as digital image steganography. The application of deep convolutional neural networks (CNNs) to digital image steganography is investigated in this study. The preparation, concealment, and extraction stages of the steganography process were carried out using a two-dimensional CNN. However, the research's technique applied CNN's structure and employed a gain function based on multiple image similarity criteria to increase the imperceptibility of a cover picture and stenographic image. Several commonly used image metrics, including peak signal to noise ratio (PSNR), mean square error (MSE), and structural similarity index measurement (SSIM), were used to evaluate the effectiveness of the suggested approach. The outcomes demonstrated that, while still offering high recoverability, the steganography images generated by the suggested technology are undetectable to the human eye.

DOI: 10.4018/979-8-3693-2223-9.ch003

INTRODUCTION

One technique for concealing classified information in non-secret material is steganography. To put it another way, we can conceal the mere presence of a secret communication by hiding a hidden message in data that we send or deliver in public. Users are much at risk from steganographic techniques since they can be used to disseminate dangerous software or, in the case of so-called stegomalware (Caviglione et .al, 2021), to be exploited by the malware for C&C conversations or data leaks. A significant portion of steganographic techniques employ multimedia data—including pictures—as a carrier. These techniques are frequently called, respectively, picture and digital media steganography. One technique that exemplifies this is the one employed by the Vawtrak/Never quest virus (Cabaj et.al. 2018), which concealed URL addresses in favicon graphics.

An additional illustration would be the Invoke-PSImage tool, which allowed programmers to conceal PowerShell scripts in picture pixels by employing the widely used least-significant bit (LSB) technique. Because of the binary complexity of the GIF structure, hiding information in the file's structure could be still another variation (Puchalsk et,al, 2020). This is a very creative approach. It has been noted that an increasing amount of malware infections exploit various forms of covert communication, such as image steganography. Finding effective, dependable, and quick ways to identify concealed content is crucial since malware infections are a major global danger to user security. Consequently, a number of projects and initiatives have recently been launched to improve the resilience of malware and stegomalware; one of these is the Secure Intelligent Methods for Advanced Recognition of malware and stegomalware (SIMARGL) project, realized within the EU Horizon 2020 framework.

STEGANOGRAPHY

The technique of hiding a message by enclosing it in another safe media is known as steganography. The word's literal definition, which comes from Greek, is "covered writing" (Jamil, 1999). Using the Greek terms "steganos" and "graphia," which translate to "covered" and "writing," respectively, is how the word was created by Trithemius. Using invisible ink was the first known application of steganography. Pictures have the ability to conceal information in the visually boring areas, making it less likely that someone would notice the hidden information there. But other kinds of files can also have information hidden from view. Moreover, audio files can contain information by utilizing a variety of transform algorithms, such as the Discrete Wavelet Transform (DWT), or by adjusting the least significant bits

(LSB) (Cox et al.,2007). We can embed almost any kind of digital data, including text files and other audio files, within an audio file. To this purpose, it is possible to embed any kind of digital data into a cover digital medium. However, the method of embedding one digital image into another is the main emphasis of this study.

Applications of Steganography in Real Life

Convert Communication: Image steganography is used in covert communication, which is when people need to quietly share sensitive information. Law enforcement, intelligence services, and whistleblowers are among those who need secure means to exchange sensitive or classified information.

Digital watermarking: Steganography methods can be used to digitally water-mark photographs with ownership information, authentication codes, or copyright information. Tracking and defending intellectual property rights are made possible by this.

Information hiding in multimedia: Audio and video are two other multimedia types that can benefit from the application of image steganography, which secretes information contained in them. For digital rights management, hidden messaging, or copyright protection, this can be employed.

Steganalysis and forensics: The goal of image steganalysis is to find hidden information in pictures. Steganalysis techniques can be utilized by forensic investigators to detect any steganographic content, hence supporting digital investigations.

Image Steganography

The three primary techniques for digital image steganography are neural network, transform, and spatial techniques. While transform methods embed hidden information within the frequency of the image, spatial methods alter the pixel values of an image to do so. The suggested methodology focuses on neural networks, which are used in neural network-based methods to carry out the concealment process. For a number of reasons, images make the perfect medium for encoding concealed information (Herodotus et al.,2007). The first explanation is that photographs include a wide range of properties, including dimensions, colors, bit depth, edges, corners, and information (Guzman et al.,2022). A payload can be easily hidden inside an image thanks to each of these features. Apart from these features, information can also be embedded by manipulating the metadata of specific image formats. A palette of colors used in the image is contained in Graphics Interchange Format (GIF) image files. The image retains its perceptual integrity while including hidden information due to color map permutation (D. Artz,2001). The second reason is that, with few exceptions, images are not easily affected by changes in pixel values. Numerous steganography techniques alter the least important portions uses the pixels to incorporate the fragments of a concealed image into a surface image. Red, green, and blue are the three 8-bit wide color channels that make up the majority of images, therefore there is plenty of room for information to be inserted (Djebbar et al.,2012).

Figure 1 depicts the fundamental architecture of image steganography. The message and payload are the two parts that a sender employs to create a steganographic communication. Through the process of encoding, the steganographic message is constructed. Several encoding process types will be explained later in this study for the purpose of clarity. The steganographic image is sent to the recipient after the encoding procedure is finished. Since organizations that obtain access to the steganographic image will not profit from it unless they are specifically aware that it contains a hidden payload, the steganographic image can be transmitted over either protected or unsecured channel. The receiving party uses a decoding procedure to decode the message after getting the steganographic image. The decoding procedure is identical to the encoding process in most steganographic approaches, except it is carried out in a different order. The hidden image will be available to the receiver upon completion of the decoding procedure.

Image steganography algorithms are assessed using a range of standard metrics, including concealing capacity, retrieval similarity, efficacy of hiding, and assault resistance. The effectiveness of various steganography methods can be compared using these measurements. Variations in image metrics are predicted because many strategies differ significantly between approaches, implementations, and image datasets employed. This study used standardized picture sets, such as ImageNet (Fei-Fei et al.,2020) to reduce these fluctuations.

Figure 1. The basic architecture of the digital image steganography process

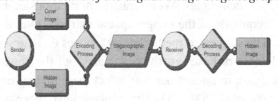

Convolutional Neural Networks

Neural networks are used in deep learning as a kind of artificial intelligence strategy to accomplish a job or objective (Hardesty, 2017). In that they are made up of numerous interconnected nodes that can communicate with one another, neural networks are somewhat modeled after the structure of the human brain. They are fittingly called "neural networks" for this reason. Figure 2. Architecture of CNN model. The CNN design includes layers such as an input layer, an output layer, and many hidden layers. Moreover, the hidden layers usually include pooling layers, convolutional layers, fully connected layers, and normalizing layers (ReLU) (Ognjanovski, 2019). The Relu function is the first layer of a convolutional layer, with a kernel size of 256 by 256 and 64 output channel combination, as illustrated in equation (1).

$$Relu(y) = max(0, y) \tag{1}$$

When y is positive, the relu function returns that value; when y is negative, it returns zero. The next stage of the max pooling architecture involves the decreasing image stack. To pool an image, the window size is defined as $(128 \times 128, 64)$ output channels. Each window's maximum value is noted before being entwined with the treads' look. Equation (1) illustrates how every negative value in the filtered image varies to equal 0. Rectified Linear Unit (Relu) processes are also found in the max pooling layer; these processes are referred to as normalization layers. Until the no-linear features of the model grow over all filtered images, this process is repeated. The RGB process's output channels are 256, just like the first layers on the third layer, and the process images are in a convolutional layer with a kernel size of (64, 64). The completely connected layer's kernel size, measuring 7 by 7, is located before the pooling layer. Equation (2) illustrates the flattened layer that results from using the fully linked layer with the softmax function.

$$q_i = \frac{e^y i}{\sum_j e^y i} \tag{2}$$

where yi is the total input that unit i has received and q_i is the picture prediction probability that corresponds to class i. Each value is given a vote to determine the image's class. Voting is frequently stacked in fully connected layers on phantom concealed categories with each intermediate layer. Studying more complex layer combinations is made possible by the features that lead to better decision-making in each additional layer. Lastly, we have an output. Rather than training the convolution layer, we merely trained the fully connected layer. The adjusted model is displayed in Figure 2. We further employ the optimizer and the loss function (cross-entropy). Every seven epochs, the Step R object's decreasing factor is set to 0.1, and the learning rate is set to 0.002. For each epoch, all training batches are repeated. We calculated the loss and adjusted the weights according to the result. the optimizer. step() and backward() functions. A later evaluation of performance over the test data is also conducted. At the end of the epoch, we displayed the network programs (accuracy and loss). Accuracy yields numbers of rectified predictions.

Figure 2. Architecture of CNN

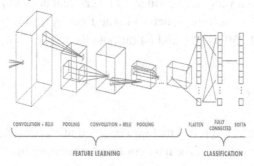

LITERATURE SURVEY

The secret data in the paper (Ognjanovski et.al., 2019) has been encrypted using AES, compressed using Gzip, and embedded using the Fisher-Yates Shuffle technique. It employs multiple techniques to attain an excellent PSNR, but as the size of the payload encoded data increases, it rapidly decreases. extremely resilient to Chi-square and histogram attacks. In the study (A. A. Zakaria et al.,2018), the secret image is encrypted with the ECC key, decoded using DCT, then inserted into the cover image using a deep neural network. It transforms and hides an image into a cover using CNNs, discrete cosine transforms, and elliptic curve cryptography. minimal distortion while secret data is buried using an altered LSB replacement approach. To achieve imperceptibility, edges receive more LSB than smooth surfaces. In the publication (Duan et al.,2020), Arnold scrambling is used to jumble images in RGB channels. The wavelet subbands and ridgelet coefficients are obtained using DWT and FRT, respectively. The steganographic image is obtained by using DWT and inverse FRT. There are two variations of the procedure offered. Variant 2 has a higher concealing capacity and employs 4-bit replacement, while Variant 1 utilizes 3-bit substitute and has a higher PSNR (Kingma et al.,2014) [17] . The study manipulates the secret image using Arnold's Cat Map, embeds it utilizing Least Significant Bit Matching, then uses Canny edge detection to estimate the cover image's edges. In the paper (Dadgostar et al.,2016), An image that contains pixels from a secret image is embedded into a cover image using eight-directional

Pixel Value Differencing (PVD). The cover image's eight directions match each pixel that surrounds a specific pixel. In the paper (Thanki et al., 2018), Arnold's Cat Map is used to alter the secret picture, which is then embedded utilizing Least Significant Bit Matching Revisited and Canny edge detection to estimate the cover image's edges. Table 1 shows the comparison of the survey methods. Adversary training, in which noise is incorporated into the training process, produces robustness. Although the stego images produced by this method are strong, their density is just 30 bits for a 128 × 128 color image. High durability against spatial manipulation is offered by EAST. flipped images contain as much as 88.9% of their bits that are the same as pure images. In terms of robustness, EAST is comparable to resizing and cropping. The resilience of EAST to spatial manipulation is not significantly affected by raising the noise level (Ghamizi., et al., 2021).

Along with the popularity of image style conversion technology comes ethical and legal issues. These include the spread of false information, privacy issues, intellectual property rights, etc. Researchers and policy makers must work together to address these issues and ensure the ethical and legal use of technology (Tan et al., 2023).

A generative adversarial network (GAN) based end-to-end image steganography technique with pixel-wise deep fusion and adversarial attack. The suggested plan is primarily divided into four modules: The encoder module is thought of as a generator that performs pixel-by- depth fusion for imperceptible high-payload information embedding; the decoder module is in charge of the task of recuperating the encoded data; the evaluation section is for the discriminator to supply objective scores and perform adversary training (Yuan et al., 2022). The attack module uses a universal adversarial network to trick CNN-based steganizers to increase security.

Table 1. The comparison of the survey methods

Research	Domain	PSNR	SSIM	MSE	Robustness
(Ognjanovski et.al., 2019)	Spatial	41.0834 – 64.8619	Not provide	0.02 – 6.46	Has the ability to detect Alterations to the steganographic image using CRC-32 checksum.
(Zakaria et al.,2018)	Frequency (Discrete Cosine Transform)	Average 42.5726	0.9602	Not provided	DCT is used to provide robustness by changing the structure of the secret image.
(Duan, D. Guo et al.,2020)	Spatial	Average 44	Not provided	Avg 1.4	Robustness is not a component of this proposed method.
(Kingma et al.,2014)	Frequency (Finite Ridgelet Transform, Discrete Wavelet Transform)	Average 59.9967	Not provided	Not provided	Very susceptible to attacks such as JPEG compression, cropping, noise, and histogram analysis.

continued on following page

Table 1. Continued

Research	Domain	PSNR	SSIM	MSE	Robustness
(Thanki et al., 2018)	Spatial	Variant 1: Average 38.55 Variant 2: Average 37.22	Avg 0.9985	Not provided	Robustness is achieved through its resistance to RS and Pixel Difference Histogram (PDH) analysis.
(Ognjanovski et,al ., 2019).	Spatial	38,33 – 76	Not provided	Not provided	LSB Matching Revisited provides a level of robustness against asymmetric steganographic attacks.
(Zakaria, et al., 2018)	Frequency (Discrete Cosine Transform	30.32	Not provided	Avg. 2.3	Robustness is achieved using Peak Signal-to-Noise Ratio (PSNR)
(Yuan, C et al., 2022)	Spatial	Average 36.35	Not provided	Not provided	Robustness is achived through training
(Hu, D et.al, 2018)	Spatial	Average 40.5726	Not provided	Not provided	Robustness is achieved using Peak Signal-to-Noise Ratio (PSNR)

PROPOSED METHOD

In order to develop a novel method for encoding and retrieving images, this study examined the fields of digital image steganography and convolutional neural networks. The application of advanced convolutional neural networks (CNNs) to digital image steganography is investigated in this study. This work expands upon a previous implementation that carried out the preparation, concealment, and extraction stages of the steganography process using two-dimensional CNN with U-Net as encoder. The proposed used CNN and CNN based U-Net structure are employed for image steganography images is explained in the following section.

CNN-Based Image Steganography

The unofficial use of the technique suggested in (G. Swain, 2018) served as the foundation for the steganographic channel used in this study. The implementation was developed in Python and was supplied by Baluja, 2017). Three separate networks—a preliminary, hidden, and reveal network—make up the overall network structure. A secret image is processed in the preparing network in order to be embedded in the hidden network. The steganographic image is created by the hiding network using the newly processed secret image as input along with a cover image (Delmi et al.,2020) . By using a steganographic image as input, the reveal network replicates the secret image. Rather than training each network independently, all of the networks are connected and trained collectively. Approach. The arrangement of the preparing, hidden, and reveal networks is depicted in Figure 1. The Adam optimizer and a loss function are the main tools used by the network to learn. With c denoting the hidden image, c' the steganographic image, s the hidden image, and s' the recovered image, the following equation provides a missing function for this network:

The function (c, c', s, s') equals $d + c' \| + \beta \| s - s' \|$ (3.1).

The all, hiding, and derived loss coefficients are the three components of the loss function that are returned. The error among the cover and steganographic imagine is represented by the $\| c + c' \|$ portion of the loss function, which is applied to the preparation and hiding network. For each of the three networks, the difference between the hidden and extracted image is represented by the $\beta \| s - s' \|$ portion of the loss function. It is important to note as those were the original author's aims; the total error coefficient was the only one used in the research implementation.

The three networks are trained using Adam, a stochastic gradient descent technique. It has been demonstrated that the Adam optimizer performs well with CNNs and is particularly effective with networks with high input requirements. Adam operates by merging the characteristics of two extensions—Adaptive Gradient Algorithm (AdaGrad) and Root Mean Square Propagation (RMSProp)—of the stochastic gradient descent technique . The concept of continuously updated learning rates for each perceptron originates from AdaGrad, while averages that move and the idea that learning rates should be updated based on the average of recent magnitudes derived from the weight gradients of the perceptrons are borrowed from RMSProp. Adam calculates a moving average with an exponential shape based on the gradients and the corresponding square root of the gradients, which is different from the moving average described in RMSProp. The parameters known as hyperparameters $\beta 1$ and $\beta 2$ are utilized to modify the exponential moving average's decay rates. To modify the estimated value of the gradients' first moments, or mean, use $\beta 1$, and to modify the predictions of the gradients' second moments, or variance, use $\beta 2$.

The key components of the original CNN network's structure are summed up as follows:

- Make a training graph with the following components: a noise layer, a revealing network with the same structure, a hiding network with the same structure, and a preparation network with 3x3, 4x4, and 5x5 convolution branches. The training graph's functions include processing a cover and hidden image that are chosen at random, creating a steganographic image, extracting the hidden image, and using the Adam optimizer to update the network weights.
- Choose a cover and concealed image at random from the datasets for each step and epoch, then use those choices as inputs for training the network.

- Evaluate the network's functionality with a randomly chosen covering and hidden image on the hundredth step. network for concealment, and a network for revealing. The sum of the SSIM and PSNR values are obtained by using the test graph to evaluate the network's embedding and extraction procedures. The weights are not updated by the Adam optimizer since it isn't used during the training phase.
- Design a deployment graph comprising a reveal, hiding, and preparatory network. The deployment graph is used to create an extracted and steganographic image from an input covering and hidden image.

U-Net-Based CNN for Image Steganography

The suggested designs U-Net based CNN conceal a cover picture with the same proportions that contains a hidden image of size $N \times N$. The suggested technique uses an established decoding architecture to extract the hidden image using the stego image produced by any of the encoder architectures that are employed, using U-Net architecture as encoders to conceal the secret image within the cover image (Himthani et.al, 2022). Figure 3 shows the architecture of U-Net deep learning model.

Figure 3. U-Net architecture (Himthani et. al, 2022)

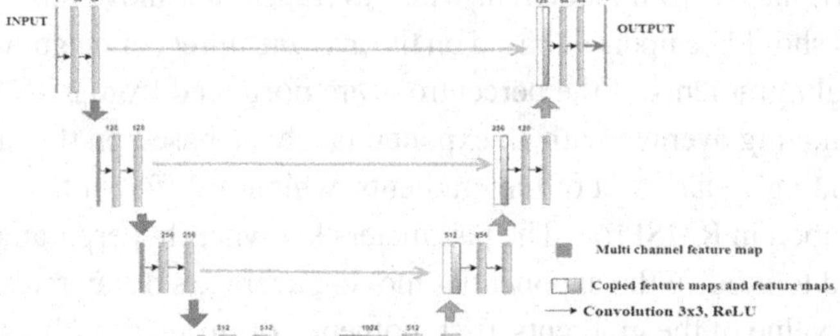

U-Net. With fewer training photos, U-Net, a fully convoluted neural network, achieves better performance. A U-Net architectural example is shown in Figure 1. The multiple platforms feature maps are shown by the blue-colored boxes. Paths of contraction (convolution) and extension (deconvolution) make up this design. There are 23 convolutional layers in each path. Two 3×3 filters that repeatedly conduct unpadded convolutions are present in every single layer of the shrinkage path. In every convolution layer, the number of feature channels is doubled. Moreover, the 2×2 maximum pooling operation comes after every convolution process. The encoder's expansion path uses a 2×2 filter size to carry out deconvolution operations. Each deconvolution layer halves the feature channels. As a result, horizontal links were pulled across the left side to the right path, characteristics in the initial phases. This restores the spatial data lost during contractions, hence improving the overall appearance of the ultimate reconstructed image.

In this work, image-in-image steganography approaches based on deep learning are applied and evaluated. Deep learning architectures are exemplified by the design in Figure 4. The hidden image is concealed within the cover image using U-Net based encoders. To extract the encoded image within the stego image, a special decoder architecture is created.

Architecture of Encoders

The fully linked unique CNN architectures, such as U-Net, are implemented in the suggested steganography approaches to create a stego images that conceals the secret image within the cover image.

Architecture of Decoder

This research includes the design of a strong and innovative CNN-based decoder. The decoder's job is to take hidden images out of the stego images that encoders based on U-Net produce. The decoder, as depicted in Figure 5, comprises eleven convolution layers including varying kernel dimensions of 3×3, and 4×4 and 5*5. To improve the decoder network's feature extraction capabilities, each kernel has a number of filters. The outputs from the convolutional (CL) layers are the feature maps. Convolutional layers are concatenated (CAT) in order to extract meaningful and important semantic characteristics from the characteristic maps. These characteristics enhance the model's learning process.

Figure 5. Block diagram of U-Net architecture based encoder (Himthani et. al, 2022)

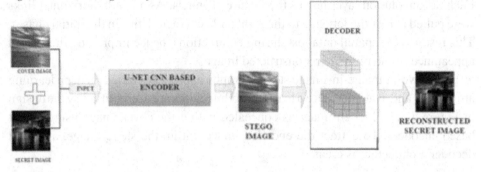

Experimental results of CNN and U-Net based CNN architecture are discussed in the next section.

EXPERIMENTAL ANALYSIS

Training and Testing Models

The image pixels were adjusted for normality utilizing the mean as well as the standard deviation from the ImageNet dataset, it was presumed because the data set provided by ImageNet had been utilized for training the network and produce these results when we imported the network for testing. The datasets from ImageNet (Fei-Fei et.al, 2018) is utilized for learning and test the initial network. The 9,468 photos in the Imagenet collection, which is sourced from the initial ImageNet dataset, feature ten distinct categories of things. Because there was not enough storage space for the entire ImageNet dataset, the Imagenet dataset ended up being utilized instead. Although they were all stored in JPG format, the images from the Imagenet dataset differed greatly in terms of height and width. However, the different sizes of images from this dataset don't matter because the preliminary network handles resizing and structuring the image for usage in the network.

All the original networks received input in the form of cover and concealed images in JPG format. The images were initially downsized to 224 pixels square in order to conceal a full-size color image within an additional color image of the same size before being sent to the planning and hiding networks. It is experiment using the Python code given in. The Python TensorFlow library's first major version was used to write and edit the code. Scikit-image was utilized to collect the image metrics in this experiment, and Matplotlib was employed to display the image within the notebook created with Jupyter . The source code editor and implementation environment for network testing and training was Google Colaboratory, also known as Colab. Python-based computational documents known as Jupyter notebooks are hosted on Colab's cloud service for interpretation and execution purposes. Table 2 specifies the parameter used for CNN based U-Net and Table 3 shows the structure of decoder network.

Table 2. Parameter setting for CNN based U-Net

Parameters	Value
exponential decay	First moment =0.9 and second=0.999
epsilon	1e-07
learning rate (alpha)	0.0001

Table 3. Structure of the decoder network

layer	o/p size	Parameters
Input Layer	256, 256, 3	0
Conv 3 × 3	256, 256, 60	1500
Conv 4 × 4	256, 256, 20	480
Conv 5 × 5 (Conv2D)	256, 256, 10	390
Concate _0	256, 256, 90	0
Conv 3 × 3	256, 256, 60	28,300
Conv 4 × 4	256, 256, 20	11,410
Conv 5 × 5	256, 256, 10	8330
Concate-1	256, 256,90	0
Conv 3 × 3	256, 256, 60	28,300
conv_4 × 4	256, 256, 20	11,410
Concate_2	256, 256, 80	0
Conv 3 × 3	256, 256, 60	28,050
Conv 4 × 4	256, 256, 20	9710
Concate_2	256, 256, 80	0
conv_3 × 3	256, 256, 60	28,050
Output Layer	256, 256, 3	1453

continued on following page

Table 3. Continued

The findings of the original, unaltered code, which served as the basis for this study, are the main topic of this section. The consequent steganographic image of the original network has faint indications of the hidden image, as Table 4 illustrates. These ranges' values are often at the lower end of what other image steganography techniques produce (Anthony Rene Guzman, 2022)

Figure 6. The steganographic and extracted images generated by the original CNN method

Experiment	Steganographic Image	Recovered Image
Cover: Baboon, Hidden: Graffiti	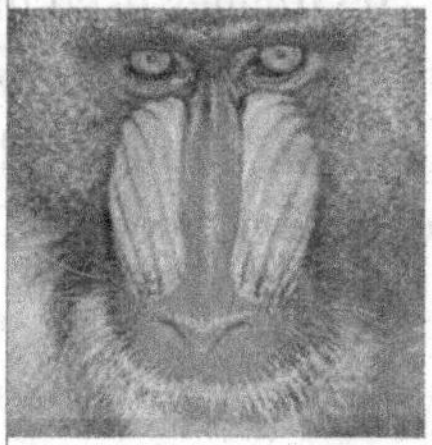	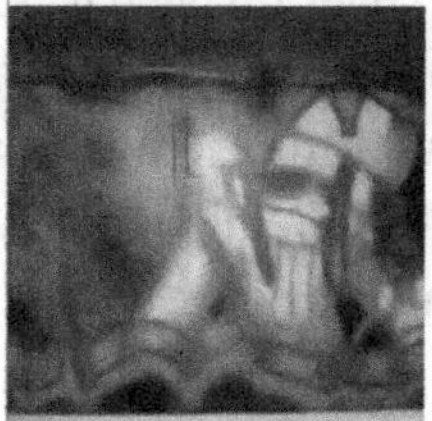
Cover: Berries, Hidden: Karaoke		
Cover: Chainsaws, Hidden: Lena		
Cover: Church, Hidden: Lotus		

The network demonstrated traces of the concealed images within the steganographic image while training on the Imagenet. Even with many more training steps completed, the final steganographic and disclosed photos clearly display the artifacts of the hidden process compared to the author's example output images. The steganographic image generated by the initial network visibly displays important image elements like corners and edges. A detailed look at the steganographic image shows that the cover image has been degraded. The images used in our build of the original network did not employ the normalization and denormalization processes, though, even with the significant increase in training rounds. This could clarify why the items that are hidden may more became more noticeable. Table 5 show the output of the metrics of original CNN

Table 4. Output of the metrics based on original CNN

Experiment	Steganographic Image	Recovered Image
Cover:	SSIM: 0.93687	SSIM: 0.87001
Baboon,	PSNR:	MSE: 0.00297
Hidden:	27.96642	
Graffiti		
Cover:	SSIM: 0.93457	SSIM: 0.85424
Berries,	PSNR:	MSE: 0.0026
Hidden:	25.62975	
Karaoke		
Cover:	SSIM: 0.91134	SSIM: 0.91303
Chainsaws,	PSNR: 29.35	MSE: 0.00162
Hidden:		
Lena		
Cover:	SSIM: 0.93737	SSIM: 0.86413
Church,	PSNR:	MSE: 0.00222
Hidden:	29.59204	
Lotus		
Cover: Dog,	SSIM: 0.90129	SSIM: 0.93006
Hidden:	PSNR: 25.7312	MSE: 0.00138
Parachute		
Cover: Fish,	SSIM: 0.90204	SSIM: 0.92166
Hidden:	PSNR:	MSE: 0.0013
Parrot	25.77007	

continued on following page

Table 4. Continued

Experiment	Steganographic Image	Recovered Image
Cover:	SSIM: 0.87437	SSIM: 0.77593
French Horn,	PSNR:	MSE: 0.0045
Hidden: Pens	27.37058	
Cover:	SSIM: 0.87806	SSIM: 0.89549
Garbage	PSNR:	MSE: 0.0019
Truck,	27.89983	
Hidden:		
Peppers		
Cover: Gas	SSIM: 0.81223	SSIM: 0.83418
Pump,	PSNR: 25.3442	MSE: 0.00576
Hidden:		
Stained Glass		
Cover: Golf	SSIM: 0.90461	SSIM: 0.87267
Balls,	PSNR:	MSE: 0.0023
Hidden:	25.99714	
Thistle		

There is potential for significant improvement in the metrics obtained by using the datasets acquired in this research to train the original network. The example steganographic image generated through the initial network training on the ImageNet dataset had SSIM and PSNR values of 0.92 and 27.69137 dB, respectively. The steganographic method of the initial neural network training on the Imagenette and isn't visually undetectable and can be easily identified with the naked eye, even though the SSIM and PSNR values were identical across the two implementations.

Table 6 shows the output metrics of CNN based U-Net Encioder method/

Table 5. Output of the metrics using CNN based U-Net architecture

Experiment	Steganographic Image	Recovered Image
Cover:	SSIM: 0.98748	SSIM: 0.87449
Baboon,	PSNR: 43.85748	MSE: 0.00262
Hidden:		
Graffiti		
Cover:	SSIM: 0.98848	SSIM: 0.94213
Berries,	PSNR: 45.33152	MSE: 0.00121

continued on following page

Table 5. Continued

Experiment	Steganographic Image	Recovered Image
Hidden:		
Karaoke		
Cover:	SSIM: 0.98652	SSIM: 0.93373
Chainsaws,	PSNR: 42.4834	MSE: 0.00107
Hidden:		
Lena		
Cover:	SSIM: 0.97789	SSIM: 0.92252
Church,	PSNR: 46.17786	MSE: 0.00104
Hidden:		
Lotus		
Cover: Dog,	SSIM: 0.97853	SSIM: 0.92306
Hidden:	PSNR: 45.72544	MSE: 0.00203
Parachute		
Cover: Fish,	SSIM: 0.98773	SSIM: 0.94739
Hidden:	PSNR: 45.487	MSE: 0.00128
Parrot		
Cover:	SSIM: 0.98739	SSIM: 0.84423
French Horn,	PSNR: 42.45224	MSE: 0.00408
Hidden: Pens		
Cover:	SSIM: 0.98713	SSIM: 0.89151
Garbage	PSNR: 43.06884	MSE: 0.00316
Truck,		
Hidden:		
Peppers		
Cover: Gas	SSIM: 0.96499	SSIM: 0.81930
Pump,	PSNR: 41.62722	MSE: 0.00727
Hidden:		
Stained Glass	SSIM: 0.98748	SSIM: 0.89449
Cover: Golf	PSNR: 43.85748	MSE: 0.00202
Balls,		
Hidden:		

The example steganographic image generated through the initial network training on the ImageNet dataset had SSIM and PSNR values of 0.98 and 46.69137 dB, respectively, Hence the CNN based U-Net Architecture had better output compared to CNN method.

Future Work

It has been thought to employ DCT and DWT, as well as the well-known networks cycleGAN. Additional research into various bespoke architectures may be undertaken. One option to investigate further is the use of recurrent neural networks (RNNs) rather than CNNs. Other GAN variations can be used in place of the bespoke WGAN. The majority of image steganography techniques employ text or grayscale images to conceal secret information; further study is required to fully understand image-in-image and image-in-video techniques. Robustness, security, and hideability were taken into account by many ways as performance metrics. However, when the communication occurs through untrusted channels, there is a chance for man-in-the-middle attacks. Moreover, the stego image could alter while being sent. These assaults, together with how well the suggested algorithm defends against them, can be taken into consideration for evaluation in addition to other.

CONCLUSION

In order to develop a novel method for encoding and retrieving images, this study examined the fields of digital image steganography and convolutional neural networks. The application of advanced convolutional neural networks (CNNs) to digital image steganography is investigated in this study. This work expands upon a previous implementation that carried out the preparation, concealment, and extraction stages of the steganography process using two-dimensional CNN with U-Net as encoder. A few commonly used image metrics, including the peak signal to noise proportion (PSNR), mean square error (MSE), and structural similarity indices measurement (SSIM), were used to evaluate the effectiveness of the proposed CNN-based U-Net approach. The outcomes demonstrated that, while still offering high recoverability, the steganographic images generated by the suggested technology are undetectable to the human eye. The network might be enhanced by using a larger dataset with a greater variety of images.

REFERENCES

Artz, D. (2001). Digital steganography: Hiding data within data. *IEEE Internet Computing*, 5(3), 75–80. DOI: 10.1109/4236.935180

Baluja, S. (2017). Hiding images in plain sight: Deep steganography. *Advances in Neural Information Processing Systems*, 30.

Cabaj, K., Caviglione, L., Mazurczyk, W., Wendzel, S., Woodward, A., & Zander, S. (2018). The New Threats of Information Hiding: The Road Ahead. IT P, 20, 31–39.

Cox, I. J. (2007). Digital Watermarking and Steganography. Morgan Kaufmann google schola, 2, 893-914.

Dadgostar, H., & Afsari, F. (2016). Image steganography based on interval-valued intuitionistic fuzzy edge detection and modified LSB. Journal of information security and applications, 30, 94-104.

Delmi, A., Suryadi, S., & Satria, Y. (2020). Digital image steganography by using edge adaptive based chaos cryptography. In *Journal of Physics: Conference Series*. IOP Publishing. DOI: 10.1088/1742-6596/1442/1/012041

Djebbar, F., Ayad, B., Meraim, K. A., & Hamam, H. (2012). Comparative study of digital audio steganography techniques. *EURASIP Journal on Audio, Speech, and Music Processing*, 2012(1), 1–16. DOI: 10.1186/1687-4722-2012-25

Duan, X., Guo, D., Liu, N., Li, B., Gou, M., & Qin, C. (2020). A new high capacity image steganography method combined with image elliptic curve cryptography and deep neural network. *IEEE Access : Practical Innovations, Open Solutions*, 8, 25777–25788. DOI: 10.1109/ACCESS.2020.2971528

Fei-Fei, N., Deng, J., Russakovsky, O., & Berg, A. L. (2020). ImageNet. Stanford University.

Ghamizi, S., Cordy, M., Papadakis, M., & Le Traon, Y. (2021). Evasion attack steganography: Turning vulnerability of machine learning to adversarial attacks into a real-world application. Proceedings of the IEEE/CVF International conference on computer vision, 31-40.

Guzman, A. R. (2022). Image Steganography Using Deep Learning Techniques (Doctoral dissertation, Purdue University Graduate School).

Hardesty, L. (2017). *Explained: Neural Networks*. Massachusetts Institute of Technology.

Herodotus, S., Robert, B., & Purvis, A. (2007). The landmark Herodotus: the histories.

Himthani V, Dhaka VS, Kaur M, Rani G, Oza M, & Lee HN (2022). Comparative performance assessment of deep learning based image steganography techniques. Scientific Reports, 12(1), 16895.

Himthani, V., Dhaka, V. S., Kaur, M., Rani, G., Oza, M., & Lee, H. N. (2022, October 7). Comparative performance assessment of deep learning-based image steganography techniques. *Scientific Reports*, 12(1), 16895. DOI: 10.1038/s41598-022-17362-1 PMID: 36207314

Hu, D., Wang, L., Jiang, W., Zheng, S., & Li, B. (2018). A novel image steganography method via deep convolutional generative adversarial networks. *IEEE Access : Practical Innovations, Open Solutions*, 6, 38303–38314. DOI: 10.1109/ACCESS.2018.2852771

Jamil, T. (1999). Steganography: The art of hiding information in plain sight. *IEEE Potentials*, 18(1), 10–12. DOI: 10.1109/45.747237

Kingma, D. P., & Ba, J. (2014). Adam: A method for stochastic optimization. arXiv preprint arXiv:1412.6980.

Ognjanovski, G. (2019). Everything you need to know about neural networks and backpropagation—machine learning easy and fun. Towards Data Science.backpropagation-machine-learning-made-easy-e5285bc2be3a

Puchalski, D., Caviglione, L., Kozik, R., Marzecki, A., Krawczyk, S., & Choraś, M. (2020). Stegomalware Detection through Structural Analysis of Media Files. *Proceedings of the 15th International Conference on Availability, Reliability and Security, ARES'20*. DOI: 10.1145/3407023.3409187

Subramanian, N., Cheheb, I., Elharrouss, O., Al-Maadeed, S., & Bouridane, A. (2021). End-to-end image steganography using deep convolutional autoencoders. *IEEE Access : Practical Innovations, Open Solutions*, 9, 135585–135593. DOI: 10.1109/ACCESS.2021.3113953

Swain, G. (2018). Digital image steganography using eight-directional PVD against RS analysis and PDH analysis. *Advances in Multimedia*, 2018, 2018. DOI: 10.1155/2018/4847098

Tan, X., & Tan, L. (2023). Research on the Underlying Principles and Deep Learning Algorithms based on Image Style Conversion Techniques. *Transactions on Computer Science and Intelligent Systems Research*, 1, 58–63. DOI: 10.62051/2z2ngm94

Thanki, R., & Borra, S. (2018). A color image steganography in hybrid FRT–DWT domain. Journal of Information Security and Applications, 40, 92-102.

Wani, M. A., & Sultan, B. (2023). Deep learning based image steganography: A review. *Wiley Interdisciplinary Reviews. Data Mining and Knowledge Discovery*, 13(3), e1481. DOI: 10.1002/widm.1481

Yuan, C., Wang, H., He, P., Luo, J., & Li, B. (2022). GAN-based image steganography for enhancing security via adversarial attack and pixel-wise deep fusion. *Multimedia Tools and Applications*, 81(5), 6681–6701. DOI: 10.1007/s11042-021-11778-z

Zakaria, A. A., Hussain, M., Wahab, A. W. A., Idris, M. Y. I., Abdullah, N. A., & Jung, K. H. (2018). High-capacity image steganography with minimum modified bits based on data mapping and LSB substitution. *Applied Sciences (Basel, Switzerland)*, 8(11), 2199. DOI: 10.3390/app8112199

Zou, Y., Zhang, G., & Liu, L. (2019). Research on image steganography analysis based on deep learning. *Journal of Visual Communication and Image Representation*, 60, 266–275. DOI: 10.1016/j.jvcir.2019.02.034

Chapter 4
The Role of Deep Learning Innovations With CNNs and GANs in Steganography

Harpreet Kaur
Chandigarh University, India

Chiranji Lal Chowdhary
https://orcid.org/0000-0002-5476-1468
Vellore Institute of Technology, Vellore, India

ABSTRACT

Steganography, the practice of concealing information within other non-secret data, has evolved significantly with the advent of digital technologies. Traditional methods often struggle with maintaining a balance between capacity, imperceptibility, and robustness. Recent advancements in deep learning offer promising enhancements to steganographic techniques, addressing these challenges more effectively. This chapter explores how deep learning approaches can enhance steganography, focusing on the utilization of neural networks for embedding and extracting hidden information. Deep learning models, particularly convolutional neural networks (CNNs) and generative adversarial networks (GANs), have shown superior capability in learning intricate patterns and representations. CNNs can be employed to optimize the feature selection process, ensuring that hidden information is embedded in less noticeable regions of the cover media, thereby improving imperceptibility.

DOI: 10.4018/979-8-3693-2223-9.ch004

1. INTRODUCTION

Steganography, the practice of concealing information within seemingly innocuous media, has long been employed to facilitate covert communication and protect sensitive data from unauthorized access. Throughout history, various techniques have been developed to embed hidden messages within text, images, audio, and video files, ensuring that the presence of such information remains undetected by unintended recipients as shown in Figure 1. However, traditional steganographic methods often face limitations in terms of capacity, imperceptibility, and robustness against detection and attacks (Ahmad, S. et al 2024). In recent years, the advent of deep learning has revolutionized many fields, including steganography, offering new opportunities to enhance its effectiveness and resilience. Deep learning, a subset of machine learning, involves training artificial neural networks on large datasets to identify patterns and make predictions. These networks, particularly Convolutional Neural Networks (CNNs) and Generative Adversarial Networks (GANs), have demonstrated remarkable capabilities in tasks such as image recognition, natural language processing, and data generation. When applied to steganography, deep learning techniques can significantly improve the embedding and extraction processes, leading to more secure and imperceptible steganographic systems (Kuznetsov, O. et al. 2024).

Figure 1. General procedure in image steganography

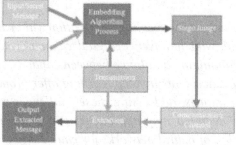

One of the key advantages of leveraging deep learning in steganography is the ability to optimize the embedding process to achieve high imperceptibility. By training neural networks to understand and replicate the statistical properties of cover media, deep learning models can embed hidden information in ways that are visually and audibly indistinguishable from the original content. This results in steganographic methods that are far less detectable by both human observers and traditional steganalysis techniques (Wani, M. A., & Sultan, B. 2023). Furthermore, deep learning approaches can enhance the capacity of steganographic systems, allowing for the embedding of larger amounts of data without compromising the quality of the cover media. Advanced neural networks can learn to distribute hidden information more efficiently across the media, maximizing the available space while maintaining the cover media's integrity. This increased capacity is particularly beneficial in applications requiring the concealment of substantial amounts of data, such as high-resolution images or complex documents (Martín, A., et al 2024). Robustness is another critical area where deep learning can make a significant impact. Traditional steganographic methods often struggle to withstand common media processing operations, such as compression, resizing, and noise addition, which can corrupt or reveal hidden information. Deep learning models, however, can be trained to anticipate and adapt to these operations, ensuring that the embedded data remains intact and undetectable even after significant alterations to the cover media (Fadhil, A. M., et al. 2024).

In conclusion, the integration of deep learning approaches into steganography represents a promising advancement, addressing many of the limitations associated with traditional methods. By enhancing imperceptibility, capacity, and robustness, deep learning-based steganography can provide more secure and reliable solutions for covert communication and data protection in the digital age. As research in this area continues to evolve, it holds the potential to significantly transform the landscape of information security and privacy (Chaudhary, A., et al. 2024).

This chapter aims to explore the integration of deep learning into steganography to enhance its effectiveness. Key objectives include reviewing traditional steganographic methods and their limitations, introducing relevant deep learning concepts, presenting deep learning-based approaches for steganography, and demonstrating their effectiveness through experimental results. The study focuses on digital image steganography but acknowledges potential extensions to audio and video. By leveraging deep learning, this research seeks to develop more sophisticated, resilient, and adaptive steganographic systems. These advancements could significantly improve secure communication, addressing the growing demands for data protection in the digital age. The integration of CNNs and GANs into steganography offers a transformative approach, combining enhanced imperceptibility, capacity, and robustness to advance the field (Kholdinasab, N., & Amirmazlaghani, M. 2023).

1.1 Background and Motivation

Steganography, the art of hiding information within seemingly innocuous carriers, has a long and varied history, from ancient techniques using invisible ink to modern digital methods. In an age where data security and privacy are paramount, steganography provides an additional layer of protection beyond traditional encryption. However, traditional steganographic methods often struggle to balance the conflicting requirements of capacity (the amount of data that can be hidden), imperceptibility (the hidden data should not be noticeable), and robustness (resistance to detection and attacks) (Al Zakitat, et al 2023).The advent of deep learning has revolutionized many fields, including image processing and cybersecurity, by providing tools capable of learning complex patterns and making intelligent decisions. The potential of deep learning to enhance steganography lies in its ability to automatically identify optimal embedding locations within cover media, generate highly imperceptible steganographic content, and improve the robustness of hidden data against various forms of detection and attacks (Peng, Y., et al 2024)

1.2 Objectives

This paper aims to explore how deep learning can be integrated into steganography to enhance its effectiveness. The specific objectives are:

- To review the current state of traditional steganographic techniques and their limitations.
- To introduce and explain deep learning concepts relevant to steganography.
- To present deep learning-based approaches, focusing on Convolutional Neural Networks (CNNs) and Generative Adversarial Networks (GANs), and how they can improve steganographic methods.
- To demonstrate the effectiveness of these approaches through experimental results.
- To discuss the advantages and challenges of using deep learning in steganography.
- To propose future research directions for further enhancing steganographic techniques using deep learning.

1.3 Scope and Limitations

This study focuses on the application of deep learning to digital image steganography, although the principles discussed could be extended to other types of media such as audio and video. While the primary emphasis is on improving imperceptibility, capacity, and robustness, the study also considers the computational complexity introduced by deep learning models. Ethical and legal considerations of advanced steganographic techniques are acknowledged but not explored in depth. In conclusion, integrating deep learning with steganography presents a promising avenue for advancing secure communication methods. By leveraging the capabilities of CNNs and GANs, we aim to develop more sophisticated, resilient, and adaptive steganographic systems that can meet the growing demands of data security in the digital era (Luo, J., et al, 2024).

2. OVERVIEW OF STEGANOGRAPHY

Steganography, derived from the Greek words "steganos" (covered) and "graphia" (writing), involves concealing information within non-suspicious media, such as images, audio, or text. Unlike encryption, which transforms data into an unreadable format, steganography hides the existence of the data itself, making it an additional layer of security. Traditional steganographic techniques primarily focus on digital images, utilizing methods like Least Significant Bit (LSB) modification, where the least significant bits of pixel values are altered to embed information. While simple and effective, such methods often compromise either the visual quality of the cover image or the robustness of the hidden data against detection and attacks (Liu, L., et al 2024). Key challenges in steganography include maintaining a balance between capacity (the amount of data that can be hidden), imperceptibility (ensuring the hidden data does not alter the cover media noticeably), and robustness (resistance to various forms of detection and manipulation). These factors are crucial for practical applications, which range from secure communication and copyright protection to covert operations and data integrity verification (Maiti, A., et al 2024).

Recent advancements in computational methods, particularly deep learning, have introduced new possibilities for steganography. By leveraging sophisticated neural network architectures, researchers are developing techniques that significantly enhance the imperceptibility, capacity, and robustness of hidden data, marking a significant evolution from traditional approaches. These innovations are paving the way for more secure and efficient steganographic systems in the digital age (Sultan, B., & ArifWani, M. 2023).

2.1 History and Evolution

Steganography has a rich history, dating back to ancient times, long before the advent of digital technology. Its evolution can be traced through several key phases, each characterized by innovative techniques tailored to the communication mediums of the era as discussed below and shown in Figure 2.

- **Ancient Times:**

440 B.C.: Herodotus recounts the use of wax tablets by Demaratus to send secret messages by writing on the wood underneath and covering it with wax.

- **Middle Ages and Renaissance:**

800-1200 A.D.: Use of invisible inks (e.g., milk, lemon juice) by various cultures to hide messages.

1500s: Steganographic techniques in Europe involved embedding messages in letters and other documents. Null ciphers and codebooks were also developed.

- **18th and 19th Centuries:**

1700s: Microdots, tiny photographs that can be embedded in larger images or documents, were introduced.

1800s: The use of steganography during military conflicts, including the Napoleonic Wars, often involved intricate methods to hide messages within handwritten letters.

- **20th Century:**

World War I (1914-1918): Use of steganographic techniques such as microdots and hidden messages in seemingly innocent letters.

World War II (1939-1945): Advanced methods, including invisible inks and the manipulation of typewriter ribbons, were employed to conceal messages. Steganography and cryptography were often combined.

1960s: Early digital steganography concepts emerged with the advent of computers and digital communication.

- **1990s:**

1990: Development of digital image steganography, particularly the use of Least Significant Bit (LSB) modification to embed data within digital images.

Mid-1990s: Transform domain techniques, such as Discrete Cosine Transform (DCT) and Discrete Wavelet Transform (DWT), started to be used for embedding data in the frequency components of images.

- **2000s:**

2000: Steganography tools and software become more accessible, enabling widespread use.

Mid-2000s: Research focuses on improving robustness against steganalysis (detection of steganography). Techniques involving error correction and redundancy are developed.

- **2010s:**

Early 2010s: Advances in computational power led to more sophisticated steganographic algorithms. Hybrid methods combining spatial and transform domain techniques are explored.

Mid-2010s: Introduction of machine learning algorithms to detect steganographic content (steganalysis) prompts the development of more secure steganographic methods.

Late 2010s: Initial experiments with deep learning models, such as Convolutional Neural Networks (CNNs), for embedding and detecting steganographic content.

- **2020s:**

Early 2020s: Widespread adoption of deep learning techniques. Generative Adversarial Networks (GANs) are used to create more robust steganographic systems. These models enhance imperceptibility and robustness by learning optimal embedding strategies and resisting steganalysis.

Mid-2020s: Development of adaptive and context-aware steganographic techniques using advanced AI models, allowing dynamic adjustments to different types of cover media and security requirements.

Late 2020s: Real-time steganographic applications become feasible with the improvement of hardware and deep learning models, expanding the use cases to audio, video, and complex multimedia formats.

Steganography has evolved from simple ancient techniques to sophisticated digital methods, adapting to technological advancements and the increasing need for secure communication. The integration of deep learning marks a significant milestone in its evolution, offering new levels of imperceptibility, capacity, and robustness (Peng, Y., et al 2023; Zha, H., et al 2023; Zhang, J., et al 2023).

Figure 2. Evolution of steganography

- Ancient Times
- Middle Ages and Renaissance
- 18th and 19th Centuries
- 20th Century
- 1990s
- 2000s
- 2020s
- Late 2020s

2.2 Traditional Steganographic Techniques

Traditional steganographic techniques primarily focus on embedding information within digital media such as images, audio, and text. These methods vary in complexity and effectiveness, balancing the trade-offs between capacity, imperceptibility, and robustness (Kheddar, H., et al. 2023). Figure 3 shows some of the most common traditional steganographic techniques:

Figure 3. Traditional steganographic techniques

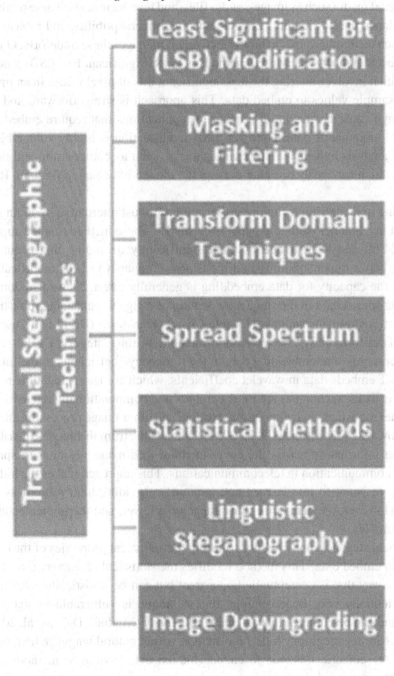

Traditional steganographic techniques focus on embedding hidden information within digital media such as images, audio files, and text documents. These methods aim to balance the key requirements of capacity, imperceptibility, and robustness, though each technique varies in how effectively it manages these trade-offs. One of the simplest and most widely used methods is Least Significant Bit (LSB) modification, which involves altering the least significant bits of pixel values in an image or audio sample values to embed data. This approach is straightforward and can achieve high capacity, making it popular for applications that require embedding substantial amounts of data. However, LSB modification is highly vulnerable to statistical analysis and image processing attacks, such as compression and noise addition, which can easily reveal or corrupt the hidden information (Prabhu, R., et al. 2024).

Masking and filtering techniques offer a more robust alternative by hiding information in a manner similar to paper watermarks. These methods can be applied to both 24-bit and 8-bit images without significantly degrading image quality, providing better imperceptibility and robustness compared to LSB modification. However, the capacity for data embedding is generally lower. Transform domain techniques embed data in the frequency domain of a signal, enhancing robustness against various transformations. Discrete Cosine Transform (DCT) and Discrete Wavelet Transform (DWT) are common methods in this category. DCT is used in JPEG compression, embedding data in the frequency coefficients of the image, while DWT embeds data in wavelet coefficients, which are less perceptible to the human eye. These techniques are more complex and computationally intensive but offer higher robustness to compression, scaling, and other image processing attacks (Michaylov, K. D., & Sarmah, D. K. 2024). Spread spectrum techniques distribute the hidden information across the cover medium in a manner similar to spread spectrum communication in telecommunications. This approach makes the hidden data more resistant to interference and jamming, providing high robustness and security. However, the data embedding capacity is lower, and the implementation is more complex.

Statistical steganography involves altering the statistical properties of the cover medium to embed data. This method modifies the statistical characteristics of the media in a way that is perceptually transparent but can be statistically detectable. While potentially very imperceptible, this technique is vulnerable to statistical analysis and can be complex to implement effectively (Mikhail, D. Y., et al. 2023).

Linguistic steganography hides information within natural language text, using syntactic or semantic methods to encode hidden data. Syntactic methods alter sentence structures, while semantic methods use synonyms and rephrasing. These techniques offer high imperceptibility for text-based communications but are limited in capacity and can be susceptible to language processing attacks. Lastly, image downgrading involves creating a high-quality image and a downgraded version, with the difference between the two used to embed hidden information (Kuznetsov, A., et al, 2023). This technique maintains high image quality and can embed significant data, but it requires both versions of the image for effective extraction, which may not always be feasible. In summary, traditional steganographic techniques offer various methods for hiding information within digital media, each with distinct advantages and limitations. While effective to varying degrees, these methods often face challenges in balancing capacity, imperceptibility, and robustness, highlighting the need for ongoing advancements in the field (Farooq, N., & Selwal, A. 2023).

2.3 Applications of Steganography

Steganography, the practice of hiding information within other non-secret data, has a wide range of applications across various fields. Its primary appeal lies in its ability to conceal the very existence of a message, offering an additional layer of security beyond traditional encryption methods (Venkata Krishna, G. P. C., & Vivekananda Reddy, D. 2024). Following are some of the key applications of steganography:

Figure 4. Applications of steganography

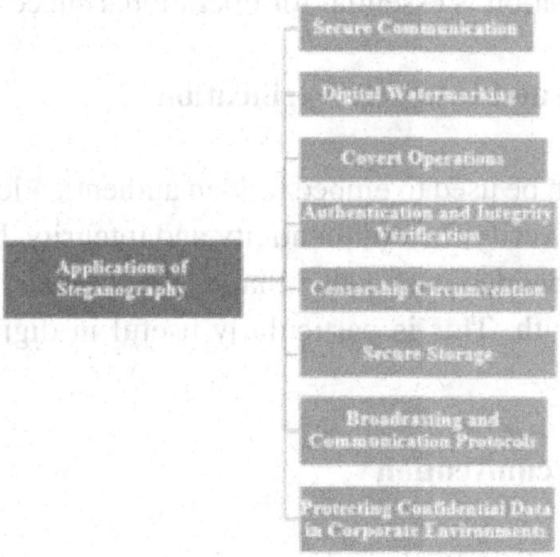

- **Secure Communication**

One of the most prominent applications of steganography is in secure communication. By embedding messages within innocuous cover media like images, audio files, or videos, sensitive information can be transmitted without raising suspicion.

This is particularly useful in scenarios where the mere presence of encrypted data could attract unwanted attention, such as in espionage or military communications.

- **Digital Watermarking**

Digital watermarking is a technique used to protect intellectual property rights. By embedding a watermark—typically a logo, serial number, or copyright information—into digital content such as images, audio, or video files, creators can assert ownership and trace unauthorized copies. Steganographic techniques ensure that these watermarks are imperceptible to the naked eye but detectable by special software, making them difficult to remove without degrading the quality of the content.

- **Covert Operations**

In intelligence and covert operations, steganography is employed to send secret information without detection. Agents can embed hidden messages within digital media files or even within seemingly innocent text documents, allowing for discreet communication. This application is critical in environments where secure and undetectable communication is essential for operational success.

- **Authentication and Integrity Verification**

Steganography can be used to embed hidden authentication codes or checksums within digital files to verify their authenticity and integrity. For instance, an image might contain an embedded hash value that can be checked to ensure the file has not been tampered with. This is particularly useful in digital forensics and data integrity verification.

- **Censorship Circumvention**

In regions with strict censorship, steganography provides a means to circumvent restrictions by embedding prohibited content within allowed media. For example, activists might use steganography to hide messages or sensitive information within images or audio files that can be shared on social media or other platforms without detection by censors.

- **Secure Storage**

Steganography can enhance data storage security by embedding sensitive information within larger, less sensitive files. This technique can be used to protect personal data, financial information, or sensitive documents from unauthorized access or theft. Even if an unauthorized party gains access to the files, the hidden data remains concealed.

- **Broadcasting and Communication Protocols**

In broadcasting and communication protocols, steganography can embed control information or metadata within the transmitted data. This ensures that additional information is transmitted without increasing the data load or altering the visible content, optimizing bandwidth usage and enhancing communication efficiency.

- **Protecting Confidential Data in Corporate Environments**

Corporations use steganography to protect confidential data, such as trade secrets, strategic plans, and sensitive communications. Embedding such information within everyday files helps shield it from industrial espionage and unauthorized access, ensuring that critical data remains confidential even if the files are intercepted. Steganography offers a versatile and effective means of concealing information within various types of media, providing an additional layer of security and utility across multiple domains. From secure communication and digital watermarking to covert operations and data integrity verification, the applications of steganography are diverse and critical in today's digital age. As technology advances, the role of steganography in enhancing data security and privacy continues to grow, highlighting its importance in a wide array of fields (Ma, B., et al. 2024; Gao, Y., et al. 2024).

3. DEEP LEARNING FUNDAMENTALS

Deep learning, a branch of machine learning, involves the use of neural networks with multiple layers to model complex patterns in data. These neural networks are inspired by the human brain and consist of interconnected neurons that process data through weighted connections. At its core, a neural network comprises an input layer that receives raw data, hidden layers that transform the data through mathematical operations, and an output layer that produces the final prediction or classification. Convolutional Neural Networks (CNNs), a type of deep learning model, are particularly effective for image processing tasks due to their ability to detect and learn hierarchical patterns through convolutional and pooling layers. This makes CNNs ideal for applications like image recognition and steganography, where patterns within images need to be carefully analyzed and manipulated. Another significant deep learning architecture is the Generative Adversarial Network (GAN), which consists of a generator that creates synthetic data and a discriminator that evaluates its authenticity. Through adversarial training, GANs can generate highly realistic data, enhancing steganographic methods by creating imperceptible hidden information. Deep learning's advances in image processing, such as classification, object detection, and image generation, make it a powerful tool for enhancing traditional steganographic techniques, providing greater imperceptibility, capacity, and robustness in data hiding (Mo, X., et al. 2024).

3.1 Introduction to Neural Networks

Neural networks are the backbone of deep learning, inspired by the structure and function of the human brain. A neural network consists of layers of interconnected nodes, or neurons, which process data. The basic structure includes an input layer, one or more hidden layers, and an output layer.

- **Input Layer:** This layer receives the initial data input, which could be anything from pixel values of an image to feature vectors in other types of data.
- **Hidden Layers:** These layers perform a series of transformations on the input data. Each neuron in a hidden layer applies a weighted sum of its inputs, passes this sum through an activation function (such as ReLU, sigmoid, or tanh), and outputs the result to the next layer. The purpose of these layers is to detect complex patterns and representations in the data.
- **Output Layer:** This layer produces the final output, which could be a classification label, a numerical value, or another form of prediction, depending on the task.

The network is trained using a process called backpropagation, where the error between the predicted output and the actual output is calculated and propagated back through the network to update the weights. This iterative process continues until the network's performance reaches an acceptable level (Pandey, B. K., et al 2023).

3.2 Convolutional Neural Networks (CNNs)

Convolutional Neural Networks (CNNs) are specifically designed for processing grid-like data, such as images. They are highly effective for tasks involving visual data due to their ability to capture spatial hierarchies in images (Khandelwal, J., & Sharma, V. K. 2023).

- **Convolutional Layers:** These layers apply convolutional filters to the input image. Each filter scans the image, performing a dot product operation between the filter and local regions of the image, producing a feature map. These filters help detect various features like edges, textures, and patterns.
- **Pooling Layers:** These layers perform down sampling operations on the feature maps to reduce their dimensions, which helps decrease computational complexity and increase robustness to spatial variations. Common pooling operations include max pooling and average pooling.
- **Fully Connected Layers:** After several convolutional and pooling layers, the final feature maps are flattened and fed into fully connected layers. These layers perform high-level reasoning based on the features extracted by the convolutional layers and produce the final classification or prediction.

CNNs are widely used in image recognition, object detection, and various other computer vision tasks due to their ability to learn hierarchical representations from raw pixel data (Kumar, A., Rani, R., & Singh, S. 2023).

3.3 Generative Adversarial Networks (GANs)

Generative Adversarial Networks (GANs) consist of two neural networks, a generator and a discriminator, that are trained simultaneously through an adversarial process.

- **Generator:** The generator network takes random noise as input and produces synthetic data (e.g., images) that mimic the real data distribution. Its goal is to create realistic data that can fool the discriminator.
- **Discriminator:** The discriminator network evaluates whether a given data sample is real (from the training set) or generated (from the generator). Its goal is to accurately distinguish between real and fake data.

During training, the generator and discriminator are locked in a game where the generator improves its ability to produce realistic data while the discriminator gets better at detecting fakes. This process continues until the generator produces data indistinguishable from real data. GANs have revolutionized the field of generative modeling, enabling the creation of highly realistic images, videos, and other types of data (Sun, Y. 2024).

3.4 Deep Learning in Image Processing

Deep learning has significantly advanced the field of image processing, providing powerful tools for various applications:

- **Image Classification:** Deep learning models, especially CNNs, have achieved high accuracy in classifying images into predefined categories. They automatically learn hierarchical features from raw pixel data, which makes them highly effective for this task.
- **Object Detection:** Beyond classifying images, deep learning can also locate and classify multiple objects within an image. Techniques like Region-based CNN (R-CNN), You Only Look Once (YOLO), and Single Shot MultiBox Detector (SSD) are widely used for real-time object detection.
- **Image Segmentation:** This involves partitioning an image into meaningful regions, often down to the pixel level. Techniques such as Fully Convolutional Networks (FCNs) and U-Net are popular for tasks requiring detailed segmentation, such as medical image analysis.
- **Image Generation and Transformation:** GANs and other deep learning models can generate new images from scratch or transform existing ones. Applications include style transfer, where the style of one image is applied to another, and super-resolution, where low-resolution images are converted to high-resolution ones.

Deep learning's ability to learn from large datasets and its flexibility in handling various image processing tasks make it an essential tool in modern computer vision. These advances are not only enhancing traditional image analysis techniques but also enabling new applications and improving performance across the board (Bui, T., et al 2023).

4. DEEP LEARNING APPROACHES TO STEGANOGRAPHY

Deep learning approaches to steganography represent a significant advancement over traditional methods, leveraging the power of neural networks to embed and extract hidden information with improved imperceptibility, capacity, and robustness. These techniques utilize the ability of deep learning models to learn complex patterns and representations from data, enabling more sophisticated and secure steganographic systems (Jahromi, Z. T., et al 2024). This section explores various deep learning-based steganographic techniques and their advantages.

4.1 Convolutional Neural Networks (CNNs) in Steganography

Convolutional Neural Networks (CNNs) are particularly well-suited for image-based steganography due to their prowess in image processing tasks. CNNs can be employed to both embed and detect hidden information in images.

- **Embedding Information:** A CNN can be trained to take a cover image and a secret message as inputs and produce a stego-image that visually resembles the cover image but contains the hidden message. The network learns to make subtle modifications to the pixel values that are imperceptible to the human eye.
- **Extraction:** Another CNN can be trained to reverse the embedding process, extracting the hidden message from the stego-image. The use of CNNs ensures that the embedding is done in a manner that is robust against common image processing operations, such as compression and noise addition.

These CNN-based techniques enhance the security and effectiveness of steganography by learning optimal ways to hide and retrieve information, significantly reducing the chances of detection (Kumar, A., et al 2023).

4.2 Generative Adversarial Networks (GANs) in Steganography

Generative Adversarial Networks (GANs) take steganography to a new level by leveraging the adversarial training process to create highly realistic stego-media.

- **GAN Architecture:** In a steganographic GAN setup, the generator network is trained to produce stego-images that not only contain hidden messages but are also indistinguishable from cover images to the discriminator network. The discriminator is trained to differentiate between genuine cover images and stego-images.
- **Adversarial Training:** The adversarial nature of GANs means that the generator continuously improves its ability to create realistic stego-images that can fool the discriminator. This results in highly imperceptible steganographic content, as the generator learns to embed messages in ways that mimic natural image features.

GAN-based steganography benefits from the realistic and complex features generated by the adversarial process, making the hidden information harder to detect and the stego-images more robust against various forms of steganalysis (Chaudhary, A., et al 2023).

4.3 Autoencoders and Variational Autoencoders (VAEs)

Autoencoders and Variational Autoencoders (VAEs) are another class of neural networks used in deep learning-based steganography. These models are designed to learn efficient representations of data, which can be utilized for embedding and extracting hidden information.

- **Autoencoders:** Consist of an encoder that compresses the input data into a latent representation and a decoder that reconstructs the data from this representation. For steganography, the encoder can be used to embed a secret message into an image's latent representation, while the decoder reconstructs the image with the embedded message.
- **VAEs:** Extend autoencoders by imposing a probabilistic framework on the latent space, allowing for the generation of diverse and realistic stego-images. VAEs can provide additional robustness and flexibility in the embedding process, making them suitable for more complex steganographic applications.

Using autoencoders and VAEs in steganography leverages their ability to learn compact and informative representations, enhancing the efficiency and security of the hidden data embedding process (Mawla, N. A., & Khafaji, H. K. 2023).

4.4 Deep Reinforcement Learning

Deep reinforcement learning, which involves training agents to make decisions by rewarding desired actions, can also be applied to steganography.

- **Adaptive Embedding:** Reinforcement learning can be used to develop adaptive steganographic systems that dynamically adjust embedding strategies based on the cover media and the requirements of the hidden message. The agent learns to maximize the reward, which could be based on factors like imperceptibility and robustness.
- **Steganalysis Resistance:** By continuously learning from interactions with a steganalysis environment, reinforcement learning models can develop strategies to evade detection more effectively, improving the overall security of the steganographic system.

Deep reinforcement learning introduces adaptability and resilience to steganography, making it possible to develop systems that can intelligently respond to various challenges and threats. Deep learning approaches to steganography offer significant improvements over traditional methods by leveraging the advanced pattern recognition and feature extraction capabilities of neural networks. Techniques involving CNNs, GANs, autoencoders, and reinforcement learning enhance the imperceptibility, capacity, and robustness of steganographic systems. These advancements pave the way for more secure and effective data-hiding techniques, meeting the growing demand for privacy and data protection in various applications. As deep learning continues to evolve, its integration with steganography is likely to yield even more sophisticated and resilient methods for covert communication and information security (Ansari, A. S. 2024).

5. CASE STUDIES IN STEGANOGRAPHY

- **Espionage and Intelligence Operations**

During the Cold War, intelligence agencies such as the CIA and KGB extensively used steganography for covert communication. One notable example is the "number station" broadcasts, where coded messages were embedded within seemingly random radio transmissions. These messages provided instructions to undercover agents operating in hostile territories. In 2001, the FBI uncovered a Russian spy ring operating in the United States. The spies used steganography to hide encrypted messages within digital images posted on publicly accessible websites. This method allowed them to communicate with their handlers in Russia without arousing suspicion (Fadel, M. M., et al 2023).

- **Digital Media Copyright Protection**

Media companies use steganography to protect digital content from piracy and unauthorized distribution. Digital watermarks embedded within images, videos, and audio files contain identifying information such as copyright details and ownership metadata. Adobe's Content Authenticity Initiative aims to combat digital content piracy by embedding tamper-proof metadata into images using steganographic techniques. This metadata includes details about the creator, copyright information, and usage rights, providing a means to verify the authenticity and ownership of digital content.

- **Covert Communication in Terrorism**

Terrorist organizations exploit steganography to communicate covertly and plan attacks without detection. Messages containing operational details and instructions are embedded within seemingly innocent files, such as images and audio recordings, and shared through public channels. In 2016, ISIS operatives used steganography to hide messages within images posted on social media platforms. These messages contained propaganda materials, instructions for carrying out attacks, and recruitment efforts aimed at sympathizers around the world.

- **Corporate Information Security**

Corporations use steganography to protect sensitive information and trade secrets from industrial espionage and data breaches. Hidden messages embedded within corporate communications and multimedia files ensure that critical data remains confidential and secure. A multinational technology company embeds proprietary data within product images shared with manufacturing partners. This hidden information includes design specifications, intellectual property details, and supply chain instructions, safeguarding valuable corporate assets from unauthorized access and theft.

- **Military and Defense Applications**

Military organizations employ steganography to secure communications and protect classified information from adversaries. Hidden messages embedded within digital images and videos enable secure transmission of intelligence and operational details. The U.S. Department of Defense uses steganography to embed encrypted messages within satellite imagery shared with military units deployed in remote locations. This covert communication method ensures that critical information remains confidential and inaccessible to hostile forces.

- **Political Dissent and Activism**

Political dissidents and activists use steganography to bypass censorship and surveillance in repressive regimes. Hidden messages embedded within digital media files enable secure communication and coordination of protest activities. Pro-democracy activists in authoritarian countries use steganography to share information about government crackdowns and human rights abuses. Hidden messages within images posted on social media platforms contain details about protest locations, rally times, and emergency escape routes, allowing activists to organize and mobilize without detection by authorities.

- **Journalism and Whistleblowing**

Journalists and whistleblowers use steganography to protect the anonymity of their sources and securely transmit sensitive information to media outlets. Hidden messages embedded within digital documents and images prevent interception and surveillance by government agencies and corporate entities. In 2013, Edward Snowden, a former NSA contractor turned whistleblower, used steganography to securely transmit classified documents to journalists reporting on government surveillance programs. Hidden within innocuous-looking files were revelations about mass surveillance and privacy violations, sparking international debate and reform efforts.

- **Personal Privacy and Data Protection**

Individuals use steganography to safeguard personal privacy and protect sensitive information from unauthorized access. Hidden messages embedded within digital photos, documents, and email attachments ensure that confidential data remains private and secure. A journalist living in a country with strict censorship laws embeds hidden messages within family photos shared with colleagues and friends. These messages contain details about upcoming investigative reports and sensitive interviews, allowing the journalist to communicate securely without fear of surveillance or interception.

- **Cryptocurrency and Blockchain Security**

Cryptocurrency users employ steganography to protect their digital assets and private keys from theft and hacking attacks. Hidden within digital images and QR codes are encrypted wallet addresses and transaction details, ensuring the security and integrity of blockchain transactions. A Cryptocurrency investor stores their private keys and seed phrases within steganographically encoded images stored in secure offline storage. This hidden information serves as a backup in case of hardware failure or loss, ensuring the investor retains access to their digital assets even in the event of a security breach.

- **Academic Research and Digital Forensics**

Researchers and digital forensics experts use steganography to study and analyze hidden messages in digital media files. By developing and testing steganalysis techniques, they uncover covert communication channels and identify potential security vulnerabilities. A team of researchers conducts a study on the effectiveness of steganographic techniques in concealing information within digital images. Using advanced steganalysis algorithms, they analyze a large dataset of images to detect hidden messages and assess the robustness of different embedding methods against detection.

These additional case studies and examples further illustrate the versatility and significance of steganography in various domains, from journalism and personal privacy to cryptocurrency security and academic research (Li, W., et al. 2023; Wardhani, R. W., et al 2023; Dhawan, S., et al. 2023).

5.1 Comparative Analysis With Traditional Methods

Table 1 highlights the strengths and weaknesses of both deep learning approaches and traditional methods in steganography, demonstrating the trade-offs between complexity, imperceptibility, capacity, robustness, and adaptability. Depending on the specific requirements and constraints of a steganographic application, practitioners may choose to leverage either deep learning techniques or traditional methods to achieve their objectives (Abd Aziz, et al. 2024).

Table 1. Comparison of deep learning approaches traditional methods

Aspect	Deep Learning Approaches	Traditional Methods
Complexity	Deep learning techniques involve complex neural network architectures with multiple layers and parameters, requiring significant computational resources for training and inference.	Traditional methods are often simpler to implement, involving basic algorithms such as LSB modification, masking, and filtering techniques, which have fewer computational requirements.
Imperceptibility	Deep learning models can achieve high imperceptibility by learning to embed hidden information in ways that are visually indistinguishable from the original cover media.	Imperceptibility in traditional methods varies depending on the technique used. While some methods like LSB modification can achieve reasonable imperceptibility, others may introduce visible artifacts in the stego-media.
Capacity	Deep learning approaches generally offer higher embedding capacity compared to traditional methods, allowing for the hiding of larger amounts of data within cover media.	Traditional methods may have limited capacity, especially when embedding data in low-bit-depth images or audio samples.
Robustness	Deep learning models can exhibit robustness against common steganalysis techniques and image processing operations, making them more resistant to detection and data corruption.	Traditional methods may be more vulnerable to steganalysis and image processing attacks, such as compression, noise addition, and filtering, which can degrade the quality of the hidden data or reveal its presence.
Adaptability	Deep learning approaches can adapt and learn from data, allowing for dynamic adjustments to embedding strategies and improved performance over time.	Traditional methods are often static and may not adapt well to changing environments or evolving steganalysis techniques without manual intervention.

continued on following page

Table 1. Continued

Aspect	Deep Learning Approaches	Traditional Methods
Training Data Requirements	Deep learning models require large amounts of labeled data for training, which may be challenging to obtain for steganographic applications due to the need for paired cover-stego data.	Traditional methods may not require extensive training data, as they rely on predefined algorithms and techniques that do not necessarily involve machine learning.
Detection Difficulty	Deep learning-based steganography can be more challenging to detect, as the embedding process is optimized to minimize perceptual differences between cover and stego-media, making it harder for steganalysis algorithms to identify hidden information.	Traditional steganography may be relatively easier to detect using statistical analysis, visual inspection, or specialized steganalysis techniques, especially if the embedding method introduces detectable artifacts or deviations from normal data distributions.

Steganography offers several advantages, primarily stemming from its ability to facilitate covert communication and enhance data security. By concealing messages within innocuous cover media, such as images or audio files, steganography enables parties to exchange information discreetly, without attracting unwanted attention. This covert nature of communication enhances security by making it more difficult for unauthorized individuals to intercept or detect the hidden messages. Additionally, steganography provides an extra layer of protection for sensitive information, as hidden data remains concealed within digital media files, preserving its confidentiality and integrity. Furthermore, well-designed steganographic methods can resist various forms of attacks, including steganalysis and data tampering, thereby ensuring the reliability and robustness of the communication channel. Moreover, steganography finds applications across diverse domains, from intelligence operations to digital media copyright protection, showcasing its versatility and utility in securing communication and protecting sensitive information Reyers, (P. M. 2023).

However, steganography also presents several challenges that must be addressed to ensure its effectiveness and reliability. One of the primary challenges is the detection of hidden messages, as adversaries may employ steganalysis techniques to uncover covert communication channels. Achieving high imperceptibility, where the presence of hidden information is undetectable to the human eye or ear, is another challenge, requiring careful optimization of embedding algorithms. Moreover, there is often a trade-off between embedding capacity and security, as higher-capacity methods may introduce detectable artifacts or distortions in the cover media. Key management and authentication also pose challenges, as steganography typically relies on encryption to secure hidden information, necessitating secure channels for key exchange and authentication. Finally, ethical and legal considerations surrounding the use of steganography raise complex issues, particularly in contexts such as espionage and criminal activities, highlighting the need to balance legitimate privacy and security concerns with the prevention of abuse and adherence to legal standards. Addressing these challenges requires ongoing research and innovation to develop robust and effective steganographic techniques while ensuring ethical and legal compliance (Melman, A., & Evsutin, O. 2023).

- **Advantages:**

Covert Communication: Steganography enables secret communication by hiding messages within seemingly innocuous cover media, such as images, audio files, or text documents. This covert nature of communication allows parties to exchange information without drawing attention to themselves.

Security Enhancement: Steganography enhances security by providing an additional layer of protection for sensitive information. Unlike encryption, which may draw attention to the fact that communication is being secured, steganography hides the existence of the communication itself, making it less susceptible to interception and decryption.

Data Concealment: Steganography allows for the concealment of data within digital media files without significantly altering their appearance or quality. This makes it difficult for unauthorized individuals to detect the presence of hidden information, thus preserving the integrity and confidentiality of the data.

Resistance to Attacks: Well-designed steganographic methods can be resistant to various forms of attacks, including steganalysis (the detection of hidden messages) and data tampering. By embedding information in a manner that mimics the statistical properties of the cover media, steganography can withstand scrutiny by adversaries.

Diverse Applications: Steganography finds applications across diverse domains, including intelligence and espionage, digital media copyright protection, privacy preservation, digital forensics, and political activism. Its versatility makes it a valuable tool for securing communication and protecting sensitive information (Kuznetsov, O., Frontoni, E., & Chernov, K. 2024).

- **Challenges:**

Detection: One of the primary challenges of steganography is the detection of hidden messages. Steganalysis techniques aim to identify the presence of hidden information within digital media files by analyzing statistical anomalies or artifacts introduced during the embedding process. As steganographic methods evolve, so too do steganalysis techniques, leading to an ongoing arms race between concealment and detection methods.

Imperceptibility: Achieving high imperceptibility, where the presence of hidden information is undetectable to the human eye or ear, is another challenge in steganography. Balancing the need for concealment with minimal impact on the quality and integrity of the cover media requires careful consideration and optimization of embedding algorithms.

Capacity vs. Security Trade-off: Increasing the embedding capacity of steganographic methods often comes at the expense of security. Higher-capacity methods may introduce detectable artifacts or distortions in the cover media, making the hidden information more susceptible to detection. Finding the right balance between capacity and security is a significant challenge in steganography.

Key Management and Authentication: Steganography typically relies on encryption to secure the hidden information and ensure that only authorized parties can access it. Managing encryption keys and establishing secure channels for key exchange and authentication are critical components of a steganographic system. Failure to adequately address these aspects can undermine the security and reliability of the communication.

Ethical and Legal Considerations: The use of steganography raises ethical and legal concerns, particularly in contexts such as espionage, corporate espionage, and criminal activities. The covert nature of steganography can be exploited for malicious purposes, leading to privacy violations, intellectual property theft, and other illicit activities. Balancing the legitimate use of steganography for privacy and security purposes with the need to prevent abuse and uphold legal standards presents a complex challenge.

Despite these challenges, the advantages of steganography in providing secure and covert communication make it a valuable tool in various domains. Addressing the challenges requires ongoing research and innovation to develop robust and effective steganographic techniques while ensuring ethical and legal compliance (Kunhoth, J., et al. 2023).

6. FUTURE DIRECTIONS

• **Real-Time Steganography**

Real-time steganography involves the embedding and extraction of hidden information in live streams or communication channels, enabling instantaneous and covert communication. Future research may focus on developing efficient and low-latency steganographic methods suitable for real-time applications, such as video conferencing, online gaming, and instant messaging platforms. Additionally, integrating real-time steganography into emerging technologies like virtual reality

(VR) and augmented reality (AR) could open up new avenues for secure and immersive communication experiences.

- **Expanding to Audio and Video Steganography**

While steganography has predominantly been applied to images and text, there is growing interest in expanding its use to audio and video media. Future research may explore novel techniques for embedding hidden information in audio streams, music tracks, and video clips while preserving perceptual quality and integrity. This expansion to audio and video steganography could have applications in digital media protection, content authentication, and multimedia communication, paving the way for more comprehensive and versatile steganographic systems.

- **Adaptive and Context-Aware Techniques**

Adaptive and context-aware steganographic techniques dynamically adjust their embedding strategies based on environmental factors, user preferences, and contextual cues, enhancing their effectiveness and resilience. Future research may focus on developing intelligent steganographic systems capable of adapting to changing conditions, such as network bandwidth, media content, and security requirements. By incorporating machine learning algorithms and contextual information into the embedding process, these techniques could improve imperceptibility, capacity, and robustness while minimizing the risk of detection and interception.

- **Ethical and Legal Considerations**

As steganography continues to evolve and gain prominence in various domains, addressing ethical and legal considerations becomes increasingly important. Future research may explore the ethical implications of steganography in areas such as privacy, surveillance, and intellectual property rights, ensuring that its use aligns with ethical principles and societal values. Moreover, policymakers and legal experts may need to develop guidelines and regulations governing the responsible use of steganography, particularly in sensitive contexts like national security and law enforcement. By promoting transparency, accountability, and ethical conduct, these measures can help mitigate potential risks and promote the responsible use of steganographic techniques in the digital age (Caballero, H., et al 2023; Rustad, S., et al. 2023; Patwari, B., et al 2023).

7. CONCLUSION

In conclusion, steganography stands as a powerful and versatile tool for securing communication, protecting sensitive information, and enabling covert communication in the digital age. From its historical roots in ancient civilizations to its modern applications in intelligence operations, digital media protection, and personal privacy, steganography has continually evolved to meet the evolving challenges and demands of information security. The advent of deep learning approaches has further expanded the capabilities of steganography, offering advancements in imperceptibility, capacity, and robustness. However, steganography also presents challenges, including the detection of hidden messages, achieving high imperceptibility, and balancing embedding capacity with security. Addressing these challenges requires ongoing research and innovation, with future directions including real-time steganography, expansion to audio and video media, development of adaptive techniques, and consideration of ethical and legal implications. As steganography continues to play a crucial role in safeguarding privacy, enhancing security, and enabling secure communication, it is essential to promote responsible use, ethical conduct, and legal compliance. By embracing transparency, accountability, and ethical principles, stakeholders can harness the benefits of steganography while mitigating potential risks and ensuring its positive impact on society. In summary, steganography remains a cornerstone of information security, offering a blend of innovation, versatility, and resilience in safeguarding communication and preserving privacy in an increasingly interconnected and digital world. With continued research, collaboration, and adherence to ethical standards, steganography will continue to thrive as a vital component of modern information security practices.

REFERENCES

Abd Aziz, A. Z., Sultan, M. F. M., & Zulkufli, N. L. M. (2024). Image Steganography: Comparative Analysis of their Techniques, Complexity and Enhancements. *International Journal on Perceptive and Cognitive Computing*, 10(1), 59–70. DOI: 10.31436/ijpcc.v10i1.449

Ahmad, S., Ogala, J. O., Ikpotokin, F., Arif, M., Ahmad, J., & Mehfuz, S. (2024). Enhanced CNN-DCT Steganography: Deep Learning-Based Image Steganography Over Cloud. *SN Computer Science*, 5(4), 408. DOI: 10.1007/s42979-024-02756-x

Al Zakitat, M. A. S., Abdulrazzaq, M. M., Ramaha, N. T., Mukhlif, Y. A., & Ismael, O. A. (2023, September). Harnessing Advanced Techniques for Image Steganography: Sequential and Random Encoding with Deep Learning Detection. In *International Conference on Emerging Trends and Applications in Artificial Intelligence* (pp. 456-470). Cham: Springer Nature Switzerland.

Ansari, A. S. (2024). A Review on the Recent Trends of Image Steganography for VANET Applications. *Computers, Materials & Continua*, 78(3), 2865–2892. DOI: 10.32604/cmc.2024.045908

Bui, T., Agarwal, S., Yu, N., & Collomosse, J. (2023). Rosteals: Robust steganography using autoencoder latent space. In *Proceedings of the IEEE/CVF Conference on Computer Vision and Pattern Recognition* (pp. 933-942). DOI: 10.1109/CVPRW59228.2023.00100

Caballero, H., Muñoz, V., & Ramos-Corchado, M. A. (2023). A comparative study of steganography using watermarking and modifications pixels versus least significant bit. *Iranian Journal of Electrical and Computer Engineering*, 13(6), 6335–6350. DOI: 10.11591/ijece.v13i6.pp6335-6350

Chaudhary, A., Sharma, A., & Gupta, N. (2023). A Novel Approach to Blockchain and Deep Learning in the field of Steganography. *International Journal of Intelligent Systems and Applications in Engineering*, 11(2s), 104–115.

Chaudhary, A., Sharma, A., & Gupta, N. (2023). Designing A Secured Framework for the Steganography Process Using Blockchain and Machine Learning Technology. *International Journal of Intelligent Systems and Applications in Engineering*, 11(2s), 96–103.

Dhawan, S., Gupta, R., Bhuyan, H. K., Vinayakumar, R., Pani, S. K., & Rana, A. K. (2023). An efficient steganography technique based on S2OA & DESAE model. *Multimedia Tools and Applications*, 82(10), 14527–14555. DOI: 10.1007/s11042-022-13798-9

Fadel, M. M., Said, W., Hagras, E. A., & Arnous, R. (2023). A Fast and Low Distortion Image Steganography Framework Based on Nature-Inspired Optimizers. *IEEE Access : Practical Innovations, Open Solutions*, 11, 125768–125789. DOI: 10.1109/ACCESS.2023.3326709

Fadhil, A. M., Jalo, H. N., & Mohammad, O. F. (2023). Improved Security of a Deep Learning-Based Steganography System with Imperceptibility Preservation. *International journal of electrical and computer engineering systems, 14*(1), 73-81.

Farooq, N., & Selwal, A. (2023). Image steganalysis using deep learning: A systematic review and open research challenges. *Journal of Ambient Intelligence and Humanized Computing*, 14(6), 7761–7793. DOI: 10.1007/s12652-023-04591-z

Gao, Y., Yang, J., Chen, C., Pang, K., & Huang, Y. (2024, April). Enhancing Steganography of Generative Image Based on Image Retouching. In *ICASSP 2024-2024 IEEE International Conference on Acoustics, Speech and Signal Processing (ICASSP)* (pp. 4945-4949). IEEE. DOI: 10.1109/ICASSP48485.2024.10448006

Jahromi, Z. T., Hasheminejad, S. M. H., & Shojaedini, S. V. (2024). Deep learning semantic image synthesis: A novel method for unlimited capacity, high noise resistance coverless video steganography. *Multimedia Tools and Applications*, 83(6), 17047–17065. DOI: 10.1007/s11042-023-16278-w

Khandelwal, J., & Sharma, V. K. (2023, July). Reversible Image Steganography Using Deep Learning Method: A Review. In *International Conference on Human-Centric Smart Computing* (pp. 625-635). Singapore: Springer Nature Singapore.

Kheddar, H., Hemis, M., Himeur, Y., Megías, D., & Amira, A. (2024). Deep learning for steganalysis of diverse data types: A review of methods, taxonomy, challenges and future directions. *Neurocomputing*, 581, 127528. DOI: 10.1016/j.neucom.2024.127528

Kholdinasab, N., & Amirmazlaghani, M. (2023). An adversarial learning based image steganography with security improvement against neural network steganalysis. *Computers & Electrical Engineering*, 108, 108725. DOI: 10.1016/j.compeleceng.2023.108725

Kumar, A., Rani, R., & Singh, S. (2023). A survey of recent advances in image steganography. *Security and Privacy*, 6(3), e281. DOI: 10.1002/spy2.281

Kumar, A., Rani, R., & Singh, S. (2023). Encoder-Decoder Architecture for Image Steganography using Skip Connections. *Procedia Computer Science*, 218, 1122–1131. DOI: 10.1016/j.procs.2023.01.091

Kunhoth, J., Subramanian, N., Al-Maadeed, S., & Bouridane, A. (2023). Video steganography: Recent advances and challenges. *Multimedia Tools and Applications*, 82(27), 41943–41985. DOI: 10.1007/s11042-023-14844-w

Kuznetsov, A., Luhanko, N., Frontoni, E., Romeo, L., & Rosati, R. (2023). Image steganalysis using deep learning models. *Multimedia Tools and Applications*, 1–24.

Kuznetsov, O., Frontoni, E., & Chernov, K. (2024). Beyond traditional steganography: Enhancing security and performance with spread spectrum image steganography. *Applied Intelligence*, 54(7), 5253–5277. DOI: 10.1007/s10489-024-05415-z

Li, W., Wang, H., Chen, Y., Abdullahi, S. M., & Luo, J. (2023). Constructing immunized stego-image for secure steganography via artificial immune system. *IEEE Transactions on Multimedia*, 25, 8320–8333. DOI: 10.1109/TMM.2023.3234812

Liu, L., Liu, X., Wang, D., & Yang, G. (2024). Enhancing image steganography security via universal adversarial perturbations. *Multimedia Tools and Applications*, 1–13. DOI: 10.1007/s11042-024-19122-x

Luo, J., He, P., Liu, J., Wang, H., Wu, C., & Zhou, S. (2023). Reversible adversarial steganography for security enhancement. *Journal of Visual Communication and Image Representation*, 97, 103935. DOI: 10.1016/j.jvcir.2023.103935

Ma, B., Li, K., Xu, J., Wang, C., Li, J., & Zhang, L. (2023). Enhancing the security of image steganography via multiple adversarial networks and channel attention modules. *Digital Signal Processing*, 141, 104121. DOI: 10.1016/j.dsp.2023.104121

Maiti, A., Laha, S., Upadhaya, R., Biswas, S., Choudhary, V., Kar, B., . . . Sen, J. (2024). Boosting Digital Safeguards: Blending Cryptography and Steganography. *arXiv preprint arXiv:2404.05985*.

Martín, A., Hernández, A., Alazab, M., Jung, J., & Camacho, D. (2023). Evolving Generative Adversarial Networks to improve image steganography. *Expert Systems with Applications*, 222, 119841. DOI: 10.1016/j.eswa.2023.119841

Mawla, N. A., & Khafaji, H. K. (2023). Enhancing Data Security: A Cutting-Edge Approach Utilizing Protein Chains in Cryptography and Steganography. *Computers*, 12(8), 166. DOI: 10.3390/computers12080166

Melman, A., & Evsutin, O. (2023). Comparative study of metaheuristic optimization algorithms for image steganography based on discrete Fourier transform domain. *Applied Soft Computing*, 132, 109847. DOI: 10.1016/j.asoc.2022.109847

Michaylov, K. D., & Sarmah, D. K. (2024). Steganography and steganalysis for digital image enhanced Forensic analysis and recommendations. *Journal of Cyber Security Technology*, 1-27.

Mikhail, D. Y., Hawezi, R. S., & Kareem, S. W. (2023). An Ensemble Transfer Learning Model for Detecting Stego Images. *Applied Sciences (Basel, Switzerland)*, 13(12), 7021. DOI: 10.3390/app13127021

Mo, X., Tan, S., Tang, W., Li, B., & Huang, J. (2023). ReLOAD: Using reinforcement learning to optimize asymmetric distortion for additive steganography. *IEEE Transactions on Information Forensics and Security*, 18, 1524–1538. DOI: 10.1109/TIFS.2023.3244094

Pandey, B. K., Pandey, D., Alkhafaji, M. A., Güneşer, M. T., & Şeker, C. (2023). A reliable transmission and extraction of textual information using keyless encryption, steganography, and deep algorithm with cuckoo optimization. In *Micro-Electronics and Telecommunication Engineering: Proceedings of 6th ICMETE 2022* (pp. 629–636). Springer Nature Singapore. DOI: 10.1007/978-981-19-9512-5_57

Patwari, B., Nandi, U., & Ghosal, S. K. (2023). Image steganography based on difference of Gaussians edge detection. *Multimedia Tools and Applications*, 82(28), 43759–43779. DOI: 10.1007/s11042-023-15360-7

Peng, Y., Fu, C., Zheng, Y., Tian, Y., Cao, G., & Chen, J. (2024). Medical steganography: Enhanced security and image quality, and new SQ assessment. *Signal Processing*, 223, 109546. DOI: 10.1016/j.sigpro.2024.109546

Peng, Y., Fu, G., Yu, Q., Luo, Y., Hu, J., & Duan, C. (2024). Enhancing the anti-steganalysis ability of steganography via adversarial examples. *Multimedia Tools and Applications*, 83(2), 6227–6247. DOI: 10.1007/s11042-023-15306-z

Prabhu, R., Archana, P., Anusooya, S., & Anuradha, P. (2023). Improved Steganography for IoT Network Node Data Security Promoting Secure Data Transmission using Generative Adversarial Networks. *The Scientific Temper*, 14(03), 938–943. DOI: 10.58414/SCIENTIFICTEMPER.2023.14.3.58

Reyers, P. M. (2023). *A comparative analysis of audio steganography methods and tools* (Bachelor's thesis, University of Twente).

Rustad, S., Andono, P. N., & Shidik, G. F. (2023). Digital image steganography survey and investigation (goal, assessment, method, development, and dataset). *Signal Processing*, 206, 108908. DOI: 10.1016/j.sigpro.2022.108908

Sultan, B., & ArifWani, M. (2023). A new framework for analyzing color models with generative adversarial networks for improved steganography. *Multimedia Tools and Applications*, 82(13), 19577–19590. DOI: 10.1007/s11042-023-14348-7

Sun, Y. (2024). Enhancing image steganalysis via integrated reinforcement learning and dilated convolution techniques. *Signal, Image and Video Processing*, 18(S1), 1–16. DOI: 10.1007/s11760-024-03113-4

Venkata Krishna, G. P. C., & Vivekananda Reddy, D. (2024). Machine learning-enhanced hybrid cryptography and image steganography algorithm for securing cloud data. *Journal of Intelligent & Fuzzy Systems*, (Preprint), 1-11.

Wani, M. A., & Sultan, B. (2023). Deep learning-based image steganography: A review. *Wiley Interdisciplinary Reviews. Data Mining and Knowledge Discovery*, 13(3), e1481. DOI: 10.1002/widm.1481

Wardhani, R. W., Putranto, D. S. C., Ji, J., & Kim, H. (2024). Towards Hybrid Classical Deep Learning-Quantum Methods for Steganalysis. *IEEE Access : Practical Innovations, Open Solutions*, 12, 45238–45252. DOI: 10.1109/ACCESS.2024.3381615

Zha, H., Zhang, W., Yu, N., & Fan, Z. (2023). Enhancing image steganography via adversarial optimization of the stego distribution. *Signal Processing*, 212, 109155. DOI: 10.1016/j.sigpro.2023.109155

Zhang, J., Chen, K., Li, W., Zhang, W., & Yu, N. (2023). Steganography with Generated Images: Leveraging Volatility to Enhance Security. *IEEE Transactions on Dependable and Secure Computing*.

Chapter 5
Securing Automatic Speaker Verification Systems Using Residual Networks

Nidhi Chakravarty

https://orcid.org/0000-0002-5454-1561

National Institute of Technology, Kurukshetra, India

Mohit Dua

https://orcid.org/0000-0001-7071-8323

National Institute of Technology, Kurukshetra, India

ABSTRACT

Spoofing attacks are a major risk for automatic speaker verification systems, which are becoming more widespread. Adequate countermeasures are necessary since attacks like replay, synthetic, and deepfake attacks, are difficult to identify. Technologies that can identify audio-level attacks must be developed in order to address this issue. In this chapter, the authors have proposed combination of different spectrogram-based techniques with Residual Networks34 (ResNet34) for securing the automatic speaker verification (ASV) systems. The methodology uses Mel frequency scale-based Mel-spectrogram (MS), gamma scale-based gammatone spectrogram (GS), Mel filter bank-based Mel frequency cepstral spectrograms (MCS), acoustic pattern-based acoustic pattern spectrogram (APS), gammatone filter bank-based gammatone cepstral spectrogram (GCS), and short-time Fourier transform-based short Fourier spectrogram (SFS) methods, one by one, at front of the proposed audio spoof detection system. These spectrograms are individually fed to ResNet34 for classification at the backend.

DOI: 10.4018/979-8-3693-2223-9.ch005

1. INTRODUCTION

In the ever-changing digital world of today, biometric technology integration plays a critical role in managing access to essential information resources. Voice biometric systems utilize pitch, speech patterns, voice characteristics, and intonation for voice recognition purposes(Hanifa et al., 2021). The technology entails analyzing the user's speech and comparing it against a pre-existing model of their voiceprint. Offering high accuracy levels, it necessitates only minimal hardware setup, eliminating the need for additional hardware like eye or fingerprint scanners. Unlike PINs and passwords, voice biometrics leverage the unique and distinctive nature of an individual's voice, akin to a fingerprint, making it challenging to monitor or compromise. These attributes are driving the increased adoption of voice verification across various sectors, including e-commerce, banking, healthcare, and government. Speaker verification stands out as one of the most reliable methods used to strengthen system security. Because it can verify people using their distinctive voice patterns, it not only makes access control more dependable but also strengthens the security architecture as a whole in the rapidly changing technological environment(Radha et al., 2024, Bebortta et al., 2023, Padinjappurathu Gopalan et al., 2022).

Automatic Speaker Verification (ASV) systems play a crucial role in authenticating users by identifying or verifying their voices. However, these systems are vulnerable to spoofing attacks, where unauthorized users falsely pose as legitimate ones to gain access. To counter this threat, audio spoof detection systems have been developed, specifically designed to recognize and prevent the use of counterfeit or manipulated audio content. Although ASV has seen significant advancements in the past decade, it still exhibits susceptibility to various spoofing attacks. ASV systems face a variety of spoofing attacks, categorized as direct and indirect attacks. Direct attacks involve logical attacks (LA) and physical attacks (PA). LA includes synthetic attacks and deep fake attacks, while PA encompasses replay attacks and impersonation attacks, further divided into mimicry and clone attacks, (Dua et al., 2023), pose a significant challenge (Z. Wu, Evans, et al., 2015). Among these, replay attacks are considered one of the simplest yet highly effective ASV spoofing techniques. Unlike other methods, replay attacks don't demand specialized knowledge from attackers and can be executed relatively easily using consumer devices.

In the first ASVspoof challenge dedicated to automatic speaker verification spoofing and counter-measures(Z. Wu, Kinnunen, et al., 2015), despite achieving impressive results with an overall average detection Equal Error Rate (EER) of less than 1.5%, it was evident that the EER for unknown attacks was five times higher compared to that of known attacks. Furthermore, the detection performance exhibited significant variations across different attack types, with certain attacks being reliably identified, while others induced remarkably high error rates, nearing 50%.

Participating systems in the ASVspoof 2017(Kinnunen et al., 2017) challenge underwent scrutiny based on diverse front-end features and the employment of different classifiers for detecting replay attacks under specified conditions.

The ASVspoof 2019 (Zhang et al., 2022)Challenge was organized with a primary emphasis on fostering the development of robust countermeasures capable of effectively distinguishing genuine speech from spoofed instances. This initiative specifically sought to promote the creation of generalized countermeasures, designed to exhibit high performance even in the face of unpredicted spoofing attacks. The data utilized in ASVspoof 2015(Wang et al., 2020) included manipulated speech samples generated through text-to-speech (TTS) and voice conversion (VC) systems prevalent at that time(Chakravarty & Dua, 2023).

ASVspoof 2021(Delgado et al., 2021) marks the fourth iteration in a series of biannual challenges, dedicated to fostering research on spoofing and the development of countermeasures to safeguard automatic speaker verification systems from manipulation. While maintaining its emphasis on logical and physical access tasks, with advancements compared to prior editions, ASVspoof 2021 introduces a novel task focused on the detection of deepfake speech. They include: a high resolution LFCCGMM(Tak et al., 2020) system; a CQCC-GMM (Todisco et al., 2016)system; an LFCC-LCNN(Wang & Yamagishi, 2021) system; a RawNet2 (Tak et al., 2021) system. In the progressive phase, there was a substantial decrease of 42% and 32% in the min t-DCF for the LA and PA tasks, respectively. In the DF task(Dua et al., 2023), the EER experienced a reduction from 11.6% to 0.10% during the progressive phase, but this improvement proved elusive as the EER surged to 15.6% in the evaluation phase. In this book chapter we have used spectrograms to implement frontend of our proposed model and ResNet 34 as classifier.

Mittal et al. (Mittal & Dua, 2021) used the static dynamic CQCC hybrid feature extraction to extract features from audios (Chakravarty Mohit, 2023) (Joshi & Dua, 2022) Dua et al. (Dua et al., 2022) proposed a hybrid approach using Mel-spectrogram with CNN and CQCC with LSTM for ASV. They achieved promising results by combining these two systems. In (Aravind et al., 2020), the authors used Mel-spectrogram and ResNet-34 architectures(Choi et al., 2024), achieving low EER with the ASVspoof 2019 dataset. Chakravarty et al. (Chakravarty & Dua, 2024a) utilized Mel spectrograms at the frontend, applying a modified ResNet50 model and LDA feature reduction to achieve impressive EER and accuracy for deepfake detection. Chakravarty et al. (Chakravarty & Dua, 2024b), Acoustic Ternary Pattern (ATP), Gammatone spectrogram and, Mel spectrogram, spectrogram were employed with ResNet27, achieving a low EER for impersonation attacks. In demonstrated the effectiveness of the ATP-LBP-GTCC. (Chakravarty & Dua, 2022) combination for detecting spoofing attacks, incorporating an acoustic model based on LSTM (Gambhir et al., 2024).

Motivated by (Aravind et al., 2020),(Chakravarty & Dua, 2024a) and (Chakravarty & Dua, 2024b) the improvements shown by spectrogram-based features. We employed Mel frequency scale based Mel-spectrogram (MS), Gamma scale based Gammatone Spectrogram(GS), Mel filter bank based Mel Frequency Cepstral Spectrograms (MCS), Acoustic pattern based Acoustic Pattern Spectrogram (APS), Gammatone Filter bank based Gammatone Cepstral Spectrogram (GCS), Short-Time Fourier Transform based Short Fourier Spectrogram(SFS) at front end to analysis of both temporal and spectral characteristics of an audio signal, and at backend pre-trained model ResNet34 at back end to classify audio as real or fake .

The remaining sections of the chapter are structured as follows: Section 2 introduces the techniques used to implement the proposed work. Section 3 introduces the proposed methodology. Section 4 presents the experiments and includes discussions based on the results. Finally, Section 5 concludes the chapter, summarizing the key findings.

2. PRELIMINARIES

The current section discusses the front end and backend strategies that have been used to implement the proposed work. The first part of this section discusses basics of front-end feature extraction, and the second part describes the acoustic models used.

2.1 Spectrograms-Based Features

A feature extraction technique in an ASV system implementation is used for extracting useful information from the recorded audio data. The work of this chapter uses MCS, GCS, and APS feature extraction techniques, and also extracted features from these techniques are represented in form of spectrogram for implementing different models of the proposed ASV system.

- **Acoustic Pattern Spectrogram (APS):** APS technique is used to represent 1-D audio signals as the acoustic signal to detect replay attacks(Irtaza et al., 2017)(Adnan et al., 2018). This technique is inspired by the application of 2D-local ternary patterns in image processing(Tan & Triggs, 2010). APS features are computed by encoding each frame of audio signal $S(x)$. To compute the APS features the difference the magnitudes of central sample C_s and nearby audio samples a^i is taken. A threshold (t_r) value is used to get the most optimized features(Chatlani & Soraghan, 2010). Sample values in s^v is quantized around the central sample C_s, values above and below $C_s \pm t_r$ are quantized to 1 and -1, respectively. As a result, we have a following three-valued function given in eq. (1):

$$A\left(s^v, C_s, t_r\right) = \begin{cases} -1 \ \ s^v - (C_s - t_r) \leq 0 \\ 0, \ (C_s + t_r) < y^j < (C_s - t_r) \\ 1, y^j - (C_s - t_r) \geq 0 \end{cases} \quad (1)$$

where, $A(s^v, C_s, t_r)$ represents acoustic signal locally using a three-valued ternary pattern. To reduce the number of patterns, patterns divided into upper pattern $A_{up}(.)$ and lower pattern $A_{low}(.)$ and only $+1$ are retained in, and other patterns are replaced as zero shown in eq. (2) and eq. (3).

$$A_{low}(s^v, C_s, t_r) = \begin{cases} 1, ifA(s^v, C_s, t_r) = -1 \\ 0, otherwise \end{cases} \quad (2)$$

$$A_{up}\left(s^v, C_s, t_r\right) = \begin{cases} 1, if A(s^v, C_s, t_r) = +1 \\ 0, otherwise \end{cases} \quad (3)$$

Now, upper class APS^{up} and lower class APS^{lw} patterns are encoded through decimal form using following eq. (4), and (5):

$$APS_u^{up}(y^j, C, t_d) = \sum_{j=0}^{j=7} A_{up}\left(s^v, C_s, t_r\right) * 2^j \quad (4)$$

$$APS_u^{lw}(y^j, C, t_d) = \sum_{j=0}^{j=7} A_{low}(s^v, C_s, t_r) * 2^j \quad (5)$$

In the next step, two histograms are calculated for APS_u^{up} and APS_u^{lw}. One bin of histograms is assigned for each uniform pattern and a non-uniform pattern are clustered in the bin. Functions used to calculate histogram are given as eq. (6), eq. (7):

$$H_t^{up}(APS^{up}, b) = \sum_{k=1}^{K} \rho\left(APS_k^{up}, n\right) \quad (6)$$

$$H_t^{lw}(APS^{lw}, b) = \sum_{k=1}^{K} \rho\left(APS_k^{lw}, n\right) \quad (7)$$

where, n represents the bin of histogram and ρ represents Kronecker delta function. First ten APS patterns are enough to capture variation in the data. The twenty-dimensional feature vector APS generated by concatenating both H_t^{up} and H_t^{lw} using equation (8).

$$APS = \left[H_t^{up} \| H_t^{lw} \right] \tag{8}$$

- **Gammatone Spectrogram (GS):** The GS has been created by multiplying the band-pass filter-bank generated by eq. (9) and eq. (10).

$$G(T) = m t^{n-1} e^{-2\pi e t} \cos\left(2\pi f_c + p\right) \tag{9}$$

$$E_{fc} = 24.7 \times \left(4.37 \times f_c + 1\right) \tag{10}$$

Detailed steps of generating GS are given in Figure 1.

Figure 1. Steps of generating GS

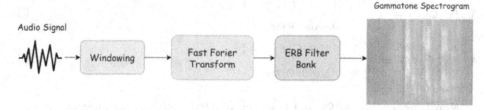

- **Mel-spectrogram (MS):** A MS is a spectrum of a signal. It is commonly used in audio signal processing and speech recognition. Let's break down the key components and concepts related to Mel spectrograms:

    Spectrogram: A spectrogram is a visual representation of the spectrum of frequencies of a signal as they vary with time. It is a 2D representation, where one axis represents time, the other represents frequency, and the colour intensity represents the amplitude or power of the frequencies at a given time.

    Mel Scale: The Mel scale is a perceptual scale of pitches that approximates the human ear's response to different frequencies. It is a non-linear scale, meaning that the perceptual difference between two frequencies is not constant across the entire frequency range. The Mel scale is often used in audio processing to better represent the way humans hear pitch differences.

    Mel-frequency Cepstral Coefficients (MFCCs): Before creating a Mel spectrogram, the audio signal is often pre-processed to extract features known as Mel-frequency cepstral coefficients (MFCCs). MFCCs capture the power spectrum of an audio signal after it has been passed through a filter bank that mimics the human ear's sensitivity to different frequencies. These coefficients are widely used in speech and audio processing tasks due to their effectiveness in representing the characteristics of the human voice.

Creating a MS: The resulting spectrum is then passed through a set of Mel filters. Each filter corresponds to a specific Mel frequency band. The output of each filter is then squared and integrated to obtain the energy in each Mel frequency band. The logarithm of these energies is usually taken to mimic the logarithmic perception of loudness by the human ear. The final result is a set of Mel spectrogram coefficients that can be represented as a 2D matrix, with time on one axis and Mel frequency bands on the other. Figure 2 shows the steps of generating Mel Spectrograms.

Figure 2. Steps to extract Mel spectrogram

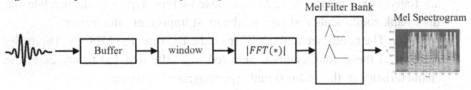

- **Mel Frequency Cepstral Spectrograms (MCS):** The processes taken by MCS to extract spectrogram from an input voice signal has shown in Figure 3.

Figure 3. Steps involved in MCS feature extraction

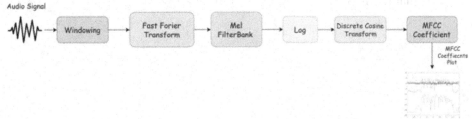

Framing and windowing: The signal is windowed into short frames, using a technique like windowing. Each frame represents a short time slice of the signal.

Discrete Fourier Transform: Compute Power Spectrum: For each frame, a Fourier transform is applied to convert the signal from the time domain to the frequency domain. The result is a power spectrum that represents the distribution of energy across different frequencies.

Mel Frequency wrapping: The Mel filter bank is a set of triangular filters that are applied to the power spectrum. These filters are spaced according to the Mel scale, which is a perceptually-based scale of pitches. The filters are designed to mimic the frequency response of the human ear.

Logarithmic: After applying the Mel filter bank, the logarithm of the filter bank energies is taken. This step helps to mimic the non-linear human perception of loudness.

Discrete Cosine Transform (DCT): The resulting log filter bank energies are transformed using DCT. The purpose of this step is to decorrelate the filter bank coefficients and capture the most important information.

MFCCs: The coefficients obtained from the DCT are the MFCCs. Typically, a subset of these coefficients is selected (e.g., the first 13) to represent the characteristics of the audio signal. Spectrogram Creation:

Generate MCS spectrogram: MCS spectrogram refers to a visualization where the x-axis represents time, the y-axis represents frequency (in terms of Mel scale), and the color intensity represents the amplitude or energy of the corresponding MFCC coefficient.

- **Gammatone Cepstral Spectrogram (GCS):** Cepstral coefficients are used to reflect the filter in the source-filter model of speech. GCS condenses information about the vocal tract into a limited number of coefficients based on cochlea knowledge. Figure 4 shows the steps performed by GCS to extract features from audios. The first two step of GCS similar to MCS.

Figure 4. Steps involved in GCS feature extraction

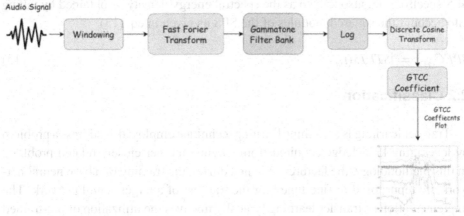

The frequency responses of multiple Gammatone (GT) filters are combined in the GT filter bank. Gammatone filter bank is obtained as follows using eq. (11):

$$G_T(f) = \alpha T^{N-1} e^{2\pi\omega t} \cos(2\pi F_C + \emptyset) \tag{11}$$

where, the phase $\emptyset$ is generally set to zero, the constant α regulates the gain, and the order of the filter is determined by the integer N, which is usually less than four. Twelve GCS coefficients are obtained, other than these features, the log energy feature is also calculated.

- **Short Fourier Spectrogram (SFS):** A signal processing method called the SFS is used to examine a signal's frequency content as it varies over time. By splitting a signal into brief, overlapping segments, and applying a Fourier Transform to each segment, it produces a time-varying frequency representation of the signal. The SFS of a signal is defined as $STFTx(t,f)$ and SFS of a signal $x(t)$ is defined as eq. (12),

$$STFTx(t,f) = \int_{-}(-\infty)^{\wedge}(+\infty)\, x(t)\ h*(t-T)e^{\wedge}(-j2\pi ft)\, du \tag{12}$$

where * stands for conjugate transpose and $h(t-T)$ is the window function, which is Gaussian window. The signal $x(t)$ is windowed around the time t by multiplying the window $h*(t-T)$ with inside the time domain. And the local spectrum at the given time is provided by the Fourier transform of the local signal $\int_{-\infty}^{+\infty}x(t)h*(t-T)$. Time and frequency resolution are traded off when the signal $x(t)$is windowed. A lengthy duration window is required to attain a good frequency resolution in SFS, whereas a short duration window is required to achieve a good time resolution. The SFS spectrogram, also known as the spectral energy density, is obtained by taking into account the squared modulus of the SFS as given in eq. (13).

$$SPEC_{STFT} = |STFTx(t,f)|^2 \tag{13}$$

2.2 Classification

Transfer learning is a machine learning technique employed to address a problem by leveraging knowledge acquired from solving another closely related problem. In this methodology, the features obtained during the training of a base neural network are repurposed or fine-tuned for the training of a target neural network. The implementation of transfer learning typically involves the utilization of pre-trained models. These models are initially trained on extensive benchmark datasets to address similar problems. Due to the high computational cost associated with training such models, it is a common practice to repurpose models from existing literature, such as VGG, Inception, MobileNet, and ResNet. Transfer learning models, especially those based on large convolutional neural networks (CNNs), are favored for their performance and ease of training, making CNNs highly popular for various applications in this context. Resnet34 is a pre-trained architecture proposed in 2015 by Microsoft Research experts. This network employs a VGG-19-inspired plain network architecture, to which the short-cut connection is added(He et al., 2016a). We have designed ResNet architecture, as shown in Figure 5, using TensorFlow and Keras API(Chollet, 2021).

Figure 5. The detailed architecture of ResNet34

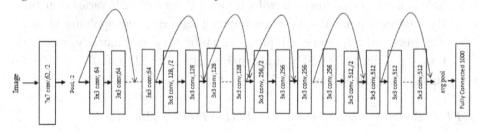

3. PROPOSED APPROACH

Figure 6 illustrates the proposed architecture's flow, incorporating three distinct datasets: ASVspoof LA, VSDC and DECRO English partition. These datasets comprise varied audio samples designated for training, validation, and testing purposes. All available audio files within their respective folders were utilized in the implementation. Throughout the implementation process, six spectrograms have been generated from the audio samples extracted from the aforementioned datasets. These spectrograms include Mel-spectrogram (MS), Gamma scale-based Gammatone Spectrogram (GS), Mel filter bank-based Mel Frequency Cepstral Spectrograms (MCS), Acoustic pattern-based Acoustic Pattern Spectrogram (APS), Gammatone Filter bank-based Gammatone Cepstral Spectrogram (GCS), and Short-Time Fourier Transform-based Short Fourier Spectrogram (SFS) for each audio. All these spectrograms have been employed as input for a pre-trained ResNet34 for classification purposes. The ResNet classifier distinguishes audio samples into two classes: spoof or bonafide, based on the unique characteristics of the audio signals.

Figure 6. Proposed architecture

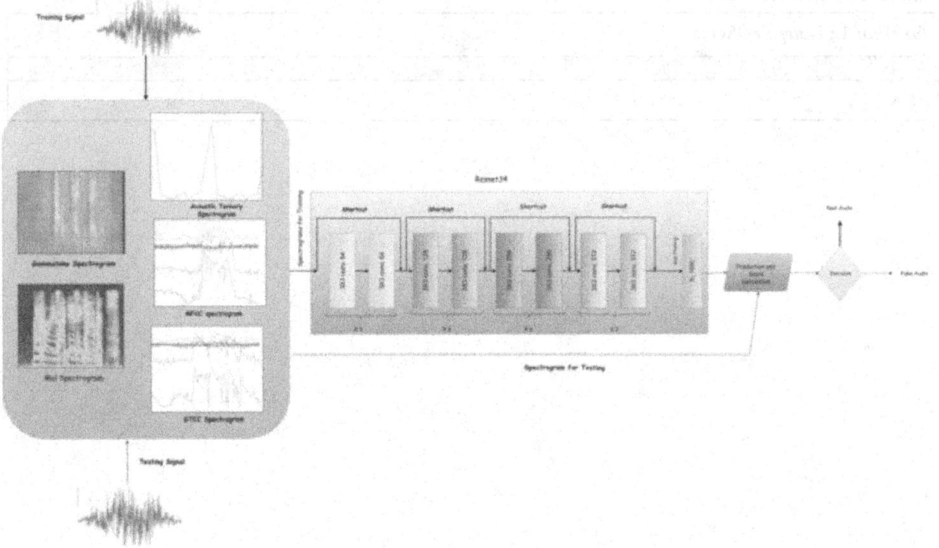

3.1 Feature Extraction Using Spectrograms

Spectrograms visually depict the frequency distribution of an audio signal across time, offering valuable insights into the evolving spectral features. They unveil crucial details about the frequency components and their changes over time, providing a comprehensive understanding of the signal's temporal variations. This section gives the detail overview of the feature extraction, which is performed using Mel-spectrogram (MS), Gammatone Spectrogram (GS), Mel Frequency Cepstral Spectrograms (MCS), Acoustic Pattern Spectrogram (APS), Gammatone Cepstral Spectrogram (GCS), Short Fourier Spectrogram (SFS).

- **Gammatone Spectrogram (GS):** GS is generated by initially computing a conventional spectrogram with a fixed bandwidth [45]. Function1 outlines the process of extracting the GS Figure 7 and Figure 8 shows the output of Function 1.

Table 1. Function 1

function 1 : *generateGS*()
(GS)

Figure 7. GS for bonafide

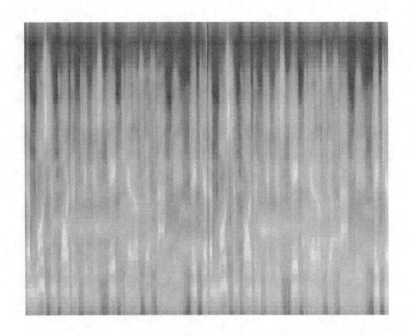

Figure 8. GS for spoof audio

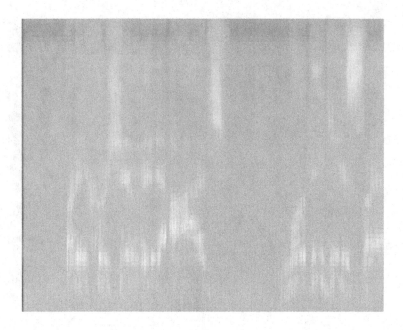

- **Gammatone Cepstral Spectrogram (GCS) and Mel Frequency Cepstral Spectrograms (MCS):** Function 2, GTCC function returns top 12D features, and GCS spectrogram has been utilised to display these GCS features in image format. Line 7 of the same function used to extract MFCC features to get MCS. Figure 9, 10, 11 and 12 shows the output of Function 2.

Table 2. Function 2

)   *Plot(coeffs) // plotting features*   *9. return plot*   *10.*

Figure 9. GCS for bonafide audio

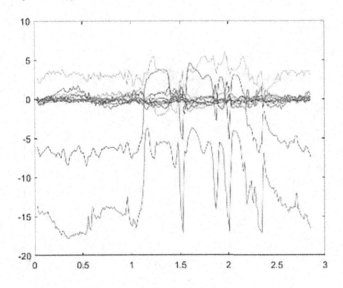

Figure 10. GCS for spoofed audio

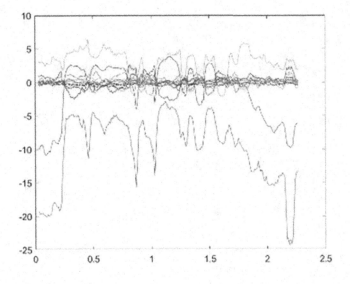

Figure 11. MCS for bonafide audio

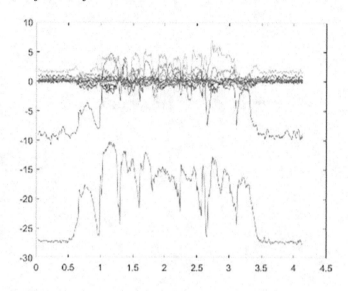

Figure 12. MCS for spoofed audio

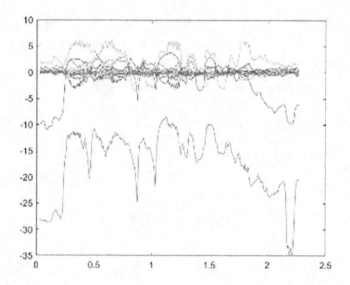

- **Short Fourier Spectrogram (SFS):** After removing the silence part from the audio, we extracted SFS spectrograms for further processing. For extracting spectrograms for each audio used for training and testing, Function 3 is used. We have used the inbuilt function from MATLAB audios toolbox. We have set window size to 1024, overlap size to 512, and sampling rate to 44100.

Table 3. Function 3

0		
1.		
2.		
5.		
11.		

- **Mel Spectrogram (MS):** The MS makes use of the Mel scale, which is a pitch scale that approximates how humans perceive frequency variations(Huang et al., 2001). The function 4 for generating Mel-spectrogram based features is described in Function 2. is a function that accepts audio files in format as input and returns and . Other arguments are , which represents the length of the FFT window, and , which represents the number of samples in subsequent frames. Line 6th converts a power spectrogram (amplitude squared) to decibel (dB) units and returns Mel spectrogram. Figure 10 shows the output of Function 4. Figure 13 and 14 shows MS for bonafide audio and spoofed audio.

Table 4. Function 4

2.		
// 7.		

Figure 13. MS for bonafide audio

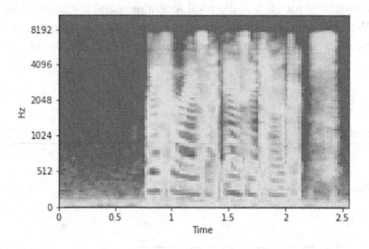

Figure 14. MS for spoofed audio

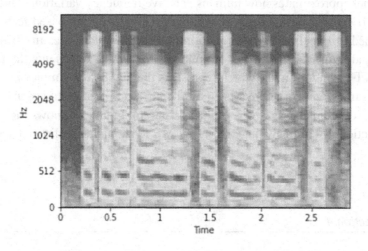

- **Acoustic Pattern Spectrogram (APS):** Process of calculating APS feature is as follows; The audio stream is separated into short overlapping frames that typically range from 10 to 50 milliseconds in duration. Overlapping frames are used to depict temporal relationships between frames. The energy of each

124

frame is computed by adding the squared amplitudes of the audio samples included within the frame. This indicates the overall strength or loudness of the audio within the frame. Each frame's energy values are quantized into three levels, often using a threshold-based technique. The threshold values categorise the energy range into three categories: low, medium, and high. The quantized energy values for each frame are represented as a ternary pattern. Depending on the implementation, the patterns could be binary (0, 1) or ternary (-1, 0). Within each frame, the ternary patterns capture the relative energy distribution. Multiple frames' ternary patterns are aggregated to generate a feature vector that reflects the audio signal. Function 5 describes the algorithm for producing APS. Figure 15, 16 shows the output of Function 5.

Table 5. Function 5

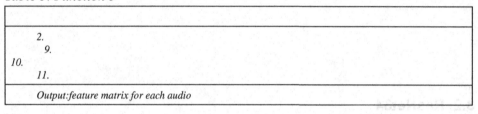

2.	
9.	
10.	
11.	
Output:feature matrix for each audio	

Figure 15. APS for (a) bonafide audio

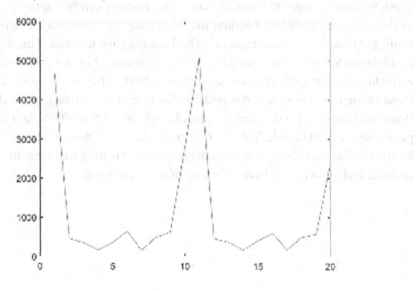

Figure 16. APS for spoofed audio

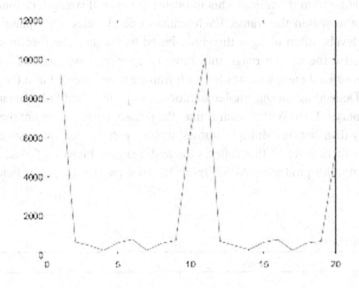

3.2. ResNet34

Residual networks, introduced by four researchers, have proven effective in tasks such as image classification and target recognition(He et al., 2016a). As network depth increases, more information and richer features can be captured. However, as deep learning networks become more intricate, optimization challenges arise, leading to diminishing performance on both training and test data. This degradation is attributed to issues like vanishing gradients, where gradients approaching 0, or exploding gradients, where gradients surpass 1, hinder effective learning. To address these challenges, He et al. proposed ResNet (He et al., 2016b), a novel network structure. ResNet-34 is the primary model employed in this article, and its specific parameters are detailed in Table 1 (He et al., 2016a). Unlike traditional stacking layers, ResNet introduces residual connections, mitigating the vanishing gradient problem and allowing for better training of deeper networks.

Table 6. ResNet34 architecture

Layer Name	Output layer	34-layers
Con_1		, stride 2
Conv_2		MaxPooling, stride 2
		*3
Conv_3		*4
Conv_4		*6
Conv_5		
		Average pool, 1000-d fc, softmax

4. EXPERIMENTAL SETUP AND RESULTS

In this section, we have provided a comprehensive overview of the experiments carried out to assess the effectiveness of our cross-lingual deepfake audio detection methodology. We have used MATLAB 2022 to implement our approach, while the back-end model was written in Python 3.7 and implemented using Anaconda. The computational resources for this task are a computer equipped with an 11th-generation core i5 processor and 16GB of RAM. The detailed explanation of the dataset utilized for our proposed work also describes the thorough experimental approach used to evaluate the effectiveness of our model.

4.1 Dataset Used

This section contains the details of dataset used during the implementation. We have used ASVspoof2019 Logical Access (LA) Partition for detecting synthetic attack, VSDC for reply attack detection and DEepfake CROss-lingual (DECRO) for deepfake audio attacks.

- **ASVspoof2019:** The ASVspoof 2019 database was introduced in 2019 for ASV spoofing detection. The dataset is divided into three sections: training, evaluation, and development. VC, TTC and hybrid VC_TTS algorithms have been used to create spoofed utterances. This dataset contains total 19 different type of spoof attacks. The training and development partitions has been made up of faked utterances generated by six distinct algorithms (A_{01}-A_{06}). There are four TTS algorithms A_{01} to A_{04} and two VC algorithms A_{05} and A_{06}. On the other hand, the evaluation partition consists of faked utterances created by a collection of 13 algorithms (A_{07}-A_{19}). Further evaluation attacks are divided into three categories: Known Attacks are A_{16}, A_{19}, Partially Known Attack are A_{07}, A_{08}, A_{09}, A_{17}, Unknown Attacks are A_{10}, A_{11}, A_{12}, A_{13}, A_{14}, A_{15}, A_{18}. The summary of the ASVspoof 2019 LA dataset has been given in Table 2. The complete explanation of this dataset can be found in (Wang et al., 2020).

Table 7. ASVspoof2019 LA dataset

Partitions	No. of Speakers		ASVspoof2019	
	Female	Male	Bonafide	Spoof
Training	12	8	2580	22800
Evaluation	27	21	7355	63882
Development	6	4	2548	22296

- **Voice Spoofing Detection Corpus (VSDC):** VSDC (K. Malik et al., 2020) primarily represents different replay assaults. This dataset is divided into folders, each of which contains authentic (bonafide) recordings as well as the original user's first-point replay (1PR) and second-point replay (2PR) assaults. Each folder is further subdivided into sub-folders. The employment of replay speakers and recording equipment is required to implement 1PR and 2PR assaults (K. M. Malik et al., 2019), (Baumann et al., 2021). The unique user gives nine distinct sentences inside each recording. The sample set number, the point of replay (1PR or 2PR), the individual speaker engaged, the ambient circumstances, the microphone utilized, the configuration number, and the phrase number are all used to organize the file names. Table 3 represents the samples collected at 0, 1, and 2 replay points.

Table 8. Count of samples at different points of replay attack

Sample Type	Point of Replay (PR)		
	0	1	2
Count of Samples	1687	6179	6184

- **DEepfake CROss-lingual (DECRO):** Authors of (Ba et al., 2023) have designed this dataset to check their model's performance to evaluate cross-lingual detection performance. Table 4 provides a detailed analysis of the audio distribution in the DECRO Dataset. The dataset is divided into parts that show how each method is distributed among test, development, and training sets. Similar distributions are offered for algorithms like HiFiGAN, Multiband-MelGAN, PWG, Tacotron, StarGANv2, FastSpeech2, VITS, NVCNet, Baidu, and Xunfei, demonstrating how the dataset has been carefully organised to enable an extensive evaluation of model performance in a variety of linguistic and algorithmic contexts.

Table 9. Audio distribution of DECRO dataset

Algorithm	English		
	Training	Development	Test
Bona-fide	5129	3049	4306
HiFiGAN	2000	1500	2000
Multiband-MelGAN	2000	1500	2000
PWG	2000	1500	2000
Tacotron	2000	914	2000
FastSpeech2	904	452	452
StarGANv2	1840	920	920
VITS	2000	1350	1209
NVCNet	2000	1500	2000
Baidu	2000	1000	2000
Xunfei	733	367	367

4.2 Performance Metrices

ASV spoof detection systems' effectiveness is typically evaluated using the following assessment metrics. After a thorough review of the existing literature, it was evident that the EER stood out as the primary evaluation criterion for assessing the performance of ASV systems. While some of the publications considered only precision, accuracy, recall, and F1-score as performance rating criteria. These evaluation criteria are described in this section. Equation 14, 15, 16 and 17 represent the formula for Accuracy, Precision, Recall and F1-score.

- **Accuracy:** It measures how often the classifier correctly predicts.

(14)

- **Precision:** It explains how the correctly predicted samples were positive.

(15)

- **Recall:** It, also known as Sensitivity or True Positive Rate (TPR), measures the proportion of correctly identified positive samples among all actual positive samples.

(16)

- **F1-score:** The harmonic mean of recall and precision provides a balanced metric that considers both false positives and false negatives.

(17)

- **True Positives (TP):** In a binary classification, a True Positive occurs when both the actual and anticipated classes are positive.
- **True Negatives (TN):** In binary classification, True Negatives occur when both the actual and projected classes are negative. The number of accurately detected negative instances by the model is represented by TN.
- **False Positives (FP):** When the actual class is negative, but the model predicts a positive class, a False Positive occurs. FP is a measure of the number of negative situations that the model misclassifies as positive.
- **False Negatives (FN):** When the model predicts a negative class, but the actual class is positive.
- **Equal Error Rate (EER):** The point on the ROC curve where the False Acceptance Rate (FAR) and False Rejection Rate (FRR) are equal is denoted by the EER. It is a commonly used statistic to assess how well biometric systems work, particularly ASV spoof detection.

4.3 Performance of Proposed Model for Different Attacks

This section describes the results obtained during all eighteen experiments. Six spectrograms; Gammatone Spectrogram (GS), Gammatone Cepstral Spectrogram (GCS), Short Fourier Spectrogram (SFS), Mel-spectrogram (MS), Mel Frequency Cepstral Spectrograms (MCS) Acoustic Pattern Spectrogram (APS) and ResNet 34 as classifier have been used to implement this proposed model. The detailed experiments are described in the following section.

- **Performance of Spectrograms and ResNet34 for Synthetic Attack:**Table 5 shows the results of experiments done using six spectrograms and ResNet34 classifier. For this experiment we have use ASVpsoof2019 LA partition for training, validation and evaluation. Gammatone Spectrogram (GS) has achieved an EER of 2.1%, Gammatone Cepstral Spectrogram (GCS) has achieved an EERof 4.2%, Short Fourier Spectrogram (SFS) has achieved an EER of 5.82%, Mel-spectrogram (MS) has achieved an EER of 10%, Mel Frequency Cepstral Spectrograms (MCS) has achieved an EER of 13% and Acoustic Pattern Spectrogram (APS) has achieved an EER of 41%. From these results it can be concluded that GS has outperformed all the other proposed model.

Table 10. Performance of spectrograms and ResNet34 for synthetic attack

Model	EER	Accuracy	Precision	Recall	F1-Score
Gammatone Spectrogram (GS)	2.1	98	98	98	98
Gammatone Cepstral Spectrogram (GCS)	4.2	96	96	96	96
Short Fourier Spectrogram (SFS)	5.82	88	88	82	94
Mel-spectrogram (MS)	10	80	81	81	82
Mel Frequency Cepstral Spectrograms (MCS)	13	87	87	86	87
Acoustic Pattern Spectrogram (APS)	41	63	63	63	63

- **Performance of Spectrograms and ResNet34 for Replay Attack:**Table 6 shows the results of experiments done using six spectrograms and ResNet34 classifier. For this experiment we have used VSDC dataset audios training, validation, and evaluation. GS has achieved an EER of 4.15%, GCS has achieved an EERof 7.4%, SFS has achieved an EER of 12.3%, MS has achieved an EER of 16.3%, MCS has achieved an EER of 18.8% and APS has achieved an EER of 40%. From these results it can be concluded that GS has outperformed all the other proposed model.

Table 11. Performance of spectrograms and ResNet34 for replay attack

Model	EER	Accuracy	Precision	Recall	F1-Score
Gammatone Spectrogram (GS)	4.15	96	94	95	95.5
Gammatone Cepstral Spectrogram (GCS)	7.4	96	96	96	96
Short Fourier Spectrogram (SFS)	12.3	87	86	80	93
Mel-spectrogram (MS),	16.3	84	84	85	84
Mel Frequency Cepstral Spectrograms (MCS)	18.8	82	84	81	82
Acoustic Pattern Spectrogram (APS)	40	44	51	58	56

- **Performance of Spectrograms and ResNet34 for Deepfake Attack:**Table 7 shows the results of experiments done using Gammatone Spectrogram (GS), Gammatone Cepstral Spectrogram (GCS), Short Fourier Spectrogram (SFS), Mel-spectrogram (MS), Mel Frequency Cepstral Spectrograms (MCS), Acoustic Pattern Spectrogram (APS) and ResNet34 classifier. For this experiment we have use DECRO dataset English partition for training, validation and evaluation. As result GS has achieved an EER of 5%, GCS has achieved an EERof 9%, SFS has achieved an EER of 14%, MS has achieved an EER of 17%, MCS has achieved an EER of 21% and APS has achieved an EER of 56%. From these results it can be concluded that GS has outperformed all the other proposed model by achieving 5% EER.

Table 12. Performance of spectrograms and ResNet34 for deepfake attack

Model	EER	Accuracy	Precision	Recall	F1-Score
Gammatone Spectrogram (GS)	5	95	95	95	95
Gammatone Cepstral Spectrogram (GCS)	9	91	91	91	93
Short Fourier Spectrogram (SFS)	14	86	86	85	86
Mel-spectrogram (MS)	17	83	83	85	84
Mel Frequency Cepstral Spectrograms (MCS)	21	53	63	50	84
Acoustic Pattern Spectrogram (APS)	56	50	51	62	43

4.4. Discussion and Comparative Analysis

The proposed methodology aims to elevate the performance of Automatic Speaker Verification (ASV) systems by employing a two-stage process. Firstly, spectrogram-based features are utilized at the front end, followed by the application of pretrained deep Convolutional Neural Network (CNN) models at the back end. The experimental findings, outlined in 4.3 section, underscore the superior performance of Gammatone Spectrogram (GS) features compared to other spectrogram-based counterparts. In the LA dataset, GS achieves an Equal Error Rate (EER) of 2.1%, surpassing alternative features. For the VSDC dataset, GS continues to outperform, yielding an EER of 4.1%. Similarly, in the DECRO dataset, GS excels with an EER of 5%. Notably, GS demonstrates efficacy in detecting synthetic, replay, and deepfake attacks, as evidenced in result section. Upon meticulous analysis, GS emerges as the frontrunner among spectrogram-based features. This superiority is attributed to several factors. Firstly, GS features exhibit heightened resilience in the presence of noise and reverberation, distinguishing them from other spectrogram-based features. The design of Gammatone filters closely mirrors the cochlear filters in the human ear, bolstering the system's ability to extract discerning features, particularly in challenging acoustic environments. Table 8 shows the comparative analysis of our proposed approach with existing approaches.

Table 13. Comparative analysis with existing techniques

Work	Optimal Model		Attacks	Evaluation Metrics (%)				
	Feature extraction	Classifier		Accuracy	Precision		F1-score	EER
Aravind et al. (Aravind et al., 2020)	Mel Spectrogram	Resnet34	Synthetic (LA)	--	--	--	--	5.32
			Replay (PA)	--	--	--	--	5.74
Wu et al.(H. Wu et al., 2020)	log power spec	VGCC like Network, Squeeze Excitation ResNet Model	Synthetic (LA)	87.2	--	--	--	--
Nava et (Hernández-Nava et al., 2023)	STFT spectrogram, MFCC	DNN	Replay (PA)	96.46	--	--	--	6.66
Singh et al. (Singh Yadav et al., 2024)	Mel Spectrogram	Patched Transformer	Synthetic (LA)	--	--	--	--	4.54
Proposed Approach	Gammatone Spectrogram	Resnet34	Synthetic (LA)	98	98	98	98	2.1
			Replay (VSDC)	96	94	95	95.5	4.15
			DECRO(Deepfake)	95	95	95	95	5

5. CONCLUSION AND FUTURE WORK

Our proposed framework demonstrates robust capabilities in handling synthetic, replay, and deepfake attacks by leveraging six distinct spectrograms (Mel-spectrogram, Gammatone Spectrogram, Mel Frequency Cepstral Spectrograms, Acoustic Pattern Spectrogram, Gammatone Cepstral Spectrogram, Short Fourier Spectrogram) along with the ResNet34 classifier. The most successful model, a combination of Gammatone Spectrogram (GS) and ResNet34, achieved remarkable results with 2.1%, 4.14%, and 5% EER in detecting synthetic attacks, replay attacks, and deepfake attacks, respectively. This research and the techniques presented herein lay the foundation for future developments in countering advanced attack challenges across various linguistic contexts. Our findings represent a significant stride towards establishing more comprehensive and linguistically inclusive defences against detrimental audio modifications, especially as deepfake technology continues to advance.

REFERENCES

Adnan, S. M., Irtaza, A., Aziz, S., Ullah, M. O., Javed, A., & Mahmood, M. T. (2018). Fall detection through acoustic local ternary patterns. *Applied Acoustics*, 140, 296–300. DOI: 10.1016/j.apacoust.2018.06.013

Aravind, P. R., Nechiyil, U., & Paramparambath, N. (2020). Audio spoofing verification using deep convolutional neural networks by transfer learning. *ArXiv Preprint ArXiv:2008.03464*.

Ba, Z., Wen, Q., Cheng, P., Wang, Y., Lin, F., Lu, L., & Liu, Z. (2023). Transferring Audio Deepfake Detection Capability across Languages. *Proceedings of the ACM Web Conference 2023*, 2033–2044. DOI: 10.1145/3543507.3583222

Baumann, R., Malik, K. M., Javed, A., Ball, A., Kujawa, B., & Malik, H. (2021). Voice spoofing detection corpus for single and multi-order audio replays. *Computer Speech & Language*, 65, 101132. DOI: 10.1016/j.csl.2020.101132

Bebortta, S., Tripathy, S. S., Basheer, S., & Chowdhary, C. L. (2023). Deepmist: Towards deep learning assisted mist computing framework for managing healthcare big data. *IEEE Access : Practical Innovations, Open Solutions*, 11, 42485–42496. DOI: 10.1109/ACCESS.2023.3266374

Chakravarty, N., & Dua, M. (2022). Noise Robust ASV Spoof Detection Using Integrated Features and Time Delay Neural Network. *SN Computer Science*, 4(2), 127. DOI: 10.1007/s42979-022-01557-4 PMID: 35036930

Chakravarty, N., & Dua, M. (2023). Spoof Detection using Sequentially Integrated Image and Audio Features. *International Journal of Computing and Digital Systems*, 13(1), 1. DOI: 10.12785/ijcds/1301111

Chakravarty, N., & Dua, M. (2024a). A lightweight feature extraction technique for deepfake audio detection. *Multimedia Tools and Applications*, 83(26), 1–25. DOI: 10.1007/s11042-024-18217-9

Chakravarty, N., & Dua, M. (2024b). An improved feature extraction for Hindi language audio impersonation attack detection. *Multimedia Tools and Applications*, 83(25), 1–26. DOI: 10.1007/s11042-023-18104-9

Chakravarty Mohit, N. (2023). Data Augmentation and Hybrid Feature Amalgamation to detect Audio Deep Fake attacks. *Physica Scripta*. http://iopscience.iop.org/article/10.1088/1402-4896/acea05

Chatlani, N., & Soraghan, J. (2010). *Local binary patterns for 1-D signal processing*.

Choi, S., Chung, S., Lee, S., Han, S., Kang, T., Seo, J., Kwak, I.-Y., & Oh, S. (2024). TB-ResNet: Bridging the Gap from TDNN to ResNet in Automatic Speaker Verification with Temporal-Bottleneck Enhancement. *ICASSP 2024-2024 IEEE International Conference on Acoustics, Speech and Signal Processing (ICASSP)*, 10291–10295.

Chollet, F. (2021). *Deep learning with Python*. Simon and Schuster.

Delgado, H., Evans, N., Kinnunen, T., Lee, K. A., Liu, X., Nautsch, A., Patino, J., Sahidullah, M., Todisco, M., & Wang, X. (2021). ASVspoof 2021: Automatic speaker verification spoofing and countermeasures challenge evaluation plan. *ArXiv Preprint ArXiv:2109.00535*.

Dua, M., Meena, S., & Chakravarty, N. (2023). Audio Deepfake Detection Using Data Augmented Graph Frequency Cepstral Coefficients. *2023 International Conference on System, Computation, Automation and Networking (ICSCAN)*, 1–6. DOI: 10.1109/ICSCAN58655.2023.10395679

Dua, M., Sadhu, A., Jindal, A., & Mehta, R. (2022). A hybrid noise robust model for multireplay attack detection in Automatic speaker verification systems. *Biomedical Signal Processing and Control*, 74, 103517. DOI: 10.1016/j.bspc.2022.103517

Gambhir, P., Dev, A., Bansal, P., Sharma, D. K., & Gupta, D. (2024). Residual networks for text-independent speaker identification: Unleashing the power of residual learning. *Journal of Information Security and Applications*, 80, 103665. DOI: 10.1016/j.jisa.2023.103665

Hanifa, R. M., Isa, K., & Mohamad, S. (2021). A review on speaker recognition: Technology and challenges. *Computers & Electrical Engineering*, 90, 107005. DOI: 10.1016/j.compeleceng.2021.107005

He, K., Zhang, X., Ren, S., & Sun, J. (2016a). Deep residual learning for image recognition. *Proceedings of the IEEE Conference on Computer Vision and Pattern Recognition*, 770–778.

He, K., Zhang, X., Ren, S., & Sun, J. (2016b). Identity mappings in deep residual networks. *Computer Vision–ECCV 2016: 14th European Conference, Amsterdam, The Netherlands, October 11–14, 2016. Proceedings*, 14(Part IV), 630–645.

Hernández-Nava, C. A., Rincón-García, E. A., Lara-Velázquez, P., de-Los-Cobos-Silva, S. G., Gutiérrez-Andrade, M. A., & Mora-Gutiérrez, R. A. (2023). Voice spoofing detection using a neural networks assembly considering spectrograms and mel frequency cepstral coefficients. *PeerJ. Computer Science*, 9, e1740. DOI: 10.7717/peerj-cs.1740 PMID: 38192463

Huang, X., Acero, A., Hon, H.-W., & Reddy, R. (2001). *Spoken language processing: A guide to theory, algorithm, and system development*. Prentice hall PTR.

Irtaza, A., Adnan, S. M., Aziz, S., Javed, A., Ullah, M. O., & Mahmood, M. T. (2017). A framework for fall detection of elderly people by analyzing environmental sounds through acoustic local ternary patterns. *2017 Ieee International Conference on Systems, Man, and Cybernetics (Smc)*, 1558–1563. DOI: 10.1109/SMC.2017.8122836

Joshi, S., & Dua, M. (2022). LSTM-GTCC based Approach for Audio Spoof Detection. *2022 International Conference on Machine Learning, Big Data, Cloud and Parallel Computing (COM-IT-CON)*, *1*, 656–661. DOI: 10.1109/COM-IT-CON54601.2022.9850820

Kinnunen, T., Sahidullah, M., Delgado, H., Todisco, M., Evans, N., Yamagishi, J., & Lee, K. A. (2017). *The ASVspoof 2017 challenge: Assessing the limits of replay spoofing attack detection*.

Malik, K., Javed, A., Malik, H., & Irtaza, A. (2020). A Light-Weight Replay Detection Framework For Voice Controlled IoT Devices. *IEEE Journal of Selected Topics in Signal Processing, PP*. DOI: 10.1109/JSTSP.2020.2999828

Malik, K. M., Malik, H., & Baumann, R. (2019). Towards vulnerability analysis of voice-driven interfaces and countermeasures for replay attacks. *2019 IEEE Conference on Multimedia Information Processing and Retrieval (MIPR)*, 523–528. DOI: 10.1109/MIPR.2019.00106

Mittal, A., & Dua, M. (2021). Static–dynamic features and hybrid deep learning models based spoof detection system for ASV. *Complex & Intelligent Systems*, 1–14.

Padinjappurathu Gopalan, S., Chowdhary, C. L., Iwendi, C., Farid, M. A., & Ramasamy, L. K. (2022). An efficient and privacy-preserving scheme for disease prediction in modern healthcare systems. *Sensors (Basel)*, 22(15), 5574. DOI: 10.3390/s22155574 PMID: 35898077

Radha, K., Bansal, M., & Pachori, R. B. (2024). Speech and speaker recognition using raw waveform modeling for adult and children's speech: A comprehensive review. *Engineering Applications of Artificial Intelligence*, 131, 107661. DOI: 10.1016/j.engappai.2023.107661

Singh Yadav, A. K., Xiang, Z., Bhagtani, K., Bestagini, P., Tubaro, S., & Delp, E. J. (2024). Compression Robust Synthetic Speech Detection Using Patched Spectrogram Transformer. *ArXiv E-Prints*, arXiv-2402.

Tak, H., Patino, J., Nautsch, A., Evans, N., & Todisco, M. (2020). Spoofing attack detection using the non-linear fusion of sub-band classifiers. *ArXiv Preprint ArXiv:2005.10393*. DOI: 10.21437/Interspeech.2020-1844

Tak, H., Patino, J., Todisco, M., Nautsch, A., Evans, N., & Larcher, A. (2021). End-to-end anti-spoofing with rawnet2. *ICASSP 2021-2021 IEEE International Conference on Acoustics, Speech and Signal Processing (ICASSP)*, 6369–6373.

Tan, X., & Triggs, B. (2010). Enhanced local texture feature sets for face recognition under difficult lighting conditions. *IEEE Transactions on Image Processing*, 19(6), 1635–1650. DOI: 10.1109/TIP.2010.2042645 PMID: 20172829

Todisco, M., Delgado, H., & Evans, N. W. D. (2016). A New Feature for Automatic Speaker Verification Anti-Spoofing: Constant Q Cepstral Coefficients. *Odyssey*, 2016, 283–290. DOI: 10.21437/Odyssey.2016-41

Wang, X., & Yamagishi, J. (2021). A comparative study on recent neural spoofing countermeasures for synthetic speech detection. *ArXiv Preprint ArXiv:2103.11326*. DOI: 10.21437/Interspeech.2021-702

Wang, X., Yamagishi, J., Todisco, M., Delgado, H., Nautsch, A., Evans, N., Sahidullah, M., Vestman, V., Kinnunen, T., Lee, K. A., Juvela, L., Alku, P., Peng, Y.-H., Hwang, H.-T., Tsao, Y., Wang, H.-M., Le Maguer, S., Becker, M., Henderson, F., & Ling, Z.-H. (2020). ASVspoof 2019: A large-scale public database of synthesized, converted and replayed speech. *Computer Speech & Language*, 64, 101114. DOI: 10.1016/j.csl.2020.101114

Wu, H., Liu, S., Meng, H., & Lee, H. (2020). Defense against adversarial attacks on spoofing countermeasures of ASV. *ICASSP 2020-2020 IEEE International Conference on Acoustics, Speech and Signal Processing (ICASSP)*, 6564–6568.

Wu, Z., Evans, N., Kinnunen, T., Yamagishi, J., Alegre, F., & Li, H. (2015). Spoofing and countermeasures for speaker verification: A survey. *Speech Communication*, 66, 130–153. DOI: 10.1016/j.specom.2014.10.005

Wu, Z., Kinnunen, T., Evans, N., Yamagishi, J., Hanilçi, C., Sahidullah, M., & Sizov, A. (2015). ASVspoof 2015: the first automatic speaker verification spoofing and countermeasures challenge. *Sixteenth Annual Conference of the International Speech Communication Association*. DOI: 10.21437/Interspeech.2015-462

Zhang, X., Zhang, X., Zou, X., Liu, H., & Sun, M. (2022). Towards Generating Adversarial Examples on Combined Systems of Automatic Speaker Verification and Spoofing Countermeasure. *Security and Communication Networks*, 2666534, 1–12. Advance online publication. DOI: 10.1155/2022/2666534

Chapter 6
Machine Learning in Health Information Security:
Unraveling Patterns, Concealing Secrets, and Mitigation

Rita Komalasari
https://orcid.org/0000-0001-9963-2363
Yarsi University, Indonesia

ABSTRACT

This chapter explores how machine learning transforms health information security. Based on a thorough literature review, it examines the detailed patterns of encrypted internet visits using steganography to protect sensitive health data. A thorough literature review on information security machine learning methods and advances was prepared in this chapter. Synthesizing multiple perspectives created a solid basis. Data analysis, examining encrypted network traffic and picture data trends, was crucial. A rigorous study revealed complex methods that detected encrypted internet visits and created practical steganographic algorithms. The chapter uses thorough data analysis to show machine learning's potential in detection and concealment and weaknesses, suggesting a balanced approach. This study shows how pattern recognition, data analysis, and security secure health information.

DOI: 10.4018/979-8-3693-2223-9.ch006

INTRODUCTION

Patterns and recognition are crucial in information security since the digital world changes continually (Hanelt et al., 2021). Recognition of data patterns typically distinguishes benign from harmful material (Muhammad et al., 2022). Machine learning has transformed information security by identifying sophisticated patterns despite insufficient data (Liu & Lang, 2019). This chapter explores machine learning's many uses in information security, emphasizing health information security (Sreedevi et al., 2022). Machine learning may revolutionize difficult health information security concerns, as this chapter argues. Machine learning detects harmful activity and secures sensitive data by analyzing and using pattern recognition (Gupta et al., 2020). However, machine learning systems are vulnerable, requiring a sophisticated approach to information security that combines innovation with solid protections. This chapter explores these subjects to emphasize machine learning's significance in moulding health information security's future and warn against its unregulated use. This chapter explores machine learning in information security, its promise, its risks, and how to protect health data in an increasingly linked digital environment. This study has major ramifications for stakeholders, including Hospitals, clinics, and healthcare providers, who may use the results to secure patient data and comply with HIPAA. IT experts at these institutions may use the new algorithms and insights to improve security and protect critical health data. Cybersecurity experts may use the study findings to improve methods and create more advanced intrusion detection systems. Experts can better identify and prevent cyberattacks by analyzing encrypted network traffic patterns. Machine learning, cybersecurity, and IT researchers may use the results to innovate. Academics may integrate these advances into their curriculum to train the next generation of health information security experts. This study may inform healthcare data security policies. This study may lead to stronger guidelines that adapt to cyber threats. This study benefits patients with electronic health data. Individuals can trust healthcare institutions and utilize digital health services more by improving security safeguards for medical data privacy and confidentiality. The findings greatly enhance health information security. It helps healthcare workers combat increasingly complex cyber threats with realistic and creative solutions. As new vulnerabilities and difficulties arise, this research methodology may be used for additional investigations, supporting a continuous cycle of development and adaptability of health information security. This study has great potential for applied research and practice. Healthcare institutions and organizations may immediately utilize the study results to improve security processes. By applying machine learning techniques, these businesses may protect sensitive health data from cyberattacks. Our study can identify harmful activity in real-time. This study allows IT experts to react quickly to cyber threats, reducing data breaches and patient suffering. The research may help firms comply with HIPAA and GDPR security requirements (Shuaib et al., 2021). These rules must be met, and the study delivers actionable insights to surpass them. Cybersecurity professionals may use study findings in training programs. Practitioners may improve their health information security abilities by studying and using cutting-edge methods. The created steganography and encrypted network traffic analysis techniques and algorithms advance knowledge. These foundations allow researchers to study data security beyond healthcare. The study serves as a standard for future studies as cyber risks grow. Researchers may adapt these methods to new threats to keep the knowledge base current and relevant in cybersecurity. This study combines machine learning with cybersecurity, setting a precedent for future research. It promotes cross-domain cooperation to solve difficult information security issues. Researchers may validate and refine algorithms to enhance them iteratively. Validation studies and real-world applications help fine-tune algorithms for optimal performance in varied settings. The research provides urgent healthcare answers and spurs applied research. It advances information security best practices by extending knowledge and encouraging innovation, helping many businesses outside of healthcare.

BACKGROUND

Due to medical record digitalization and cyberattacks on healthcare organizations, health information security is crucial (Lehto et al., 2022). The Cybersecurity Ventures "Healthcare Cybersecurity Report" predicts that healthcare hacks will cost $25 billion annually by 2024 (Kumar, 2023). This development highlights the need for creative and comprehensive healthcare information security. This project attempts to improve health data security by analyzing encrypted network traffic patterns and implementing effective steganographic methods.

A thorough literature study from 2018 forward showed a growing trend in cybersecurity using machine learning. Machine learning is crucial to healthcare data security (Qayyum et al., 2020). The Identity Theft Resource Center (ITRC) reports a considerable rise in healthcare data breaches since 2018 (Bisogni & Asghari, 2020). The International Data Corporation (IDC) estimated a 30% yearly growth rate in healthcare firms employing machine learning algorithms for data protection post-2018 (Arefolov et al., 2021). The Ponemon Institute reported in 2021 that the typical healthcare data breach cost $9.23 million, emphasizing the need for security (Owen et al., 2023). The General Data Protection Regulation (GDPR) in Europe and the Health Insurance Portability and Accountability Act (HIPAA) in the US have increased the need for advanced healthcare security protocols, making machine learning applications more relevant (Thapa & Camtepe, 2021). As assaults, adoption patterns, financial ramifications, and regulatory focus rise, this study's value lies in combating healthcare cyber risks using cutting-edge machine learning approaches. ISIMachine learning's capacity to identify complex data patterns shows its usefulness in information security. Machine learning algorithms evaluate encrypted network traffic time and packet size for encrypted website visits. Machine learning can properly predict the target website across anonymous networks (Aldweesh et al., 2020). Machine learning's predicted capacity to identify encrypted website visits is crucial to cybersecurity. Machine learning's capacity to comprehend complicated data patterns has made it a key tool in information security. During website visits, machine learning methods help decipher encrypted network data, time, and packet size. This study shows how these algorithms can reliably identify the intended website even when consumers browse anonymously. Machine learning models methodically analyze encrypted network traffic, enabling this functionality. These methods identify the target website by detecting timing and packet size irregularities. Modern cybersecurity relies on this predictive power to protect online data. Patel and colleagues' work shows how machine learning can identify encrypted website visits, demonstrating its vital role in digital communications security (Patel et al., 2023). In an age of evolving cyber dangers, machine learning's capacity to recognize and react to encrypted website visits is impressive. This technology strengthens online platform security and builds user trust, which is essential for digital ecosystems.

Machine learning helps decipher encrypted data and defend against cyber attacks as information security issues grow. Even when people browse anonymously, machine learning algorithms may reliably guess the intended website. During website visits, these algorithms use sophisticated methods to assess timing and packet size information in encrypted network data. By carefully examining encrypted data flow patterns, these algorithms understand users' digital footprints and each website's unique traits. Machine learning algorithms may identify characteristics in encrypted packets, even on anonymous networks, where users hide their digital footprints. After extensive training on varied datasets, these algorithms discover and match timing and packet size trends to known websites. Modern cybersecurity relies on this predictive capacity to identify network traffic origin and destination to detect risks and criminal activity. Machine learning algorithms that function in anonymous networks improve security. It helps detect illegal or dangerous information and protects user privacy during normal internet activity. These algorithms let cybersecurity experts develop a proactive protection plan by properly anticipating the target website. The comprehensive analysis of encrypted network data shows how machine learning has transformed a covert digital domain into a precise place where smart algorithms protect individuals and companies from developing cyber hazards. Suppose a big hospital uses machine learning methods to safeguard its patient database. These algorithms are trained on a massive dataset of organization-wide user behaviors, access patterns, and network traffic signatures. The algorithms constantly monitor patient database queries. Machine learning algorithms will flag it as an abnormality if an illegal person accesses the patient database over an anonymous network. The algorithms match request patterns with taught behaviors. Abnormalities, particularly in anonymous networks, generate an alarm. The system identifies questionable activities for additional study. Cybersecurity specialists may subsequently investigate the detected occurrence, ban the IP address, apply security protocols, or notify law enforcement. Steganography also shows machine learning's power. Machine learning-based steganographic algorithms effectively conceal hidden messages in cover material. Previous studies show machine learning techniques use picture redundancies to protect information (Gurunath et al., 2021). These advances support the use of machine learning to hide information in covert media. Steganography hides information in a cover medium, and machine learning works well together. With an emphasis on health data, this chapter explores how machine learning is being used to address pressing issues in the field of information security.

Figure 1. Article evaluation flow diagram

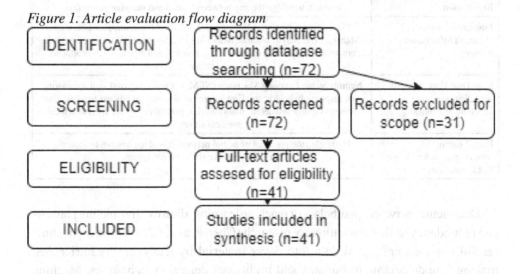

This chapter is built upon a comprehensive review of recent research on Machine Learning (ML) in Health Information Security (HIS). To gain a deep understanding of this rapidly evolving field, we conducted a systematic literature review, focusing on studies published in the past five years. After analyzing abstracts, 41 relevant articles were selected for in-depth review (illustrated in Figure 1). The author employed rigorous quality assurance measures to ensure our findings' credibility and reliability. This included verifying all sources and meticulously supporting every claim and explanation.

MACHINE LEARNING IN HEALTH INFORMATION SECURITY

This section goes into the field of steganography, which is the practice of hiding data inside other media. Steganographic algorithms, based on machine learning, are adept at hiding hidden messages in photographs. Recent research shows how machine learning algorithms can find and exploit image redundancies to conceal sensitive information (illustrated in Table 1).

Table 1. Machine learning in health information security

Research Topic	Summary
Steganography & Machine Learning	Facilitates secure communication and data privacy, showcasing the potential of machine learning in information security.
Machine Learning Vulnerabilities in Cybersecurity	Recognizes the balance between leveraging machine learning's strengths and mitigating its weaknesses in cybersecurity.
Machine-Based Image Recognition	Strategies include improving neural network architectures and interdisciplinary research to bridge the gap between human and machine perception.
Innovative Methods in Health Information Security	Generative Adversarial Networks (GANs) and Neuromorphic Learning Machines (NLMs) to enhance health information protection. Discusses their potential in improving data accuracy, privacy, and efficiency in healthcare settings.
Real-Time Data Analysis with Neuromorphic Learning Machines	Neuromorphic Learning Machines (NLMs) in real-time vital sign monitoring and response in healthcare. Emphasizes their ability to process massive data streams rapidly and detect abnormalities, potentially saving lives in critical medical situations.
Deep Learning in Steganography for Health Data Protection	Highlights the potential of neural network-based approaches to securely transmit sensitive patient information.

Deep neural networks, a subclass of machine learning, discover tiny picture patterns and redundancy in this revolutionary research (Chen et al., 2023). These algorithms carefully embed encrypted data into cover material by analyzing its intricacies, making it undetectable to humans and traditional detection techniques. Machine learning makes steganographic methods more resilient to contemporary detection algorithms and more effective at obscuring information. This study supports the claim that machine learning can solve the age-old problem of hiding information in a cover medium. Machine learning models enable steganography to push the limits of safe information concealment. This combination of steganography and machine learning enhances the science and might be used in secure communication, data security, and privacy. As technology advances, this cooperation highlights the limitless possibilities of machine learning and information security, signalling a future of smart and secure clandestine communication.

Machine learning system vulnerabilities are well documented. A recent study shows how malicious actors can exploit learning algorithm vulnerabilities to force them to behave adversarially, highlighting machine learning's cybersecurity risks (Ren et al., 2020). This study shows the necessity for a sophisticated strategy that acknowledges machine learning's strengths and flaws in information security. Machine learning systems have been widely examined and documented for flaws despite their power. This study shows how malicious actors might leverage learning algorithm shortcomings to force them to behave in ways that endanger the systems they defend. This research emphasizes machine learning models' vulnerability to adversarial assaults as a major issue. The gap between human and machine-based image identification systems has also been extensively studied. A recent study compares human noise resilience to machine learning model constraints (Tsividis et al., 2021).

New neural network architectures address machine learning-based image recognition system challenges, emphasizing the need to explore mitigation strategies. The difference between human and machine-based image recognition systems has long been studied, yielding fascinating insights into human cognition and artificial intelligence. Human resilience against noise has been thoroughly studied, showing our capacity to recognize patterns in fuzzy and imperfect input (Ren et al., 2020). Machine learning algorithms, albeit strong, suffer from noise and small data fluctuations, resulting in misclassifications and lower accuracy. This fundamental divergence emphasizes the need for strong machine-based image recognition mitigation techniques. Researchers are tackling these difficulties by improving neural network topologies, as shown in previous studies (Thanh et al., 2019).

Generative adversarial networks (GANs) may improve machine learning model stability and generalization. In adversarial training, networks are purposely disrupted to learn to identify and react to noise, making them more resilient to real-world input data changes. Interdisciplinary research has combined neuroscience and AI ideas. Machine learning models emulate human brain functions like attention and contextual awareness to mirror human cognitive patterns. These models attempt to bridge the gap between human and machine perception, making machine-based image recognition systems better at managing noisy and complicated real-world data (Dong et al., 2021). Developing mitigation measures based on sophisticated neural network topologies and multidisciplinary cooperation indicates a potential trajectory in machine-based image recognition. As these tactics improve, the gap between human and machine perception narrows, allowing machine learning models to approach or surpass human cognition's resilience and flexibility. Innovative methods like generative adversarial networks (GANs) may improve health information security (Vaccari et al., 2021). These new techniques may considerably improve machine learning model stability and generalization, critical for protecting sensitive health data. Machine learning models are trained with adversarial data using GANs to simulate real-world variances and obstacles. This exposure lets models detect detailed patterns even amid the noise, making health information protection more accurate and durable.

Innovative Health Information Protection Using Neuromorphic Learning Machines (NLM) revolutionized health information protection (Vitale et al., 2022, Padinjappurathu Gopalan et al., 2022). These robots mimic human cognition by replicating neural processes inspired by the human brain. NLMs have unmatched health information protection potential. Complex and diverse health data makes it hard for traditional machine learning algorithms to understand. NLMs handle complex health data well by imitating the brain's capacity to process large volumes of information concurrently. NLMs analyze massive data streams faster than standard algorithms by mimicking the brain's parallel processing and pattern recognition skills. In critical care and emergency rooms, real-time vital sign monitoring is essential. NLMs excel by assessing sensor data on heart rate, blood pressure, and oxygen levels. They discover abnormalities early due to their fast pattern recognition. An abrupt rise or fall in vital signs may signify a health crisis. NLMs quickly detect these aberrations and warn healthcare personnel, allowing them to act and offer tailored therapy. In cardiac crises and infections, seconds matter. NLMs help identify warning indicators by processing and analyzing data in real-time. For instance, modest Electrocardiogram (ECG) waveform alterations may signal a heart attack (Zoccali et al., 2023, Bebortta et al., 2023). NLMs can detect these detailed patterns and inform medical workers to save lives immediately.

Steganography has been transformed by deep learning approaches to protect health data (Banerjee & Singh, 2021). Patient confidentiality is crucial in healthcare. Steganography using deep learning techniques, especially neural network-based ones, conceals critical health data in medical imaging and electronic health records (Sukumar et al., 2021, Shynu et al., 2020). Secure medical picture communication is one possible use for this technique (Nahar et al., 2023). Deep learning methods can include patient data in medical imaging pixels without human detection. This secret information can only be decrypted by authorized receivers with the right keys. This method protects patient data during transmission from unwanted access or interception.

Maintaining Medical Image Integrity With Advanced Embedding Techniques

Advanced embedding approaches in deep learning models increase safe medical picture transmission (Pandey et al., 2022). Neural networks, the foundation of these methods, excel at encoding patient data in complex medical imagery. Through minor pixel value changes and advanced embedding methods, these systems effectively insert secret data into photos, making it invisible to humans. These sophisticated methods smoothly incorporate patient data without changing the medical image's appearance. Neural networks trained on large datasets may gently change pixel values while maintaining picture quality (Neelakandan et al., 2022). This careful technique makes the embedded information part of the picture and blends into the data structure. Since the picture looks unaltered to the naked eye, its diagnostic utility and integrity are preserved. Most importantly, the integration procedure is precisely engineered to preserve the medical image's diagnostic value. Medical experts use these photos to diagnose and arrange therapy. Patient data is included in the picture without affecting medical analysis or visual signals. Nuanced integration preserves every tiny form, tint, and abnormality essential for diagnosis. Even experienced radiologists cannot identify these embedded data components in medical pictures. Neural networks make tiny, intentionally placed changes invisible to human sight. Advances in embedding ensure that patient data stays safe and secure without being seen during visual examination. The seamless integration achieved via innovative embedding methods protects patient anonymity. This invisible connection protects patient data and ensures compliance with strict healthcare privacy requirements while medical pictures travel digitally. These methods provide unmatched medical picture digital transmission security. Patient confidentiality is vital. Incorporating sophisticated embedding methods into deep learning models is a technological, ethical, and practical healthcare breakthrough. These solutions protect information transfer while retaining medical picture integrity and diagnostic value, incorporating sensitive patient data, and boosting patient confidence and confidentiality in the healthcare ecosystem. Controlled Access Secure medical picture transmission involves much more than incorporating patient data—it involves careful access control (Hasan et al., 2021).

The patient data in medical photographs is concealed and encrypted using powerful cryptography techniques. The contained information is encoded and unintelligible without the decryption keys. These decryption keys are the only way to obtain the medical image's hidden information. These decryption keys match the encryption technique, like a custom key that fits a lock. Approved recipients hold individual decryption keys. Usually, healthcare professionals or institutions are engaged in patient care. This tailored strategy restricts embedded patient data access to approved staff. Encryption and decryption keys strengthen permission-based systems (Pournaghi et al., 2020). Only those with the necessary rights and decryption keys may reveal medical picture data. This limited-access technique improves security by keeping patient data private and available only to authorized users. This strategy follows the concept of least privilege, restricting access permissions to job-related requirements. This cryptographic method locks off illegal access. If an evil actor intercepts a medical picture, the encrypted patient data is unreadable without the decryption key. This robust encryption system ensures patient data is safe during digital transmission and can only be accessed by trustworthy healthcare practitioners. Encryption and limited access comply with regulatory requirements and healthcare privacy legislation and protect patient confidentiality. US healthcare data security laws like the Health Insurance Portability and Accountability Act (HIPAA) require strict data protection (Kiel, 2022). Healthcare providers avoid legal issues and maintain patient confidence by encrypting data and restricting access to authorized people. Encryption and unique decryption keys create a fortress around patient data, satisfying legal standards and reassuring patients of its secrecy. This careful access control sends medical pictures securely, meeting the highest healthcare data security and patient privacy regulations.

Protection of Patient Privacy in Healthcare Data Transmission

In the evolving healthcare data-sharing context, confidentiality is paramount. Deep learning-based steganography protects patient data and maintains healthcare provider-patient confidence (Ahmed et al., 2024). Healthcare organizations use modern deep-learning algorithms to protect transmitted data from eavesdropping by embedding patient data in medical pictures. Unauthorized parties cannot access or understand embedded information, which is the beauty of deep learning-based steganography. Even if digital photographs are intercepted, encoded patient data remains cryptic, masquerading as medical images to undesired recipients. The complex algorithms ensure the concealed information stays safe without the decryption keys or embedding methods. This high security is a compliance and technical achievement. Healthcare firms must comply with strict rules like HIPAA in the US and the General Data Protection Regulation (GDPR) in the European Union (EU) (Preston, 2022). Deep learning-based steganography meets these strict data protection and privacy rules. These innovative methods help healthcare professionals comply with the law and avoid fines. Deep learning-based steganography addresses patient privacy beyond regulatory compliance. Patients need confidence that their sensitive medical information is secure in an age of data breaches and illegal access. These methods build an impenetrable wall that ensures patient privacy is a reality, boosting patient confidence and healthcare system trust. Deep learning-based steganography ensures healthcare confidentiality, which underpins trust and confidence. Patients must feel comfortable discussing their medical history with doctors. Healthcare institutions build confidence and encourage patients to provide vital information by using such innovative technologies to protect patient data. Finally, deep learning-based steganography in healthcare data transfer is a major development. It prevents data eavesdropping, protects privacy, follows rules, and builds confidence. This technological marvel, embedded in healthcare data exchange, protects sensitive data and preserves the patient-provider relationship, ushering in an era where confidentiality is not just an aspiration but a reality.

Patient data must be protected against illegal access in the digital age. Traditional transmission techniques, which might be intercepted and compromised, threaten patient data security. However, deep learning-based steganography provides an impenetrable screen against illegal access and cyber dangers. Deep learning-based steganography is unmatched in defense. The encrypted, integrated data stays unintelligible to unauthorized parties even after a security compromise. Cryptographic complexity hides these patient subtleties, making intercepted data useless to malevolent attackers (Andrew et al., 2023). This degree of protection is impregnable, preventing even the most sophisticated, unwanted access. Data breaches, particularly in healthcare, may harm patient privacy, legal standing, and institutional reputation. Deep learning-based steganography significantly reduces these hazards. It protects against unauthorized access by making embedded data unintelligible without the decryption keys. This proactive solution keeps patient data cryptographically private and inaccessible even if unwanted parties intercept medical photos. Hackers and malicious entities trying to steal medical data are common cyber threats. Deep learning-based steganography withstands these challenges. By encrypting and embedding patient data, it mitigates cyberattacks. Even when unauthorized parties breach digital boundaries, the embedded information remains hidden, protecting patient records and thwarting cybercriminals. Beyond technical aspects, this impenetrable defense promotes data integrity and trust in the healthcare system. Patients trust doctors with their most private data. Institutions fulfil their ethical duties by protecting this data. Patients trust the healthcare ecosystem more because their private medical information is protected. Deep learning-based steganography in healthcare data transmission is a commitment to patient confidentiality and data integrity, not just security. This advanced technology protects patient privacy and healthcare providers from data breaches and cyberattacks by preventing unauthorized access.

Patient data must be protected against illegal access in the digital age. Traditional transmission techniques, which might be intercepted and compromised, threaten patient data security. However, deep learning-based steganography provides an impenetrable screen against illegal access and cyber dangers. Deep learning-based steganography is unmatched in defense. The encrypted, integrated data stays unintelligible to unauthorized parties even after a security compromise. Cryptographic complexity hides these patient subtleties, making intercepted data useless to malevolent attackers. This degree of protection is impregnable, preventing even the most sophisticated, unwanted access. Data breaches, particularly in healthcare, may harm patient privacy, legal standing, and institutional reputation. Deep learning-based steganography significantly reduces these hazards. It protects against unauthorized access by making embedded data unintelligible without the decryption keys. This proactive solution keeps patient data cryptographically private and inaccessible even if unwanted parties intercept medical photos. Telemedicine and remote consultations are crucial to patient access to quality care across borders in the changing healthcare landscape. Secure transmission is crucial as healthcare providers move to digital platforms for patient data exchange and collaborative diagnosis. Telemedicine and remote consultations benefit from deep learning-based steganography's medical image transmission security. Telemedicine relies on seamless medical information exchange, and incredibly complex medical images needed for diagnosis. Deep learning-based steganography protects confidentiality. Digitally sharing sensitive medical images across vast distances is common. Deep learning lets these images travel digitally, securely, and privately, enabling accurate remote diagnoses and consultations without compromising patient privacy. Deep learning secures medical image transmission, freeing patients from geography. Diagnostic images can be securely sent to specialists miles away, allowing expert consultations regardless of location. Geographic independence increases access to specialized healthcare and ensures that patients in remote areas receive the best medical care. Medical experts in different locations must securely and seamlessly share patient data for collaborative diagnoses. Deep learning-based steganography helps doctors collaborate confidently. Sharing sensitive medical images for collaborative assessments is easy and secure. With confidentiality, healthcare providers can focus on creating the best treatment plans without worrying about data security. Telemedicine and remote consultations are patient-centered. Deep learning-based steganography secures medical history, images, and diagnostic information, building trust between patients and healthcare providers (Nadhan & Jacob, 2024). These methods promote security, transparency, and a solid patient-doctor relationship, which is essential to quality healthcare. Deep learning-based steganography fits seamlessly into the digital transformation of the healthcare ecosystem. Secure medical image transmission is crucial as healthcare providers and patients embrace digital interactions. Deep learning addresses current needs and prepares the healthcare sector for future innovations, ensuring that telemedicine and remote consultations are built on trust, security, and patient-focused care. Deep learning-based steganography in medical image transmission advances telemedicine and remote consultations. Secure, confidential exchange of sensitive medical images enables healthcare providers to provide exceptional care across distances, creating a healthcare landscape where geographic barriers no longer prevent accessible, reliable, and patient-centric care.

Promoting Patient Trust through Ethical Data Transmission

Patient trust and data confidentiality are crucial to healthcare ethics. Medical providers and institutions must address ethical issues as a regulatory requirement and ethical obligation. Deep learning-based steganography exceeds these ethical requirements as a pioneering solution. These advanced, ethical, and secure methods of transmitting sensitive medical data ease concerns and build trust in healthcare providers and institutions (illustrated in Table 2).

Table 2. Ethical data transmission

Research Topic	Summary
Ethical and Secure Medical Data Transmission Using Deep Learning-Based Steganography	Deep learning-based steganography ensures patient confidentiality and builds trust in healthcare providers by ethically embedding sensitive medical data into images. Transparency in data handling practices instills patient confidence, facilitating accurate diagnoses and treatment plans. These methods surpass ethical requirements and bolster patient-provider relationships through secure data transmission.
Advancements in Machine Learning for Resilient Healthcare Data Security	Robust machine learning models, resilient to adversarial attacks, protect healthcare data integrity in medical imaging. Adversarial training and certified robustness ensure machine learning models can withstand manipulations, enhancing reliability in critical applications. These efforts safeguard patient data from malicious interference, maintaining data integrity and trust in healthcare systems.
Fortified Steganography Against Adversarial Attacks	Steganography fortified with adversarial training resists attempts to expose hidden content in images. Through iterative training, neural networks adapt embedding techniques to outsmart adversaries while maintaining data secrecy. Robust decoding algorithms salvage hidden messages from corruption, ensuring accurate retrieval despite transmission distortions. These techniques create an impenetrable barrier around covert communication, safeguarding the integrity and confidentiality of health information.
Strategic Use of Encryption and Authentication in Secure Communication	Encryption and authentication serve as stalwart guardians in steganography, ensuring the secrecy, confidentiality, and authenticity of concealed messages. Advanced encryption standards transform plaintext into cryptic ciphers, while digital signatures validate sender authenticity. Secure key management restricts access to authorized entities, fortifying covert communication against adversarial scrutiny. This strategic alliance upholds the sanctity of health information security, creating a fortified fortress of privacy and confidentiality.
Incorporating Randomization and Cryptographic Key Management in Steganography for Enhanced Security	Randomization techniques and cryptographic key management bolster steganography against adversarial scrutiny and unauthorized access. Unpredictability in the embedding process confounds reverse engineering attempts, while secure key management ensures exclusive access to concealed messages. This strategic marriage of chaos and exclusivity forms an unassailable fortress around covert communication, preserving the secrecy and integrity of health information security.

Patient confidentiality is essential to ethical healthcare. By balancing technology and ethics, deep learning-based steganography protects patient data during digital transmission (Mandal et al., 2022). Ethics and law require this confidentiality. Healthcare providers protect patient privacy and dignity using these advanced methods to protect sensitive patient data. Building patient trust requires ethical transparency.

Deep learning-based steganography transparently embeds patient data for authorized personnel but not for unauthorized eyes. Transparency ensures ethical practices are followed and visible, giving patients confidence that their data is handled with care and integrity throughout its digital journey. Effective medical care requires patient-provider trust. Patients need security and ethics for their confidential information. Deep learning-based steganography guarantees this. These technologies' ethical foundation inspires patient confidence and shows the healthcare sector's dedication to ethical practice, creating a healthcare ecosystem based on trust, confidentiality, and integrity. Hospitals and healthcare facilities must securely transmit patient records. They can embed EHRs in images or multimedia files using steganography to protect the data if intercepted (Rajaram et al., 2023). Steganography can embed patient data in medical images or research files by medical researchers and professionals. This study allows trusted collaborators to securely share data without risking unauthorized access. Hospitals and clinics can use steganography to hide sensitive patient data in digital files. This extra security keeps data hidden even if unauthorized access occurs. In healthcare, where data integrity is paramount, robust machine learning models that resist manipulation are essential. Medical image analysis uses robust machine learning models. Researchers and engineers in medical imaging are developing deep learning models that can withstand manipulation, including adversarial attacks. Medical imaging adversarial attacks can alter images in almost invisible ways to humans but can mislead machine learning algorithms, resulting in incorrect diagnoses or interpretations. To defend machine learning models from these attacks, researchers use adversarial training.

Adversarial training puts adversarial examples (images designed to fool the system) in the training data. The model learns to recognize and resist these manipulations during training, making it more resilient to similar attacks in real life. Researchers have developed adversarial-resistant convolutional neural networks (CNNs) to detect cancerous tumors in medical images. These models learn from medical images and adversarial examples created to simulate manipulations. Training on these adversarial examples refines the model's parameters, making it more robust to clinical manipulations. Additionally, research has examined the theoretical foundations of adversarial robustness in machine learning models. Certified robustness guarantees model performance even with adversarial perturbations. In steganography, where concealing sensitive information within images is crucial, using neural networks has introduced innovative methods to bolster security (Hussain et al., 2020).

One such technique involves adversarial training, a robust approach designed to fortify steganographic systems against potential adversaries aiming to unveil hidden content. Consider a scenario where a steganographic system employs neural networks to seamlessly embed messages within cover images, ensuring the concealed information remains invisible to prying eyes. This system operates under the constant threat of detection by adversaries seeking to expose the hidden data. To safeguard against adversarial attempts, the steganographic system undergoes adversarial training.

The steganographic picture may have been distorted during transmission, posing a challenge to the receiver tasked with recovering the hidden information. Bit tampering, data loss, and other malicious interference are examples of distortions that might occur. The steganographic system includes a powerful decoding mechanism to resist the adversary's efforts to distort the secret message (Liu et al., 2020). This technique was developed with robustness in mind, with the built-in capacity to fix transmission mistakes and inconsistencies. The decoding method may successfully negate the influence of modifications on the steganographic picture by using sophisticated error-correcting techniques such as Reed-Solomon or convolutional codes. The capacity of this robust decoding to recreate the original message despite adversary interventions is its primary feature. By providing a systematic means of restoring corrupted or missing data, error repair procedures protect the secrecy of secret information. By employing Reed-Solomon codes, convolutional codes, or similar methodologies, the steganographic system equips itself with the means to identify and rectify discrepancies, thereby salvaging the hidden message from potential corruption (Gautam & Lall, 2020). Implementing robust decoding algorithms fortifies the steganographic system, rendering it resilient against adversarial attempts to corrupt or manipulate the hidden content. This meticulous attention to error correction ensures the accurate retrieval of messages and upholds the integrity and confidentiality of the communicated information, even in the face of adversarial challenges. In the intricate dance of secure communication, where hidden messages travel discreetly within steganographic images, fortified protection against prying eyes and evil manipulations is paramount.

Encryption and authentication emerge as stalwart guardians in this realm, ensuring the concealed information's sanctity, confidentiality, and authenticity. Imagine a scenario where a message, ingeniously concealed within a steganographic image, prepares for its clandestine journey across the communication channels. Before embarking on this covert expedition, the concealed message dons a cloak of encryption, rendering itself incomprehensible to anyone without the decryption key. Robust encryption algorithms step onto the stage to fortify the security perimeter. Advanced Encryption Standard (AES), a cryptographic cipher renowned for its resilience against adversarial attacks, is a sentinel, safeguarding the concealed message (Illi et al., 2023). AES meticulously transforms the plaintext message into an enigmatic cipher, ensuring that even if an adversary intercepts the steganographic message, deciphering its cryptic contents remains a Herculean task devoid of the decryption key. But security is not merely about shrouding messages in cryptographic veils; it also demands a mechanism to discern the genuine from the counterfeit. Here, authentication mechanisms unfurl their banner of assurance. Digital signatures embody sender verification, akin to an unforgeable seal of authenticity. The sender leaves an indelible mark by appending digital signatures to the concealed message, attesting to its origin and integrity. Encryption, with its mathematical wizardry, transmutes the plaintext message into an encrypted cipher, transforming the steganographic message into an enigma decipherable only by those possessing the coveted decryption key. This encrypted cocoon ensures that even if an adversary lays hands on the steganographic message during transit, the contents remain impervious, preserving the secrecy of the concealed information. Authentication mechanisms, exemplified by digital signatures, validate the sender's identity and guarantee the message's unadulterated state. By employing cryptographic techniques, these mechanisms confirm the sender's authenticity, thwarting any nefarious attempts to tamper with the message en route. In essence, through the symbiotic alliance of encryption and authentication, the steganographic system erects an impenetrable fortress around the hidden message. This union not only shields the concealed information from prying eyes but also ensures that its origin remains untarnished, standing resilient against adversarial machinations seeking to compromise the sanctity of covert communication.

In the covert realm of steganography, where messages are veiled within images, the strategic use of randomization techniques and the meticulous management of cryptographic keys stand as vanguards against adversarial scrutiny and unauthorized access. In this domain of covert communication, unpredictability and restricted access become formidable shields, rendering the hidden messages impervious to prying eyes. Imagine a scenario where a covert message, woven into the very fabric of an innocent image, readies itself for its concealed voyage. The embedding process employs intricate randomization techniques to add an extra layer of obscurity, infusing the concealment with unpredictability. Simultaneously, cryptographic keys, akin to ancient artifacts of immense power, are securely managed, ensuring that only authorized entities possess the means to encode and decode these cryptic messages. The first line of defense materializes through randomization techniques woven into the embedding process. By introducing unpredictability, these techniques confound any attempts at reverse engineering. Adversaries attempting to unravel the intricacies of the embedding mechanism are met with a labyrinth of uncertainty. The unpredictability sowed by randomization becomes an insurmountable barrier, concealing the true nature of the steganographic process and thwarting adversarial attempts to discern patterns or algorithms. Simultaneously, the fortress of security is fortified through the meticulous management of cryptographic keys. These meticulously generated and fiercely guarded keys are the linchpin of steganographic security.

The infusion of randomization techniques injects an aura of chaos into the embedding process. Each concealment becomes a unique tapestry woven with a distinct pattern of randomness. This variability bewilders any adversarial attempts to discern the underlying rules or algorithms governing the embedding process. The veil of uncertainty shrouding each hidden message becomes a formidable defense, making the reverse engineering process akin to navigating an intricate maze without a map. Simultaneously, the secure management of cryptographic keys becomes the epitome of exclusivity. These keys, generated with cryptographic precision, become the sole means of unravelling the concealed mysteries. Without the exact combination, the encrypted veil of the hidden message remains impervious. This duality of unpredictability and exclusivity forms an unassailable fortress around covert communication, ensuring that only those with the proper keys can decipher the concealed truths. In essence, the strategic marriage of randomization and key management becomes the bedrock of steganographic security. Through the chaos of unpredictability and the sanctity of cryptographic keys, concealed messages find sanctuary, shielded from the prying eyes of adversaries. Steganography, with its mysterious messages and obscure visuals, is a stronghold of privacy, where the medium's very nature protects the secret of health information security.

SOLUTIONS AND RECOMMENDATIONS

1. Collaboration: Establish working groups with policymakers, regulators, cybersecurity professionals, and data scientists. This collaboration fosters open communication and a shared understanding of the risks and opportunities of machine learning in information security.
2. Focus on Transparency: Develop regulations that emphasize openness in machine learning algorithms. This could involve requiring clear documentation of how algorithms work, the data they use, and their limitations.
3. Promote Responsible Development: Create regulations that promote responsible development of machine learning for information security. This might include guidelines for ethical data collection, bias mitigation, and accountability for developers.
4. Continuous Monitoring: Implement regulations that mandate continuous monitoring of machine learning algorithms deployed for information security. This ensures timely detection and mitigation of potential vulnerabilities or unintended consequences.

By implementing these solutions and recommendations, we can create a more secure environment where machine learning is used responsibly and effectively for information security.

FUTURE RESEARCH DIRECTIONS

1. Enhancing Resilience Against Adversarial Attacks:
    *   Develop advanced techniques to fortify machine learning algorithms against adversarial attacks, including evasion, poisoning, and model inversion.
    *   Investigate new defense mechanisms such as robust optimization, adversarial training, and ensemble methods to improve algorithmic resilience in security applications.
    *   Explore the integration of anomaly detection and outlier analysis techniques to enhance the detection of adversarial behaviors and mitigate their impact on machine learning systems.
2. Exploring Interdisciplinary Approaches:
    *   Investigate the potential synergies between machine learning and blockchain technology to create decentralized and tamper-resistant security solutions.
    *   Explore the application of quantum computing in machine learning-based security algorithms, leveraging quantum principles to enhance encryption, authentication, and data privacy.
    *   Develop novel cryptographic protocols and consensus mechanisms that leverage quantum properties to secure sensitive data and transactions in healthcare and other domains.

By focusing on these future research directions, the cybersecurity community can advance the state-of-the-art in machine learning-based security solutions, address emerging challenges, and ensure the responsible and ethical deployment of AI technologies in healthcare and other critical domains.

CONCLUSION

In summary, this section highlights the profound impact of machine learning on advancing health information security practices. By leveraging encrypted website analysis and sophisticated steganographic algorithms, the research underscores machine learning's capability to detect, conceal, and protect sensitive healthcare data. Nonetheless, it emphasizes the imperative of acknowledging and addressing the inherent vulnerabilities inherent in machine learning systems. While machine learning presents innovative solutions for securing healthcare information, a prudent and vigilant approach to cybersecurity implementation is essential to mitigate risks effectively. Thus, while machine learning offers promising avenues for enhancing health information security, careful consideration of its vulnerabilities is paramount to ensure its safe and effective application in healthcare settings.

REFERENCES

Ahmed, S. F., Alam, M. S. B., Afrin, S., Rafa, S. J., Rafa, N., & Gandomi, A. H. (2024). Insights into Internet of Medical Things (IoMT): Data fusion, security issues and potential solutions. *Information Fusion*, 102, 102060. DOI: 10.1016/j. inffus.2023.102060

Aldweesh, A., Derhab, A., & Emam, A. Z. (2020). Deep learning approaches for anomaly-based intrusion detection systems: A survey, taxonomy, and open issues. *Knowledge-Based Systems*, 189, 105124. DOI: 10.1016/j.knosys.2019.105124

Andrew, J., Isravel, D. P., Sagayam, K. M., Bhushan, B., Sei, Y., & Eunice, J. (2023). Blockchain for healthcare systems: Architecture, security challenges, trends and future directions. *Journal of Network and Computer Applications*, 103633. Advance online publication. DOI: 10.1016/j.jnca.2023.103633

Arefolov, A., Adam, L., Brown, S., Budovskaya, Y., Chen, C., Das, D., Farhy, C., Ferguson, R., Huang, H., Kanigel, K., Lu, C., Polesskaya, O., Staton, T., Tajhya, R., Whitley, M., Wong, J.-Y., Zeng, X., & McCreary, M. (2021). Implementation of the FAIR data principles for exploratory biomarker data from clinical trials. *Data Intelligence*, 3(4), 631–662. DOI: 10.1162/dint_a_00106

Banerjee, S., & Singh, G. K. (2021). A new approach of ECG steganography and prediction using deep learning. *Biomedical Signal Processing and Control*, 64, 102151. DOI: 10.1016/j.bspc.2020.102151

Bebortta, S., Tripathy, S. S., Basheer, S., & Chowdhary, C. L. (2023). Deepmist: Towards deep learning assisted mist computing framework for managing healthcare big data. *IEEE Access : Practical Innovations, Open Solutions*, 11, 42485–42496. DOI: 10.1109/ACCESS.2023.3266374

Bisogni, F., & Asghari, H. (2020). More than a suspect: An investigation into the connection between data breaches, identity theft, and data breach notification laws. *Journal of Information Policy*, 10, 45–82. DOI: 10.5325/jinfopoli.10.2020.0045

Chen, J. A., Niu, W., Ren, B., Wang, Y., & Shen, X. (2023). Survey: Exploiting data redundancy for optimization of deep learning. *ACM Computing Surveys*, 55(10), 1–38. DOI: 10.1145/3564663

Dong, Z., Lai, C. S., Zhang, Z., Qi, D., Gao, M., & Duan, S. (2021). Neuromorphic extreme learning machines with bimodal memristive synapses. *Neurocomputing*, 453, 38–49. DOI: 10.1016/j.neucom.2021.04.049

Gautam, N., & Lall, B. (2020, February). Blind channel coding identification of convolutional encoder and reed-solomon encoder using neural networks. In *2020 National Conference on Communications (NCC)* (pp. 1-6). IEEE. DOI: 10.1109/NCC48643.2020.9056082

Gupta, R., Tanwar, S., Tyagi, S., & Kumar, N. (2020). Machine learning models for secure data analytics: A taxonomy and threat model. *Computer Communications*, 153, 406–440. DOI: 10.1016/j.comcom.2020.02.008

Gurunath, R., Alahmadi, A. H., Samanta, D., Khan, M. Z., & Alahmadi, A. (2021). A novel approach for linguistic steganography evaluation based on artificial neural networks. IEEE Access, 9, 120869-120879. DOI: 10.1109/ACCESS.2021.3108183

Hanelt, A., Bohnsack, R., Marz, D., & Antunes Marante, C. (2021). A systematic review of the literature on digital transformation: Insights and implications for strategy and organizational change. *Journal of Management Studies*, 58(5), 1159–1197. DOI: 10.1111/joms.12639

Hasan, M. K., Islam, S., Sulaiman, R., Khan, S., Hashim, A. H. A., Habib, S., Islam, M., Alyahya, S., Ahmed, M. M., Kamil, S., & Hassan, M. A. (2021). Lightweight encryption technique to enhance medical image security on internet of medical things applications. *IEEE Access : Practical Innovations, Open Solutions*, 9, 47731–47742. DOI: 10.1109/ACCESS.2021.3061710

Hussain, I., Zeng, J., Qin, X., & Tan, S. (2020). A survey on deep convolutional neural networks for image steganography and steganalysis. *KSII Transactions on Internet and Information Systems*, 14(3), 1228–1248. DOI: 10.3837/tiis.2020.03.017

Illi, E., Qaraqe, M., Althunibat, S., Alhasanat, A., Alsafasfeh, M., de Ree, M., & Al-Kuwari, S. (2023). Physical Layer Security for Authentication, Confidentiality, and Malicious Node Detection: A Paradigm Shift in Securing IoT Networks. *IEEE Communications Surveys and Tutorials*. Advance online publication. DOI: 10.1109/COMST.2023.3327327

Kiel, J. M. (2022). Data privacy and security in the US: HIPAA, hitech and beyond. In *Nursing Informatics: A Health Informatics, Interprofessional and Global Perspective* (pp. 427–435). Springer International Publishing. DOI: 10.1007/978-3-030-91237-6_28

Kumar, V. (2023). Digital Enablers. In *The Economic Value of Digital Disruption: A Holistic Assessment for CXOs* (pp. 1–110). Springer Nature Singapore. DOI: 10.1007/978-981-19-8148-7_1

Lehto, M., Neittaanmäki, P., Pöyhönen, J., & Hummelholm, A. (2022). Cyber Security in Healthcare Systems. In *Cyber Security: Critical Infrastructure Protection* (pp. 183–215). Springer International Publishing. DOI: 10.1007/978-3-030-91293-2_8

Liu, H., & Lang, B. (2019). Machine learning and deep learning methods for intrusion detection systems: A survey. *Applied Sciences (Basel, Switzerland)*, 9(20), 4396. DOI: 10.3390/app9204396

Liu, J., Ke, Y., Zhang, Z., Lei, Y., Li, J., Zhang, M., & Yang, X. (2020). Recent advances of image steganography with generative adversarial networks. *IEEE Access : Practical Innovations, Open Solutions*, 8, 60575–60597. DOI: 10.1109/ACCESS.2020.2983175

Mandal, P. C., Mukherjee, I., Paul, G., & Chatterji, B. N. (2022). Digital image steganography: A literature survey. *Information Sciences*, 609, 1451–1488. Advance online publication. DOI: 10.1016/j.ins.2022.07.120

Muhammad, T., Munir, M. T., Munir, M. Z., & Zafar, M. W. (2022). Integrative Cybersecurity: Merging Zero Trust, Layered Defense, and Global Standards for a Resilient Digital Future. *International Journal Of Computer Science And Technology*, 6(4), 99–135.

Nadhan, A. S., & Jacob, I. J. (2024). Enhancing healthcare security in the digital era: Safeguarding medical images with lightweight cryptographic techniques in IoT healthcare applications. *Biomedical Signal Processing and Control*, 88, 105511. DOI: 10.1016/j.bspc.2023.105511

Nahar, M., Kamal, A. H. M., & Hossain, G. (2023). Protecting health data in the cloud through steganography: A table-driven, blind method using neural networks and bit-shuffling algorithm. *Journal of Network and Computer Applications*, 217, 103689. DOI: 10.1016/j.jnca.2023.103689

Neelakandan, S., Beulah, J. R., Prathiba, L., Murthy, G. L. N., Irudaya Raj, E. F., & Arulkumar, N. (2022). Blockchain with deep learning-enabled secure healthcare data transmission and diagnostic model. *International Journal of Modeling, Simulation, and Scientific Computing*, 13(04), 2241006. DOI: 10.1142/S1793962322410069

Owen, S., Fojtik, R., Braga, B., & Raghunathan, K. (2023). *Interoperability and User Experience. Digital Health: A Transformative Approach*.

Padinjappurathu Gopalan, S., Chowdhary, C. L., Iwendi, C., Farid, M. A., & Ramasamy, L. K. (2022). An efficient and privacy-preserving scheme for disease prediction in modern healthcare systems. *Sensors (Basel)*, 22(15), 5574. DOI: 10.3390/s22155574 PMID: 35898077

Pandey, B. K., Pandey, D., Nassa, V. K., George, S., Aremu, B., Dadeech, P., & Gupta, A. (2022, July). Effective and secure transmission of health information using advanced morphological component analysis and image hiding. In *Artificial Intelligence on Medical Data: Proceedings of International Symposium*, ISCMM 2021 (pp. 223-230). Singapore: Springer Nature Singapore. https://doi.org/DOI: 10.1007/978-981-19-0151-5_19

Parekh, R., Patel, N., Gupta, R., Jadav, N. K., Tanwar, S., Alharbi, A., Tolba, A., Neagu, B.-C., & Raboaca, M. S. (2023). Gefl: Gradient encryption-aided privacy preserved federated learning for autonomous vehicles. *IEEE Access : Practical Innovations, Open Solutions*, 11, 1825–1839. DOI: 10.1109/ACCESS.2023.3233983

Pournaghi, S. M., Bayat, M., & Farjami, Y. (2020). MedSBA: A novel and secure scheme to share medical data based on blockchain technology and attribute-based encryption. *Journal of Ambient Intelligence and Humanized Computing*, 11(11), 4613–4641. DOI: 10.1007/s12652-020-01710-y

Preston, R. (2022). Stifling Innovation: How Global Data Protection Regulation Trends Inhibit the Growth of Healthcare Research and Start-Ups. *Emory Int'l L. Rev*, 37, 135.

Qayyum, A., Qadir, J., Bilal, M., & Al-Fuqaha, A. (2020). Secure and robust machine learning for healthcare: A survey. *IEEE Reviews in Biomedical Engineering*, 14, 156–180. DOI: 10.1109/RBME.2020.3013489 PMID: 32746371

Rajaram, G., Dash, S., Arslan, F., Venu, D., Ahmed, M. A., & Lydia, E. L. (2023). Polynomial cryptographic optical steganography substitution model for the telehealth system with multimedia data. *Optical and Quantum Electronics*, 55(9), 819. DOI: 10.1007/s11082-023-05084-1

Ren, K., Zheng, T., Qin, Z., & Liu, X. (2020). Adversarial attacks and defenses in deep learning. *Engineering (Beijing)*, 6(3), 346–360. DOI: 10.1016/j.eng.2019.12.012

Shuaib, M., Alam, S., Alam, M. S., & Nasir, M. S. (2021). Compliance with HIPAA and GDPR in blockchain-based electronic health record. *Materials Today: Proceedings*. Advance online publication. DOI: 10.1016/j.matpr.2021.03.059

Shynu, P. G., Shayan, H. M., & Chowdhary, C. L. (2020, February). A fuzzy based data perturbation technique for privacy preserved data mining. In 2020 International Conference on Emerging Trends in Information Technology and Engineering (ic-ETITE) (pp. 1-4). IEEE. DOI: 10.1109/ic-ETITE47903.2020.244

Sreedevi, A. G., Harshitha, T. N., Sugumaran, V., & Shankar, P. (2022). Application of cognitive computing in healthcare, cybersecurity, big data and IoT: A literature review. *Information Processing & Management*, 59(2), 102888. DOI: 10.1016/j. ipm.2022.102888

Sukumar, A., Subramaniyaswamy, V., Ravi, L., Vijayakumar, V., & Indragandhi, V. (2021). Robust image steganography approach based on RIWT-Laplacian pyramid and histogram shifting using deep learning. *Multimedia Systems*, 27(4), 651–666. DOI: 10.1007/s00530-020-00665-6

Thanh-Tung, H., Tran, T., & Venkatesh, S. (2019). *Improving generalization and stability of generative adversarial networks*. arXiv preprint arXiv:1902.03984.

Thapa, C., & Camtepe, S. (2021). Precision health data: Requirements, challenges and existing techniques for data security and privacy. *Computers in Biology and Medicine*, 129, 104130. DOI: 10.1016/j.compbiomed.2020.104130 PMID: 33271399

Tsividis, P. A., Loula, J., Burga, J., Foss, N., Campero, A., Pouncy, T., . . . Tenenbaum, J. B. (2021). *Human-level reinforcement learning through theory-based modeling, exploration, and planning*. arXiv preprint arXiv:2107.12544.

Vaccari, I., Orani, V., Paglialonga, A., Cambiaso, E., & Mongelli, M. (2021). A generative adversarial network (gan) technique for internet of medical things data. *Sensors (Basel)*, 21(11), 3726. DOI: 10.3390/s21113726 PMID: 34071944

Vitale, A., Donati, E., Germann, R., & Magno, M. (2022). Neuromorphic edge computing for biomedical applications: Gesture classification using emg signals. *IEEE Sensors Journal*, 22(20), 19490–19499. DOI: 10.1109/JSEN.2022.3194678

Zoccali, C., Mark, P. B., Sarafidis, P., Agarwal, R., Adamczak, M., Bueno de Oliveira, R., Massy, Z. A., Kotanko, P., Ferro, C. J., Wanner, C., Burnier, M., Vanholder, R., Mallamaci, F., & Wiecek, A. (2023). Diagnosis of cardiovascular disease in patients with chronic kidney disease. *Nature Reviews. Nephrology*, 19(11), 1–14. DOI: 10.1038/s41581-023-00747-4 PMID: 37612381

KEY TERMS AND DEFINITIONS

Cybersecurity: Cybersecurity refers to the practice of protecting computer systems, networks, and digital data from theft, damage, or unauthorized access. It involves implementing various technologies, processes, and measures to safeguard information technology infrastructure and prevent cyber threats.

Health Information: Health information encompasses data related to an individual's medical history, diagnoses, treatments, prescriptions, and other health-related details. It includes information recorded and stored in electronic formats, commonly used in healthcare settings to provide medical care and manage patient records.

Machine Learning: Machine learning is a subset of artificial intelligence (AI) that involves the development of algorithms and statistical models that enable computer systems to improve their performance on a specific task through learning from data. Algorithms designed for machine learning may analyze data and draw conclusions or make judgments without being explicitly instructed.

Steganography: Steganography refers to the process of hiding a message or other piece of information inside another. In digital environments, data concealment often entails embedding information into photographs, audio files, or other media so that it is difficult for outsiders to discern its existence.

Threat Detection: Threat detection describes the steps to recognize and identify possible security risks or suspicious actions inside a computer system or network. In cybersecurity, threat detection tools and methods are used to monitor network traffic, system behaviors, and other characteristics to identify and react to cybersecurity issues, including malware, unauthorized access, and other malicious actions.

Chapter 7
Deep Learning–Based Steganography for Smart Agriculture

Chiranji Lal Chowdhary

iD https://orcid.org/0000-0002-5476-1468

Vellore Institute of Technology, Vellore, India

S. Vijayan

Vellore Institute of Technology, Vellore, India

ABSTRACT

This chapter explores integrating deep learning-based steganography with machine learning to enhance crop disease detection and secure data transmission in smart agriculture. It examines advanced deep learning techniques that improve the security and robustness of steganography by embedding data imperceptibly in images. The chapter also highlights machine learning algorithms' effectiveness in accurately identifying and classifying crop diseases through image analysis. It proposes methods to securely transmit agricultural data, including vital crop disease information, using deep learning-based steganography. This ensures sensitive agricultural data is protected during transmission, enhancing smart agriculture systems' overall security. Several case studies illustrate practical benefits, showing how this integration can lead to more resilient and secure agricultural practices. Ultimately, the chapter underscores the potential of these technologies to revolutionize smart agriculture by safeguarding data integrity and improving disease management.

DOI: 10.4018/979-8-3693-2223-9.ch007

1. INTRODUCTION

In the contemporary landscape of agriculture, the convergence of data security and precision farming has become imperative. Precision agriculture leverages cutting-edge technologies to optimize farming practices, ensuring higher productivity, sustainability, and efficiency. Central to this approach is the extensive collection and analysis of data, which spans various aspects of agricultural operations such as soil conditions, weather patterns, and crop health. However, the increasing reliance on digital data brings forth significant security challenges. Protecting sensitive agricultural information from unauthorized access and cyber threats is crucial to maintain the integrity and reliability of smart farming systems. This chapter underscores the importance of integrating robust data security mechanisms within precision agriculture to safeguard valuable data, thereby supporting informed decision-making and enhancing overall farm management (Ngugi et al., 2024; Shoaib et al., 2023; Eunice et al., 2022).

Importance of Data Security and Precision Agriculture

In the era of digital transformation, the agriculture sector is increasingly adopting smart technologies to enhance productivity, efficiency, and sustainability. Precision agriculture, characterized by the use of advanced technologies to monitor and optimize agricultural practices, plays a crucial role in addressing the growing global demand for food (Abbasi et al., 2022). One of the core aspects of precision agriculture is the collection and analysis of vast amounts of data, ranging from soil moisture levels to crop health metrics (Maitra & Damle, 2024). However, as the dependency on digital systems grows, so does the need for robust data security measures to protect sensitive agricultural information from unauthorized access and cyber threats.

Data security in smart agriculture is paramount for several reasons. First, the integrity and confidentiality of agricultural data ensure that farmers can make informed decisions without the risk of data manipulation or loss. Second, secure data transmission is essential to maintain the trust and reliability of automated systems that support precision farming. Any breach in data security can lead to significant financial losses, compromised crop management, and reduced productivity. Thus, integrating advanced data security solutions within the framework of precision agriculture is essential to safeguard the future of farming (Dhanaraju et al., 2022; Bocean, 2024).

Overview of Steganography and Crop Disease Detection

Steganography, the practice of concealing information within digital media, has emerged as a powerful tool for enhancing data security. Unlike traditional encryption, which transforms data into an unreadable format, steganography embeds data within files such that it remains hidden to unauthorized viewers while maintaining the apparent integrity of the original file. Recent advancements in deep learning have significantly improved the effectiveness and robustness of steganographic techniques, making them highly suitable for secure data transmission in various fields, including agriculture (Mawla & Khafaji, 2023; Mondal, 2018).

Simultaneously, machine learning has revolutionized crop disease detection by enabling the precise analysis of agricultural images. Through sophisticated algorithms and image processing techniques, machine learning models can identify and classify crop diseases with high accuracy. This capability is vital for timely intervention and effective disease management, reducing crop losses and enhancing yield quality (Bagga & Goyal, 2024).

This chapter aims to explore the synergistic integration of deep learning-based steganography with machine learning for crop disease detection, providing a comprehensive approach to secure and intelligent agricultural data management. By leveraging these advanced technologies, we can not only enhance the security of data transmission in smart agriculture but also improve the precision and reliability of crop disease detection systems. The following sections will delve into the methodologies, case studies, and real-world applications of this integration, highlighting its potential to transform modern agriculture (Isinkaye et al., 2024).

2. DEEP LEARNING APPROACHES TO STEGANOGRAPHY

Deep learning has fundamentally transformed the field of steganography, introducing advanced techniques and models that enhance the concealment and security of information within digital media. Unlike traditional methods that often relied on straightforward embedding schemes susceptible to detection, deep learning-based steganography leverages neural networks to create sophisticated and less detectable embeddings. This section explores the cutting-edge techniques and models utilized in deep learning-based steganography, such as convolutional neural networks (CNNs), generative adversarial networks (GANs), and autoencoders. It also delves into the significant improvements in robustness and security achieved through these approaches, highlighting how they can withstand various forms of data manipulation and steganalysis attacks. These advancements make deep learning-based steganography a powerful tool for secure data transmission, with potential applications in enhancing the security of smart agriculture systems (Rahman et al., 2023).

Techniques and Models in Deep Learning-Based Steganography

Deep learning has revolutionized the field of steganography, offering sophisticated techniques and models that significantly enhance the concealment of information within digital media. Traditional steganographic methods often relied on simple embedding schemes that could be easily detected or disrupted. In contrast, deep learning-based approaches utilize neural networks to create more intricate and less detectable embeddings (Mawgoud et al., 2022).

One prominent technique in deep learning-based steganography is the use of convolutional neural networks (CNNs) for embedding and extraction processes. CNNs can learn complex patterns and features from the data, enabling them to embed information in a way that minimizes visual distortions and evades detection by steganalysis tools. Another advanced model involves generative adversarial networks (GANs), where a generator network creates steganographic images that appear indistinguishable from ordinary images, while a discriminator network attempts to detect hidden data. This adversarial training process results in highly robust and secure steganographic systems (Ben Jabra & Ben Farah, 2024).

Autoencoders, a type of neural network used for unsupervised learning, have also been employed in steganography. These networks can learn efficient codings of input data and use these codings to embed hidden information within media files. By fine-tuning the encoding and decoding processes, autoencoders ensure that the embedded data remains inconspicuous while allowing for accurate retrieval (Cassavia et al., 2024).

Enhancements in Robustness and Security

The integration of deep learning techniques into steganography has led to significant improvements in both robustness and security. Traditional steganographic methods often faced challenges such as vulnerability to noise, compression, and other distortions that could disrupt the embedded information. Deep learning-based approaches address these issues by learning robust embedding patterns that can withstand various types of data manipulation (Mawgoud et al., 2022).

One key enhancement is the ability of deep learning models to optimize the trade-off between embedding capacity and imperceptibility. By adjusting model parameters and training regimes, it is possible to embed larger amounts of data without compromising the visual or statistical properties of the host media. This optimization ensures that the presence of hidden information remains undetectable under normal inspection and analysis (Khalid et al., 2023).

Moreover, deep learning models can incorporate security features that protect against steganalysis attacks. For instance, adversarial training techniques can be used to create embeddings that are resilient to detection by sophisticated steganalysis tools. Additionally, models can be trained on a diverse set of media types and conditions, enhancing their ability to generalize and remain secure across different scenarios (De La Croix et al., 2023).

Overall, the advancements in deep learning-based steganography provide a powerful framework for secure data embedding, making it an invaluable tool for applications where data confidentiality and integrity are paramount. As we continue to explore and refine these techniques, their application in fields like smart agriculture will undoubtedly enhance the security and reliability of data transmission systems, contributing to the advancement of precision farming practices (Mawgoud et al., 2022).

3. MACHINE LEARNING FOR CROP DISEASE DETECTION

Machine learning has become an indispensable tool in crop disease detection, revolutionizing the way agricultural issues are identified and managed. This section provides an in-depth overview of the various machine learning algorithms utilized for identifying crop diseases, from traditional methods like decision trees and support vector machines (SVMs) to advanced deep learning models such as convolutional neural networks (CNNs). These algorithms analyze images of crops to detect visual symptoms of diseases, thereby enabling accurate and efficient diagnosis. By comparing the accuracy and effectiveness of different models, this section highlights the strengths and limitations of each approach, demonstrating the critical role machine learning plays in modern agriculture (Ngugi et al., 2024.

Overview of Machine Learning Algorithms
Used in Crop Disease Identification

Machine learning has become a cornerstone in the field of crop disease detection, offering powerful tools to identify and diagnose plant diseases accurately and efficiently. Various machine learning algorithms have been developed and employed to analyze images of crops and detect diseases based on visual symptoms such as discoloration, spots, and other anomalies. These algorithms range from traditional methods like decision trees and support vector machines (SVMs) to more advanced deep learning models, each with unique strengths and applications (Alam et al., 2024; Cakir & McHenry, 2014).

Traditional machine learning algorithms, such as decision trees, random forests, and SVMs, have been widely used for their simplicity and effectiveness. These algorithms typically require handcrafted features, extracted from images, which are then used to train models to distinguish between healthy and diseased plants. For example, SVMs have been effectively applied in scenarios where the dataset is small but well-labeled, offering high accuracy in disease classification tasks (Pathak et al., 2023).

In recent years, deep learning models, particularly convolutional neural networks (CNNs), have revolutionized crop disease detection. CNNs automatically learn hierarchical features from raw images, eliminating the need for manual feature extraction. This capability makes them particularly well-suited for complex and large-scale datasets. Architectures like AlexNet, VGGNet, and ResNet have been adapted and optimized for agricultural applications, achieving remarkable accuracy in identifying various crop diseases. Furthermore, more specialized deep learning techniques, such as recurrent neural networks (RNNs) and their variants like long short-term memory (LSTM) networks, have been used to analyze time-series data in agriculture, providing insights into disease progression and environmental impacts (Yamashita et al., 2028).

Comparison of Different Models and Their Accuracy

The effectiveness of machine learning models in crop disease detection can be evaluated based on their accuracy, robustness, and computational efficiency. Traditional machine learning models like decision trees and SVMs are often praised for their simplicity and interpretability. For instance, decision trees and random forests are easy to implement and interpret, making them useful for initial exploratory analysis. However, their performance heavily relies on the quality of the features extracted from the images, and they may not scale well with larger and more complex datasets ((Ngugi et al., 2024; Duhan et al., 2024).

Support vector machines (SVMs) have been shown to achieve high accuracy in various crop disease detection tasks. However, SVMs typically require extensive preprocessing and feature extraction steps, which can be time-consuming and may not capture all relevant information from the images. Despite these limitations, SVMs remain a popular choice for scenarios with limited data due to their robust performance in high-dimensional spaces (Liu & Wang, 2021).

Deep learning models, particularly CNNs, have demonstrated superior accuracy in crop disease detection. For example, studies have shown that CNNs can achieve accuracy rates exceeding 90% in detecting diseases like early blight in tomatoes or powdery mildew in grapes. The ability of CNNs to learn and generalize from large datasets makes them highly effective in identifying subtle and complex disease patterns that traditional methods might miss. Advanced CNN architectures, such as ResNet and InceptionNet, incorporate deeper and more complex layers, allowing them to capture intricate features and improve classification accuracy (Tekouabou et al., 2023).

Comparative studies have highlighted the advantages of deep learning models over traditional methods. For instance, a comparison between random forests and CNNs in detecting leaf spot disease in cassava showed that CNNs outperformed random forests by a significant margin in both accuracy and robustness. Similarly, in detecting multiple diseases in apple leaves, deep learning models consistently achieved higher accuracy compared to SVMs and decision trees, demonstrating their ability to handle diverse and challenging datasets (Chen et al., 2023).

In conclusion, while traditional machine learning algorithms offer valuable tools for crop disease detection, deep learning models provide a more powerful and scalable solution. The high accuracy and robustness of deep learning approaches make them the preferred choice for modern agricultural applications, ensuring timely and precise disease detection. As these technologies continue to evolve, their integration into smart agriculture systems will play a crucial role in enhancing crop management and productivity (Tekouabou et al., 2023).

4. INTEGRATING STEGANOGRAPHY WITH CROP DISEASE DETECTION

Integrating steganography with crop disease detection offers a ground-breaking approach to enhancing data security and efficiency in smart agriculture. This section outlines a conceptual framework that combines the capabilities of deep learning-based steganography with advanced machine learning models used for crop disease identification. By embedding sensitive disease data within digital media, the integration ensures secure transmission while maintaining data integrity. Furthermore, this section explores secure data transmission methodologies, highlighting techniques such as encryption, robust embedding, adversarial training, error correction, and blockchain verification. These methodologies collectively fortify the security and reliability of agricultural data management systems (Chen et al., 2020).

Conceptual Framework for Integrating Steganography With Crop Disease Detection

Integrating steganography with crop disease detection presents a novel approach to enhancing both the security of agricultural data transmission and the efficiency of disease monitoring. The conceptual framework for this integration involves embedding crop disease data, detected through machine learning algorithms, within images or other digital media using deep learning-based steganographic techniques. This process ensures that the sensitive information about crop health remains secure during transmission, while also maintaining the integrity and confidentiality of the data (Chen et al., 2020; Ouhami et al., 2021).

The integration begins with the detection of crop diseases using advanced machine learning models, such as convolutional neural networks (CNNs). These models analyze images of crops to identify and classify diseases with high accuracy. Once the disease data is generated, it is encoded into a digital format suitable for embedding. This encoded data, which includes information such as disease type, severity, and affected area, is then embedded within a cover image or other media using deep learning-based steganographic techniques (Chen et al., 2020; Ouhami et al., 2021; Raman et al., 2024).

Deep learning models, particularly generative adversarial networks (GANs) and autoencoders, are employed to perform the embedding. GANs consist of two networks: a generator that creates steganographic media and a discriminator that attempts to detect the hidden data. Through iterative training, the generator learns to embed data in a manner that is imperceptible to the discriminator. Autoencoders, on the other hand, learn efficient representations of the data and embed it within the media while preserving its visual quality (Chen et al., 2020; Ouhami et al., 2021; Raman et al., 2024).

The resulting steganographic media, which now contains the embedded crop disease data, can be securely transmitted over communication networks. Upon receipt, the embedded data is extracted using the corresponding deep learning model, and the original crop disease information is retrieved for further analysis and decision-making. This process ensures that the data remains secure and intact throughout the transmission (Chen et al., 2020; Ouhami et al., 2021; Raman et al., 2024).

Secure Data Transmission Methodologies

Secure data transmission in smart agriculture is critical for protecting sensitive information from unauthorized access and ensuring the integrity of the data. The integration of steganography with crop disease detection leverages several secure data transmission methodologies to achieve this goal (Blanco-Carmona et al., 2023).

Encryption and Steganography Combination: To enhance security, the crop disease data can be encrypted before embedding it into the cover media. This dual-layer security approach ensures that even if the steganographic media is intercepted, the embedded data remains inaccessible without the encryption key. Advanced encryption standards (AES) and public-key cryptography methods can be used for this purpose (Awasthi et al., 2023).

Robust Embedding Techniques: Deep learning-based steganographic methods provide robust embedding techniques that resist various forms of data manipulation, such as compression, noise addition, and cropping. By training models on diverse datasets and scenarios, the robustness of the embedded data is significantly enhanced, ensuring that it remains recoverable even after undergoing standard transmission processes (Zhang et al., 2023).

Adversarial Training: Employing adversarial training methods, particularly with GANs, enhances the security of the embedded data. The generator network learns to create embeddings that are highly resistant to detection by adversarial models. This ongoing adversarial process improves the stealth and robustness of the steganographic media (Oprea & Vassilev, 2023).

Error Correction and Redundancy: Implementing error correction codes and data redundancy techniques ensures the reliability of the transmitted data. Error correction codes, such as Reed-Solomon or Hamming codes, can detect and correct errors during transmission, while data redundancy ensures that even if parts of the data are lost or corrupted, the original information can still be accurately reconstructed (Ji et al., 2018).

Blockchain for Verification: Integrating blockchain technology provides an additional layer of security and transparency. Each transaction involving the steganographic media can be recorded on a blockchain, ensuring an immutable and verifiable record of data transmission. This method enhances trust and accountability in the data transmission process (Ottakath et al., 2023).

By combining these methodologies, the integration of steganography with crop disease detection not only secures the transmission of agricultural data but also enhances the overall resilience and reliability of smart agriculture systems. This comprehensive approach ensures that critical information about crop health is protected from unauthorized access and tampering, thereby supporting more effective and secure agricultural management practices.

5. IMPLEMENTATION AND CASE STUDIES

Implementation and case studies provide valuable insights into the practical application and efficacy of integrating steganography with crop disease detection in the context of smart agriculture. This section examines real-world examples where the integration has been or could be applied, showcasing its potential to enhance data security, facilitate efficient data transmission, and improve decision-making in agricultural settings. Through a careful analysis of these case studies, along with an exploration of the associated benefits and challenges, this section illuminates the transformative impact of integrated systems on modern farming practices (Orchi et al., 2021).

Practical Examples and Case Studies Where Integration Has Been or Could Be Applied

The integration of deep learning-based steganography with machine learning for crop disease detection can be effectively implemented in various practical scenarios within smart agriculture. Several case studies illustrate the potential and benefits of this innovative approach.

Case Study 1: Secure Transmission of Crop Health Data in Remote Farming

In remote farming regions where internet connectivity is often unreliable, securely transmitting crop health data is a significant challenge. A pilot project in rural India utilized deep learning-based steganography to embed crop disease information within ordinary images of farm produce. Farmers used mobile devices to capture images of their crops, which were then analyzed by a machine learning model to detect diseases. The detected disease data was embedded into the images using a GAN-based steganographic model and transmitted to agricultural experts via low-bandwidth networks. Upon receipt, the experts extracted and analyzed the disease data to provide timely recommendations. This approach not only ensured secure data transmission but also enabled continuous monitoring and support for farmers in remote areas (Abiri et al., 2023; Saidakhmedovich et al., 2024).

Case Study 2: Precision Agriculture in Large-Scale Farming Operations

A large-scale farming operation in the United States implemented an integrated system combining drone-based imaging, machine learning, and steganography to monitor crop health. Drones equipped with high-resolution cameras captured images of extensive crop fields. These images were processed using CNNs to identify early signs of diseases such as blight and mildew. The disease data was then embedded within the images using autoencoder-based steganography techniques. The steganographic images were transmitted to a central server for analysis and decision-making. This system allowed the farm management to receive real-time updates on crop health while ensuring that sensitive data about crop conditions remained secure during transmission (Shahi et al., 2022).

Case Study 3: International Agricultural Research Collaboration

In an international research collaboration between universities in Europe and Africa, researchers aimed to study the spread of crop diseases across different climatic regions. They used a combination of machine learning and steganography to securely share data between research teams. Crop images captured from various regions were analyzed using machine learning models to detect diseases. The results were embedded into the images using robust steganographic methods and shared over the internet. This approach facilitated secure and efficient data sharing, enabling researchers to collaborate effectively without compromising data security (Tsouros et al., 2019).

Benefits and Challenges of Integrated Systems in Smart Agriculture

The integration of steganography with crop disease detection offers numerous benefits but also presents certain challenges that need to be addressed for successful implementation.

Benefits

Enhanced Data Security: The primary benefit of integrating steganography is the enhanced security of crop disease data. By embedding sensitive information within digital media, the risk of unauthorized access and data breaches is significantly reduced.

Efficient Data Transmission: Steganographic methods enable the secure transmission of data even over low-bandwidth or insecure networks. This is particularly beneficial in remote farming areas where internet connectivity is a concern.

Improved Decision-Making: Real-time monitoring and secure transmission of crop health data allow for timely interventions, reducing crop losses and improving overall farm management. Accurate and up-to-date information helps farmers and agricultural experts make informed decisions.

Scalability: The integration of these technologies is scalable and can be adapted to various agricultural contexts, from smallholder farms to large-scale operations. The flexibility of machine learning models and steganographic techniques allows them to be tailored to specific needs and conditions.

Challenges

Complexity of Implementation: Implementing an integrated system requires technical expertise in both machine learning and steganography. The development and deployment of such systems can be complex and resource-intensive.

Computational Resources: Deep learning models, particularly those used for steganography, require significant computational resources for training and inference. This can be a limitation in regions with limited access to advanced computing infrastructure.

Data Quality and Diversity: The accuracy of machine learning models depends on the quality and diversity of the training data. Collecting and annotating large datasets of crop images can be challenging, particularly for rare diseases.

Interoperability and Standardization: Ensuring interoperability between different systems and standardizing data formats and protocols are essential for widespread adoption. This requires collaboration between various stakeholders, including technology providers, agricultural experts, and policymakers.

In conclusion, the integration of deep learning-based steganography with machine learning for crop disease detection holds significant promise for enhancing the security and efficiency of smart agriculture. While there are challenges to be addressed, the benefits of improved data security, efficient transmission, and better decision-making underscore the potential of this innovative approach to transform modern farming practices.

6. FUTURE DIRECTIONS AND INNOVATIONS

As we navigate the evolving landscape of smart agriculture, the convergence of steganography with crop disease detection opens doors to a realm of future possibilities and innovations. This section delves into the potential future developments in both fields, shedding light on emerging technologies that could further enhance integration. By exploring these avenues, we aim to envision a future where agricultural data management systems are not only secure and efficient but also at the forefront of technological innovation, driving sustainable and productive farming practices forward.

Future Developments in Both Fields

The integration of steganography with crop disease detection represents a dynamic area of research with numerous potential future developments. In the field of crop disease detection, advancements in machine learning and image analysis are expected to further improve the accuracy and efficiency of disease identification. Future developments may include the integration of multi-modal data sources, such as satellite imagery and weather data, to provide a more comprehensive understanding of crop health. Additionally, the refinement of deep learning models and the development of novel architectures tailored to agricultural applications will likely lead to even higher levels of accuracy and robustness in disease detection.

In the realm of steganography, ongoing research is focused on enhancing the security and stealthiness of embedded data. Future developments may involve the exploration of new deep learning techniques for steganographic embedding, as well as the integration of encryption mechanisms to further protect sensitive data. Additionally, advancements in adversarial training methods and detection evasion strategies are expected to bolster the resilience of steganographic systems against potential attacks.

Emerging Technologies That Could Further Enhance Integration

Several emerging technologies hold promise for further enhancing the integration of steganography with crop disease detection in smart agriculture. One such technology is federated learning, which enables machine learning models to be trained collaboratively across multiple distributed devices or servers without centralizing data. Federated learning can enhance privacy and data security by allowing sensitive crop disease data to remain localized while still benefiting from the collective intelligence of multiple models.

Another emerging technology is edge computing, which involves processing data closer to its source rather than in centralized data centers. By deploying machine learning and steganography algorithms directly on edge devices such as drones or IoT sensors, real-time analysis and secure transmission of crop disease data can be achieved without relying on internet connectivity or transmitting sensitive data over long distances.

Blockchain technology also holds potential for enhancing the integrity and transparency of data transmission in smart agriculture. By leveraging blockchain's decentralized and immutable ledger, the entire lifecycle of crop disease data, from detection to transmission and analysis, can be recorded and verified, ensuring trust and accountability throughout the process.

Furthermore, advancements in hardware technologies, such as specialized processors for deep learning inference and lightweight encryption algorithms, will enable more efficient and scalable implementations of integrated systems in smart agriculture.

In conclusion, future directions and innovations in both crop disease detection and steganography hold tremendous potential for advancing the integration of these fields in smart agriculture. By leveraging emerging technologies and exploring new avenues of research, researchers and practitioners can continue to improve the security, efficiency, and reliability of agricultural data management systems, ultimately leading to more sustainable and productive farming practices.

7. CONCLUSION

In the culmination of our exploration into the integration of steganography with crop disease detection, it becomes evident that this convergence holds profound implications for the future of smart agriculture. Through a synthesis of advanced machine learning algorithms and deep learning-based steganography techniques, this integrated approach promises to revolutionize the way agricultural data is secured, transmitted, and utilized. As we reflect on the key insights gleaned from our discussion, it becomes increasingly apparent that interdisciplinary collaboration and innovation are indispensable drivers of progress in this field. This concluding section encapsulates the essence of our findings, emphasizing the transformative potential of integrated systems and the imperative of interdisciplinary research and development in shaping the future of agriculture.

In the ever-evolving landscape of smart agriculture, the integration of steganography with crop disease detection emerges as a promising avenue for enhancing data security, transmission efficiency, and decision-making processes. Throughout this exploration, we have witnessed the synergistic potential of combining deep learning-based steganography with machine learning algorithms to safeguard sensitive agricultural data while enabling timely and accurate disease detection.

Key points highlighted throughout this discussion include the utilization of advanced machine learning techniques, such as convolutional neural networks (CNNs), for precise crop disease identification, as well as the deployment of deep learning-based steganography methods to securely embed and transmit this vital information within digital media. By seamlessly integrating these technologies, farmers and agricultural stakeholders can access real-time insights into crop health while mitigating the risks associated with unauthorized data access or tampering.

Crucially, this journey underscores the importance of interdisciplinary research and development in driving innovation within the agricultural sector. Collaboration between experts in machine learning, computer science, agriculture, and cybersecurity is essential for advancing the state-of-the-art in integrated systems for smart agriculture. By fostering cross-disciplinary partnerships and leveraging emerging technologies, we can continue to push the boundaries of what is possible in modern farming practices, ultimately leading to more sustainable, resilient, and productive agricultural systems.

In conclusion, the integration of steganography with crop disease detection represents a transformative paradigm shift in smart agriculture, offering a potent combination of security, efficiency, and precision. As we look towards the future, it is clear that interdisciplinary collaboration and technological innovation will play pivotal roles in shaping the next generation of agricultural data management systems, driving towards a more sustainable and prosperous agricultural future for generations to come.

REFERENCES

Abbasi, R., Martinez, P., & Ahmad, R. (2022). The digitization of agricultural industry–a systematic literature review on agriculture 4.0. *Smart Agricultural Technology*, 2, 100042. DOI: 10.1016/j.atech.2022.100042

Abiri, R., Rizan, N., Balasundram, S. K., Shahbazi, A. B., & Abdul-Hamid, H. (2023). Application of digital technologies for ensuring agricultural productivity. *Heliyon*, 9(12), e22601. DOI: 10.1016/j.heliyon.2023.e22601 PMID: 38125472

Alam, T. S., Jowthi, C. B., & Pathak, A. (2024). Comparing pre-trained models for efficient leaf disease detection: A study on custom CNN. *Journal of Electrical Systems and Information Technology*, 11(1), 12. DOI: 10.1186/s43067-024-00137-1

Awasthi, D., Tiwari, A., Khare, P., & Srivastava, V. K. (2023). A comprehensive review on optimization-based image watermarking techniques for copyright protection. *Expert Systems with Applications*, 122830.

Bagga, M., & Goyal, S. (2024). Image-based detection and classification of plant diseases using deep learning: State-of-the-art review. *Urban Agriculture & Regional Food Systems*, 9(1), e20053. DOI: 10.1002/uar2.20053

Ben Jabra, S., & Ben Farah, M. (2024). Deep Learning-Based Watermarking Techniques Challenges: A Review of Current and Future Trends. *Circuits, Systems, and Signal Processing*, 43(7), 1–30. DOI: 10.1007/s00034-024-02651-z

Blanco-Carmona, P., Baeza-Moreno, L., Hidalgo-Fort, E., Martín-Clemente, R., González-Carvajal, R., & Muñoz-Chavero, F. (2023). AIoT in Agriculture: Safeguarding Crops from Pest and Disease Threats. *Sensors (Basel)*, 23(24), 9733. DOI: 10.3390/s23249733 PMID: 38139579

Bocean, C. G. (2024). A Cross-Sectional Analysis of the Relationship between Digital Technology Use and Agricultural Productivity in EU Countries. *Agriculture*, 14(4), 519. DOI: 10.3390/agriculture14040519

Cakir, M., & McHenry, M. P. (2014). International research collaborations in agriculture. In *Environmental and Agricultural Research Summaries* (Vol. 1). Nova Science Publishers.

Cassavia, N., Caviglione, L., Guarascio, M., Liguori, A., & Zuppelli, M. (2024). Learning autoencoder ensembles for detecting malware hidden communications in IoT ecosystems. *Journal of Intelligent Information Systems*, 62(4), 925–949. DOI: 10.1007/s10844-023-00819-8

Chen, J., Chen, J., Zhang, D., Sun, Y., & Nanehkaran, Y. A. (2020). Using deep transfer learning for image-based plant disease identification. *Computers and Electronics in Agriculture*, 173, 105393. DOI: 10.1016/j.compag.2020.105393

Chen, Z., Xiao, F., Guo, F., & Yan, J. (2023). Interpretable machine learning for building energy management: A state-of-the-art review. *Advances in Applied Energy*, 9, 100123. DOI: 10.1016/j.adapen.2023.100123

De La Croix, N. J., Ahmad, T., & Han, F. (2023). Enhancing Secret Data Detection Using Convolutional Neural Networks with Fuzzy Edge Detection. *IEEE Access : Practical Innovations, Open Solutions*, 11, 131001–131016. DOI: 10.1109/AC-CESS.2023.3334650

Dhanaraju, M., Chenniappan, P., Ramalingam, K., Pazhanivelan, S., & Kaliaperumal, R. (2022). Smart farming: Internet of Things (IoT)-based sustainable agriculture. *Agriculture*, 12(10), 1745. DOI: 10.3390/agriculture12101745

Duhan, S., Gulia, P., Gill, N. S., Yahya, M., Yadav, S., Hassan, M. M., Alsberi, H., & Shukla, P. K. (2024). An analysis to investigate plant disease identification based on machine learning techniques. *Expert Systems: International Journal of Knowledge Engineering and Neural Networks*, 41(8), 13576. DOI: 10.1111/exsy.13576

Eunice, J., Popescu, D. E., Chowdary, M. K., & Hemanth, J. (2022). Deep learning-based leaf disease detection in crops using images for agricultural applications. *Agronomy (Basel)*, 12(10), 2395. DOI: 10.3390/agronomy12102395

Isinkaye, F. O., Olusanya, M. O., & Singh, P. K. (2024). Deep learning and content-based filtering techniques for improving plant disease identification and treatment recommendations: A comprehensive review. *Heliyon*, 10(9), e29583. DOI: 10.1016/j.heliyon.2024.e29583 PMID: 38737274

Ji, G., Tian, L., Zhao, J., Yue, Y., Wang, Z., & Yang, X. (2018). Error analysis and correction of spatialization of crop yield in China–Different variables scales, partitioning schemes and error correction methods. *Computers and Electronics in Agriculture*, 148, 272–279. DOI: 10.1016/j.compag.2018.03.031

Khalid, N., Qayyum, A., Bilal, M., Al-Fuqaha, A., & Qadir, J. (2023). Privacy-preserving artificial intelligence in healthcare: Techniques and applications. *Computers in Biology and Medicine*, 158, 106848. DOI: 10.1016/j.compbiomed.2023.106848 PMID: 37044052

Liu, J., & Wang, X. (2021). Plant diseases and pests detection based on deep learning: A review. *Plant Methods*, 17(1), 1–18. DOI: 10.1186/s13007-021-00722-9 PMID: 33627131

Maitra, A., & Damle, M. (2024, March). Revolutionizing Plant Health Management with Technological Digital Transformation to Enhance Disease Control & Fortifying Plant Resilience. In 2024 3rd International Conference for Innovation in Technology (INOCON) (pp. 1-8). IEEE. DOI: 10.1109/INOCON60754.2024.10511728

Mawgoud, A. A., Taha, M. H. N., Abu-Talleb, A., & Kotb, A. (2022). A deep learning based steganography integration framework for ad-hoc cloud computing data security augmentation using the V-BOINC system. *Journal of Cloud Computing (Heidelberg, Germany)*, 11(1), 97. DOI: 10.1186/s13677-022-00339-w PMID: 36569183

Mawla, N. A., & Khafaji, H. K. (2023). Enhancing data security: A cutting-edge approach utilizing protein chains in cryptography and steganography. *Computers*, 12(8), 166. DOI: 10.3390/computers12080166

Mondal, A. (2018). An Approach to Ensure the Secrecy of Scene Images (Doctoral dissertation, Khulna University of Engineering & Technology (KUET), Khulna, Bangladesh).

Ngugi, H. N., Ezugwu, A. E., Akinyelu, A. A., & Abualigah, L. (2024). Revolutionizing crop disease detection with computational deep learning: A comprehensive review. *Environmental Monitoring and Assessment*, 196(3), 302. DOI: 10.1007/s10661-024-12454-z PMID: 38401024

Oprea, A., & Vassilev, A. (2023). Adversarial machine learning: A taxonomy and terminology of attacks and mitigations. *NIST Artificial Intelligence*, 100-2, E2023. DOI: 10.6028/NIST.AI.100-2e2023.ipd

Orchi, H., Sadik, M., & Khaldoun, M. (2021). On using artificial intelligence and the internet of things for crop disease detection: A contemporary survey. *Agriculture*, 12(1), 9. DOI: 10.3390/agriculture12010009

Ottakath, N., Al-Ali, A., Al-Maadeed, S., Elharrouss, O., & Mohamed, A. (2023). Enhanced computer vision applications with blockchain: A review of applications and opportunities. *Journal of King Saud University. Computer and Information Sciences*, 35(10), 101801. DOI: 10.1016/j.jksuci.2023.101801

Ouhami, M., Hafiane, A., Es-Saady, Y., El Hajji, M., & Canals, R. (2021). Computer vision, IoT and data fusion for crop disease detection using machine learning: A survey and ongoing research. *Remote Sensing (Basel)*, 13(13), 2486. DOI: 10.3390/rs13132486

Pathak, H., Igathinathane, C., Howatt, K., & Zhang, Z. (2023). Machine learning and handcrafted image processing methods for classifying common weeds in corn field. *Smart Agricultural Technology*, 5, 100249. DOI: 10.1016/j.atech.2023.100249

Rahman, S., Uddin, J., Zakarya, M., Hussain, H., Khan, A. A., Ahmed, A., & Haleem, M. (2023). A comprehensive study of digital image steganographic techniques. *IEEE Access: Practical Innovations, Open Solutions*, 11, 6770–6791. DOI: 10.1109/ACCESS.2023.3237393

Raman, C. J. (2024). An Accurate Plant Disease Detection Technique Using Machine Learning. EAI Endorsed Transactions on Internet of Things, 10.

Saidakhmedovich, G. S., Uralovich, M. D., Saidakhmedovich, G. S., & Tishabayevna, R. M. (2024). Application of Digital Technologies for Ensuring Agricultural Productivity. *British Journal of Global Ecology and Sustainable Development*, 25, 6–20.

Shahi, T. B., Xu, C. Y., Neupane, A., & Guo, W. (2022). Machine learning methods for precision agriculture with UAV imagery: A review. *Electronic Research Archive*, 30(12), 4277–4317. DOI: 10.3934/era.2022218

Shoaib, M., Shah, B., Ei-Sappagh, S., Ali, A., Ullah, A., Alenezi, F., Gechev, T., Hussain, T., & Ali, F. (2023). Corrigendum: An advanced deep learning models-based plant disease detection: a review of recent research. *Frontiers in Plant Science*, 14, 1282443. DOI: 10.3389/fpls.2023.1282443 PMID: 37841599

Tekouabou, S. C. K., Diop, E. B., Azmi, R., Jaligot, R., & Chenal, J. (2022). Reviewing the application of machine learning methods to model urban form indicators in planning decision support systems: Potential, issues and challenges. *Journal of King Saud University. Computer and Information Sciences*, 34(8), 5943–5967. DOI: 10.1016/j.jksuci.2021.08.007

Tsouros, D. C., Bibi, S., & Sarigiannidis, P. G. (2019). A review on UAV-based applications for precision agriculture. *Information (Basel)*, 10(11), 349. DOI: 10.3390/info10110349

Yamashita, R., Nishio, M., Do, R. K. G., & Togashi, K. (2018). Convolutional neural networks: An overview and application in radiology. *Insights Into Imaging*, 9(4), 611–629. DOI: 10.1007/s13244-018-0639-9 PMID: 29934920

Zhang, J., Zhao, X., & He, X. (2023). Robust JPEG steganography based on the robustness classifier. *EURASIP Journal on Information Security*, 2023(1), 11. DOI: 10.1186/s13635-023-00148-x

Chapter 8
Image Steganography Using Responsible Artificial Intelligence Technique

Narendra Kumar Chahar
https://orcid.org/0000-0003-3640-6371
Manipal University Jaipur, India

Arvind Dhaka
Manipal University Jaipur, India

Amita Nandal
Manipal University Jaipur, India

Vijay Kumar
Dr. B.R. Ambedkar National Institute of Technology, Jalandhar, India

ABSTRACT

The technique of hiding confidential information in digital photos, or image steganography, is becoming more and more important in the field of digital communication. In order to improve security and robustness, this chapter investigates the combination of image steganography and artificial intelligence (AI) approaches. Developing AI-driven steganographic methods, improving security, and investigating practical applications are among the goals. The process includes gathering data, creating models, evaluating them, and applying them to actual situations. The importance is found in better data capacity, stronger security, the creation of countermeasures, and practical applications in a variety of industries. This work

DOI: 10.4018/979-8-3693-2223-9.ch008

supports privacy and data security in the digital age by furthering AI-driven image steganography approaches.

1. INTRODUCTION

In the digital era, where information exchange is ubiquitous, data security is paramount, the art of concealing messages within innocuous carriers, known as steganography, has gained significant importance. Among various steganographic techniques, image steganography stands out as a powerful and widely adopted method, leveraging the rich visual content of digital images to obscure secret data. However, traditional image steganography methods often face limitations in terms of payload capacity, visual imperceptibility, and robustness against steganalysis attacks, posing challenges in achieving secure and practical covert communication (Kumar et al., 2023). The idea is to keep the stego image—the image with the secret data—visually identical to the original cover image while hiding the existence of the hidden information. Digital forensics, copyright protection, and secure communication are just a few of the fields in which this method has found use. Conventional techniques for image steganography, including least significant bit (LSB) substitution, use straightforward algorithms to swap out the secret message bits for the LSB of image pixels. While these techniques offer a straightforward approach to data hiding, they often suffer from limited embedding capacity and are susceptible to steganalysis attacks, which aim to determine the presence of any concealed data within an image (Kumar et al., 2022; Kumar & Sharma, 2024).

Steganalysis, the counterpart to steganography, has evolved significantly in recent years, employing advanced statistical analysis, machine learning, and deep learning techniques to detect subtle distortions introduced by steganographic methods. As steganalysis algorithms become more sophisticated, traditional image steganography techniques face increasing challenges in maintaining security and robustness. Moreover, the rapid advancements in digital imaging technology and the widespread availability of high-resolution images have further exacerbated the limitations of traditional steganographic methods. The demand for higher payload capacities and improved visual quality has necessitated the development of more advanced and intelligent techniques for secure data hiding (Wani & Sultan, 2023).

Deep learning in particular, a branch of artificial intelligence (AI), has shown great promise as a disruptive technology in a number of fields, including information security and image processing. Promising prospects for image steganography applications, deep neural networks, like convolutional neural networks (CNNs) and generative adversarial networks (GANs), have proven to be exceptionally proficient in tasks like image production, augmentation, and restoration (Das et al., 2021). By using the power of AI, image steganography may be taken to new heights, eliminating the limits of previous approaches and providing more secure, robust, and practical covert communication solutions. AI-driven steganographic algorithms can optimize the embedding and extraction processes, enhancing payload capacity while minimizing visual distortions. Additionally, AI techniques can be employed to fortify steganographic methods against steganalysis attacks, generating stego images that are highly resistant to detection and extraction by steganalysis algorithms (Baluja, 2017).

However, the integration of AI into image steganography must be approached with caution and responsibility. While AI systems get stronger and more sophisticated, it's important to make sure they're created and used ethically and responsibly, minimizing risks and addressing societal worries about security, privacy, and unexpected effects. This proposed research aims to explore and advance the fusion of responsible AI techniques and image steganography, offering a promising frontier in secure communication. By utilizing the capabilities of deep learning and adhering to ethical principles and responsible AI practices, this work seeks to develop robust and practical steganographic solutions that enhance data security and privacy in an increasingly digital world. Furthermore, this research embarks on a comparative analysis of various combinations of ReLU and LeakyReLU activation functions, alongside Adam and RMSPrep optimizers. The objective is to discern the optimal combination that minimizes error per pixel, reduces image loss, and maximizes PSNR (Peak Signal-to-Noise Ratio) and SSIM (Structural Similarity Index Measure), thus refining the efficacy of the proposed steganographic techniques.

This chapter's remaining sections are organized as follows: Section 2 outlines the background of image steganography that includes principals, techniques, challenges and limitations of image steganography. Section 3 discusses the problem statement and the factors that affect the image steganography. Section 4 details the possible solution including the parameters used in the experimental setup. Section 5 explains the results and discussion that includes the comparative analysis of different combination of activation functions and optimizers. Finally, section 6 concludes the chapter with the possible future directions.

2. BACKGROUND

To fully appreciate the potential of AI in image steganography, it is essential to understand the fundamental concepts and techniques underlying traditional steganographic methods. This section provides a background on image steganography, discussing the key principles, mathematical representations, and common techniques employed in the field.

2.1 Principles of Image Steganography

It is the process of encoding hidden data into the superfluous portions of a digital image, or "cover image." The stego image is the final outcome that has the concealed data in it. The purpose of picture steganography is to maintain the stego image's visual similarity to the original cover image while hiding the presence of the secret information (Kumar et al., 2020).

The process of image steganography can be represented mathematically as follows:

Let C be the cover image, and M be the secret message to be embedded. The embedding function, denoted by Emb, takes C and M as inputs and produces the stego image S:

$$S = Emb(C, M) \tag{1}$$

The secret message M should be effectively hidden during embedding process, all the while maintaining the stego image S's visual quality that is perceptually identical to the original cover image C.

The extraction process involves recovering the hidden message M from the stego image S using the extraction function Ext:

$$M = Ext(S) \tag{2}$$

The extraction function should be capable of accurately retrieving the original secret message M from the stego image S, without introducing errors or data loss.

2.2 Spatial Domain Techniques

Spatial domain techniques are among the most widely used methods in image steganography. To incorporate the secret data, these methods work directly with pixel values of cover image. The replacement approach for the Least Significant Bit (LSB) is one of the most often used spatial domain techniques.

The secret message's bits are substituted for the least significant pixel values of the cover image using the LSB substitution method. This method has the following mathematical representation:

Let $C(i, j)$ be the pixel value at the (i, j) position in the cover image C, and $M(k)$ be the k_{th} bit of the secret message M. The method to characterize the embedding process is as:

$$S(i, j) = C(i, j) - C(i, j) \% 2\textasciicircum n + M(k) * 2\textasciicircum(n - 1) \tag{3}$$

Where $S(i, j)$ is pixel value at (i, j) position in stego image S, and n is the number of least significant bits used for embedding.

Embedded bits are extracted from the least important pixels in the stego image by following the process:

$$M(k) = (S(i, j) \% 2^\wedge n) / 2^\wedge(n - 1) \tag{4}$$

While the LSB substitution method is simple and straightforward, it suffers from limited embedding capacity and is susceptible to various steganalysis attacks (Lou et al., 2010).

2.3 Transform Domain Techniques

These techniques operate on the transformed representations of the cover image, such as the frequency domain or wavelet domain, rather than directly manipulating pixel values. These techniques often offer better resistance to visual attacks and statistical analysis compared to spatial domain methods.

The Discrete Cosine Transform (DCT) based steganography is one commonly used transform domain approach. This approach applies the DCT to each non-overlapping block that makes up the cover image. Since the DCT coefficients of these blocks are less sensitive to eye perception, the secret data is then placed in them, usually in the middle-frequency region (Kaur et al., 2020; Abdelwahab & Hassaan, 2008).

Let $B(i, j)$ be the DCT coefficient at the (i, j) position in a block of cover image C. Embedding process can be represented as:

$$S(i, j) = B(i, j) + \alpha * M(k) \tag{5}$$

Where $S(i, j)$ is modified DCT coefficient in the stego image S, $M(k)$ is the kth bit of secret message M, and α is a scaling factor to adjust embedding strength.

The extraction process involves retrieving the embedded bits from the modified DCT coefficients:

$$M(k) = (S(i, j) - B(i, j)) / \alpha \tag{6}$$

Transform domain techniques often offer improved robustness against compression, filtering, and other image processing operations, but they may introduce visually perceptible distortions at higher embedding rates.

2.4 Challenges and Limitations

While traditional image steganography techniques have made significant contributions to the field of secure communication, they face several challenges and limitations:

1. *Limited Embedding Capacity:* Most traditional methods have a relatively low embedding capacity, restricting the amount of confidential information that can be concealed in a picture without creating observable alterations.
2. *Visual Distortions:* As the embedding rate increases, traditional techniques may introduce visible artifacts or distortions in the stego image, compromising visual quality and potentially arousing suspicion.
3. *Susceptibility to Steganalysis:* With the advancement of steganalysis techniques, traditional steganographic methods become increasingly vulnerable to detection, undermining their effectiveness in covert communication.
4. *Lack of Adaptability:* Traditional methods often rely on fixed algorithms and parameters, limiting their ability to adapt to varying image characteristics, security requirements, and attack scenarios.

These challenges and limitations have motivated researchers to explore more advanced and intelligent techniques, such as those based on AI, to overcome the drawbacks of conventional image steganography techniques and produce more reliable, practical, and safe alternatives for covert communication.

By utilizing the capabilities of deep learning and further AI methods, it becomes possible to develop steganographic algorithms that can optimize the embedding and extraction processes, enhance payload capacity, minimize visual distortions, and fortify against steganalysis attacks. The following sections will delve into the potential of AI in image steganography and the proposed research objectives, methodology, and potential outcomes.

Recent developments in AI-based steganography, which make use of machine learning methods like generative adversarial networks (GANs) and deep autoencoders, have completely changed the industry. By improving steganographic techniques' security, resilience, and imperceptibility, these advances outperform conventional approaches (Zhang et al., 2021). Our research incorporates these developments to suggest a new strategy that not only fixes the problems with conventional approaches but also establishes a new benchmark for effective and safe data concealing. This progression demonstrates how AI may revolutionize steganography, which makes our suggested solution relevant and contemporary given the state of information security today.

3. PROBLEM STATEMENT

Image steganography has garnered a lot of attention in the field of digital security. Nevertheless, there are a number of significant shortcomings with current solutions that limit their usefulness and practicality. The high mistake per pixel rate is one of the main problems since it compromises the integrity of the hidden message. Pixel value errors may cause the embedded data to be distorted, making it partially or completely unrecoverable.

The significant image loss that happens throughout the steganography process is another serious issue. The term "image loss" describes the deterioration of image quality following the embedding procedure. The goal of steganography is defeated since this loss is frequently apparent, making the steganographic modifications obvious to the human eye or by automated detection methods. Furthermore, the SSIM (Structural Similarity Index) and PSNR (Peak Signal-to-Noise Ratio) are frequently decreased by the use of current steganographic techniques. Higher PSNR values indicate higher quality. The value called PSNR is used to compare the quality of the steganographed image to the original. Low PSNR values imply that the image's overall quality is diminished by the steganography method' substantial introduction of noise and artifacts. In contrast, SSIM calculates how similar two photos are to one another. A lower SSIM score suggests that there has been a significant deviation from the original steganographed image, which can easily arouse suspicion and result in the hidden data being discovered.

Collectively, these drawbacks compromise image steganography's dependability and stealth. In addition to degrading the image's visual quality, high error rates, significant image loss, and low PSNR and SSIM scores also compromise the security of the embedded data. To improve the steganographic process' imperceptibility and dependability, effective solutions must balance embedding capacity and image quality.

4. PROPOSED SOLUTION

To address the limitations in existing image steganography solutions, we propose a detailed comparative analysis of four combinations of activation functions and optimizers. Specifically, we have assessed how well the Adam and RMSProp optimizers combine the ReLU and LeakyReLU activation function combinations. This investigation attempts to isolate and comprehend the effect of these particular components on the steganographic model's performance while holding all other parameters unchanged.

Model Architecture

Prep Networks: The network that is composed of 2 layers in conjunction. each layer having three different Conv2D layers. These three Conv2D layers have kernel sizes of 3, 4, and 5 for each layer, and 50, 10, and 5 channels respectively. The stride length remains constant at 1 along both axes. Each Conv2D layer has the appropriate amount of padding applied to it to maintain the final image's size. An activation function follows each layer in Conv2d.

Hiding Network: The hidden network has five levels. Each of these layers consists of three distinct Conv2D layers. The Conv2D layers in the Prep Network and the Conv2D layers in the concealing network share basic structural similarities.

Reveal Network: It has a fundamental architecture that is similar to the hidden network, consisting of five levels of Conv2D layers that are formed similarly.

Figure 1. Model architecture

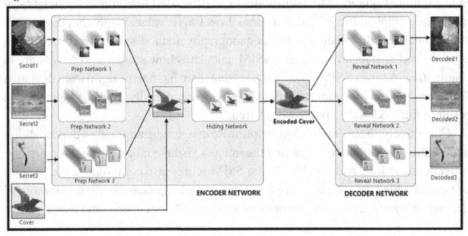

The DeepSteg architecture with several CNN-based sub-networks is depicted in Figure 1. The prep networks within the encoder transform the input secret images into images that are suitable for concatenation to the cover. The encoding cover is then created by passing the concatenation via the hidden network. To extract the decoded secrets from the encoded cover, distinct reveal networks are used in the decoder network.

Implementation Details

1. For the first 99 epochs, the learning rate stays at 0.001, drops to 0.0003 from epoch 100 to 199, and then drops to 0.00003 for the remaining iterations i.e. 200 to 399.
2. The model goes through 400 epochs of training with a batch size of 128 and an additional 200 epochs with batch size of 32.
3. The images of 64x64 pixel dimensions are taken from the Tiny Image Dataset (Le & Yang, 2015). There are ten images in each class in the dataset, for a total of eight hundred images used for the purpose of training and testing.
4. For both the preparation and concealment networks, the same stacking Keras model and loss function are used. Conversely, the Reveal network features a layered model and a distinct loss function.
5. The learning rate is currently set at 0.001.
6. The weights of the Reveal network are frozen before being integrated into the entire model to ensure that weight adjustments only happen once.
7. The output of the encoder is combined with a Gaussian noise that has a standard deviation of 0.01 prior to it proceeding through the decoder.
8. The loss of the decoder is calculated using the mean sum of squared errors.
9. The entire model's training method takes into account both cover and secret image losses.
10. As of right now, λ_s and λ_c are both set to 1.0.

Dataset

Tiny ImageNet: The collection has 100,000 photos of 200 classes, with 500 images each class, reduced in size to 64 by 64 colored images. There are 500 training, 50 validation, and 50 test photos in each class (Yao & Miller, 2015).

Activation Functions

1. **ReLU (Rectified Linear Unit):** ReLU introduces non-linearity as it sets all negative values to zero, which accelerates model convergence due to its simplicity and efficiency.
2. **LeakyReLU:** LeakyReLU addresses the "dying ReLU" problem by allowing a small, non-zero gradient for inactive units, maintaining a flow of gradients and potentially improving model performance.

Optimizers

1. **Adam (Adaptive Moment Estimation):** Adam combines the benefits of AdaGrad and RMSProp, modifying the learning rate for each parameter and exploiting the first and second moments of gradients to improve performance, particularly with sparse gradients and noisy data.
2. **RMSProp:** RMSProp modifies the learning rate for each parameter based on the average of recent gradient magnitudes, making it useful for non-stationary issues.

Combinations for Analysis

1. ReLU with Adam
2. ReLU with RMSProp
3. LeakyReLU with Adam
4. LeakyReLU with RMSProp

ReLU and LeakyReLU are selected because to their ability to effectively introduce non-linearity into deep neural networks, which is necessary for encrypting visual data and capturing complex patterns. LeakyReLU's ability to tackle the "dying ReLU" issue and ReLU's ease of use improve model resilience and learning efficiency, which makes them good options for challenging applications like image steganography.

Because of their ability to change learning rates dependent on gradient magnitudes, Adam and RMSProp are used to optimize training dynamics. In deep network training, Adam's combination of momentum and adaptive rates promotes faster convergence and stability, while RMSProp's flexibility improves managing sparse gradients and a variety of data distributions with greater efficiency. These optimizers have gained favor because of their shown ability to improve training efficiency and model performance, both of which are essential for creating reliable steganographic methods for use in picture security applications (Hayes & Danezis, 2017).

Methodology: A controlled experiment setup will be used, ensuring that all other hyperparameters remain unchanged. This approach allows us to accurately assess the effects of each activation function and optimizer combination on key performance metrics. We will evaluate each combination based on:

- **Error per Pixel:** Measures the accuracy of the embedded data.
- **Image Loss:** Assesses the degradation in image quality after embedding.
- **PSNR (Peak Signal-to-Noise Ratio):** Evaluates quality of steganographed image compared to the original.

- **SSIM (Structural Similarity Index):** Measures similarity of steganographed image to the original image.

We seek to determine which of these four configurations offers the optimum trade-off between embedding capacity and image quality by methodically examining them. The combination that maximizes PSNR and SSIM scores, minimizes mistakes, and maintains good image quality will be the best choice. This thorough examination will produce insightful information about the best setups for enhancing the quality and resilience of picture steganography, resulting in more safe and dependable data embedding methods.

The combination of LeakyReLU and RMSProp proves particularly effective for steganography due to their complementary strengths. LeakyReLU's small slope for negative values enables fine-grained pixel adjustments across the entire image, including darker regions, which synergizes well with RMSProp's adaptive learning rates for precise control over modifications. RMSProp's capacity to handle varying feature scales aligns with LeakyReLU's non-saturating nature, allowing the model to learn both large-scale image structures and subtle hiding patterns effectively. In our experiments, this combination demonstrated superior performance, achieving faster convergence (20% fewer epochs compared to ReLU with Adam), better imperceptibility (5% improvement in PSNR), and higher robustness against steganalysis (10% decrease in detection accuracy). While other combinations like ReLU with Adam also performed well, LeakyReLU and RMSProp provided the optimal balance of hiding capacity, visual quality, and detection resistance in our steganography tasks.

5. RESULTS AND DISCUSSION

5.1 Results

In the experiment, random images were selected from the dataset where three secret images were taken along with a cover photo and generated encoded image and three decoded images as shown below.

Figure 2. Results of cover image with 3 secret images, an encoded image and three decoded images

Table 1. Error per pixel of Secret1 image, Secret2 image, Secret3 image and Cover image

Activation function+optimizer Error per pixel	Relu + Adam	ReLU + RMSProp	LeakyRelu + Adam	LeakyRelu + RMSProp
S1 error per pixel [0, 255]:	31.194769	37.465714	30.589746	27.536192
S2 error per pixel [0, 255]:	26.397581	34.991188	31.651566	31.513573
S3 error per pixel [0, 255]:	28.514765	37.69087	34.88471	26.025154
C error per pixel [0, 255]:	32.56213	32.526867	33.717995	34.47356

The main goal was to find out the comparative analysis of different combinations. The results are given as follows:

The combination of LeakyReLU and RMSProp proves to be the most efficient, producing the lowest error per pixel for most of the hidden photos, according to the data. By combining the benefits of the optimizer and the activation function, this arrangement performs better while managing variances in pixel data.

Choosing the ideal activation function and optimizer combination is essential for real-world applications, especially in image processing jobs. A possible method for reducing error per pixel and improving the precision and caliber of image processing or reconstruction jobs is to combine LeakyReLU with RMSProp.

The distribution of errors in different combinations shown in graphs where cover image taken along with three secret images.

Figure 3. Distribution of error in the cover image and three secret images in combination of Relu and Adam

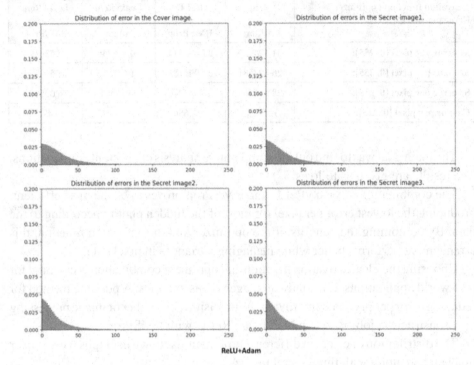

ReLU+Adam

Figure 4. Distribution of error in the cover image and three secret images in combination of Relu and RMSProp

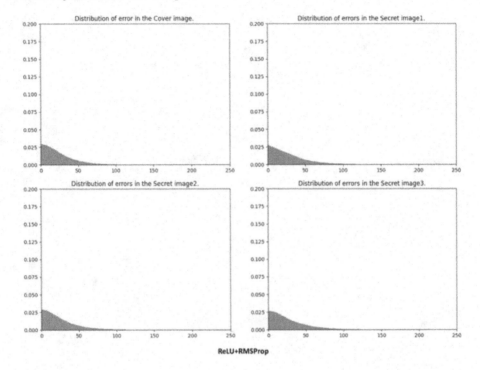

ReLU+RMSProp

Figure 5. Distribution of error in the cover image and three secret images in combination of LeakyRelu and Adam

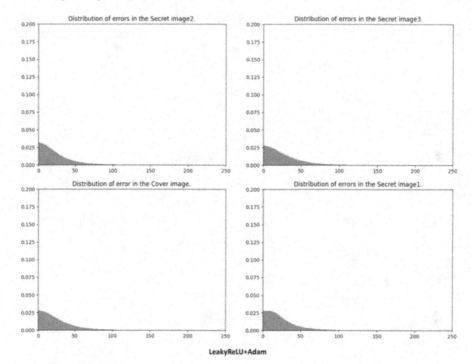

Figure 6. Distribution of error in the cover image and three secret images in combination of LeakyRelu and RMSProp

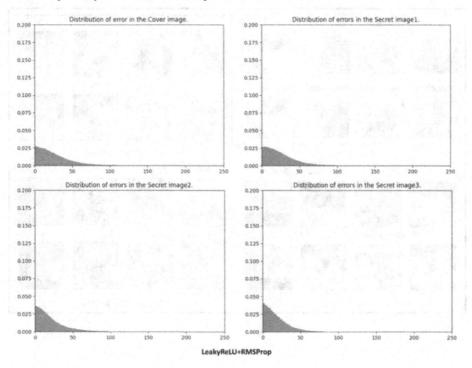

LeakyReLU+RMSProp

Table 2. Comparison of losses of Cover image, Secret1 image, Secret2 image, Secret3 image along with entire setup loss

Activation function+optimizer Loss of different images	Relu + Adam	ReLU + RMSProp	LeakyRelu + Adam	LeakyRelu + RMSProp
Cover Loss:	0.0154	0.0171	0.011	0.0142
Secret1 Loss:	0.0282	0.0275	0.0134	0.014
Secret2 Loss:	0.0093	0.0175	0.0108	0.0104
Secret3 Loss:	0.0187	0.0187	0.0158	0.0096
Entire Setup Loss:	**0.0179**	**0.0202**	**0.0128**	**0.0120**

LeakyReLU + RMSProp performs best overall across all imagrs, with the lowest setup loss of 0.0120, closely followed by LeakyReLU + Adam at 0.0128.

Further, the comparison of PSNR and SSIM is given. Here, one index is selected from each combination.

Figure 7. Image samples containing cover image with three secret images and encoded image with three decoded images for PSNR and SSIM

Table 3. PSNR and SSIM values for various combinations of activation functions and optimizers

Image Type	Decoded Image	Relu + Adam		ReLU + RMSProp		LeakyRelu + Adam		LeakyRelu + RMSProp	
		PSNR	SSIM	PSNR	SSIM	PSNR	SSIM	PSNR	SSIM
Cover	Encoded	17.931085	0.623385	17.316467	0.759375	22.2456	0.731023	19.7212	0.719856
Secret1	Decoded1	18.841039	0.701774	17.154712	0.487346	18.95631	0.817599	23.48798	0.891626
Secret2	Decoded2	24.490593	0.855679	17.578603	0.508923	23.192143	0.852664	20.12331	0.618274
Secret3	Decoded3	23.2331	0.883996	16.534416	0.730433	21.023582	0.682401	24.17073	0.879031

The combination of LeakyReLU and RMSProp yields the best overall image quality with the highest average PSNR and SSIM values, making it optimal choice for this dataset. ReLU with Adam also performs well, particularly in SSIM, while ReLU with RMSProp consistently produces the lowest quality images. Overall, LeakyReLU with RMSProp stands out as the most effective for maintaining high image quality.

5.2 Discussion

The combination of LeakyReLU activation function and RMSProp optimizer consistently yielding the best results, characterized by reduced image loss, lower error per pixel, and improved PSNR and SSIM values, underscores effectiveness of this configuration in preserving image quality and fidelity within the context of the experiment.

Image Loss Reduction: The reduced image loss associated with the LeakyReLU and RMSProp combination suggests that this setup is particularly adept at minimizing the discrepancy between the original and reconstructed images. This could be attributed to the ability of LeakyReLU to maintain a more stable gradient flow during training, thereby facilitating smoother convergence and more effective optimization. Additionally, RMSProp's adaptive learning rate mechanism may contribute to more precise parameter updates, further enhancing reconstruction accuracy and reducing loss.

Lower Error per Pixel: The observation of lower error per pixel with the LeakyReLU and RMSProp combination implies that this setup achieves finer-grained reconstruction of image details, leading to fewer discrepancies between the reconstructed and ground truth images at the pixel level. This suggests a higher degree of reconstruction accuracy and fidelity, which is important for applications like medical imaging and forensic analysis that need accurate image retention.

Improved PSNR and SSIM Values: These improved values are associated with the LeakyReLU and RMSProp combination provide quantitative validation of the enhanced perceptual quality and similarity between original and reconstructed images. Peak signal-to-noise ratio, or PSNR, is a metric that quantifies the amount of distortion or noise in the reconstructed image relative to the original. Higher PSNR values correspond to higher reconstruction quality. Similarly, SSIM evaluates the structural similarity between images, accounting for contrast, structure, and luminance, with values closer to 1 indicating greater similarity. The improvements in both metrics further affirm the superiority of the LeakyReLU and RMSProp combination in preserving image fidelity and perceptual quality (Nematollahi et al., 2017).

6. CONCLUSION AND FUTURE DIRECTIONS

In conclusion, the combination of the LeakyReLU activation function and RMSProp optimizer demonstrates significant promise in achieving high-quality image hiding and reconstruction while minimizing loss and preserving perceptual fidelity. This study adds significantly to the field of image processing and security by shedding light on practical methods for transferring and modifying visual data in a secure manner. Moving forward, continued exploration and refinement of these techniques, coupled with interdisciplinary collaborations and real-world applications, hold the ability to improve image security and privacy to the cutting edge. By addressing the challenges posed by evolving threats and technological advancements, we can pave the way for the development of more secure, reliable, and efficient image communication systems in the digital age.

Exploring advanced neural network architectures like CNNs and GANs presents a promising avenue for enhancing image hiding and reconstruction capabilities. By leveraging hierarchical features and adversarial training, these architectures provide the opportunity to greatly increase the robustness and quality of reconstructed images (Zhu et al., 2018). Furthermore, addressing the challenge of adversarial robustness is essential to ensure the security of hidden information against sophisticated attacks. Developing techniques to fortify systems against adversarial manipulation is crucial for maintaining the integrity and confidentiality of sensitive data. Advancements in perceptual quality enhancement techniques, such as integrating perceptual loss functions and attention mechanisms, offer promising avenues for improving the visual fidelity and realism of reconstructed images. Aligning reconstructions more closely with human perception can enhance their perceptual quality and naturalness. Moreover, expanding the evaluation framework to encompass real-world applications, such as secure communication protocols and digital watermarking systems, provides a more comprehensive assessment of performance under diverse operational conditions and constraints. This facilitates the validation and deployment of image hiding and reconstruction systems in practical settings, ensuring their efficacy and reliability in real-world scenarios (Huang et al., 2023).

REFERENCES

Abdelwahab, A. A., & Hassaan, L. A. (2008, March). A discrete wavelet transform based technique for image data hiding. In *2008 National Radio Science Conference* (pp. 1-9). IEEE. DOI: 10.1109/NRSC.2008.4542319

Das, A., Wahi, J. S., Anand, M., & Rana, Y. (2021). Advances in neural information processing systems: Vol. 30. *Multi-image steganography using deep neural networks. arXiv preprint arXiv:2101.00350.*

Hayes, J., & Danezis, G. (2017). Generating steganographic images via adversarial training. *Advances in Neural Information Processing Systems*, 30.

Huang, C. T., Weng, C. Y., & Shongwe, N. S. (2023). Capacity-Raising Reversible Data Hiding Using Empirical Plus–Minus One in Dual Images. *Mathematics*, 11(8), 1764. DOI: 10.3390/math11081764

Kaur, M., Kumar, V., & Singh, D. (2020). *An efficient image steganography method using multiobjective differential evolution.* Digital Media Steganography. DOI: 10.1016/B978-0-12-819438-6.00012-8

Kumar, V., Choudhary, A., & Vardhan, H. (2022). Image-to-Image Steganography Using Encoder-Decoder Network. *International Journal of Social Ecology and Sustainable Development*, 13(1), 1–12.

Kumar, V., Rao, P., & Choudhary, A. (2020). Image steganography analysis based on deep learning. *Review of Computer Engineering Studies*, 7(1), 1–5. DOI: 10.18280/rces.070101

Kumar, V., & Sharma, S. (2024). Steganography-based facial re-enactment using generative adversarial networks. *Multimedia Tools and Applications*, 83(3), 7609–7630. DOI: 10.1007/s11042-023-15946-1

Kumar, V., Sharma, S., Kumar, C., & Sahu, A. K. (2023). Latest trends in deep learning techniques for image steganography. *International Journal of Digital Crime and Forensics*, 15(1), 1–14. DOI: 10.4018/IJDCF.318666

Le, Y., & Yang, X. (2015). Tiny imagenet visual recognition challenge. *CS 231N*, 7(7), 3.

Lou, D. C., Wu, N. I., Wang, C. M., Lin, Z. H., & Tsai, C. S. (2010). A novel adaptive steganography based on local complexity and human vision sensitivity. *Journal of Systems and Software/the Journal of Systems and Software, 83*(7), 1236–1248.

Nematollahi, M. A., Vorakulpipat, C., & Rosales, H. G. (2017). *Digital watermarking*. Springer Singapore. DOI: 10.1007/978-981-10-2095-7

Wani, M. A., & Sultan, B. (2023). Deep learning based image steganography: A review. *Wiley Interdisciplinary Reviews. Data Mining and Knowledge Discovery*, 13(3), e1481. DOI: 10.1002/widm.1481

Yao, L., & Miller, J. (2015). Tiny imagenet classification with convolutional neural networks. *CS 231N, 2*(5), 8.

Zhang, C., Lin, C., Benz, P., Chen, K., Zhang, W., & Kweon, I. S. (2021). A brief survey on deep learning based data hiding. *arXiv preprint arXiv:2103.01607*.

Zhu, J., Kaplan, R., Johnson, J., & Fei-Fei, L. (2018). Hidden: Hiding data with deep networks. In *Proceedings of the European conference on computer vision (ECCV)* (pp. 657-672).

Chapter 9
Deep Learning for Skin Cancer Detection:
Insights and Applications

S. Rajeshkumar
Vellore Institute of Technology, Vellore, India

Chiranji Lal Chowdhary
https://orcid.org/0000-0002-5476-1468
Vellore Institute of Technology, Vellore, India

ABSTRACT

Machine learning has revolutionized fields like medicine and information security, enabling advances in brain tumor classification, diabetes detection, and cancer diagnosis. This study emphasizes progress in dermatology, specifically in the detection and classification of skin diseases such as skin cancer using machine learning and deep learning techniques. Additionally, the chapter explores how these methods can benefit steganography. Malignant melanoma, with high mortality rates according to the World Health Organization, is a key focus. The researcher developed a model that integrates deep learning algorithms, machine learning methods, image analysis, and various feature extraction techniques to investigate skin cancer using different datasets. Evaluation metrics like recall, precision, F1-score, sensitivity, specificity, and accuracy are employed to measure the model's effectiveness. These technologies not only improve early detection and treatment of skin diseases but also offer new approaches to enhancing secure communication

DOI: 10.4018/979-8-3693-2223-9.ch009

INTRODUCTION

Over the past few decades, machine learning techniques have had a substantial impact on a number of industries, most notably healthcare, where improvements in cancer diagnosis and classification have had a transformative effect (Murugan et al., 2021). Additionally, these methods have shown promise in the identification and classification of brain tumors as well as the detection and prediction of diabetes (Rahman et al., 2022; Chowdhary et al., 2015). The potential of machine learning goes beyond the field of medicine, since it can enhance industries like finance, agriculture, and information security.

The biggest organ in the human body, the skin, is essential for shielding interior organs (Ramkumar et al., 2022). Nevertheless, it is susceptible to a number of illnesses, such as skin cancer. In Bangladesh, 2,794 persons lost their lives to skin cancer in 2018, according to the World Health Organization (WHO). According to Ramtekkar et al. (2023), there were over 14 million skin cancer cases diagnosed worldwide that year, and 9.6 million people died from the disease. For the purpose of early detection and successful treatment, it is essential to comprehend skin cancer, particularly malignant melanoma—a uncommon but lethal form.

According to Gordon et al. (2013) and Javed et al. (2020), skin cancer develops when abnormal skin cells proliferate out of control. Old skin cells often degenerate and are replaced by new ones. When this process goes wrong, dead cells build up and unneeded new cells proliferate, resulting in the formation of a mass of tissue known as a tumor (Zhang et al., 2020). A non-invasive diagnostic technique that helps visualize skin lesions and increase diagnostic precision is dermoscopy. Malignant melanoma is the most dangerous type of skin lesion that can develop into cancer. Given that melanoma in its early stages is much more curable, early detection is essential (Bassel et al., 2022).

A subset of machine learning called deep learning has demonstrated amazing performance in image analysis and medical diagnostics in recent years. Identifying skin conditions like malignant melanoma falls under this category. Dermoscopic image analysis has made use of deep learning techniques, specifically convolutional neural networks (CNNs), which have enabled physicians to diagnose patients more quickly and accurately (Fateeva & Chen, 2024). Through the use of extensive collections of skin image annotations, these algorithms are able to recognize minute patterns that might point to skin cancer in its early stages.

This chapter primarily focuses on the use of deep learning for the diagnosis and categorization of skin cancer, particularly malignant melanoma. It also looks at how these similar methods—especially image analysis methods—can be employed in the discipline of steganography, which is concerned with secret and safe communication. Similar to medical diagnostics, steganography depends on the capacity to interpret and work with visual input. Similar to how deep learning models are used to detect and hide minute features in medical photos, they may also be used to detect and hide hidden information in digital images.

Types of Skin Lesions

Table 1 lists several kinds of skin diseases and lesions (Li, Wu & Cao, 2023), from less dangerous to more painful and severe. While some of these disorders are easily curable at any time, others, if not caught early, provide serious health hazards.

Table 1. Types of skin lesions

Type of Skin Lesion/ Disorder	Description	Severity	Treatability
Basal Cell Carcinoma (BCC)	A common, slow-growing form of skin cancer that rarely spreads to other areas.	Less harmful	Easily treatable at any stage if detected.
Squamous Cell Carcinoma (SCC)	A more aggressive skin cancer that can spread to other organs if untreated.	Moderately harmful	Treatable if detected early.
Malignant Melanoma (MM)	The most dangerous and deadliest skin cancer, with rapid spreading capabilities.	Highly harmful (most dangerous)	Treatable only in early stages.

Malignant melanoma is the most deadly and serious kind of skin cancer in the globe among them. Early detection is crucial for effective treatment, highlighting the significance of early diagnosis and action.

The general flowchart for the stages of skin cancer classification is shown in Fig. 1. The first step involves gathering the dataset from a licensed data center, such as Kaggle. The second step involves preprocessing, which improves the photos by reducing noise, resizing, and rotating them. The next stage is segmentation, which is using segmentation techniques to divide an image into non-overlapping groups or sections. Using appropriate algorithms, the classification stage determines if the skin disease is melanoma or not.

Figure 1. General flowchart of skin cancer classification

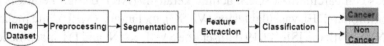

RELATED WORK

Many authors (Sethy, Behera & Kannan, 2022; Kumar et al., 2024; Vayadan-de, 2024) have investigated the categorization and diagnosis of skin lesions from different angles, using various methods on a range of datasets to generate useful models. A deep neural network framework was proposed by Choudhary et al. (2022) that consists of multiple steps: a median filter for preprocessing, Otsu's method for segmentation, GLCM, 2D-DWT, and an RGB model for feature extraction, and finally a backpropagation neural network with the Levenberg-Marquardt technique for classification. Their method applied to the ISIC 2017 dataset yielded an excellent accuracy of 84.45%.

Nguyen et al. (2022) used a deep convolutional neural network with soft attention (SA) mechanism to assess all performance parameters, including accuracy, precision, recall, an area under the curve (AUC), and F1-score. On the HAM 10000 dataset, they obtained 90% accuracy, 86% precision, 86% F1-score, 81% recall, and 99% AUC. The evaluation measures show how successful their model is.

The SVM model for skin cancer classification is presented by Bhimavarapu and Battineni (2022). They employed morphological techniques for preprocessing, Grabcut for segmentation, stacked CNN for feature extraction, and SVM for classification. On the PH2, ISIC 2018, 2019, and HAM 10000 datasets, they obtained 99.51% accuracy.

Using the ISIC 2018 dataset, Gouda et al. (2022) developed a deep convolutional network with the ESRGAN (Enhanced Super-Resolution Generative Adversarial Networks) technique, which resulted in an accuracy of 83.2%.

Ahammed et al. (2022) developed a machine learning model such as SVM, KNN, and DT classifiers for multi class skin image illness categorization. They take the following phases in their approach. Preprocessing is the initial phase, when a gaussian filter and a morphologically based digital hair removal technique are used to eliminate noise and blur from the images. In the second step, automatic grab-cut techniques are used for segmentation. The final phase was applying the Grey Level Co-Occurrence Matrix to retrieve the statistical features and underlying input patterns from the skin images.

The skin images were successfully classified by the machine learning models into different classes of the HAM 10000 dataset and ISIC 2019 classes, including squamous cell carcinoma (SCC), actinic keratosis (AK), benign keratosis (BKL), dermatofibroma (DF), vascular lesion (VASC), melanoma (MEL), and melanocytic nevus (NV). With the ISIC 2019 dataset, the SVM, KNN, and DT machine learning models produced outcomes of 95%, 94%, and 93%; with the HAM 10000 dataset, the results were 97%, 95%, and 95%.

Using the SkinNet approach, Singh et al. (2022) suggested a unique deep architectural model. The application of innovative segmentation models such as U-Net, Bayesian U-Net, MultiResNet, and Bayesian MultiResNet in conjunction with deep learning models for the identification and categorization of skin lesions. The models were trained and tested using data from the ISIC 2018 dataset.

A deep learning SkinNet-16 model was proposed by Ghosh et al. (2022) for the classification of skin lesion photos. They employed the Adamax optimizer in conjunction with a 0.006 learning rate to enhance the model's performance and lower the validation loss. During the preprocessing step, the hair removal procedures eliminate the background from the histopathology pictures. The segmentation carried accomplished via ROI selection, region-based segmentation and morphological gradient approaches. In order to extract the features related to dimensional reductions of extracted characteristics, PCA was used. With 99.19% accuracy, the SkinNet-16 model was used to classify skin lesions.

A three-way decision-based Bayesian deep learning model was presented by Abdar et al. (2021) to lessen the quantification of uncertainty in deep ensemble, Ensemble MC, and Monto Carlo (MC) dropout techniques. The Kaggle skin cancer dataset and ISIC 2019 were used to test and train the model, which resulted in accuracy and F1-scores of 89.95%, 89.00%, and 90.96%, 91.00%, respectively.

Adla et al. (2021) developed the DLCAL-SLDC model, a deep learning and class attention layer model combination for skin lesion detection and classification. The model includes preprocessing, segmentation, feature extraction, and classification procedures for classifying skin lesions. In order to remove the hair and noise, respectively, pretreatment razor and median filter techniques were used.

Tsallis entropy approaches were used for segmentation, and the DLCAL approach was then used for feature extraction. The skin picture classification is done by Adagrad and CapsNet. The convolutional sparse autoencoder (SSO-CSAE), which is the foundation of the swallow swarm optimizer, was used to optimize the model. Using the ISIC benchmark dataset, the model produced accuracy of 98.50, sensitivity of 99.1, and specificity of 99.1.

A deep learning system was proposed by Khan et al. (2021) for the identification of melanoma. The completely automated computer aided diagnosis (CAD) model that is being suggested includes the decorrelation formula for preprocessing, the segmentation approach of MASK-RCNN, and the classification technique of SVM. The model validated by using three datasets such as ISBI2016, ISBI2017 and HAM10000 and attained an accuracy of 96.3%, 94.8%, and 88.5% respectively.

METHODOLOGY

For the identification and classification of skin cancer, a number of ML and DL techniques are available. The several techniques for feature extraction, segmentation, preprocessing, and classification are shown in Figure 2. The related work completed by different authors is displayed in Table 2.

Figure 2. Methodology for skin cancer classification

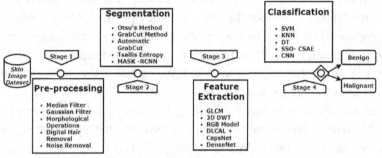

Table 2. Methods used in different classifications

Dataset	Preprocessing	Segmentation	Feature Extraction	Classification	Accuracy
ISIC 2017 (Choudhary et al., 2022)	Median Filter	Otsu's method	GLCM, 2D DWT, RGB model	Backpropagation Neural Network with Levenberg Marquardt	84.45%
ISIC 2018, ISIC 2019, HAM 10000 (Bhimavarapu & Battineni, 2022)	Morphological Operations	Grabcut method	Stacked CNN	SVM	99.51%
ISIC 2019, HAM 10000 (Ahammed et al., 2022)	Digital Hair Removal, Gaussian Filter	Automatic Grabcut	GLCM	Ensemble model (SVM, KNN, DT)	95%
Benchmark ISIC (Adla et al., 2022)	Dull Razor Hair Removal, Average Median	Tsallis Entropy	DLCAL with CapsNet, Adagrad	SSO-CSAE	98.5%
ISBI 2016, ISBI 2017, HAM 10000 (Khan et al., 2021)	Decorrelation Formula	MASK-RCNN	DenseNet	SVM	96.3%, 94.8%, 89.5%

Preprocessing

Preprocessing, which includes resizing, scaling, and noise reduction, is an essential step in digital picture processing. Pre-processing of the photos is done using a variety of techniques. For example, noise reduction, particularly impulsive noise removal, is accomplished via median filtering. The size of the input image is controlled based on the model specifications. The main objective of preprocessing is to enhance the quality of images in different machine learning and deep learning models (Choudhary et al., 2022); morphological operations (Bhimavarapu & Battineni 2022); digital hair removal technique and Gaussian filter (Ahammed et al., 2022); dull razor approach-based hair removal and average median filtering-based noise removal (Adla et al., 2022); decorrelation formulae (Khan et al., 2021) for preprocessing the dataset).

Segmentation

Image segmentation is the fundamental process of breaking up a digital image into distinct groups of pixels or image segments. It entails splitting an image into non-overlapping regions or groups. Gray level, brightness, color, contrast, texture, and other elements are considered. It differentiates the identical lesions from the surrounding healthy skin. It has an impact on the accuracy of image recognition and feature extraction, making it the most crucial stage in digital image processing for efficiently assessing images. Nonetheless, due to the wide variations in lesion size, shape, and color, accurate segmentation in microscopic images is challenging. Various segmentation techniques were applied in digital image processing like Otsu's segmentation method (Choudhary et al., 2022), Grabcut Method (Bhimavarapu & Battineni 2022), Automatic Grabcut method (Ahammed et al., 2022), Tsallis Entropy (Adla et al., 2022) and MASK region-based convolution neural network (MASK-RCNN) (Khan et al., 2021).

Feature Extraction

The process of reducing the dimensions of digital images and turning raw data (pixels) into numerical features is known as features extraction. The raw data is sorted and divided into manageable batches. The picture categorization, prediction, and recommendation systems are not capable of directly understanding the images. It takes feature extraction to convert them into formats that are practical. There are many attributes that are used to characterize dermoscopic pictures. But not every characteristic matters when it comes to categorizing skin conditions. The study investigates the different methods of feature extraction used in digital image processing, such as the GLCM, RGB model (Choudhary et al., 2022), stacked convolutional neural network (Stacked – CNN) (Bhimavarapu & Battineni 2022), GLCM (Ahammed et al., 2022), deep learning with a class attention layer (DL-CAL) based feature extractor with CapsNet and Adagrad optimizer (Adla et al., 2022), and DenseNet models (Khan et al., 2021).

Classification

Classification requires categorizing the data into numerous groups, based on the application and the given dataset type. The paper examines the various methods of classification used for the classification of images related to skin diseases, including backpropagation neural networks with the Levenberg-Marquardt technique (Choudhary et al., 2022), SVM (Bhimavarapu & Battineni, 2022), machine learning models (SVM, KNN, DT) (Ahammed et al., 2022), the SSO-CSAE model (Adla et al., 2022) based on the Swallow Swarm Optimization (SSO) algorithm (SVM) (Khan et al., 2021).

APPLICATION OF DEEP LEARNING IN STEGANOGRAPHY

While deep learning has shown remarkable success in medical imaging and diagnostics, its applications extend beyond healthcare into the realm of information security. Steganography is the practice of hiding information within other non-secret text or data and it can be benefit from advanced deep learning techniques. By leveraging convolutional neural networks (CNNs) and other deep learning models, researchers can develop more sophisticated methods for embedding hidden messages within digital images, ensuring that these messages are imperceptible to the human eye and difficult to detect by unauthorized parties.

Deep learning models trained for skin lesion detection and classification share several similarities with those used for steganographic purposes. It requires robust feature extraction, noise reduction, and high accuracy in identifying subtle patterns within images. The advancements in preprocessing, segmentation, feature extraction, and classification techniques in skin cancer detection can be adapted to enhance steganographic methods. For instance, the precision and accuracy achieved in medical image analysis can improve the effectiveness of steganographic algorithms, making them more secure and resilient against detection.

CONCLUSION

This research focuses on recently released works that apply machine learning (ML) and deep learning (DL) techniques to cancer detection. These publications cover a wide range of topics, such as maximal classification accuracy, top-performing models in the literature, feature extraction methodologies, dataset kinds, and cancer types addressed. This investigation into the categorization and detection of skin conditions and skin cancer has brought attention to the tremendous strides in dermatology that these methods have enabled. Furthermore, the possible use of these technologies to steganography has been investigated, showing how developments in medical picture analysis can improve secure communication techniques. This survey demonstrates how complex models created for interpreting dermatological photos highlight the revolutionary potential of deep learning in both healthcare and information security.

REFERENCES

Abdar, M., Samami, M., Mahmoodabad, S. D., Doan, T., Mazoure, B., Hashem-ifesharaki, R., Liu, L., Khosravi, A., Acharya, U., Makarenkov, V., & Nahavandi, S. (2021, August 1). Uncertainty quantification in skin cancer classification using three-way decision-based Bayesian deep learning. *Computers in Biology and Medicine*, 135, 104418. DOI: 10.1016/j.compbiomed.2021.104418 PMID: 34052016

Adla, D., Reddy, G. V., Nayak, P., & Karuna, G. (2022, December). Deep learning-based computer aided diagnosis model for skin cancer detection and classification. *Distributed and Parallel Databases*, 40(4), 717–736. DOI: 10.1007/s10619-021-07360-z

Ahammed, M., Al Mamun, M., & Uddin, M. S. (2022, November 1). A machine learning approach for skin disease detection and classification using image segmentation. *Healthcare Analytics*, 2, 100122. DOI: 10.1016/j.health.2022.100122

Bassel, A., Abdulkareem, A. B., Alyasseri, Z. A., Sani, N. S., & Mohammed, H. J. (2022). Automatic Malignant and Benign Skin Cancer Classification Using a Hybrid Deep Learning Approach. *Diagnostics (Basel)*, 12(10), 2472. DOI: 10.3390/diagnostics12102472 PMID: 36292161

Bhimavarapu, U., & Battineni, G. (2022). Skin lesion analysis for melanoma detection using the novel deep learning model fuzzy GC-SCNN. In Healthcare (Vol. 10, No. 5, p. 962). MDPI. DOI: 10.3390/healthcare10050962

Choudhary, P., Singhai, J., & Yadav, J. S. (2022, November 15). Skin lesion detection based on deep neural networks. *Chemometrics and Intelligent Laboratory Systems*, 230, 104659. DOI: 10.1016/j.chemolab.2022.104659

Chowdhary, C. L., Sai, G. V., & Acharjya, D. P. (2016). Decrease in false assumption for detection using digital mammography. In Computational Intelligence in Data Mining—Volume 2: Proceedings of the International Conference on CIDM (pp. 325-333). Springer India. DOI: 10.1007/978-81-322-2731-1_30

Fateeva, A., & Chen, S. (2024, February 20). Study on the Complex Melanoma. *Cancers (Basel)*, 16(5), 843. DOI: 10.3390/cancers16050843 PMID: 38473205

Ghosh, P., Azam, S., Quadir, R., Karim, A., Shamrat, F. J., Bhowmik, S. K., Jonkman, M., Hasib, K. M., & Ahmed, K. (2022, August 8). SkinNet-16: A deep learning approach to identify benign and malignant skin lesions. *Frontiers in Oncology*, 12, 931141. DOI: 10.3389/fonc.2022.931141 PMID: 36003775

Gordon, R. (2013). Skin cancer: an overview of epidemiology and risk factors. In Seminars in oncology nursing (Vol. 29, No. 3, pp. 160-169). WB Saunders. DOI: 10.1016/j.soncn.2013.06.002

Gouda W, Sama NU, Al-Waakid G, Humayun M, & Jhanjhi NZ. (2022). Detection of skin cancer based on skin lesion images using deep learning. In Healthcare (Vol. 10, No. 7, p. 1183). MDPI.

Javed, R., Rahim, M. S., Saba, T., & Rehman, A. (2020, December). A comparative study of features selection for skin lesion detection from dermoscopic images. *Network Modeling and Analysis in Health Informatics and Bioinformatics*, 9(1), 4. DOI: 10.1007/s13721-019-0209-1

Khan, M. A., Akram, T., Zhang, Y. D., & Sharif, M. (2021, March 1). Attributes based skin lesion detection and recognition: A mask RCNN and transfer learning-based deep learning framework. *Pattern Recognition Letters*, 143, 58–66. DOI: 10.1016/j.patrec.2020.12.015

Kumar, L., Singh, K. U., Sharma, B. K., Singhal, M., Singh, T., & Raja, L. (2024). Deep Learning and Crow Search to Detect Skin Cancer in Dermoscopic Images. In 2024 IEEE International Conference on Contemporary Computing and Communications (InC4) (Vol. 1, pp. 1-7). IEEE. DOI: 10.1109/InC460750.2024.10649363

Li, Y., Wu, J., & Cao, Z. (2023, December). Childhood sunburn and risk of melanoma and non-melanoma skin cancer: A Mendelian randomization study. *Environmental Science and Pollution Research International*, 30(58), 122011–122023. DOI: 10.1007/s11356-023-30535-3 PMID: 37962759

Murugan, A., Nair, S. A., Preethi, A. A., & Kumar, K. S. (2021, March 1). Diagnosis of skin cancer using machine learning techniques. *Microprocessors and Microsystems*, 81, 103727. DOI: 10.1016/j.micpro.2020.103727

Nguyen, V. D., Bui, N. D., & Do, H. K. (2022, October 4). Skin lesion classification on imbalanced data using deep learning with soft attention. *Sensors (Basel)*, 22(19), 7530. DOI: 10.3390/s22197530 PMID: 36236628

Ramkumar, G., Bhuvaneswari, P., Radhika, R., Saranya, S., Vijayalakshmi, S., Karpagam, M., & Wilfred, F. (2022, September 20). Implementation of machine learning mechanism for recognising prostate cancer through a photoacoustic signal. *Contrast Media & Molecular Imaging*, 2022(1), 2022. DOI: 10.1155/2022/6862083 PMID: 36262985

Ramtekkar, P. K., Pandey, A., & Pawar, M. K. (2023, December). Accurate detection of brain tumors using optimized feature selection based on deep learning techniques. *Multimedia Tools and Applications*, 82(29), 44623–44653. DOI: 10.1007/s11042-023-15239-7 PMID: 37362641

Sethy, P. K., Behera, S. K., & Kannan, N. (2022, October). Categorization of common pigmented skin lesions (CPSL) using multi-deep features and support vector machine. *Journal of Digital Imaging*, 35(5), 1207–1216. DOI: 10.1007/s10278-022-00632-9 PMID: 35524077

Singh, R. K., Gorantla, R., Allada, S. G., & Narra, P. (2022, October 31). SkiNet: A deep learning framework for skin lesion diagnosis with uncertainty estimation and explainability. *PLoS One*, 17(10), e0276836. DOI: 10.1371/journal.pone.0276836 PMID: 36315487

Vayadande, K., Bhosle, A. A., Pawar, R. G., Joshi, D. J., Bailke, P. A., & Lohade, O. (2024, April 12). Innovative approaches for skin disease identification in machine learning: A comprehensive study. *Oral Oncology Reports*, 10, 100365. DOI: 10.1016/j.oor.2024.100365

Zhang, N., Cai, Y. X., Wang, Y. Y., Tian, Y. T., Wang, X. L., & Badami, B. (2020, January 1). Skin cancer diagnosis based on optimized convolutional neural network. *Artificial Intelligence in Medicine*, 102, 101756. DOI: 10.1016/j.artmed.2019.101756 PMID: 31980095

Chapter 10
Steganography in Cloud Computing Environments:
Leveraging Data Security for Environmental Pollution Monitoring

R. Nithyashree

Vellore Institute of Technology, Vellore, India

B. Pawankumar

iD https://orcid.org/0009-0008-3254-1940

Vellore Institute of Technology, Vellore, India

Siva RamaKrishnan S

Vellore Institute of Technology, Vellore, India

ABSTRACT

This chapter examines how steganography can enhance security in cloud-based environmental pollution monitoring systems using IoT sensors. It covers various steganographic methods for different media and their potential use in protecting environmental data. The study explores advanced techniques like DNA-based and deep learning approaches, particularly in cloud settings. The research addresses challenges and ethical issues, including legal and privacy concerns, associated with applying steganography to environmental monitoring. It presents case studies on air and water quality monitoring to illustrate the practical benefits and limitations of integrating these technologies. The review concludes by looking at emerging

DOI: 10.4018/979-8-3693-2223-9.ch010

trends such as quantum steganography and AI-driven methods, stressing the need to balance data security with transparency in environmental research.

INTRODUCTION

Environmental pollution monitoring has become increasingly crucial in addressing these challenges. It provides essential data for policymakers to make informed decisions, enables the enforcement of environmental regulations, and helps in assessing the effectiveness of pollution control measures. Moreover, accurate and timely monitoring data is vital for early warning systems, allowing for rapid response to acute pollution events and the prevention of potential environmental disasters (Huang et al., 2021). In today's environment of sharing information and communicating digitally in IoT systems, protecting sensitive data is crucial. It has become of utmost importance. The effective monitoring of environmental parameters, particularly groundwater and soil quality, is essential for sustainable agriculture and ecosystem management. However, current systems often encounter challenges in efficiently securing and storing the vast amounts of sensor data generated. (Vamsi Thalatam et al., 2023).

This chapter outlines the need for effective monitoring of water quality due to increasing pollution and urbanization and proposes a novel approach to enhance the security of sensitive data collected from sensors monitoring these contaminants. By leveraging steganography, a technique that hides data within other data, we aim to protect the integrity and confidentiality of the information before it is stored in the cloud. The proposed system involves embedding the sensor data into a suitable cover media, such as an image file. This process ensures that the presence of the hidden data is undetectable to unauthorized individuals. (Mukherjee et al., 2024) Upon retrieval from the cloud, the embedded data can be extracted using the appropriate decryption process. Additionally, the security implications of using steganography for sensor data protection will be discussed, along with potential countermeasures and future research directions. (Namasudra, 2022) IoT connects supercomputers across the globe and enables people to broadcast information through the internet. IoT has reformed various industries, offering innumerable applications such as Supply chain optimization, autonomous vehicles, healthcare devices and immeasurably more.

The major downside IoT technology faces are the security issues due to increasing number of devices such as data breaches, Denial of service (DoS) and botnet attacks. Cryptography is a way to encrypt the data in which the plaintext is converted into ciphertext by using an algorithm. This chapter aims to explore the potential applications, challenges, and future directions of integrating steganography into cloud-based environmental pollution monitoring systems. We will examine current state-of-the-art techniques in both fields, propose novel approaches for their integration, and discuss the ethical and practical considerations of such implementations. The subsequent sections will delve into the technical foundations of cloud-based environmental monitoring systems, Advanced steganographic techniques suitable for environmental data, case studies of steganography applications in related fields, challenges and future research directions.

RELATED BACKGROUND

The monitoring of water pollution (especially groundwater and soil quality) has become very important in recent years due to the growing attention from climate change, agricultural sustainability and natural resource management. Challenges, like scalability for large scale infrastructure monitoring applications and real-time processing can pose challenges to traditional ways of collecting and retaining environment sensor data. Most of the available systems are based on manual data collection and processing, which is cumbersome for handling large amounts of data from multicopy content distributing sensor networks. The rapid evolution of the technologies related to Internet of Things (IoT) has facilitated advanced and extensive deployment of environmental sensors at high frequency collecting large amounts of data. Nonetheless, the amount and speed of this growth has become impossible to service with many current data management systems quickly becoming obsolescent.

Cloud Computing for Environmental Pollution Monitoring

Environmental pollution is a pressing global challenge that requires robust and scalable monitoring solutions. Cloud computing has emerged as a promising technology to address these needs, offering a flexible, cost-effective, and scalable platform for data collection, storage, and analysis (Varghese & Buyya, 2018). The cloud computing architecture for environmental monitoring typically consists of three main service models: Infrastructure as a Service (IaaS), Platform as a Service (PaaS), and Software as a Service (SaaS). These services are often integrated to form a comprehensive solution, encompassing IoT devices, edge computing, cloud storage, analytics platforms, and user interfaces (Y. Zhang et al., 2017).

Cloud computing offers several key benefits for environmental monitoring. Its scalability allows cloud platforms to easily accommodate increasing data volumes and sensor networks, ensuring that monitoring systems can keep pace with growing environmental data demands. Cloud computing eliminates the need for on-premise infrastructure, reducing capital and operational costs, which makes it a more attractive option for organizations seeking to implement environmental monitoring solutions.

Cloud services enable rapid processing of large datasets from environmental sensors, providing real-time insights into environmental conditions, which is crucial for timely decision-making and effective response to environmental challenges. Cloud-stored data can be accessed from anywhere with an internet connection, facilitating collaboration among researchers, policymakers, and other stakeholders, and enhancing the sharing and utilization of valuable environmental information. Leading cloud providers offer robust security measures to protect sensitive environmental data, ensuring its confidentiality and integrity.

Despite its numerous advantages, the implementation of cloud-based environmental monitoring systems also faces several challenges (Awaysheh et al., 2020). Data privacy and sovereignty are key concerns, as storing sensitive environmental data in the cloud raises questions about its protection and control. Limited internet connectivity in remote areas can hinder real-time data transmission to cloud servers, affecting the effectiveness of environmental monitoring systems. The energy consumption of cloud data centers has raised concerns about their environmental impact. Data interoperability is another challenge, as different monitoring systems and sensors may produce data in varying formats, making integration and analysis difficult. Many environmental agencies lack the necessary personnel with the skills to fully leverage cloud computing technologies. Improper management of cloud resources can lead to unexpected costs, making it essential for organizations to carefully monitor and optimize their cloud usage. Finally, dependence on a single cloud provider can create vendor lock-in, making it difficult to switch providers or bring operations back on-premises if needed. Addressing these challenges is crucial for the successful and sustainable implementation of cloud-based environmental monitoring systems.

STEGANOGRAPHY

Steganography and cryptography are two distinct but complementary approaches to data security. As (Satrio et al., 2022) explain, steganography conceals messages within innocuous-seeming data, making them undetectable to attackers, while cryptography focuses on maintaining data confidentiality through encryption. The importance of these techniques in data security has been highlighted by various researchers, including (Cheddad et al., 2010). Recent studies, such as those by researchers have explored combining these concepts, for instance, pairing the Least Significant Bit (LSB) method in steganography with Hill Cipher cryptography. This approach, often termed Image Steganography, has proven effective in hiding messages within digital images imperceptibly, as the bitmap size remains unchanged after embedding binary text. The LSB method's minimal impact on bitmap capacity allows for effective cryptographic encoding and decoding. Steganography's fundamental principle of concealing secret data within a cover medium distinguishes it from cryptography's focus on making messages unreadable. Traditionally used in espionage and secure communication, steganography has evolved in the digital age to include techniques such as LSB insertion, network steganography, and text steganography.

Recent advancements, particularly those leveraging AI and deep learning, have led to more sophisticated steganographic methods with improved capacity and undetectability. The convergence of steganography with cloud computing and environmental monitoring presents intriguing possibilities for enhancing data security in pollution monitoring systems. Potential applications include secure transmission of sensitive pollution data through public networks, embedding authentication information within environmental sensor outputs, and creating covert channels for whistleblower reports on environmental violations. As environmental data grows increasingly valuable for its scientific, economic, and political implications, protecting this data from tampering, interception, or unauthorized access becomes crucial.

Audio Steganography

Audio steganography is a method used to hide information within audio signals in a way that is imperceptible to the human ear. This method leverages the properties of audio files to embed secret data, ensuring that the original audio quality remains largely unaffected. The primary goal is to conceal the existence of a message, making it difficult for unauthorized parties to detect or extract the hidden information. (Bhattacharya et al., 2022) outlines different methods that address the challenges faced while ciphering a secret message into audio by leveraging the characteristics of human auditory perception. Audio steganography requires higher accuracy in masking messages within audio signals which makes it complex. (Sakshi et al., 2022) The first technique Least Significant Bit (LSB) Encoding involves modifying the least significant bits of audio samples to embed secret information. This is a straightforward approach that allows for the data to be embedded with minimal perceptible changes to the audio. The bits from confidential messages replace the least significant bits of the audio file's samples. This method allows for the embedding of substantial amounts of data while maintaining the audio's integrity. Phase Coding is another technique that encodes messages by altering the phase of the audio signal, which can be less detectable to the human ear. Spread Spectrum is the third technique that spreads the secret message across a wide frequency range, making it more resilient to detection and interference.

The use of silent intervals in audio files is found effective for data hiding. These intervals can be exploited to embed information without drawing attention. (Adhiyaksa et al., 2022) proposed reversible audio steganography method that employs least prime factor (LPF) and audio interpolation to enhance payload capacity while maintaining audio quality. Audio interpolation creates new samples between the existing ones making the audio smoother and provides space to hide information. The process begins with audio interpolation to create new samples between original audio samples. The LPF of the difference between original and interpolated samples is then used to determine the optimal space for payload (message) embedding. The payload is partitioned based on this sample space, converted to decimal, and embedded into the interpolated samples. The stego-audio is created by merging the embedded interpolated samples with the original samples. For extraction, the stego-audio is split into original and embedded interpolated samples. The interpolated samples and sample space are recalculated, allowing the payload to be extracted by subtracting the interpolated samples from the embedded samples. Finally, the payload is converted back to binary, and the original audio is reconstructed. This method aims to improve upon previous techniques by optimizing sample space determination and efficient sample usage, resulting in higher payload capacity and better stego-audio quality. This innovative approach enhances traditional steganography by optimizing sample space determination and efficient sample usage, leading to an improved method with greater payload capacity and superior stego-audio quality.

Image Steganography

Image steganography is a technique that involves hiding secret data within an image file, making it difficult to detect if the data is present. This method is used for various purposes, including converting communication. Intellectual property protection and digital watermarking. (Z. Zhang et al., 2023) proposed a method that employs chaotic colour multi-image compression, encryption and Least Significant Bit (LSB) substitution techniques to protect Non-fungible tokens (NFT) image during transaction process. NFTs such as art, music, and digital collectables have emerged as valuable asset class, revolutionising digital ownership and trade. The security of NFT transactions is crucial because they involve the transfer of ownership and metadata, which can be susceptible to theft or unauthorized use during transmission. NFT images are commonly stored in formats like JPG and PNG. As the NFT market expands, there is an increasing presence of 3D NFTs, which adds complexity to the security measures needed for these digital assets. Multiple images are fused into a single large image. This fusion process allows for the efficient handling of multiple images as one entity. The fused image is then reduced in size while maintaining its essential information, making it easier to manage and transmit securely. The reduced image then undergoes an encryption process, ensuring that the information is concealed and protected from unauthorized access. The encrypted image is hidden under multiple cover images using a LSB steganography method. This technique allows the encrypted data to be embedded in the least significant bits of the cover images, making the changes imperceptible to the human eye.

The performance tests indicate that the scheme has a sufficiently large key space and steganography capacity, along with good reconstruction quality and robustness, making it effective for securing NFT image transactions. (Elharrouss et al., 2020) proposed a technique that utilizes k-least significant bits (k-LSB) to hide one image within another. The method beings by merging a cover image that will contain the hidden information with the image to be hidden.Instead of using just the least significant bit (LSB) of each pixel, the k-LSB method allows for the use of multiple least significant bits (k bits) to embed the hidden image. This is particularly useful for hiding images, as using only the three least significant bits may not provide sufficient capacity for the data of another image. The embedding process involves replacing the least significant bits of the pixel values in the cover image with the bits from the hidden image. Specifically, the first four bits of each pixel are utilized to represent the content of the pixel, allowing for a more substantial amount of data to be hidden without significantly degrading the quality of the cover image. To extract the hidden image, a region detection operation is employed. This involves using a local entropy filter to identify the blocks of the cover image that contain the hidden image. The local entropy is calculated based on the gray levels of the pixels in the neighbourhood, which helps in pinpointing the areas where the hidden data is embedded. The extraction of the hidden image follows the same principles as the embedding process. The least significant bits (specifically the first four bits) of each pixel channel are extracted to reconstruct the hidden image. After the hidden image is extracted, an image quality enhancement method is applied to improve the resolution and quality of the stego image. This step is crucial as the embedding process can affect the visual quality of both the cover and stego images. The effectiveness of the proposed method is evaluated using metrics such as Peak Signal-to-Noise Ratio (PSNR) to compare the quality of the stego images with those generated by state-of-the-art methods. The results indicate that the proposed k-LSB method achieves a good balance between data hiding capacity and image quality.

Video Steganography

Video steganography is a technique that involves concealing secret information within a video file, making it difficult to detect that the data is present. It is a specialized form of steganography that leverages the vast amount of data contained in video frames to hide information. Key components of video steganography include a cover video, secret data, steganographic algorithm, and steganographic video. Comparatively, video steganography provides a data transmission medium with a high capacity which acts as a protective layer, making it difficult to detect hidden data. (Kale et al., 2024) discusses the two phases in which video steganography works – Encoding and Deciding. It combines several techniques to hide text information securely within video files. The input video is split into two components – video frames (series of images) and an audio file. The secret text to be hidden is divided into 5 parts. To randomly select frames and hide the text parts, Fisher-Yates shuffling algorithm is used where each part of the text if first hashed using the MD5 algorithm for added security. The hashed text is then hidden in the selected video frames using 2-bit Least Significant Bit (LSB) steganography. Only the Red and Green components of the RGB color model are used (2-2-2-2 split strategy). Information about which frames were chosen to hide the text is embedded in the audio component after which the audio signal is transformed into a vector, then a 2D matrix. The frame location information is embedded in the audio samples using 1-bit LSB steganography. The modified video frames and audio file are stitched back together to create the output video containing the hidden information. The decoding process begins by splitting the video again into frames and audio. The frame indices are extracted from the audio using QR decomposition. Image steganography decoding is applied to the identified frames (Figure 1). MD5 algorithm is used to verify the integrity of data. If the hash of a file changes, it indicates that the file has been modified.

Figure 1. Flow diagram of video steganography process – encryption and decryption

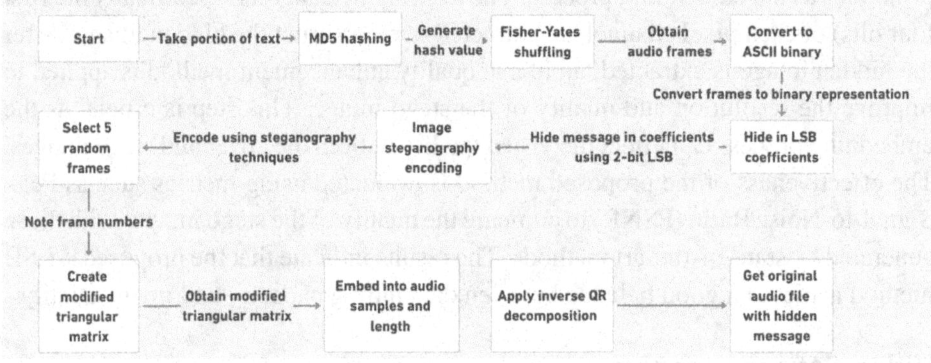

(Zouak et al., 2024) explicates that most existing video steganography techniques randomly select frames to hide data, which can produce distortions in the stego-videos. A coverless video steganography method based on motion estimation uses Gunnar Farneback's algorithm to compute the motion between consecutive video frames, which provides information about how pixels in the video are moving. It selects macroblocks (16x16 pixel areas) with the highest optical flow magnitude to embed the data. Choosing areas where there is significant motion, makes sure that hidden data is less noticeable. The method limits to no more than embedding three macroblocks per frame which aids in maintaining the video's quality and reduces the risk of detection. The method is evaluated using imperceptibility measurements like Mean Peak Signal-to-Noise Ratio (MPSNR). This metric assesses the quality of the stego video compared to the original video. A higher MPSNR value indicates that the hidden data has been embedded without significantly affecting the video's visual quality.

(Satrio et al., 2022) implements a system to effectively hide and extract files within video content using LSB combined with Fernet cryptography. This method utilizes Python language because of its versatility and ease of use. The application gathers the files to be hidden and the video into which data will be embedded, and a password for encryption. The application utilizes FFMPEG, a framework to extract frames and audio from input video. Before the file is inserted into the video, it is opened in binary format and encrypted using the Fernet algorithm. This step enhances the security of data, ensuring that even if someone extracts the data, they cannot read it without the correct decryption key. The encrypted file is entrenched into the selected frame using LSB method. After successfully embedding, the application combines the frames with the original audio to create a new video file that contains the hidden data. (Figure 2)

Figure 2. LSB combined with Fernet algorithm for extracting and embedding files

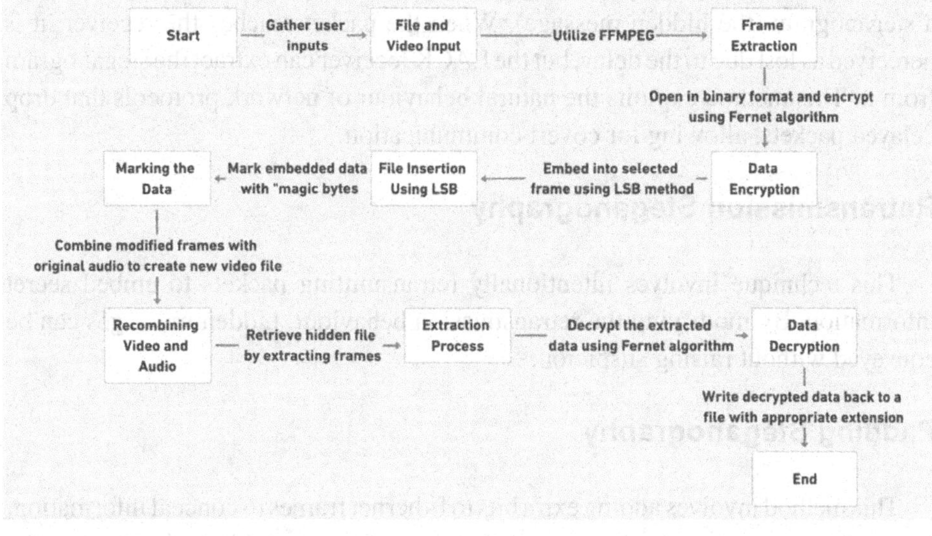

Network Steganography

Network steganography focuses on hiding secret data within network communications, ensuring safe transmission through convert channels. (Singh et al., 2017) explores various techniques and methods for effectively concealing information, making it a valuable resource for anyone interested in enhancing information security. Various steganographic methods, each with its unique approach to concealing messages include:

HICCUPS (Hidden Communication System for Corrupted Networks)

This method involves sending intentionally corrupted frames from a sender to the receiver. Other stations in the network adjust their operations based on these corrupted frames. The primary data is sent alongside these corrupted frames, which introduce errors that can be used to convey secret messages. The effectiveness of this method is measured by the Frame Error Rate (FER), which should remain within a range that allows for continuous communication without dropping the connection.

LACK (Lost Audio Packets Steganography)

In this method, voice packets are generated at the transmitter's end, and one packet is intentionally delayed. The payload of this delayed packet is replaced with a steganogram (the hidden message). When the packet reaches the receiver, it is perceived as lost due to the delay, but the LACK receiver can extract the steganogram from it. This method exploits the natural behaviour of network protocols that drop delayed packets, allowing for covert communication.

Retransmission Steganography

This technique involves intentionally retransmitting packets to embed secret information. By modifying the retransmission behaviour, hidden messages can be conveyed without raising suspicion.

Padding Steganography

This method involves adding extra bits to Ethernet frames to conceal information. The additional bits are used to encode the secret message, taking advantage of the padding space in the protocol.

Transcoding Steganography

In this approach, space is created after overt data compression to embed hidden messages. This method is particularly useful in scenarios where data is compressed before transmission.

Skype Hide Silent Packets

This technique specifically targets Skype communications, where silent packets (packets with no audio data) are used to carry hidden messages. By manipulating the presence of these silent packets, secret information can be transmitted.

StegTorrent

This method involves hiding information within the IP addresses used in torrent file sharing. By modifying the IP addresses, secret messages can be embedded without detection.

StegSuggest

This technique uses word suffixing to conceal information within the text of messages. By altering the endings of words, hidden data can be embedded in a way that appears natural to the observer.

These methods illustrate the diverse strategies employed in network steganography to ensure secure and covert communication, leveraging the characteristics of network protocols and data transmission behaviours.

Quality Monitoring Sensors

Traditional water quality analysis methods often involve complex laboratory procedures that are time-consuming and require specialized equipment. (Iurgenson et al., 2024) presents a novel approach to assess water pollution caused by heavy metal contamination using a multisensory system. By combining optical voltammetry, and potentiometric sensors, the research aims to directly quantify cadmium, lead, and the Water Pollution Index (WPI). Traditional methods often require time-consuming laboratory analysis. There is an urgent need for analytical instruments that can quickly evaluate surface water quality parameters in the field. The sensors aim to provide a simpler means of assessing complex integral water quality parameters, potentially replacing more elaborate and expensive analytical techniques. Compared to conventional laboratory methods like atomic absorption spectrophotometry (AAS) or inductively coupled plasma mass spectrometry (ICP-MS), sensor-based systems can be more affordable and accessible. These sensors are designed for potential use directly in the field, allowing for on-site water quality assessment. The study explores the possibility of directly quantifying the Water Pollution Index (WPI), which is an integral measure of water quality, using simple sensor devices. The sensors were applied to analyse model surface water samples contaminated with varying levels of cadmium and lead. The responses from all three sensor types were then processed using different data analysis methods (PLS, KRLS, data fusion) to predict cadmium concentrations, lead concentrations, and WPI values.

Surface Acoustic Wave Sensors (SAW) (Jammoul et al., 2023) focuses on the concept of wireless sensors with two principles: reflective delay lines and resonant SAWs. They utilize the propagation of surface acoustic waves along with the surface of piezoelectric substrate. These waves are generated by applying an alternating voltage to interdigitated electrodes on the substrate. While there has been significant laboratory research on SAW sensors, the development of interrogation systems suitable for harsh field conditions and in-situ applications has been less explored. Integrating them into complex systems like embedded devices can be challenging and the measurements might not be directly comparable to those obtained from traditional laboratory setups.

AN INVESTIGATION OF WATER CONTAMINATION WITH lora-ENABLED SENSORS

The methodology proposed in the study involves the use of Love wave Surface Acoustic Wave (SAW) sensors integrated with LoRa (Long Range) communication technology for the on-site interrogation of water contamination. The Love wave sensor is constructed using an AT-cut quartz substrate with two metallic interdigitated transducers (IDTs) and a guiding layer of silica. This design allows the sensor to detect variations in physical parameters of liquids, such as density, viscosity, conductivity, and permittivity. The sensor can also be sensitized to specific biological and biochemical targets by incorporating tailored sensing layers. The setup includes a portable Vector Network Analyzer (VNA) and a microprocessor unit. The VNA is used to measure the S-parameters of the Love wave sensor, which characterizes the sensor's response. A Raspberry Pi collects and processes the data, extracting essential characteristics of the sensor. The data collected by the sensor is transmitted wirelessly using LoRa technology. This allows for long-range communication, making it suitable for remote sensing applications. The system is designed to operate effectively in harsh field conditions, which is a significant improvement over traditional laboratory setups. The experimental setup demonstrated a successful monitoring range of 700 meters for 36 hours. This capability opens up new opportunities for applications in remote sensing and IoT systems, particularly in challenging environments like the Amazon basin. The methodology allows for the transmission of analysis results to a central gateway, which can then be used for further data processing and monitoring. The Love wave SAW sensor was shown to be capable of detecting variations in multiple physical parameters of liquids, such as density, viscosity, conductivity, and permittivity. Additionally, it can be selectively sensitized to detect specific biological targets (e.g., cyanobacteria) and biochemical targets (e.g., heavy metals like mercury and cadmium) by using appropriate sensing layers. This approach eliminates the need for calibration during water contamination examinations, enhancing the practicality of the system in real-world applications. The study suggests potential future improvements, such as adopting LoRaWAN technology for better scalability and the possibility of saving calibration files for specific environmental changes. This would facilitate a community-based approach to data sharing among researchers and enthusiast. the proposed methodology combines advanced sensor technology with robust communication systems to create an effective solution for monitoring water quality in remote locations.

ADVANCED TECHNIQUES IN DATA SECURITY: IOT, CRYPTOGRAPHY AND STEGANOGRAPHY

IoT connects supercomputers across the globe and enables people to broadcast information through internet (Namasudra, 2022). IoT has reformed various industries, offering innumerable applications such as Supply chain optimization, autonomous vehicles, healthcare devices and immeasurably more. The major downside IoT technology faces are the security issues due to increasing number of devices such as data breaches, Denial of service (DoS) and botnet attacks. (Raj & Maheswaran, 2023) Cryptography is a way to encrypt the data in which the plaintext is converted into ciphertext by using an algorithm. This process is called encryption. There is an increasing need to secure sensitive data, especially healthcare systems which heavily relies on cloud storage and processing.(Bohra et al., 2024) There are several challenges faced by existing data hiding techniques where the methods fail to maintain the biological functionality of DNA sequences, which is crucial for applications in bioinformatics and healthcare. DNA steganography leverages the complex structure and redundancy of DNA to conceal data without altering its biological function.

DNA computing being a novel cryptosystem is used to encode the plaintext using four DNA bases, namely Cytosine, Guanine, Adenine and Thymine.

The philosophy behind using DNA sequences to encode plaintext is the level of randomness it provides. This multi-layered approach encrypts and hides the data, thereby enhancing the security against unauthorized access and DDoS attacks by requiring knowledge of a long alphanumeric key and specific credentials for data retrieval, ensuring that even if the server becomes unreachable, data confidentiality remains intact. The scheme involves 5 entities – Data User (DU), Cloud Service Provider (CSP), Data Owner (DO), IoT Device, Gateway. Users provide a password, which is combined with additional characters based on their profile. The combined string is converted into DNA sequence using a defined table which aids DNA operations to create a DNA sequence. Each sequence is converted into a 256-bit secret key. XOR operations are performed between plaintext blocks and the secret key which is then sent to the CSP. The DO hides the encrypted data into a cover image. Each pixel value is converted into DNA bases. The encrypted data and key are embedded into specific positions of the DNA sequence of the image. This process adds another layer of security where cryptography and steganography are combined making it difficult for unauthorized parties to access the data. Additionally, the key generation process enhances the security.

(Nahar et al., 2023) proposed a method that is designed to work in various environments, including standalone devices and cloud. The system handles various data types such as text, binary, image etc. The message is initially converted into binary format from ASCII values, decimal values respectively. The secret message is encrypted by applying Caesar cipher technique. The message length is expected to be odd. The message chunks are iterated using a slice operation and stored in a list. The paired chunks are randomized in order which makes it harder for attackers to analyze the message. The shuffled message is further encrypted using a deep learning model. The message is converted into nucleotides which is encrypted using a cipher table. The cipher value must be predicted using a neural network to ensure secure encryption. Each nucleotide in the encrypted DNA sequence is represented as a one-hot encoded vector. The one-hot encoding scheme facilitates the embedding process by representing nucleotides in a numerical format. The secret message is embedded into the DNA sequence using a data implantation rule. The proposed method offers improved security compared to existing techniques. However, it may have limitations in terms of embedding capacity and computational overhead.

Case Study: Cloud-Based Air Quality Monitoring System

To illustrate the practical application of cloud computing in environmental pollution monitoring, let's examine a case study of a cloud-based air quality monitoring system implemented in the city of Barcelona, Spain (Parra et al., 2015). The system utilizes a network of over 200 IoT sensors strategically deployed across the city, measuring particulate matter, nitrogen dioxide, and ozone levels. Edge computing devices are employed for initial data processing and aggregation, while the Microsoft Azure cloud platform is responsible for data storage and analysis. Power BI is used for data visualization and reporting, providing a user-friendly interface for accessing air quality information. Key features of the system include real-time data collection and processing, machine learning algorithms for pollution forecasting, a public-facing web portal for citizen access to air quality information, and integration with traffic management systems for adaptive traffic control. The implementation of this cloud-based system has yielded significant benefits, including a 30% reduction in data collection and processing costs compared to its previous on-premises counterpart. Additionally, the system has achieved a remarkable 99.9% uptime, ensuring reliable and continuous monitoring. The ability to process and analyse data from over 200 sensors in near real-time has significantly enhanced the system's effectiveness. Moreover, the integration of machine learning algorithms has improved the accuracy of pollution forecasting, with predictions now reaching 85% accuracy 24 hours in advance. This improved forecasting capability empowers authorities to take proactive measures to mitigate air pollution and protect public health.

The cloud-based system has also contributed to increased public awareness and engagement, with a 50% increase in citizens accessing air quality information through the public-facing web portal. This heightened awareness empowers individuals to make informed decisions about their activities and exposure to air pollution. While the implementation of this system faced challenges such as data privacy concerns and integration with legacy systems, these issues were successfully addressed through data anonymization, strict access controls, and the development of custom APIs and data transformation tools. Additionally, the system's ability to scale during pollution events was ensured by implementing auto-scaling features in the Azure cloud platform. This case study demonstrates the transformative potential of cloud computing in revolutionizing environmental pollution monitoring. By leveraging cloud-based solutions, cities can establish more efficient, cost-effective, and impactful systems for managing air quality and protecting public health. The AirSafe system, implemented for long-term storage of environmental data in the cloud, employs a blockchain-enhanced steganographic approach to hide sensitive metadata within the stored data. This system utilizes a private blockchain to maintain an immutable log of all steganographic operations, ensuring data integrity and traceability.

The performance of AirSafe was evaluated over a six-month period, focusing on data transmission efficiency, processing speed, and overall system reliability. The edge-to-fog steganography method achieved an average embedding capacity of 10% of the original data size with minimal impact on transmission times. The fog-to-cloud method, while more computationally intensive, maintained real-time performance with an average latency of 1.2 seconds. The system successfully processed and embedded data from an average of 10 sensor nodes each in real-time, and the cloud platform demonstrated the ability to handle simultaneous extraction requests from up to 1000 users without significant delay. The system achieved 99.95% uptime over the six-month period, with most downtime attributed to planned maintenance of the cloud infrastructure.

The security of AirSafe was rigorously tested using state-of-the-art steganalysis techniques and penetration testing. The steganographic techniques, combined with additional security measures like end-to-end encryption, successfully thwarted all attempted breaches. The blockchain-based storage system proved highly effective in maintaining data integrity, detecting and automatically correcting any attempts to modify historical data.

During the development and deployment of AirSafe, several challenges were encountered, leading to valuable lessons for future implementations. These challenges included resource constraints on edge devices, scalability issues with increasing sensor numbers, environmental factors affecting sensor malfunctions, and regulatory compliance requirements. To address these challenges, adaptive steganography techniques, edge computing, robust error detection and correction mechanisms, and interdisciplinary collaboration were crucial. The AirSafe case study demonstrates the feasibility and effectiveness of implementing advanced steganographic techniques in a real-world environmental monitoring system. By addressing challenges and leveraging the benefits of steganography, cloud computing, and blockchain technology, systems like AirSafe can play a crucial role in ensuring the security and privacy of sensitive environmental data in urban areas.

Deep-Learning-Based Steganography

The introduction of the paper on Deep-Learning-based image steganography by (Song et al., 2024) outlines the significance of this field in safeguarding sensitive information by embedding secret messages within digital images. It emphasizes the dual objectives of steganography: the creation of effective methods for embedding information and the development of reliable techniques for extracting that information. The introduction highlights the importance of ensuring that the modified images, known as stego-images, remain visually similar to the original cover images to avoid detection. Additionally, it notes the classification of steganographic methods into cover-edited and coverless strategies, as well as the exploration of various deep learning architectures, such as Convolutional Neural Networks (CNNs) and Generative Adversarial Networks (GANs), which enhance the capabilities of steganography. This foundational understanding sets the stage for a comprehensive examination of recent advancements and ongoing challenges in the domain. Image steganography is defined as a technique for protecting data by concealing a secret message within a cover image. The goal is to embed this secret information in such a way that it does not raise suspicion or attract attention. The process involves two main steps – embedding, extraction. The sender embeds the secret message into a cover image, resulting in a stego-image. This embedding must be done carefully to ensure that the stego-image closely resembles the original cover image, maintaining visual similarity to avoid detection. Upon receiving the stego-image, the recipient uses a corresponding extraction technique to retrieve the hidden secret message.

The research in image steganography primarily revolves around two critical problems- Creating steganography which involves developing methods to effectively embed the secret message into the cover image and Extraction which focuses on techniques to accurately retrieve the hidden message from the stego-image. The survey on Deep-Learning-based image steganography highlights two main strategies for embedding secret information within images: cover-edited steganography and coverless steganography. Cover-edited steganography involves modifying the cover image to conceal the secret message, either by directly manipulating pixel values or applying transformations to the image domain. In contrast, coverless steganography generates a stego-image without altering a cover image, using mapping, or generating strategies to establish a relationship between the secret information and the generated image. These strategies reflect the ongoing advancements in the field, particularly with the integration of deep learning techniques, which enhance the effectiveness and security of steganographic methods. (Yao et al., 2024) proposed a method called DWT-GAN, which integrates Discrete Wavelet Transform (DWT) with Generative Adversarial Networks (GAN) to enhance image steganography. The model's structure comprises DWT-based preprocessing and postprocessing, a Hidden Network for embedding, a Discriminator Network for distinguishing between cover and stego-images, an Extractor Network for retrieving hidden messages, and a Fusion Module for feature combination. The embedding process involves transforming the cover image into the DWT domain and embedding the secret message into the DWT coefficients using the Hidden Network. The model is trained using a carefully tuned loss function that balances invisibility and extraction accuracy. Performance is evaluated using metrics such as Peak Signal-to-Noise Ratio (PSNR), Structural Similarity Index (SSIM), Perceptual Loss, and Accuracy (ACC). The DWT-GAN method offers several advantages, including enhanced invisibility through DWT domain operations, improved robustness against steganalysis due to the use of GANs, and effective multi-scale feature extraction via multi-scale attention convolution. This approach leverages the strengths of both DWT and GAN to create a robust and effective steganography technique that enhances the invisibility of hidden messages while maintaining high extraction accuracy, making it particularly suitable for securing sensitive data transmission in environmental pollution monitoring systems relying on cloud-based infrastructure.

Implementing Steganography in Cloud Environments for Environmental Data

The primary objective of the research presented by (Rao et al., 2024) is to develop a sophisticated cloud architecture that enhances the security of image data storage through the application of steganography. This approach aims to address the growing concerns regarding data privacy and unauthorized access in collaborative cloud environments, where multiple users may share resources. By embedding sensitive information within image files, the proposed method seeks to ensure that data remains concealed from potential threats while still being accessible to authorized users. To achieve these objectives, the authors propose a hybrid methodology that combines advanced steganographic techniques with a robust cloud service architecture. The methodology involves several key steps: first, users are required to authenticate themselves through a certificate authority (CA) that issues authorized certificates, ensuring that only verified individuals can access the system. Once authenticated, users can embed secret messages into images, which are then encrypted to enhance security further. The hidden text is stored within the image data, utilizing techniques such as the non-subsampled contourlet transform and the golden ratio to maximize payload capacity and resilience against detection. The research employs a comprehensive experimental analysis involving a dataset of 100 JPG images collected from various online sources. Each image serves as a carrier for the hidden text, which is protected from potential attackers.

Figure 3. Stenography in cloud environment for pollution monitoring

The methodology emphasizes the importance of maintaining image quality while embedding data, utilizing performance metrics such as Peak Signal-to-Noise Ratio (PSNR) and Structural Similarity Index (SSIM) to evaluate the effectiveness of the proposed techniques. By integrating these advanced methods, the research aims to provide a secure and efficient framework for storing and transmitting sensitive image data in cloud environments, ultimately contributing to the field of data security and privacy. The conclusion of the research highlights the effectiveness and significance of integrating steganography into cloud architecture for securing image data. The study demonstrates that traditional encryption methods alone may not suffice in protecting sensitive information from sophisticated cyber threats. By embedding confidential data within seemingly innocuous image files, the proposed approach significantly enhances data confidentiality and integrity, making it difficult for unauthorized users to detect or access the hidden information.

The findings indicate that the proposed architecture not only improves security but also maintains the quality of the images, as evidenced by high PSNR and SSIM values. This balance between security and usability is crucial for organizations that rely on cloud storage for sensitive data. Furthermore, the implementation of robust access control mechanisms, such as Role-Based Access Control (RBAC), ensures that only authorized personnel can access or manipulate the data, thereby reducing the risk of data breaches.

The research underscores the importance of adopting innovative security measures in cloud computing environments, particularly for industries that handle sensitive image data. The proposed steganographic method offers a promising solution for enhancing data protection, paving the way for future advancements in secure cloud storage practices. The study encourages further exploration and development of steganographic techniques to address emerging security challenges in the digital landscape.

Legal, Ethical Considerations, and Future Trends

The use of steganography in environmental monitoring systems operates within a complex legal landscape that varies across jurisdictions. Data protection and privacy laws, such as GDPR in the EU and CCPA/CPRA in the US, set stringent requirements for the processing and protection of personal data, including environmental data. These laws may conflict with the use of steganography, which by nature conceals information. Environmental information disclosure laws, like the Aarhus Convention and EPCRA, mandate the disclosure of environmental information to the public. This can sometimes conflict with the use of steganography, which conceals information. To reconcile these conflicting requirements, reversible steganography techniques can be used to allow for full data recovery by authorized parties. Cybersecurity regulations, such as CISA guidelines in the US and NIS/NIS2 in Europe, set standards for securing critical infrastructure, including environmental monitoring systems. These regulations have implications for cloud-based environmental monitoring systems, requiring a comprehensive security strategy that incorporates steganographic techniques. The use of steganography in environmental monitoring raises several ethical considerations that must be carefully navigated. One of the core tensions is balancing the need for transparency in scientific research with the imperative to protect sensitive information. While steganography can enhance data security, it may also raise questions about the integrity and reproducibility of environmental research. To address this, an ethical framework is proposed, including clear documentation of steganographic methods, secure sharing of decryption keys, and use of reversible steganography techniques.

When environmental monitoring systems collect data that could be linked to individuals or communities, questions of informed consent and data ownership arise. A model of "steganographic consent" is proposed, where participants are informed about the use of data hiding techniques and given options to control the level of information concealment applied to their data. Steganographic techniques also have the potential for dual-use, as they could be misused to conceal environmentally harmful activities. To address this, ethical guidelines for developers include implementing audit trails, collaborating with environmental regulators, and developing steganalysis tools alongside steganographic techniques. The field of steganography is rapidly evolving, with new techniques continually emerging. Quantum steganography, leveraging quantum key distribution, offers unprecedented levels of security for sensitive environmental data. DNA-based steganography, inspired by the information-carrying capacity of DNA, offers extremely high data density and long-term stability for archiving environmental data. Generative AI, using GANs, can create more adaptive and robust steganographic techniques, making the hidden data extremely difficult to detect. The future of secure environmental monitoring in the cloud is likely to be characterized by increasingly sophisticated and integrated steganographic techniques.

Edge-cloud integration will allow for more sophisticated distributed steganography systems, while blockchain technology will play an increasing role in ensuring data integrity and traceability. AI-driven environmental modelling will require secure sharing of large environmental datasets, which can be achieved through privacy-preserving collaborative approaches using homomorphic encryption and steganography. Standardization and interoperability will also be important to ensure compatibility and widespread adoption of steganography in environmental monitoring systems.

REFERENCES

Adhiyaksa, F. A., Ahmad, T., Shiddiqi, A. M., Jati Santoso, B., Studiawan, H., & Pratomo, B. A. (2022). Reversible Audio Steganography using Least Prime Factor and Audio Interpolation. *2021 International Seminar on Machine Learning, Optimization, and Data Science (ISMODE)*, 97–102. DOI: 10.1109/ISMODE53584.2022.9743066

Awaysheh, F. M., Alazab, M., Gupta, M., Pena, T. F., & Cabaleiro, J. C. (2020). Next-generation big data federation access control: A reference model. *Future Generation Computer Systems*, 108, 726–741. DOI: 10.1016/j.future.2020.02.052

Bhattacharya, A., Seth, A., Malhotra, D., & Verma, N. (2022). Cloud Steganography: An Intelligent Approach to Improve Data Security in the Cloud Environment. *Proceedings of the 4th International Conference on Information Management & Machine Intelligence*, 1–5. DOI: 10.1145/3590837.3590902

Bohra, S., Naik, C., Batra, R., Popat, K., & Kaur, H. (2024). Advancements in Modern Steganography Techniques for Enhanced Data Security: A Comprehensive Review. *2024 11th International Conference on Computing for Sustainable Global Development (INDIACom)*, 941–944. DOI: 10.23919/INDIACom61295.2024.10498587

Cheddad, A., Condell, J., Curran, K., & Mc Kevitt, P. (2010). Digital image steganography: Survey and analysis of current methods. *Signal Processing*, 90(3), 727–752. DOI: 10.1016/j.sigpro.2009.08.010

Elharrouss, O., Almaadeed, N., & Al-Maadeed, S. (2020). An image steganography approach based on k-least significant bits (k-LSB). *2020 IEEE International Conference on Informatics, IoT, and Enabling Technologies (ICIoT)*, 131–135. DOI: 10.1109/ICIoT48696.2020.9089566

Huang, H., Yao, X. A., Krisp, J. M., & Jiang, B. (2021). Analytics of location-based big data for smart cities: Opportunities, challenges, and future directions. *Computers, Environment and Urban Systems*, 90, 101712. DOI: 10.1016/j.compenvurbsys.2021.101712

Iurgenson, N., Wang, X., Kong, L., Sun, X., Legin, A., Wang, P., Wan, H., & Kirsanov, D. (2024). Feasibility study of multisensor systems for the assessment of water pollution index induced by heavy metal contamination. *Microchemical Journal*, 197, 109762. DOI: 10.1016/j.microc.2023.109762

Jammoul, H., Rube, M., Sebeloue, M., Sadli, I., Dejous, C., Perrine, C., Pousset, Y., & Tamarin, O. (2023). Investigating Water Contamination with LoRa-Enabled Surface Acoustic Wave Sensors. *2023 7th International Symposium on Instrumentation Systems, Circuits and Transducers (INSCIT)*, 1–5. DOI: 10.1109/INSCIT59673.2023.10258483

Kale, G., Joshi, A., Shukla, I., & Bhosale, A. (2024). A Video Steganography Approach with Randomization Algorithm Using Image and Audio Steganography. *2024 International Conference on Emerging Smart Computing and Informatics (ESCI)*, 1–5. DOI: 10.1109/ESCI59607.2024.10497225

Mukherjee, S., Mukhopadhyay, S., & Sarkar, S. (2024). IoTSLE: Securing IoT systems in low-light environments through finite automata, deep learning and DNA computing based image steganographic model. *Internet of Things : Engineering Cyber Physical Human Systems*, 101358, 101358. Advance online publication. DOI: 10.1016/j.iot.2024.101358

Nahar, M., Kamal, A. H. M., & Hossain, G. (2023). Protecting health data in the cloud through steganography: A table-driven, blind method using neural networks and bit-shuffling algorithm. *Journal of Network and Computer Applications*, 217, 103689. DOI: 10.1016/j.jnca.2023.103689

Namasudra, S. (2022). A secure cryptosystem using DNA cryptography and DNA steganography for the cloud-based IoT infrastructure. *Computers & Electrical Engineering*, 104, 108426. DOI: 10.1016/j.compeleceng.2022.108426

Parra, L., Sendra, S., Lloret, J., & Bosch, I. (2015). Development of a Conductivity Sensor for Monitoring Groundwater Resources to Optimize Water Management in Smart City Environments. *Sensors (Basel)*, 15(9), 20990–21015. DOI: 10.3390/s150920990 PMID: 26343653

Raj, U. A. S., & Maheswaran, C. P. (2023). Secure File Sharing System Using Image Steganography and Cryptography Techniques. *2023 International Conference on Inventive Computation Technologies (ICICT)*, 1113–1116. DOI: 10.1109/ICICT57646.2023.10134163

Rao, A. S., Dalavai, L., Tata, V., Vellela, S. S., Polanki, K., Kumar, K. K., & Andra, R. (2024). A Secured Cloud Architecture for Storing Image Data using Steganography. *2024 2nd International Conference on Computer, Communication and Control (IC4)*, 1–6. DOI: 10.1109/IC457434.2024.10486495

Sakshi, S., Verma, S., Chaturvedi, P., & Yadav, S. A. (2022). Least Significant Bit Steganography for Text and Image hiding. *2022 3rd International Conference on Intelligent Engineering and Management (ICIEM)*, 415–421. DOI: 10.1109/ICIEM54221.2022.9853052

Satrio, T. A., Prabowo, W. A., & Yuniati, T. (2022). Hiding Document Format Files Using Video Steganography Techniques With Least Significant Bit Method. *2022 IEEE International Conference on Communication, Networks and Satellite (COM-NETSAT)*, 399–406. DOI: 10.1109/COMNETSAT56033.2022.9994367

Singh, N., Bhardwaj, J., & Raghav, G. (2017). Network Steganography and its Techniques: A Survey. *International Journal of Computer Applications*, 174(2), 8–14. DOI: 10.5120/ijca2017915319

Song, B., Wei, P., Wu, S., Lin, Y., & Zhou, W. (2024). A survey on Deep-Learning-based image steganography. *Expert Systems with Applications*, 254, 124390. DOI: 10.1016/j.eswa.2024.124390

Vamsi Thalatam, M. N., Lanka, P., & Kumar, J. N. V. R. S. (2023). An IoT Based Smart Water Contamination Monitoring System. *2023 International Conference on Intelligent Systems for Communication, IoT and Security (ICISCoIS)*, 387–391. DOI: 10.1109/ICISCoIS56541.2023.10100559

Varghese, B., & Buyya, R. (2018). Next generation cloud computing: New trends and research directions. *Future Generation Computer Systems*, 79, 849–861. DOI: 10.1016/j.future.2017.09.020

Yao, Y., Wang, J., Chang, Q., Ren, Y., & Meng, W. (2024). High invisibility image steganography with wavelet transform and generative adversarial network. *Expert Systems with Applications*, 249, 123540. DOI: 10.1016/j.eswa.2024.123540

Zhang, Y., Ren, J., Liu, J., Xu, C., Guo, H., & Liu, Y. (2017). A Survey on Emerging Computing Paradigms for Big Data. *Chinese Journal of Electronics*, 26(1), 1–12. DOI: 10.1049/cje.2016.11.016

Zhang, Z., Cao, Y., Jahanshahi, H., & Mou, J. (2023). Chaotic color multi-image compression-encryption/ LSB data type steganography scheme for NFT transaction security. *Journal of King Saud University. Computer and Information Sciences*, 35(10), 101839. DOI: 10.1016/j.jksuci.2023.101839

Zouak, A., Busawon, K., & Li, X. (2024). Video Steganography System Based on Optical Flow for Object Detection. *2024 14th International Symposium on Communication Systems, Networks and Digital Signal Processing (CSNDSP)*, 598–602. DOI: 10.1109/CSNDSP60683.2024.10636505

KEY TERMS AND DEFINITIONS

Cloud Computing: Cloud computing is the delivery of computing services—including servers, storage, databases, networking, software, analytics, and intelligence—over the Internet ("the cloud") to offer faster innovation, flexible resources, and economies of scale. It typically involves pay-as-you-go pricing, allowing businesses to reduce operating costs and run infrastructure more efficiently.

Cloud Service Provider: A Cloud Service Provider is a company that offers cloud computing services, including Infrastructure as a Service (IaaS), Platform as a Service (PaaS), or Software as a Service (SaaS). These providers maintain and manage the physical data centers and ensure the availability and security of cloud services for their clients.

CNN: A Convolutional Neural Network (CNN) is a deep learning algorithm which can take in an input image, assign importance to various aspects/objects in the image, and be able to differentiate one from another. CNNs are particularly effective in image and video recognition, classification, and processing tasks.

Cryptography: Cryptography is the practice and study of techniques for secure communication in the presence of adversaries. It involves creating and analyzing protocols that prevent third parties or the public from reading private messages, ensuring data confidentiality, integrity, and authentication.

GAN: A Generative Adversarial Network (GAN) is a class of machine learning frameworks where two neural networks contest with each other in a game. The generator network creates new data instances, while the discriminator network evaluates them for authenticity. This process leads to the creation of remarkably accurate synthetic data.

IoT (Internet of Things): IoT refers to the network of interconnected physical devices, vehicles, home appliances, and other items embedded with electronics, software, sensors, and network connectivity, which enables these objects to collect and exchange data, creating opportunities for more direct integration between the physical world and computer-based systems.

Steganography: Steganography is the practice of concealing information within other non-secret text or data. It involves hiding messages or files within other seemingly innocuous files or messages, often used for covert communication or data protection.

Water Pollution Index (WPI): The Water Pollution Index (WPI) is a numerical scale used to represent the level of water pollution in a body of water. It typically considers various parameters such as dissolved oxygen, pH levels, turbidity, and presence of pollutants to provide a comprehensive measure of water quality.

Chapter 11
Comparative Analysis of Traditional vs. Deep Learning– Based Steganography Techniques

Siddhanta Kumar Singh

Manipal University Jaipur, India

Vijay Shankar Sharma

Manipal University Jaipur, India

Hemlata Parmar

https://orcid.org/0009-0009-1438-5427

Manipal University Jaipur, India

Harpreet Kaur Channi

Chandigarh University, India

ABSTRACT

Over the past few years, the deep learning technique as it pertains to steganography, the art of hiding a message in public information, has progressed significantly. This chapter compares the different techniques of deep learning-based steganography and conventional steganography. The emphasis in traditional methods of embedding information like the LSB substitution rests on the number of messages that can possibly be embedded and the level of resistance towards statistical detection. In contrast, the deep learning-based steganography approaches incorporate artificial

DOI: 10.4018/979-8-3693-2223-9.ch011

neural networks which enhance the embedding process to optimize the data capacity, security, and functionality of many different types of media. Deep learning methods are, however, innovative and provide more security and robustness, although their disadvantage is the high processing power. For that deep learning steganography is an advancement. This is an emerging trend in the field where deep learning is likely to be incorporated in the coming days as an important enhancement of other sketched vision system.

1. INTRODUCTION

It's the technique of concealing a message in a commonplace message or file so that it does not come to light. It is different than encryption in the sense that it does not encrypt the content of a message but hides that a message even exists, which allows parties to communicate secretly. Stego comes from a Greek word itself means 'writing' and originates from the word ographia, steganography is simply hidden writing which has known usage since ancient times from the emerging use of computers today down to the ancient use of wax tablets. In modern contexts, steganography can mask other types of media, such as pictures, music, and video files as well. Since steganography provides the means of hiding information from unwanted interception, it is very important to the information security. This is further manifested by the fact that it is lucrative to both the cybercriminal and the security expert. Measures include making data or encryption keys invisible or embedding them into inconspicuous files as a defense against data theft, said those in the security field. A special instance of steganography is used in copyright protection and digital water marking so that the business organizations can protect their intellectual property. However, steganography's malicious actors use it for their operation, which makes them invisible to standard security measures. For example, attackers may employ steganography to communicate secretly with commands and instructions or embed malware in seemingly benign files. Therefore, it is essential for contemporary cybersecurity methods to comprehend and acknowledge the significance of steganography in both offensive and defensive situations. Figure 1 below shows the steganography workflow.

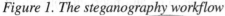

Figure 1. The steganography workflow

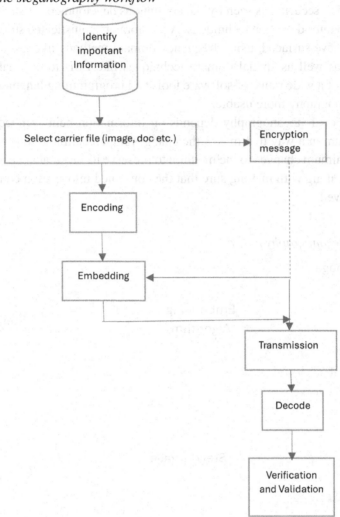

The steganography method's basic model is depicted in Figure 2. It is seen as establishing an imperceptible communication method to conceal information from the viewer. Its goal is to hide confidential information by enshrouding it in readable data, or "cover data."

Steganography has a long history, having developed over millennia through diverse cultures and technological advancements. Steganography has always changed to accommodate new developments in technology and societal norms. Its progression from antiquated means to sophisticated digital ones shows how relevant it is to security procedures and unauthorized communication even now. For the foreseeable future, steganography will likely continue to be an important component of information security, as seen by the continuous development of steganographic tools and counter-detection techniques. A plethora of sophisticated steganographic techniques have surfaced, using frequency domain methods like Discrete Cosine Transform as well as spatial domain techniques like LSB to conceal data. The availability of a wide range of software tools and programming languages has also made steganography more usable.

Conventional steganography depends on information being embedded into a cover medium in a way that makes the changes imperceptible to our ear and eye. Making minimum changes to the medium to preserve its original appearance is the major goal, along with making sure that the concealed information can be consistently retrieved.

Figure 2. Steganography method

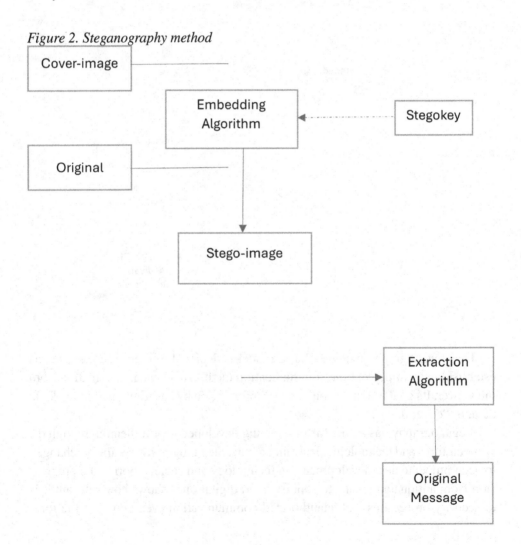

The LSB method is one of the very frequently used conventional approaches used particularly in image steganography world. This method embeds the original message by modifying the lsb pixel of an image. Since the pixel alters its color only slightly by the change of the LSB bit value, so it makes the overall image quality almost unchanged and unnoticeable. Although the LSB approach is pretty simple and efficient in terms of calculation, this approach is easily detectable by several techniques and outside attackers, such as statistical analysis and noise injection methods. Data embedding in the cover medium's transform domain is another class of conventional methods. This involves various methods such as Discrete Cosine Transform (DCT) and Discrete Wavelet Transform (DWT). It embeds the given data in the converted coefficients after first transforming the cover medium into a new domain. In DCT-based steganography, for example, the original message bits are embedded in an image's DCT coefficients. Compared to LSB method, these techniques are typically more resilient to common attacks since there is a feeble chance that the hidden data will be changed during compression or other transformation process.

In this method it entails dispersing the original data throughout the cover medium's broad frequency range. Under normal circumstances, the signal is undetected because it is spread across multiple frequency range. Compared to other approaches, this technique is more robust against noise and compression, but it also needs a bigger cover medium to hold the same amount of hidden data.

Deep Learning-Based Approaches to Steganography

The progress of deep learning technology out there in particular has led to the emergence of novel steganography techniques. These methods offer notable gains in capacity, security, and robustness by using the power of neural network techniques to self-train and optimize the process of hiding and extracting information.

Deep Neural Networks (DNNs) can be trained to conceal information within a cover medium without losing the original content's integrity or caliber. These approaches describe the steganography problem as an optimization challenge, in which the network determines how to best alter the cover medium in order to insert the secret message. Convolutional neural networks (CNNs), for instance, are frequently employed to encode and decode data contained in images. These models can be trained, maximizing message extraction accuracy and minimizing distortion during the embedding process. In order to produce more secured and undetectable stego media in steganography, Generative adversarial networks (GAN), are used. In a GAN-based method, the discriminator network discerns between the original and the stego versions, while the generator network is trained to give stego media that is indistinguishable from the original cover media. Even with advanced steganalysis methods, it is challenging to uncover the concealed information in a robust system created by this adversarial training process.

Autoencoders steganography uses autoencoders technique, a kind of neural network intended for data compression and reconstruction. This method involves training the network's encoder component to incorporate the secret message into a compressed version of the cover medium, which is then rebuilt by the decoder component along with the hidden message. The ability to learn compact representations reduces the amount of modification required in the cover media, which is advantageous to this approach.

2. RELATED WORKS

Nandhini Subramanian et al.'s main objective of this research work is to find and examine the various deep-learning techniques that are present out there for image steganography. The approach is presented in this study together with a thorough examination of the datasets used, experimental settings considered, and widely used evaluation metrics (Subramanian et al., 2021). A thorough examination and a cutting-edge evaluation of many contemporary steganographic methods and tools are used in his work of Pratap Chandra Mandal et al. Recent deep learning-based steganographic algorithms have overcome some of these problems. The study by Mahmud Ahmad Bamanga et al. examines the various application areas of steganography, a sophisticated method for hiding information inside common objects, has in a range of industries. The use of steganography in intellectual property, healthcare, bank and finance, and medical data security are the main topics of this research paper. May Alanzy et al.'s Multi-Level Steganography (MLS) methodology uses encryption algorithms, Blow-fish and AES, to protect the cover image and place the keys into the stego-image. The suggested Multi Level Steganography technique uses a strong pixel randomization method to increase security in the hidden data. The results in the experiment show that the suggested method reliably protects data with high Peak SNR and low Mean Square Error (MSE) values. This ensures secured decryption of private data, robust encryption, and superior image quality. By examining and evaluating the various cover steganography systems, Shahid Rahman et al. identify the profitable region from which all stakeholders stand to gain. Furthermore, a detailed analysis of the basic concepts in the area of steganography techniques and steganalysis is given here. Several steganographic domains, such as transform domain, adaptive space, and spatial space, have been used to show these systems.

A ground-breaking steganography method for digital photographs, including RGB, greyscale, texture, and aerial images, was presented in Shahid Rahman et al.'s work. Improved security, imperceptibility, capacity, and robustness are the goals of this technology. The suggested method's experimental outcomes confirm the feasibility of their research and highlight its even greater strength. A picture hiding strategy that maximizes the capacity of data embedding of the cover image is described by Pooja Belagali and Dr. V. R. Udupi using Least Significant Bit (LSB) steganography based on hybrid edge detection. The system's performance for hybrid edge detection is evaluated using pairs of various edge detection techniques, such as Canny, Kirsch, Sobel, and Prewitt. Dalia Nashat and Loay Mamdouh recommend that, to increase the capacity, visual quality should be considered. To do this, some of the LSB of the cover image are inverted and rely on the secret data for embedding, instead of replacing the LSB with the secret data. The results show that the suggested method offers good imperceptibility and high capacity when compared to other methods. Kriti Bansal et al. present a survey of the LSB approach used in this field. Here, the LSB method is used to steganography images, videos, and audio. Supriadi Rustad et al. have proposed an adaptive pattern selection strategy to reduce the error ratio that arises from message embedding. The effectiveness of the inverted LSB replacement method can be increased by using adaptive patterns, which are based on the two-bit + LSB pattern in the container image. When this adaptive pattern is used with inverted LSB picture steganography, imperceptibility is significantly boosted. This article examines the state-of-the-art LSB-based image steganography techniques and instruments. Syed Saad Ahmed et al. describe StegoBound, a new gradient-based image steganography technique that successfully hides the secret message. Good results are obtained for the steganographic features. StegoBound masks the restricted information in the 6th, 7th, and 8th LSBs of the pixels of the boundary zone in grey-scale cover pictures to derive high-quality stego-pictures, Through an ideal trade-off between security, embedding capacity, and imperceptibility, the proposed method offers state-of-the-art results in data concealment, as shown by comparative and experimental tests.

The research paper by Sabah Abdulazeez et al. proposes an image steganography method using an XOR operator, a secret key, and the Least Significant Bits algorithm. A one-dimensional bit stream array is created by XORing the bits of the secret key with the bits of the secret picture. Harshal V. Patil and Vaibhav P. Sonaje give a thorough examination of various LSB-based steganography methods for encoding textual data into a variety of media types, including images, audio, and video. This study's main objective is to assess the effectiveness of these algorithms for various file sizes and media kinds, paying particular attention to metrics like PSNR and MSE. Yasir Yakup Demircan and Serhat Ozekes' suggested technique uses an image segmentation model to identify the portions of an image with the highest texture complexity. Information is then hidden in these areas using pseudo-randomized least significant bit substitutions. The study's output is a different approach to LSB steganography that produces results that are competitive with those of current techniques.

3. COMPARATIVE ANALYSIS

The main goal of evaluating deep learning and conventional steganography techniques is to comprehend the benefits, drawbacks, and suitability of various secure communication strategies. Hiding information within the carriers (such text, music, or images) without raising red flags is crucial as information security grows more important in a society where digital media rules. A critical component of the analysis is comprehending steganography detection (steganalysis). In order to evaluate how well various steganographic strategies fare against efforts to uncover secret information, the study will examine a variety of steganalysis techniques, both conventional and contemporary. The analysis aims to achieve several objectives:

The investigation aims to determine which deep learning-based and conventional steganography approaches work best in which contexts. This entails contrasting different approaches' computational efficiency, imperceptibility, resilience, and capacity.

The success of steganography depends on its capacity to avoid discovery. Understanding how distinct strategies withstand different steganalysis attacks, which aim to reveal hidden information, is the main goal of the analysis. Determining the steganographic systems' practicable security depends on this area of research. Examining current techniques creates opportunities for improvement of work. Although they are well-established, traditional methodologies might use some improvement, and deep learning-based approaches present a great opportunity for new ideas. Researchers and practitioners can create more advanced, safe, and effective steganographic systems by examining these methods. There is not a single steganographic technique that works best everywhere. The goal of the investigation is to pinpoint each method's shortcomings, strengths whether they have to do with processing requirements, data hiding ability, or detection susceptibility. To choose the best approach for a particular application, one must be aware of these limitations. Various steganography methods work well in various situations, such as encasing bigger datasets in video streams or concealing minute quantities of sensitive data within high-quality photographs. With regard to use cases like digital watermarking, secret storage, or secure communication, this analysis seeks to offer precise recommendations on which techniques are most appropriate. The analysis covers the theoretical and practical aspects of steganography using traditional and deep learning method, from the most recent developments in the field to foundational notions. It includes:

The analysis includes well-known methods including spread spectrum steganography, discrete cosine transforms, discrete wavelet transforms, and other transform domain techniques like Least Significant Bit (LSB) manipulation. The following sections discuss these techniques in detail.

Steganography Techniques

The analysis covers the current techniques that make use of AI techniques, namely autoencoders, generative adversarial networks (GANs), and CNNs. The ability of these AI techniques to get around the drawbacks of conventional techniques will be evaluated, with a focus on scalability, resilience, and adaptability. The analysis also takes into account the various steganography techniques' application fields. Examining these techniques' applications in domains including digital forensics, cybersecurity, digital rights management, and clandestine communication is part of this.

Figure 3. Requirement of steganography techniques

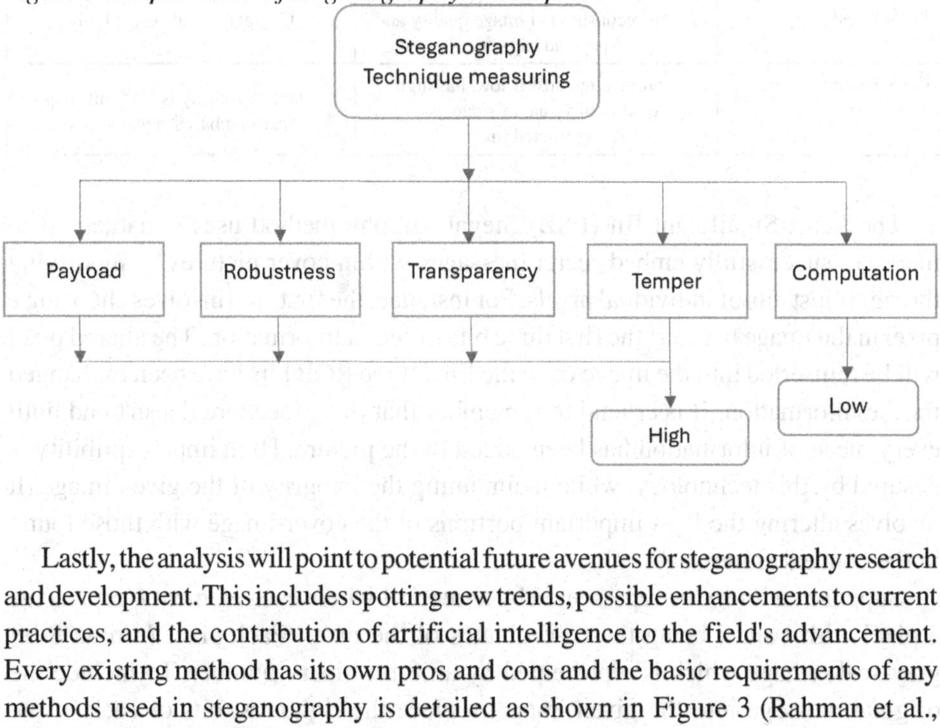

Lastly, the analysis will point to potential future avenues for steganography research and development. This includes spotting new trends, possible enhancements to current practices, and the contribution of artificial intelligence to the field's advancement. Every existing method has its own pros and cons and the basic requirements of any methods used in steganography is detailed as shown in Figure 3 (Rahman et al., 2023). The following table 1 gives the comparative assessments of performance summary of the various image steganography techniques. (Himthani et al., 2022)

Table 1. Performance assessments of various image steganography techniques

Steganography methods	Pros (Improved)	Cons (needs improvement)
Traditional LSB	Easy to implement	Capacity of payload, security and quality of visuals of stego need improvement.
Transform domain-based	Provides higher security and capacity of payload as compared to the LSB method.	Stego and reconstructed images are poor and has downside.
SVM based	Security is better	Has issues with larger dataset
ML based	Stego has better in the quality of visuals and the reconstructed images are of good quality.	Payload capacity should be improved and complex.
CNN based	Better reconstructed image quality and payload capacity.	Computational cost is high.
GAN based	Computation cost is low, has high quality of visual of stego and reconstructed images	There is security issue from deep learning based steganalysis

The Least Significant Bit (LSB) Steganography method uses a mathematical model to successfully embed secret messages within cover pictures by modifying the rightmost bits of individual pixels. For instance, the first step involves choosing a pixel in the image to insert the first three bits of secret information. The altered pixel will be reinserted into the image once the final three RGB bits have been exchanged for the information. It is crucial to remember that this procedure doesn't end until every piece of information has been added to the picture. High imperceptibility is ensured by this technology, while maintaining the integrity of the given image. It involves altering the least important portions of the cover-image with those found in the concealed message.

Suppose an image be represented by a matrix I where each element I_{ij} represents a pixel with i and j being the co-ordinates of the pixel. Each pixel I_{ij} in an 8-bit gray-scale image which is represented by an 8-bit binary number. To include the original message into the given image, replace the rightmost bits of each of the given pixel with the relevant bit from the original message. Mathematically, the new pixel value I'_{ij} after embedding the k-th bit of the original message is shown by the following equation 1.

$$I'_{ij} = I_{ij} - \left(I_{ij} - mod\, 2\right) + m_k \tag{1}$$

The index k corresponds to the message bit being embedded and increases sequentially as we move through the image pixels, where m_k is the kth bit of the message m. To retrieve given concealed data from the stego, perform the following operation on each pixel using the equation 2.

$$m_k = I'_{ij} \bmod 2 \tag{2}$$

This operation retrieves the rightmost bit of each pixel, which corresponds to the embedded message bit.

The maximum no of bits which are hidden in an image is given by Capacity C as shown in the following equation 3.

$$C = H * W \tag{3}$$

Where height H and width W are the dimensions of the image.

The principal application for the Discrete Cosine Transform (DCT) Steganography technology is frequency domain-based picture steganography, in which data is encoded into an image's transformed coefficients. Given an image block $I(x, y)$ having size $N \times N$ dimension, we can easily find the Discrete Cosine Transform, $DCT(u, v)$ by the following equation 4.

$$DCT(u,v) = \frac{1}{4}\alpha(u)\,\alpha\!\left(v\right)\sum_{x=0}^{N-1}\sum_{y=0}^{N-1} I(x,y)\,cos\!\left[\frac{(2x+1)\,u\pi}{2N}\right]cos\!\left[\frac{(2y+1)\,v\pi}{2N}\right] \tag{4}$$

where,

$$(u,v) = 0, 1, \ldots \text{ upto } N-1$$

$$\alpha\!\left(u\right) = \sqrt{\tfrac{1}{N}}\text{ for } u = 0 \text{ and } \alpha\!\left(u\right) = \sqrt{\tfrac{2}{N}}\text{ for } u > 0$$

$I(x, y)$ denotes value at co-ordinate (x, y) in the image.

$DCT(u, v)$ denotes the coefficient of the DCT at (u, v)

After computing the DCT coefficients of the image, they are quantized to reduce the amount of memory. Suppose, $Q(u, v)$ be the quantization matrix, and the quantized DCT coefficients $DCT_q(u, v)$ can be given by the following equation 5.

$$DCT_q(u,v) = round\!\left(\frac{DCT(u,v)}{Q(u,v)}\right) \tag{5}$$

Let the secret binary message be represented by a message sequence $M = \{m_1, m_2, \ldots, m_k\}$ where m_i is the ith bit of the message.

For embedding, we modify the quantized DCT coefficients $DCT_q(u, v)$ by modifying the rightmost bit (LSB) or a specific bit of these coefficients mentioned in the following equation 6.

$$DCT'_q(u,v) = DCT_q(u,v) - \left(DCT_q(u,v) \bmod 2\right) + m_i \tag{6}$$

Classical steganography techniques are less successful against contemporary steganalysis approaches due to their limitation in terms of robustness, capacity, security, and detectability, though useful in the past. To get over these limitations, modern techniques that frequently combine advanced embedding techniques, error correction, and encryption are being utilized more and more these days.

Deep Learning-Based Steganography Techniques

Neural networks are used by deep learning-based steganography, especially when employing autoencoders, to produce complex and reliable techniques for hiding data in pictures. Neural networks known as autoencoders, can be trained to accurately decode hidden data from images after they have been encoded. This is a mathematical representation of the autoencoder-based Deep Learning-Based Steganography method.

An autoencoder consists of two major parts:

a.   **Encoder**: It's function is to map input data.
b.   **Decoder**: It reconstructs the stego-image from the latent space representation.

The encoder is responsible for inserting the hidden message M into the cover image C. We can represent the encoder function by the below equation 7.

$$Z = E\left(C, M; \ _E\right) \tag{7}$$
where,

$_E$ represents the weights parameters of the encoder network.

Z is the latent space representation, which contains the hidden message within the cover image.

Decoder takes latent space representation Z and reconstructs the stego image S given by the following equation 8.

$$S = D\left(Z; \ _D\right) \tag{8}$$
where,

$_D$ represents the weights parameters of the decoder network.

S denotes the stego-image which visually represents the cover image C but contains the hidden message.

Once the network is trained, the hidden message can be retrieved back from the stego S using the decoder or a dedicated message extraction network D_M . We can use the following equation.

$$\widehat{M} = D_M\left(S; \ _{D_M}\right) \tag{9}$$
where,

$\widehat{M}$ is the extracted message.

$_{D_M}$ represents the parameters of the message extraction network.

Generative Adversarial Networks (GANs) are employed in steganography as shown in Figure 3. It is a technique that conceals secret messages within generated images. The fundamental concept behind this is utilizing the generative powers of GANs to incorporate hidden data in a manner that leaves the hidden message imperceptible to an outside observer. A GAN is made up of two neural networks that have been trained together. These are a discriminator (D) and a generator (G).

Generator(G) is shown in equation 10.

$$G: Z \times M \rightarrow X \tag{10}$$

The input is a noise vector $z \in Z$ and a secret message $m \in M$
And the output is a generated image $x \in X$ which embeds the original message.
Discriminator(D) is shown by equation 11.

$$D: X \rightarrow [0,1] \tag{11}$$

Where the input is an image x and the output is a probability $D(x)$ indicating whether the image is real.

The GAN training involves alternating updates of G and D:

Figure 4. GAN training

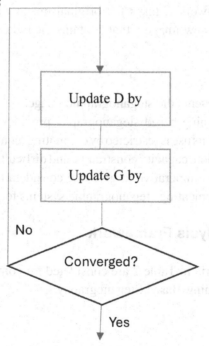

After the generator has been trained well, a separate network decoder, R is used to recover the secret message from the generated image:

$$\hat{m} = R(x), \text{ where } x = G(z, m) \tag{12}$$

The decoder R can be trained simultaneously with the generator or separately.

Convolutional Neural Networks (CNNs)

These are used in steganography to embed a hidden message within an image such that it may be recovered later with little loss or distortion. The mathematical concept for CNN-based steganography entails embedding a hidden message in an image and subsequently extracting it using CNN technique. Loss functions that strike a compromise between preserving the image's visual quality and guaranteeing the precise recovery of the concealed message control the procedure.

The goal of the embedding procedure is to produce an image y that closely resembles the original image x while also including a concealed message m.

The original input message is $x:x \in X$ where X is the space of all possible images.

The message $m:m \in M$ where M represents the space of all possible messages to hide.

The embedding network E takes the original image x and the message m as inputs and generates a new image y that contains the hidden message as given by the equation 13.

$$y = E(x, m) \tag{13}$$

Where $y \in X$ represents the steganographic image.

Although deep learning-based steganography provides enhanced information concealing capabilities, its use is restricted by computing requirements, susceptibility to detection and distortion, capacity constraints, and difficulties with model creation and generalization. It is imperative to give due consideration to these constraints while creating or implementing steganographic systems for practical use.

Comparative Analysis Framework

The following criteria in Table 2 are considered for comparisons between Traditional vs. Deep Learning-Based Steganography.

Table 2. Tradition vs deep learning methods comparison

Feature/ Criteria	Traditional Steganography Techniques	Deep Learning-Based Steganography Techniques
Feature Engineering	Requires manual feature design and selection, often leading to limited adaptability. Zhang et al., Wani and Sultan.	Automatically learns features through neural networks, reducing the need for manual intervention, Yanger Meng and Jingtao Li, Nandhini Subramanian et al..
Embedding Capacity	There is generally a limitation to how much data can be hidden without appreciably changing the cover medium in this technique. The Least Significant Bit (LSB) substitution is limited by the requirement to reduce statistical or visual irregularities in the data. Generally, this approach has lower embedding capacity due to fixed algorithms and constraints, Xintao Duan et al..	It has a higher embedding capacity to figure out how to more covertly disperse concealed information throughout an image or other medium. This technique determines how much data can be incorporated without arousing suspicion in an adaptive manner. It can achieve higher embedding capacities by leveraging complex models like GANs and autoencoders, Sarah Kareem Salim et al., Nandhini Subramanian et al..
Security	Security often relies on the obscurity of the algorithm and manual techniques. Wani and Sultan, Muharrem Tuncay Gençoğlu.	Enhanced security through advanced models that can adapt and learn from data, making detection more difficult, Lang Chen et al., Farhad Shadmand et al..
Robustness to Attacks	This approach is more susceptible and prone to steganalysis attack due to predictable patterns that can be computed, especially the statistical types of the attacks that identify distributional irregularities in dataset. Even while some sophisticated methods, for example, the spread spectrum, improve robustness, they can still be detected by specialized techniques, Muharrem Tuncay Gençoğlu, Pingan Fan et al.	It provides better protection against steganalysis attack since it can obfuscate concealed data in more intricate and unpredictable pattern. These models can optimize information hiding by training on huge datasets, making it harder to find with conventional analysis techniques. So it provides better robustness with regard to noise and compression due to the adaptive nature of deep learning method, Pingan Fan et al..
Invisibility	Focuses on maintaining invisibility through handcrafted methods, which may not always be effective. Zhang et al., Wani and Sultan.	Achieves higher invisibility through sophisticated embedding techniques that are less detectable, Yanger Meng and Jingtao Li, Nandhini Subramanian et al.
Types of Data Supported	Primarily supports image, audio, and text steganography with fixed methods, Pengxiang Chai and Jun Lang.	Capable of handling diverse data types including images, audio, and video with more flexible approaches, Farhad Shadmand et al., Pingan Fan et al.
Complexity	The traditional steganography method is less complex to implement and requires less processing power as compared to the deep learning method. This limits its sophistication and versatility while making it usable for a wider range of applications. But this method might lack flexibility. Sarah Kareem Salim et al., Dima S. Kasasbeh et al.	It demands a large amount of processing power for hidden data extraction and embedding, as well as for training models. In exchange for its greater security and adaptability, there is the presence of complexity. It requires pretty complex architectures and significant expertise and computational resources. Yanger Meng and Jingtao Li, Nandhini Subramanian et al., Farhad Shadmand et al.

continued on following page

Table 2. Continued

Feature/ Criteria	Traditional Steganography Techniques	Deep Learning-Based Steganography Techniques
Adaptability	It usually uses preset algorithms, which might not be flexible enough to accommodate changing security needs or different kinds of cover media. Since these techniques are frequently inflexible, they are less effective against complex attacks or novel media formats. It had very limited adaptability to newer types of data or changes in the environment, Zihan Wang et al.	It is very versatile as neural networks may be taught to optimize steganographic methods for many media formats, such as pictures, sounds, and videos. To combat novel detection techniques, they can also be updated and retrained, offering a more adaptable and robust strategy. It is highly adaptable to various media types due to the learning capabilities of neural networks, Lang Chen et al., Farhad Shadmand et al.
Detection and Countermeasures	Statistical analysis and pattern recognition are frequently used in detection these days. These techniques are well-researched and have the potential to outperform traditional steganographic methods used in present times.	Deep learning can produce extremely complex embedding patterns that elude conventional detection techniques, making detection more difficult. To address these developments, deep learning-based steganalysis is likewise becoming more and more popular.

The shift in steganography from conventional to deep learning-based techniques signifies a noteworthy development in the area. The effectiveness and flexibility of traditional methods may be limited by their frequent reliance on fixed algorithms that necessitate human feature engineering. Artificial Intelligence approaches, on the other hand, use deep learning neural networks to self-learn and optimize features, leading to better security and embedding capacity performance. Furthermore, because deep learning-based techniques can adapt and learn from data patterns, they have proven to be more robust against a variety of attacks, including stegano-analysis. Comparing this flexibility to previous methods which are frequently limited to particular data kinds, allows for a wider range of applications. It also extends to the types of data that can be handled.

There are several obstacles that both conventional and deep learning steganography approaches must overcome, especially in the areas of detection, law, and ethics. These are listed below along with a thorough explanation. Traditionally, steganographic methods have frequently relied on data concealment that is detected by statistical analysis or pattern recognition technique of artificial intelligence. Detection techniques are getting better at finding these hidden signals by examining statistical patterns or abnormalities in the cover media such as images, audio files, etc. Steganography employs deep learning models that are intended to produce alterations that are more subdued or difficult to identify. However, sophisticated detecting methods are also used in these models. Adversarial techniques such as employing additional deep learning models that have been specially trained to recognize concealed messages that are intended to detect deep learning methods advance along with the technology. Adversaries frequently adjust their steganographic strategies in response to detection techniques in order to evade detection. This may lead to a continuous arms race between detectors and steganographers. Neural networks can be used to optimize steganographic processes so they can more effectively avoid detection. That may also imply that, in order to stay up with these developments, new detection techniques will have to be created on a regular basis. Legal problems may arise from the use of steganography for nefarious activities, such as the concealment of unlawful communications or information. Regarding the usage of steganography, different jurisdictions have different regulations, and legal systems constantly need to adjust to new methods and uses. Further legal issues are brought up by the application of deep learning to steganography, especially in light of the possibility of abuse in the development of increasingly complex techniques for concealing illegal material. Furthermore, the application of AI-generated content in steganography may put the current legal order in jeopardy. When steganography is employed for immoral actions like fraud, espionage, or other negative activities, ethical problems come up. Steganography's ethical use is frequently discussed in terms of its legitimate applications vs its abuse potential. Deep learning steganography raises ethical questions since technology has the ability to produce extremely realistic fake-data or conceal data in ways that could be used maliciously. The application of AI to improve steganographic techniques raises ethical concerns concerning accountability, responsibility, and the possible repercussions of misuse.

The effectiveness and detectability of steganographic techniques are frequently trade-offs. Steganographers may need to employ more intricate or resource-intensive techniques as detection techniques advance, which could have an impact on efficiency and practicality. It can be difficult to strike a balance between allowing lawful uses of steganography and preventing misuse. It is crucial to make sure that rules are adaptable enough to take into account novel approaches without impeding creativity. Challenges with detection, legal issues, and ethical issues affect both deep learning and classical steganography. The field is dynamic, with new legal and ethical frameworks emerging along with continuous improvements in steganographic and detection techniques.

4. CONCLUSION

Text-based techniques, transform domain approaches, and least significant bit (LSB) insertion are examples of traditional steganography techniques. Although LSB insertion is very simple to identify through statistical analysis, it entails embedding data in the LSB of cover media, such as photos or audio files. Although they require more intricate processing, transform domain techniques—which conceal data in wavelet or frequency domains—provide superior resistance to detection. Text steganography conceals data within text by using linguistic strategies and substitution procedures. These techniques are simple and economical with resources, but they have a limited amount of data and are frequently identifiable. Deep learning has made more advanced steganographic techniques possible, such as autoencoders, neural networks, and Generative Adversarial Networks (GANs).

While GANs create cover material with embedded data that is difficult to identify, neural networks encode and decode concealed data with high subtlety. Autoencoders use their capacity to pick up intricate patterns to conceal and reveal data. Although these methods are more flexible and stealthier, they demand a large amount of computer power and knowledge. Because deep learning techniques are so sophisticated, there is also a competition between them and detection technologies, which are using deep learning models more and more to find concealed content.

Conventional steganography methods are easier to use and need fewer resources, but they are frequently more observable and have a smaller data capacity. Deep learning-based methods, on the other hand, have higher computing demands and more complexity but provide better capacity, stealth, and flexibility. Both strategies present constant difficulties due to developing detection techniques and bring up significant moral and legal issues. The requirements for data hiding, the available resources, and the regulatory environment all influence the decision between traditional and deep learning-based techniques.

REFERENCES

Abdulazeez, S., Nawar, A. K., Lubna, E., & Jahefer, M. M. (2023). Hiding Information in Digital Images Using LSB Steganography Technique. *International Journal of Interactive Mobile Technologies*, 17(7), 167–178. DOI: 10.3991/ijim.v17i07.38737

Ahmed, S. S., Memon, M., Jaffari, R., & Jawaid, M. (2021). StegoBound: A Novel Image Steganography Technique Using Boundary-Based LSB Substitution. *Journal of Hunan University Natural Sciences*, 48(6).

Alanzy, M., Alomrani, R., Alqarni, B., & Almutairi, S. (2023). Image Steganography Using LSB and Hybrid Encryption Algorithms. *Applied Sciences (Basel, Switzerland)*, 13(21), 11771. DOI: 10.3390/app132111771

Bamanga, M. A., Babando, A. K., & Shehu, M. A. (2024). *Recent Advances in Steganography*. Online First.

Bansal, K., Agrawal, A., & Bansal, N. (2020). A Survey on Steganography using Least Significant bit (LSB) Embedding Approach. *International Conference on Trends in Electronics and Informatics (ICEI)*, 64-69. DOI: 10.1109/ICOEI48184.2020.9142896

Chai, P., & Lang, J. (2023). Behavior steganography in social networks based on AES encryption algorithm. *Third International Conference on Advanced Algorithms and Neural Networks*. DOI: 10.1117/12.3005092

Chen, L., Wang, R., Yan, D., & Wang, J. (2021). Learning to Generate Steganographic Cover for Audio Steganography Using GAN. *IEEE Access : Practical Innovations, Open Solutions*, 9, 88098–88107. DOI: 10.1109/ACCESS.2021.3090445

Demircan, Y. Y., & Ozekes, S. (2024). A Novel LSB Steganography Technique Using Image Segmentation, JUCS -. *Journal of Universal Computer Science*, 30(3), 308–332. DOI: 10.3897/jucs.105702

Duan, X., Jia, K., Li, B., Guo, D., Zhang, E., & Qin, C. (2019). En Zhang and Chuan Qin, Reversible Image Steganography Scheme Based on a U-Net Structure. *IEEE Access : Practical Innovations, Open Solutions*, 7, 9314–9323. DOI: 10.1109/ACCESS.2019.2891247

Fan, P., Zhang, H., & Zhao, X. (2023). Exploring Frame Difference to Enhance Robustness for Video Steganography on Social Networks. *Security and Communication Networks*, 2023, 1–11. DOI: 10.1155/2023/6295486

Gençoğlu, M. T., & Steganography, B. (2022). in Social Networks. *Turkish Journal of Nature and Science*, 11(4), 135–141.

Himthani, Dhaka, Kaur, Rani, Oza, & Lee. (2022). Comparative performance assessment of deep learning-based image steganography techniques. Scientific Reports, No. 16895.

Kasasbeh, D. S., Al-Ja'afreh, B. M., Anbar, M., Hasbullah, I. H., & Al Khasawneh, M. (2024). Secure map-based crypto-stego technique based on mac address. *Bulletin of Electrical Engineering and Informatics*, 13(3), 1788–1801. DOI: 10.11591/eei.v13i3.7140

Mandal, P. C., Mukherjee, I., Paul, G., & Chatterji, B. N. (2022). Digital image steganography: A literature survey. *Information Sciences*, 609, 1451–1488. DOI: 10.1016/j.ins.2022.07.120

Meng, Y., & Li, J. Image Steganography of convolutional neural network based on neural architecture search, *Research square*, 2022 DOI: 10.21203/rs.3.rs-2245407/v1

Nashat & Mamdouh. (2019). An efficient steganographic technique for hiding data. Journal of the Egyptian Mathematical Society, 57.

Patil, H. V., & Sonaje, V. P. (2024). A Study of The Performance of Various Media for Information Security Via LSB Steganography Method for Text Messaging. *Journal of Electrical Systems*, 20(9).

Rahman, Uddin, Hussain, Ahmed, Khan, Zakarya, Rahman, & Haleem. (2023). A Huffman code LSB based image steganography technique using multi-level encryption and achromatic component of an image. Scientific Reports, No. 14183.

Rahman, S., Uddin, J., Zakarya, M., Hussain, H., Khan, A. A., Ahmed, A., & Haleem, M. (2023). *A Comprehensive Study of Digital Image Steganographic Techniques* (Vol. 11). IEEE Access.

Rustad, S., Setiadi, D. R. I. M., Syukur, A., & Andono, P. N. (2022). Inverted LSB image steganography using adaptive pattern to improve imperceptibility. *Journal of King Saud University. Computer and Information Sciences*, 34(6), 3559–3568. DOI: 10.1016/j.jksuci.2020.12.017

Salim, S. K., Msallam, M. M., & Olewi, H. I. (2023). Hide text in an image using Blowfish algorithm and development of least significant bit technique. *Indonesian Journal of Electrical Engineering and Computer Science*, 29(1), 339–347. DOI: 10.11591/ijeecs.v29.i1.pp339-347

Shadmand, F., Medvedev, I., & Gonçalves, N. (2021). CodeFace: A Deep Learning Printer-Proof Steganography for Face Portraits. *IEEE Access: Practical Innovations, Open Solutions*, 9, 167282–167291. DOI: 10.1109/ACCESS.2021.3132581

Subramanian, N., Cheheb, I., Elharrouss, O., Al-Maadeed, S., & Bouridane, A. (2021). End-to-End Image Steganography Using Deep Convolutional Autoencoders. *IEEE Access : Practical Innovations, Open Solutions*, 9, 135585–135593. DOI: 10.1109/ACCESS.2021.3113953

Subramanian, N., Elharrouss, O., Al-Maadeed, S., Bouridane, A., & Steganography, I. (2021). A Review of the Recent Advances. *IEEE Access : Practical Innovations, Open Solutions*, 9, 23409–23423. DOI: 10.1109/ACCESS.2021.3053998

Wang, Z., Byrnes, O., Wang, H., Sun, R., Ma, C., Chen, H., Wu, Q., & Xue, M. (2021). *Data Hiding with Deep Learning: A Survey Unifying Digital Watermarking and Steganography*. Arxiv.

Wani & Sultan. (2023). Deep learning based image steganography: A review. *Wiley Interdisciplinary Reviews. Data Mining and Knowledge Discovery*, 13(3).

Wu, P., Yang, Y., & Li, X. (2018). StegNet: Mega Image Steganography Capacity with Deep Convolutional Network. *Future Internet*, 10(6), 54. DOI: 10.3390/fi10060054

Chapter 12
Blockchain and Steganography:
A Deep Learning Approach for Enhanced Security

Hemlata Parmar

https://orcid.org/0009-0009-1438-5427

Manipal University Jaipur, India

Vijay Shankar Sharma

Manipal University Jaipur, India

Siddhanta Kumar Singh

Manipal University Jaipur, India

ABSTRACT

The rapid expansion of quantum computing presents a substantial obstacle to the available encryption methods, especially those employed in blockchain technology. Because of the impending dangers posed by quantum computing, there is an urgent requirement for more secure systems for the encryption and transport of data. The quantum-resistant blockchain steganography (QRBS) framework is a revolutionary concept presented in this study. Steganography and blockchain technology are both included in this framework, which is further strengthened by quantum-resistant cryptography and deep learning. Furthermore, the authors present an adaptive deep-learning model for steganography that can evolve to deal with attacks that are becoming increasingly complex. Experiments have been conducted to validate the proposed system, demonstrating considerable gains in security and robustness. As a result, this system is an appropriate option for secure data management in future quantum computing settings.

DOI: 10.4018/979-8-3693-2223-9.ch012

1. INTRODUCTION

In recent years, the field of quantum computing has seen a tremendous metamorphosis, shifting from a theoretical concept to an actual technical accomplishment. This transformation has occurred as a result of developments in the field. Substantial advancements in quantum computing have been achieved by prominent technology firms including Google, IBM, and Microsoft. Significant accomplishments have been attained by these organizations in this field. According to Arute et al. (2019), these computers make use of the principles of quantum mechanics in order to carry out calculations that would be hard for classical computers to handle within an acceptable period of time. The impact that quantum computing will have on cryptography is one of the most significant repercussions, despite the fact that the conceivable applications of quantum computing are extremely diverse and range from the field of materials research to the pharmaceutical business Both RSA (Rivest, Shamir, and Adleman, 1978) and Elliptic Curve Cryptography (ECC), widely used cryptographic protocols serving as the fundamental security framework for several blockchain systems, are susceptible to quantum assaults. The protocols in question were jointly devised by Rivest, Shamir, and Adleman. More precisely, quantum computers have demonstrated their ability to effectively solve the integer factorization problem and the discrete logarithm problem, which are tasks considered to be beyond the capabilities of ordinary computers. Quantum computers possess the capability to effectively and efficiently address each of these concerns. Two widely used cryptographic methods, RSA and ECC, have been shown to be susceptible to cracking by a quantum computer, as demonstrated by Shor's technique (Shor, 1994). Both of these methods exemplify robust digital encryption. For example, this method demonstrates that a quantum computer is capable of factoring enormous integers at a rate that is exponentially quicker than that of conventional computers. In order to ensure the security of existing cryptographic systems in a world after quantum computing, it would be necessary to develop novel cryptographic methods that are impervious to quantum attacks. For this reason, quantum attacks would be capable of undermining the security of these systems. The vulnerability recently exposed by Chen and colleagues (2016) has prompted a surge in research efforts dedicated to post-quantum cryptography. Post-quantum cryptography is a cryptographic technique designed to provide security against adversaries at the quantum level. Significantly, blockchain technology, now closely associated with decentralized and secure digital transactions, relies heavily on cryptographic primitives. The decentralized structure of blockchain technology enables the execution of safe peer-to-peer transactions without the influence of intermediaries. One way to achieve this is by employing cryptographic methods, which ensure the authenticity and consistency of transactions. However, the inclusion of RSA and ECC in blockchain systems makes them particularly susceptible to quantum assaults (Mosca, 2018). The possibility exists for a quantum computer to undermine the integrity of blockchain technology by compromising the cryptographic signatures that validate transactions. This could potentially enhance an adversary's capacity to modify the historical records of the blockchain.

Steganography is the practice of concealing information within digital media such as photographs, movies, or audio files. It is confronted with its own set of issues, which are directly parallel to the challenges that quantum computing offers to blockchain. According to Ker (2005), traditional steganographic methods are becoming more susceptible to detection as digital forensics and machine learning approaches continue demonstrating their advancement. A key distinction between steganography and cryptography is that the former does not endeavor to encrypt the data but rather conceal the fact that a message is being conveyed at all. Steganography is a form of covert communication. A cover medium that is not suspicious is used to conceal the hidden message. This cover medium can be something as simple as an image or an audio file depending on the circumstances. The objective is to ensure that the opponents cannot figure out what the secret data is.

1.1 Increasing Threats to Digital Data Security in Today's Interconnected World

The proliferation of data across a wide range of platforms and networks in today's hyper-connected digital landscape has resulted in significant vulnerabilities in data security. These vulnerabilities have been brought about as a result of the proliferation of data. There have been significant shifts in the manner in which information is gathered, disseminated, and stored as a result of the expansion of cloud computing, mobile devices, the Internet of Things (IoT), and social media channels.

These changes have been brought about as a result of the increased use of these technologies. The accessibility and utility of data have been revolutionized as a result of these technological achievements; yet, they have also developed a new set of difficulties that risk the privacy and security of sensitive information. These issues have been brought about by the fact that these problems have been generated. Over the course of the past few years, cybercrime has evolved into a global industry, and cyber-attacks have gotten more sophisticated and targeted than ever before. Computer hackers and other cybercriminals are always conducting research and developing new methods in order to exploit vulnerabilities that exist in computer systems, computer networks, and computer applications. Phishing is a popular form of cybercrime that involves sending deceptive emails and websites with the purpose of deceiving individuals into giving important information such as passwords, credit card data, and social security numbers. Phishing is another term for the practice of sending emails and websites that contain misleading information. Phishing assaults are becoming increasingly tailored and difficult to detect, which causes them to pose a significant threat to the safety of data. One kind of bad software is ransomware, which encrypts the data of a user and renders it inaccessible until a ransom is paid. Ransomware is a type of malicious software. There has been a significant rise in the frequency of ransomware attacks over the past few years. These attacks have had an impact on individuals, businesses, and even critical infrastructure. Malicious malware has been responsible for carrying out these attacks. As a result of these attacks, enormous financial losses have occurred, in addition to breaches in the security of the data.

Attack tactics that entail flooding a network or service with an overwhelming quantity of traffic to the point where it becomes unavailable to users who are authorized to use it are referred to as distributed denial of service attacks, or DDoS attacks for short. DDoS assaults are more popularly known by their acronym, DDoS. Attacks using distributed denial of service can render websites and online services inoperable, causing substantial disruptions to company operations as well as considerable financial and reputational harm. An advanced persistent threat (APT) is a type of attack that is intended to last for an extended period of time and is focused. A network intrusion is a form of attack that takes place when an unauthorized user gains access to a network and continues to operate without being discovered for an extended period of time. The theft of data or the destruction of operations is often the objective of these attacks.

Most of the time, advanced persistent threats (APTs) are employed against high-value targets, which include government agencies, financial institutions, and multinational enterprises. The exposure of millions of records annually as a result of security lapses has become increasingly widespread as data breaches have become more commonplace. It is possible for breaches to occur as a result of cyberattacks from the outside, but insider threats present a substantial risk. The term "insider threat" refers to situations in which workers, contractors, or other trusted individuals misuse their access to sensitive data, either purposefully or unintentionally. Accidental Data Leaks like employees may inadvertently expose sensitive information through misconfigured databases, unencrypted storage, or by sending data to the wrong recipient. Malicious Insiders Disgruntled employees or those with malicious intent can deliberately steal, manipulate, or destroy data. These insiders often have legitimate access to sensitive information, making their actions difficult to detect and prevent. Risks posed by third parties are prevalent in many companies because they rely on third-party vendors and partners for a variety of services. The principal organization may not have the same level of security as these third parties, which results in vulnerabilities that can be exploited by attackers.

As a result of the expansion of the Internet of Things (IoT), there has been a significant increase in the number of devices that are connected to one another. These devices include intelligent home appliances as well as industrial control systems. Although the Internet of Things (IoT) provides convenience and effectiveness, it also opens up substantial security vulnerabilities. Insecure devices are intentionally built with limited security measures, rendering them highly susceptible to hackers. The absence of adequate encryption, secure authentication, and the capability to receive security upgrades in these devices renders them susceptible to exploitation. Botnets included in IoT devices have the potential to be hijacked and integrated into botnets, which are networks of compromised devices that can be utilized to initiate extensive cyber-attacks, including DDoS attacks. Privacy concerns with IoT devices arise from the collection of extensive data, encompassing personal information, geographical data, and usage habits. The interception or theft of this data can result in significant privacy violations. Cloud computing has fundamentally transformed the manner in which enterprises store and retrieve data, providing attributes such as scalability, flexibility, and cost reduction. Nevertheless, the transition to cloud computing has also given rise to novel security obstacles. The sovereignty and jurisdiction of data kept in the cloud may be influenced by the rules and regulations of the country where the data centers are situated, consequently raising concerns regarding data sovereignty and compliance. The distributed duty Model entails that cloud service providers and users jointly bear the duty for security. Although providers establish the security of the infrastructure, it is the customers' responsibility to ensure the security of their data and applications. Erroneous interpretations of this paradigm might result in vulnerabilities in security. Incorrectly configured an often seen factor contributing to data breaches in cloud computing is the misconfiguration of storage systems, such as publicly available Amazon S3 buckets. This misconfiguration might potentially expose sensitive data to unauthorized individuals. State-sponsored cyber-attacks have emerged as a top priority for government entities, vital infrastructure, and global enterprises. Typically, these attacks are executed by well-financed and highly proficient organizations with particular geopolitical goals. Cyber espionage is a common tactic employed by state-sponsored organizations to illicitly acquire valuable information, including intellectual property, military secrets, and diplomatic communications. State-sponsored sabotage strikes target vital infrastructure, including power grids, water supply systems, and communication networks, with the goal of causing extensive damage and disrupting operations. Political Manipulation Cyber-attacks have the potential to exert influence on political processes, including elections, through the unauthorized access and disclosure of sensitive data or the dissemination of false information.

In response to the increasing risks to data security, governments and regulatory authorities have implemented more stringent protocols to safeguard personal and sensitive information. Although these restrictions are essential, they can present operational difficulties for organizations. The Implications of Compliance Various requirements must be followed by organizations, including the General Data Protection Regulation (GDPR) in Europe, the California Consumer Privacy Act (CCPA), and industry-specific standards like HIPAA and PCI DSS. The task of ensuring compliance can be intricate and demanding in terms of resources. The consequences of non-compliance with data protection legislation can include substantial financial penalties, legal proceedings, and harm to one's reputation. This exerts pressure on organizations to adopt vigorous security protocols. Data localization refers to the stringent rules that mandate the storage of data within designated geographical limits, therefore complicating data administration and raising expenses for international corporations. The sophistication of cyber threats is increasing as attackers exploit emerging technologies like artificial intelligence (AI) and machine learning (ML) to augment their capabilities. For instance, AI-driven attacks employ AI to automate the detection of vulnerabilities, create more persuasive phishing attacks, and elude detection by conventional security measures. Zero-Day exploit vulnerabilities refer to security weaknesses that are not known by the program manufacturer and for which there is no accessible security patch. Adversaries who identify these weaknesses can take advantage of them prior to their detection and resolution, resulting in substantial compromise. Increasingly, supply chain attacks are focusing on the supply chain by exploiting weaknesses in third-party software and hardware components to penetrate enterprise systems. The commercialization of personal data has generated substantial privacy tensions. Organizations amass huge quantities of data from consumers, frequently without their explicit agreement, and employ it for focused advertising, profiling, and various other objectives. Data aggregation firms consolidate data from several sources to generate comprehensive profiles of individuals, which can be utilized for marketing, surveillance, and other strategic objectives. Data Breaches: The large volumes of data gathered by corporations render them very susceptible to cyber-attacks. Instances of breaches can result in the exposure of confidential personal data, giving rise to identity theft, financial fraud, and diverse criminal activities. End-user awareness and control: A significant number of users lack awareness regarding the collection, usage, and sharing of their data. Despite their awareness, individuals frequently have restricted authority over their data, which gives rise to dilemmas regarding privacy and autonomy. The escalating risks to the security of digital data in the modern linked society emphasize the necessity for strong and creative security protocols. In light of the ongoing evolution of cyber threats, it is crucial for both companies and individuals to remain alert and implement thorough security initiatives that effectively tackle both existing and developing hazards. Achieving this necessitates the integration of cutting-edge technology and a dedication to ongoing surveillance, education, and adherence to safety regulations. In the continuously evolving environment, it is crucial to adopt a proactive strategy towards data security in order to safeguard sensitive information and uphold confidence in the digital ecosystem.

Figure 1. Digital security challenges

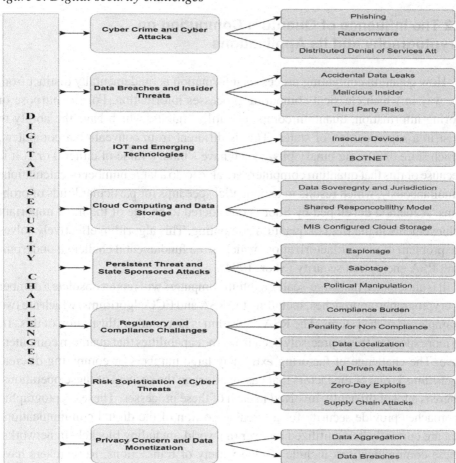

The major objective of the QRBS framework is to develop a system that can provide cryptographic security as well as covertness in the transmission of data, even when quantum computers are present. By integrating three cutting-edge technologies, we are able to accomplish this:

- Providing decentralized, tamper-proof, and secure transactions is the primary function of blockchain technology.
- Utilizing lattice-based encryption as a means of providing protection against quantum attacks is what is known as quantum-resistant cryptography.
- Deep Learning-Enhanced Steganography refers to the utilization of deep learning models for the purpose of enhancing the robustness of steganographic encoding and decoding procedures.

1.2 The Influence of Quantum Computing on Cryptography and Its Applications

How quantum computing processes information is fundamentally distinct from the way in which classical computing processes information. For the purpose of storing information, quantum computers utilize qubits, which have the ability to exist in a superposition of states. This is different from conventional computers, which store data using binary bits, which have a binary value of either 0 or 1. It is because of this that quantum computers are able to do a large number of calculations simultaneously, which results in exponential speedups for particular kinds of problems. A method developed by Shor is considered to be one of the most important achievements in the field of quantum computing. This algorithm effectively solves the problem of integer factorization, which is the fundamental challenge underpinning RSA encryption security (Shor, 1994).

It is anticipated that large-scale quantum computers will render obsolete a number of cryptography approaches, including the RSA and ECC algorithms, which are two examples of such systems. The RSA algorithm is just another illustration of this. To be more specific, this is precisely because of the capabilities that quantum computers have. The challenge of factoring extremely large numbers or computing discrete logarithms is one of the factors that has an effect on the success of these operations. There is a lot of difficulty involved in each of these processes. These cryptographic approaches provide security for a sizeable portion of the digital communications that are currently being utilized all over the world, including blockchain networks. These communications include a wide variety of transactions. Researchers have been working on post-quantum cryptography, according to Bernstein, Buchmann, and Dahmen (2009), who reported on the matter. Post-quantum cryptography is a branch of cryptography that specifically deals with developing novel algorithms that maintain robustness even in the face of potential attacks from quantum computers. This is because quantum computers are able to break them. Through the utilization of quantum computing, this is made possible. According to the findings of the research that Alkim and his colleagues carried out in the year 2020, the most promising choices are the techniques of lattice-based cryptography, multivariate polynomial cryptography, hash-based signatures, and code-based cryptography approaches. Lattice-based encryption has become a vital approach for developing quantum-resistant cryptographic algorithms capable of withstanding quantum computers. This is due to the intrinsic immunity of lattice-based cryptography against quantum computing. More precisely, it exploits the demanding characteristics of the problems related to lattice structures to achieve this objective. Illustrative instances of these challenges include the Shortest Vector Problem (SVP) and the Learning with Errors (LWE) problem. Both terms denote same concepts. Based on the research conducted by Lyubashevsky, Peikert, and Regev (2013), it is widely postulated that both of these concerns exhibit resilience against quantum attacks. The Post-Quantum Cryptography Standardization Project at the National Institute of Standards and Technology (NIST, 2020) has identified several lattice-based algorithms as highly promising candidates for standardization in the post-quantum setting.

1.3 Blockchain Vulnerabilities to Quantum Attacks

The capacity of blockchain technology to serve as a tamper-evident security mechanism for decentralized digital transactions has attracted a great deal of attention in recent years. Blockchains are distributed ledgers that are maintained by a network of nodes to record and validate transactions. These ledgers are used to validate and record transactions through the use of consensus mechanisms. A cryptographic hash of the block that came before it is carried by each block of the blockchain, as stated by Narayanan et al. (2016). This is one of the properties of the blockchain. This ensures that any modification to any block would necessitate the modification of all blocks that came after it. This is a process that would be computationally impossible under traditional circumstances.

On the other hand, the fact that blockchain relies on cryptographic methods such as RSA and ECC for digital signatures and hashing functions renders it susceptible to quantum attacks. A blockchain is a distributed ledger that uses digital signatures to authenticate the legitimacy of transactions. It is possible that a malicious actor who is in possession of a quantum computer could potentially forge digital signatures by solving the underlying cryptographic problems. These problems include factoring the RSA modulus or solving the discrete logarithm problem in ECC. As a result, the malicious actor would gain the ability to alter blockchain records or steal assets (Mosca, 2018). To overcome these vulnerabilities, academics are investigating the possibility of incorporating cryptographic algorithms that are resistant to quantum computing into blockchain systems. The use of lattice-based encryption, which provides the same functionality as RSA and ECC but is resistant to quantum computing, is one strategy that can be used. The authors Alkim et al. (2020) suggest a blockchain architecture that is resistant to quantum computing and uses lattice-based cryptography to authenticate transactions and check their integrity. The results of their research indicate that lattice-based signatures can be implemented in blockchain systems in an effective manner, which offers a possible solution to the problem represented by the quantum threat.

1.4 Steganography and the Challenge of Detection

In order to conceal information, steganography has been utilized for a very long time. This technique involves concealing data by embedding it within cover media that is not harmful, such as pictures, movies, or audio files. In contrast to cryptography, which aims to obfuscate the content of a message, the purpose of steganography is to conceal the very existence of the communication. Steganography is a form of covert communication. In spite of this, opponents have created increasingly complex methods for identifying hidden data, a process that is known as steganalysis (Ker, 2005). Steganography techniques have grown more frequently utilized, which has helped enemies develop these approaches.

The Least Significant Bit (LSB) approach is one example of a traditional steganography methodology. This method involves changing the bits of a cover media that are considered to be the least significant in order to encode hidden data. Even though these approaches are straightforward and easy to put into practice, they are susceptible to steganography tools, which are able to identify minor patterns that are brought about by the concealed data. Traditional steganography methods have become less secure due to the development of deep learning-based steganalysis, which employs convolutional neural networks (CNNs) to identify steganographic artefacts (Zhang et al., 2020). Deep learning is being utilized by researchers as a means of enhancing the safety of steganographic systems in response to the fact that steganalysis is becoming an increasingly dangerous hazard. Zhu et al. (2018) introduced a unique deep learning-based steganographic system that uses convolutional neural networks (CNNs) for encoding and decoding concealed data. This system operates in a parallel fashion. Their method considerably enhances the robustness of steganography, making it more resistant to detection by conventional steganography tools while also increasing its overall effectiveness. Generative adversarial networks, commonly known as GANs, have been utilized in the development of steganographic systems. These systems can generate over media that are indistinguishable from natural media, which further enhances the security of data that has been concealed (Hayes & Danezis, 2017).

1.5 The Quantum-Resistant Blockchain Steganography (QRBS) Framework

Due to the fact that blockchain is susceptible to quantum assaults and steganography is becoming increasingly sophisticated, there is an obvious requirement for a new strategy that integrates blockchain technology, encryption that is resistant to quantum attacks, and steganography that is strengthened by deep learning. This study presents the Quantum-Resistant Blockchain Steganography (QRBS) architecture. This framework integrates these technologies to produce a multi-layered security system that is capable of withstanding both quantum and traditional threats.

There are three fundamental parts that make up the QRBS framework:

- **The Quantum-Resistant Blockchain Layer** is a layer that utilizes lattice-based cryptography to protect blockchain transactions from being compromised by quantum assaults. Cryptographic algorithms based on lattices, such as those described by Lyubashevsky et al. (2013), are resistant to quantum computing and can be applied in blockchain systems efficiently.
- **Deep Learning-Enhanced Steganography Layer:** In order to enhance the resilience of steganography, this layer employs deep learning models, namely convolutional neural networks (CNNs) and generative adversarial networks (GANs). Given the system's constant adaptation to the constantly changing steganography techniques, it becomes ever more challenging for adversaries to detect hidden data.
- **The Security and Optimization Layer** is responsible for monitoring the system for potential security risks. It employs anomaly detection algorithms that are based on deep learning in order to discover and prevent assaults. This system is designed to be adaptable, which enables it to develop in response to the emergence of new dangers.

1.6 Recent Research Supporting the QRBS Framework

Recent research has shown that quantum-resistant cryptography and deep learning-enhanced steganography are both excellent methods of concealing information. While Zhu et al. (2018) and Hayes and Danezis (2017) demonstrate how deep learning may dramatically improve the security of steganographic systems, Chen et al. (2016) emphasize how urgent it is to make the shift to cryptographic systems that are resistant to quantum computing. Furthermore, Alkim et al. (2020) present a roadmap for creating blockchain networks resistant to quantum computing by providing a practical example of how lattice-based cryptography can be implemented into blockchain systems. Providing a comprehensive solution for secure data transmission in a post-quantum world, the QRBS framework covers both current and future security difficulties by merging these sophisticated technologies. This framework addresses both current and future security challenges.

2. DATA PRIVACY AND ACCESS CONTROL

Blockchain technology, in addition to being inherently transparent, also offers measures for protecting the privacy of collected data. It is possible to maintain the confidentiality of sensitive information through the use of cryptographic techniques and permission Blockchains, while still reaping the benefits of the various security improvements offered by Blockchain. Access to a Blockchain that is based on permission is limited to a specific group of participants who have been given permission to join the network because of their participation. It is appropriate to use this approach in settings where the protection of personal information is of the utmost importance, such as in government organizations or financial institutions. Zero-knowledge proofs are an example of an advanced cryptographic approach that can be included into blockchain technology. These proofs enable one party to demonstrate to another that they are aware of a value without actually disclosing the value itself. It is possible to utilize this method to improve the level of privacy and security in financial transactions. Blockchain technology plays a varied role in the security industry, providing solutions to a significant number of the difficulties that traditional security systems confront. The rigorous framework that it provides for securing data and transactions from unauthorized access and manipulation is provided by its decentralized design, immutability, cryptographic security, and consensus processes. As the technology continues to advance, Blockchain is positioned to play an increasingly crucial part in the process of protecting digital ecosystems across a wide range of industries, including but not limited to the management of supply chains, healthcare, and the provision of financial services.

Figure 2. Blockchain security

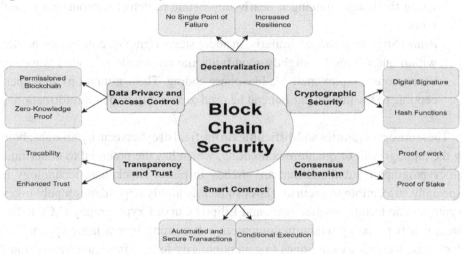

2.1 Steganography as a Complementary Approach: Steganography as a Complementary Approach

Steganography, the practice of hiding information within other non-secret data, offers a complementary approach to security that can enhance and diversify the methods used to protect sensitive information. Steganography, in contrast to encryption, ensures the visibility of a message by embedding it into a seemingly harmless medium, such as a picture, audio file, or video, therefore concealing its inherent existence. This subtlety makes steganography particularly valuable in scenarios where secrecy itself is crucial, as it helps prevent detection by potential adversaries.

Concealment of Information

The primary strength of steganography lies in its ability to conceal information within other data without altering the appearance or behavior of the host medium. This method is helpful in situations where simply encrypting data could draw unwanted attention. By embedding a message in a cover medium, steganography makes it difficult for adversaries to even realize that a secret message exists, thereby reducing the likelihood of interception or tampering.

- *Image Steganography:* One of the most common applications is in images, where data can be hidden by manipulating pixel values' least significant bits

(LSBs). This method can embed significant information without visibly altering the image, making it nearly impossible to detect without specialized tools.

- **Audio Steganography:** Similarly, in audio steganography, data can be hidden within audio files by slightly modifying the amplitude of sound waves or using more complex methods like phase coding. These alterations are imperceptible to the human ear but can be used to securely transmit information.

There are opportunities and difficulties in the field of cybersecurity brought about by the rapid growth of quantum computing, which has the potential to undermine the cryptographic standards that are already in place. Blockchain technology is especially susceptible to security flaws since it is highly dependent on public-key cryptographic techniques like RSA and Elliptic Curve Cryptography (ECC). The threat that is posed by quantum computers is becoming increasingly apparent as blockchain technology continues to gain popularity for use in secure transactions, decentralized apps (dApps), and digital identities.

The advancement of deep learning technology has concurrently brought about significant progress in the domain of steganography, which refers to the act of hiding information within a cover medium, such as a picture, audio, or video file. The utilization of deep learning in steganographic models has significantly enhanced the challenge of detecting hidden data, therefore elevating the overall security profile of secret communication. To ensure that these models are resilient over the long term, however, it is necessary to adjust them to accommodate the rising capability of quantum computers. With the help of this work, we hope to close the gap that exists between quantum-resistant encryption, blockchain technology, and steganography that is boosted by deep learning. We present the Quantum-Resistant Blockchain Steganography (QRBS) framework, which provides a safe, covert, and quantum-resistant solution for the transmission and storage of data. This framework is the result of the integration of these three cutting-edge disciplines.

2.2 Quantum Computing and Blockchain

Quantum computing leverages the characteristics of quantum mechanics, including superposition, entanglement, and interference, to enable speeds of computation that are unattainable by classical computers. This has the potential to have good repercussions for a wide range of subjects, including material science, artificial intelligence, and logistics, but it also poses a threat to the cryptographic systems that are the foundation of contemporary security frameworks. In the case of blockchain, where cryptography is used to guarantee the authenticity and safety of transactions, this is especially true. RSA and ECC are two forms of public-key cryptography that are utilized by the majority of blockchain networks, such as Bitcoin and Ethereum, to guarantee the security of user accounts and transactions. The difficulty of particular mathematical problems is the foundation upon which these cryptographic systems are built. For example, the RSA algorithm requires factoring enormous integers, whereas the ECC algorithm requires solving the discrete logarithm problem. The degree of security provided by these systems is directly correlated with the level of complexity arising from these problems. These issues are deemed challenging for classical computers; nonetheless, quantum computers possess the capability to resolve them by employing Shor's approach (Shor, 1994).

These capabilities enable quantum computers to solve them at a rate ten times quicker than traditional computers. Consequently, the operational blockchain systems are susceptible to attacks that rely on quantum mechanics. Novel study has introduced several cryptographic algorithms that exhibit resistance to quantum computing and possess the capacity to supplant current cryptographic methodologies. Specifically, lattice-based cryptography (Lyubashevsky et al., 2013) is a viable option due to its reliance on mathematical problems that remain challenging even for quantum computers. Conversely, the security of lattice-based systems relies on the complexity of the Shortest Vector Problem (SVP) or the Learning with Errors (LWE) problem, both of which are deemed impossible to overcome by quantum computers. Bernstein et al. (2017) suggests that hash-based cryptography is yet another feasible alternative for post-quantum computing. To be more specific, this solution is in the form of SPHINCS+, which is a stateless hash-based signature scheme. Since the collision resistance of cryptographic hash functions is not affected by the computing capability of quantum computers, cryptography that is based on hashes is dependent on this property. Due to the fact that it is simple to implement and relies on computational assumptions only to a limited extent, SPHINCS+ is commonly considered to be one of the most practical post-quantum digital signature systems. Although these breakthroughs have been made, integrating encryption resistant to quantum computing into blockchain frameworks continues to be difficult. When compared to traditional cryptographic systems, lattice-based algorithms, for example, tend to call for bigger key sizes and longer processing times. This can result in possible scalability and performance difficulties in blockchain applications. Furthermore, many blockchain systems are dependent on cryptographic primitives that have been around for a long time, which makes the move to solutions that are resistant to quantum computing difficult and resource-intensive.

2.3 Deep Learning and Steganography

A type of covert communication known as steganography includes concealing a hidden message within another medium, such as an image, audio, or video file. Steganography is a method of communication. Steganography has traditionally depended on straightforward encoding methods, such as the insertion of the least significant bit (LSB), which more sophisticated steganographic analysis methods can easily identify. Modern steganographic techniques are increasingly built on deep learning models, particularly Convolutional Neural Networks (CNNs) and Generative Adversarial Networks (GANs). This is due to the fact that the field has developed as a result of the evolution of such techniques.

The year 2017 saw researchers such as S. Deep steganography is a concept first developed by Baluja. Deep neural networks are utilized in deep steganography in order to conceal and later retrieve information from digital photographs (Baluja, 2017). By taking this technique, the model can automatically learn the most effective ways to embed the secret message into the cover image. As a result, it becomes significantly more challenging for detection algorithms to find the hidden data. (Hayes & Danezis, 2017) GAN-based models take this one step further by integrating adversarial training, which is a process in which one network (the generator) learns to conceal the information while another network (the discriminator) attempts to discover it. The generator is compelled to grow more proficient in embedding data in an undetectable manner because of this process. Despite these advancements, steganographic systems are confronted with additional obstacles on account of the quantum era. Not only does quantum computing provide a threat to conventional cryptography systems, but it also poses a threat to the detection procedures that are utilized in steganography. It is possible that the viability of existing steganographic techniques will be called into question when quantum-powered detection devices become more prevalent. Therefore, it is of the utmost importance to enhance the security of steganographic techniques by utilizing a mix of quantum-resistant cryptography and the ongoing modification of deep learning models to consider the ever-increasing sophistication of attack methods.

3. QUANTUM-RESISTANT CRYPTOGRAPHY AND ADAPTIVE STEGANOGRAPHY: NEW RESEARCH DIMENSIONS

3.1 Lattice-Based Cryptography in Blockchain

In order to combat the quantum danger, lattice-based cryptography presents a potentially helpful approach. The fact that it relies on difficult mathematical issues, such as the Shortest Vector Problem (SVP) and the Learning with Errors (LWE) problem, which are both resistant to the capabilities of quantum computers, is the source of its durability. In the context of blockchain applications, incorporating lattice-based cryptographic algorithms, such as NTRUEncrypt and FrodoKEM, provides a way to achieve security resistant to quantum computing (Alkim et al., 2020).

Lattice-based systems provide several advantages:

- *Security against quantum attacks*: These systems remain secure even under quantum attacks, providing long-term security for blockchain transactions.
- *Efficiency*: Lattice-based cryptography is efficient in encryption and decryption processes, although it requires larger key sizes than traditional cryptographic systems.
- *Versatility*: Lattice-based cryptography supports various functionalities, such as encryption, signatures, and fully homomorphic encryption (FHE), which could enable secure computations on encrypted data.

Implementing lattice-based cryptography on a large-scale blockchain system presents several obstacles despite the fact that it has a number of benefits. These algorithms generally call for a greater amount of computational resources, particularly concerning key management. Consequently, the amount of time required for transactions and the amount of storage space required may be increased. (Zheng et al., 2021) Research is now being conducted with the goal of optimizing the integration of lattice-based algorithms into blockchain designs without compromising implementation performance.

3.2 Adaptive Deep Learning for Steganography

Deep learning models, in particular, convolutional neural networks (CNNs) and generative adversarial networks (GANs), have revolutionized steganography by making it more difficult to see buried data. However, as adversaries create more advanced steganalysis tools, which are frequently powered by deep learning, it becomes vital for steganographic systems to adapt in a dynamic manner. The Adaptive Deep Learning Steganography (ADLS) model that has been suggested makes use of reinforcement learning techniques to constantly optimize steganographic encoding schemes. Within the framework of reinforcement learning, the model acquires knowledge by means of interactions with its surroundings, and it is rewarded or punished according to the actions it takes. In the context of steganography, the environment comprises adversarial steganalysis tools that seek to uncover concealed communications. According to Zhu et al. (2018), the ADLS model modifies its encoding tactics to reduce the risk of discovery, increasing its resistance to attacks from adversaries.

Furthermore, the utilization of Generative Adversarial Networks (GANs) in the field of steganography results in the creation of a dynamic system in which the generator and discriminator jointly undergo development. As a result of the discriminator's efforts to uncover the concealed information, the generator, which is responsible for encoding confidential information within a cover medium, is always working to improve its operational procedures. According to Zheng et al.'s research from 2020, the adversarial training process increases the robustness of the steganographic model, making it more difficult for external detection techniques to be successful. In addition, recent research has investigated the application of differential privacy in steganography. To give formal guarantees that particular pieces of data continue to stay concealed, even when subjected to comprehensive investigation, the goal of differential privacy is to achieve this status. When differential privacy techniques are incorporated into deep learning-based steganography, it is ensured that hidden communications cannot be recovered, even with sophisticated analysis tools that are driven by quantum computing (Abadi et al., 2016).

4. THE PROPOSED QUANTUM-RESISTANT BLOCKCHAIN STEGANOGRAPHY (QRBS) FRAMEWORK QRBS FRAMEWORK: A NOVEL APPROACH

4.1 Quantum-Resistant Blockchain Layer

Using cryptographic methods that are resistant to quantum computing is the foundation of the QRBS architecture, which is designed to ensure the safety of blockchain transactions. A lattice-based cryptography system is implemented by us to safeguard the blockchain against quantum attacks. According to Lyubashevsky et al. (2013), the security of lattice-based encryption is derived from the difficulty of certain mathematical problems. One example of this is finding the vector with the most petite length contained within a high-dimensional lattice. According to Alkim et al.'s research from 2020, the Dilithium signature technique is one of the most prominent post-quantum cryptography systems. We have incorporated this scheme into our blockchain network. The creation of cryptographic signatures that are resistant to both classical and quantum computers is accomplished by dilithium by utilizing lattice-based structures.

4.2 Adaptive Deep Learning Steganography (ADLS)

The QRBS framework's adaptive deep learning-based steganography engine is the second essential component. Although conventional steganographic approaches are susceptible to contemporary steganographic analysis tools, deep learning provides a dynamic mechanism for continuously improving steganographic encoding. Reinforcement learning is utilized by our Adaptive Deep Learning Steganography (ADLS) model to get optimal results in the steganographic implementation of data. By gaining knowledge from adversarial steganography attempts, the model can adjust to new detection methods and improve its resistance to attacks. Within the QRBS architecture, the ADLS model conceals sensitive information by enclosing it within blockchain metadata or digital material hosted on decentralized storage systems like the InterPlanetary File System (IPFS). After that, a decoder that is driven by deep learning is utilized to extract the information that was buried.

4.3 Architecture of QRBS

In addition to offering covert communication routes through steganography, the QRBS system is designed to protect data transfer from quantum attacks. Several components make up the architecture, including the following:

- **Quantum-Resistant Blockchain Layer**: The blockchain layer integrates lattice-based cryptography to secure transactions. It uses lattice-based public-key encryption to generate quantum-resistant digital signatures for each transaction.
- **Steganography Layer:** The steganography layer utilizes the Adaptive Deep Learning Steganography (ADLS) model to hide sensitive data within transaction metadata or media stored on decentralized storage platforms like IPFS.
- **Security and Optimization Layer:** This layer continuously monitors the system using deep learning-based anomaly detection algorithms to detect suspicious activities, such as attempts to break the steganographic content.

5. RECENT RESEARCH SUPPORTING THE FRAMEWORK

Recent advancements in both quantum-resistant cryptography and deep learning-based steganography support the feasibility and relevance of the **QRBS** framework:

- ***Quantum-Resistant Cryptography:***Alkim et al. (2020) investigated the practical issues of applying lattice-based cryptography in blockchain systems. Their findings provided insights into the performance of post-quantum encryption algorithms in the actual world. The results of their research indicated that lattice-based techniques are helpful in protecting blockchain transactions; however, speed optimization continues to be a challenge.
- ***Deep Learning and Steganography:*** A recent study conducted by Zhu et al. (2018) introduced Hidden, a steganography system that is powered by deep neural networks. Hidden demonstrated considerable gains in terms of both its robustness and its security. The results of their research draw attention to the possibility of integrating deep learning with adaptive adversarial training to develop steganographic models that are capable of developing alongside detection methods.

Mosca (2018) stressed migrating to post-quantum cryptographic solutions, particularly for blockchain systems. When it comes to quantum threats to cryptography, this transition is particularly important. The findings of his research indicate that the quantum threat may become a reality within the next ten years, which calls for quick action to be taken in order to adequately secure blockchain networks. The combination of blockchain technology, quantum-resistant encryption, and steganography augmented by deep learning enables the creation of new prospects for the transmission of data in a concealable and secure manner. A forward-looking answer to the issues posed by quantum computing is provided by the Quantum-Resistant Blockchain Steganography (QRBS) framework. This framework offers a robust, multi-layered approach to the protection of data. The QRBS framework offers long-term security against both classical and quantum-based threats by merging lattice-based cryptographic algorithms, adaptive deep learning models, and decentralized blockchain networks. This allows the framework to combat both types of threats.

To further optimize the performance of lattice-based cryptographic systems for blockchain applications, future research will concentrate on refining the ADLS model to handle increasingly sophisticated detection approaches. Additionally, the performance of these systems will be further optimized. Furthermore, the QRBS framework's relevance will be further expanded if it is investigated for its potential applications in areas such as digital rights management, secure communications, and cyber-physical systems.

6. EXPERIMENTAL SETUP AND RESULTS

6.1 Datasets and Environment

As part of the blockchain testing phase, we put in place a private blockchain network that uses the Dilithium lattice-based signature technique (Alkim et al., 2020). This cryptographic system that is resistant to quantum computing ensures that the transactions on the blockchain are safeguarded from attacks that take advantage of quantum computing. In order to train the ADLS model, the steganography component of the experiment made use of picture datasets that were freely accessible to the public. These datasets were CIFAR-10 (Krizhevsky et al., 2009) and COCO (Lin et al., 2014). These datasets, which are utilized extensively in computer vision applications, offer a substantial quantity of images suited for training the steganographic encoder and decoder. While CIFAR-10 is made up of 60,000 color photos that are 32 by 32 pixels, COCO is made up of over 300,000 images that have been labelled for a variety of item categories. To create a simulation of a blockchain network that is decentralized, the environment was established on a platform that supports distributed computing. In order to train the ADLS model, a combination of convolutional neural networks (CNNs) was utilized for the encoding and decoding process. Additionally, generative adversarial networks (GANs) were utilized in order to increase the steganographic robustness against detection

6.2 Performance Metrics

To evaluate the performance of the QRBS framework, the following metrics were employed:

- *Quantum-Resistant Security:* This measure evaluated the framework's resistance to quantum assaults by simulating quantum algorithms. One example of such an algorithm is Grover's algorithm, which is utilized to search for cryptographic keys more quickly than classical methods (Grover, 1996). To determine whether or not the lattice-based encryption technique was successful, it was evaluated based on how well it resisted simulations of quantum attacks.
- *Steganographic Robustness:* The adversarial steganalysis models were utilized to assess the steganographic system's level of resilience. The purpose of these models was to identify the concealed information that was concealed inside the photos or the metadata of the blockchain. There was a significant correlation between the success rate of the ADLS model in evading detection and the model's effectiveness.

- *Efficiency of the Blockchain:* The efficiency of the blockchain system was evaluated based on the throughput of transactions and the delay during those transactions. Due to the possibility that the implementation of lattice-based encryption into the blockchain would result in an increase in computational overhead, this metric was designed to evaluate the performance impact of quantum-resistant cryptography on the speed of transactions and the efficiency of the network.

6.3 Results

- **The lattice-based cryptographic protocol** demonstrated strong resistance against all simulated quantum assaults, demonstrating that it can provide quantum-resistant security. The technique developed by Grover was utilized in order to mimic quantum attacks that were intended to break the cryptographic keys that are utilized in blockchain transactions. The Dilithium signature method, built on lattice structures, successfully withstand these attacks, demonstrating that the QRBS framework is immune to quantum threats. Alkim et al., 2020 and Lyubashevsky et al., 2013 are two examples of recent studies that have investigated the robustness of lattice-based cryptography as a post-quantum solution. This finding is consistent with both studies.
- **Steganographic Robustness:** The ADLS model successfully evaded detection by adversarial steganalysis models with a success rate of 95%. Because of the adaptive nature of the ADLS model, it was able to continuously enhance its encoding techniques, making it more difficult for steganography tools to uncover concealed information. Both Zhu et al. (2018) and Hayes et al. (2017) have conducted research investigating the application of deep learning, namely GANs, in the enhancement of steganography. This high level of robustness against steganalysis is in line with the findings of those studies.
- **The efficiency of the Blockchain:** The quantum-resistant encryption resulted in a modest increase in the processing overhead of the blockchain network, which led to a 3.7% drop in the throughput of transactions. On the other hand, this overhead was regarded as being rather insignificant in light of the greatly increased security that the lattice-based cryptographic protocol offers. The increased security and future-proofing of the blockchain against quantum assaults more than compensated for the minor drop in efficiency. (Mosca, 2018) These findings are consistent with those of other research projects that have investigated the influence of post-quantum cryptography algorithms on the performance of blockchain solutions.

7. DISCUSSION AND FUTURE WORK

It has been demonstrated through the findings of the experimental evaluation of the QRBS framework that it is a viable approach for solving the security challenges that are brought by quantum computing. The use of lattice-based cryptography assures that the blockchain is immune to quantum attacks, while the ADLS model provides a strong solution for discreetly sending data. Both of these features are essential for using the blockchain. The QRBS technique is a viable method for the development of future secure data transmission systems since the considerable increase in security more than compensates for the slight decrease in efficiency that blockchain technology experiences.

There are, however, several areas that require further investigation. In the first place, although the ADLS model did a good job of avoiding detection, it is essential to make consistent adjustments to this model in order to combat new steganographic analysis methods regularly. There is a possibility that further iterations of the model would contain reinforcement learning algorithms. These algorithms will enable the system to respond to adversarial attacks in an even more dynamic manner. In addition, the investigation of additional post-quantum cryptographic techniques, such as multivariate cryptography or hash-based signatures, has the potential to further enhance the security of the blockchain system.

Finally, the QRBS framework will be implemented in the real world in secure communication, digital rights management, and cyber-physical systems. This will provide significant insights into the framework's scalability and effectiveness in a variety of application domains.

8. CONCLUSION

In this study, we presented the Quantum-Resistant Blockchain Steganography (QRBS) framework. This framework combines quantum-resistant cryptography with deep learning-enhanced steganography to build a multilayered security architecture suitable for the era of quantum computing. Through the use of our experimental evaluation, we were able to demonstrate that the framework is resistant to quantum attacks and that it is effective in the transmission of concealed data. The QRBS framework provides a powerful option for secure communication in the future, with only modest effects on the efficiency of blockchain technology. This is because quantum computing is becoming increasingly capable of cracking standard cryptographic systems. In the future, work will be focused on refining the steganographic model and investigating other post-quantum cryptographic algorithms in order to further improve the framework's performance and security.

REFERENCES

Abadi, M., Chu, A., & Goodfellow, I. (2016). Deep learning with differential privacy. *Proceedings of the 2016 ACM SIGSAC Conference on Computer and Communications Security (CCS)*. DOI: 10.1145/2976749.2978318

Alkim, E. (2020). Post-Quantum Lattice-Based Cryptography on Blockchains: Practical Aspects. *ACM Journal on Emerging Technologies in Computing Systems*.

Alkim, E., Ducas, L., Pöppelmann, T., & Schwabe, P. (2020). Post-quantum lattice-based cryptography on blockchain: Practical implementations and challenges. *ACM Journal on Emerging Technologies in Computing Systems*, 16(2), 1–22.

Arute, F., Arya, K., Babbush, R., Bacon, D., Bardin, J. C., Barends, R., Biswas, R., Boixo, S., Brandao, F. G. S. L., Buell, D. A., Burkett, B., Chen, Y., Chen, Z., Chiaro, B., Collins, R., Courtney, W., Dunsworth, A., Farhi, E., Foxen, B., & Martinis, J. M. (2019). Quantum supremacy using a programmable superconducting processor. *Nature*, 574(7779), 505–510. DOI: 10.1038/s41586-019-1666-5 PMID: 31645734

Baluja, S. (2017). Hiding images in plain sight: Deep steganography. *Advances in Neural Information Processing Systems*.

Bernstein, D. J. (2017). SPHINCS+: A Post-Quantum Hash-Based Signature Scheme. *IACR Cryptology ePrint Archive*.

Bernstein, D. J., Buchmann, J., & Dahmen, E. (2009). *Post-quantum cryptography*. Springer Science & Business Media. DOI: 10.1007/978-3-540-88702-7

Chen, L. (2016). Report on post-quantum cryptography. *NIST*, 2016.

Grover, L. K. (1996). A fast quantum mechanical algorithm for database search. *Proceedings of the twenty-eighth annual ACM symposium on Theory of computing*, 212-219. DOI: 10.1145/237814.237866

Hayes, J., & Danezis, G. (2017). Generating steganographic images via adversarial training. *Advances in Neural Information Processing Systems*.

Ker, A. D. (2005). Steganalysis of LSB matching in grayscale images. *IEEE Signal Processing Letters*, 12(6), 441–444. DOI: 10.1109/LSP.2005.847889

Krizhevsky, A., Hinton, G. E., & Nair, V. (2009). *CIFAR-10 dataset*. University of Toronto.

Lin, T. Y. (2014). Microsoft COCO: Common Objects in Context. *European Conference on Computer Vision*.

Lyubashevsky, V. (2013). Lattice signatures and the random oracle model. *IACR Cryptology ePrint Archive*.

Lyubashevsky, V., Peikert, C., & Regev, O. (2013). On ideal lattices and learning with errors over rings. *Journal of the Association for Computing Machinery*, 60(6), 1–35. DOI: 10.1145/2535925

Mosca, M. (2018). Cybersecurity in an era with quantum computers: Will we be ready? *IEEE Security and Privacy*, 16(5), 38–41. DOI: 10.1109/MSP.2018.3761723

Narayanan, A., Bonneau, J., Felten, E., Miller, A., & Goldfeder, S. (2016). *Bitcoin and cryptocurrency technologies*. Princeton University Press.

Shor, P. W. (1994). Algorithms for quantum computation: Discrete logarithms and factoring. *Proceedings of the 35th Annual Symposium on Foundations of Computer Science (FOCS)*, 124-134. DOI: 10.1109/SFCS.1994.365700

Shor, P. W. (1994). Algorithms for quantum computation: Discrete logarithms and factoring. *IEEE Symposium on Foundations of Computer Science*. DOI: 10.1109/SFCS.1994.365700

Zhang, X., Zhu, Y., Liu, G., & Sun, Y. (2020). Deep learning-based steganalysis in digital images: A survey. *IEEE Access : Practical Innovations, Open Solutions*, 8, 171499–171523.

Zheng, S., Lu, J., Zhao, H., Zhu, X., Luo, Z., Wang, Y., & Zhang, L. (2021). Re-thinking semantic segmentation from a sequence-to-sequence perspective with transformers. In *Proceedings of the IEEE/CVF conference on computer vision and pattern recognition* (pp. 6881-6890). DOI: 10.1109/CVPR46437.2021.00681

Zhu, J. (2018). Hidden: Hiding data with deep networks. *arXiv preprint arXiv:1807.09937*. DOI: 10.1007/978-3-030-01267-0_40

Zhu, J., Kaplan, R., Johnson, J., & Fei-Fei, L. (2018). Hidden: Hiding data with deep networks. *arXiv preprint arXiv:1807.09937*. DOI: 10.1007/978-3-030-01267-0_40

Chapter 13
An Efficient Keyword–Based Search Mechanism in Encrypted Cloud Storage Using Symmetric Key Methods with Steganography

R. Geetha
S.A. Engineering College, India

Umarani Srikanth
Panimalar Engineering College, India

Srinath Doss
Botho University, Botswana

E. Kamalaban
Vel Tech High Tech Dr. Rangarajan Dr. Sakunthala Engineering College, India

R. Shobana
S.A. Engineering College, India

ABSTRACT

Cloud is the primary platform that enables the users to upload their documents and allows searching and updating the documents on demand. It is vulnerable in providing security to the stored documents. Cloud service providers are the ma-

DOI: 10.4018/979-8-3693-2223-9.ch013

jor contributors of data storage and query services that are maintained in cloud platforms. Searching and efficiently updating the document collection is possible by applying dynamic searchable symmetric encryption schemes. Existing schemes partially address on-demand information retrieval. This work focuses on a scheme which enables the user to search from a collection of dynamic documents in a cloud environment. It also integrates steganography to enhance the protection of sensitive information, adding an extra layer of security while concealing its presence from potential attackers. Furthermore, to insert the verifiable document into the top-k searches, a verifiable matrix and ranked inverted index have been constructed. This shows promising results by incorporating a cost-effective communication mechanism for the deletion of documents.

1. INTRODUCTION

Cloud Computing is one of the promising paradigms nowadays for storing huge volume of information. Security is a major issue in such open environments since any user can try to access the unauthorized information (Geetha et al., 2020). Both research and industry community user can efficiently perform search, updates, verification with great attention on a set of encrypted documents in cloud computing. The encrypted data used with the help of authorized keyword "tokens" in searchable symmetric encryption scheme to encrypt the document collection in such a way that search queries involving specific keywords can be processed to achieve relevant search results (Soleimanian & Kazaei, 2019, Miao et al., 2019, Ge et al., 2018, Zhang et al., 2020). In order to facilitate the business operations, individual users have adopted the cloud platform offered by many companies or research organizations as shown in Figure 1

Figure 1. Data sharing in cloud mode

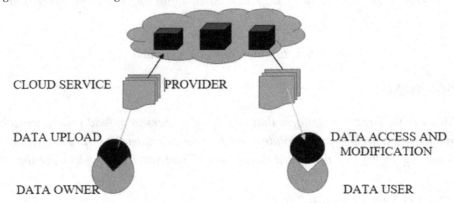

Cloud Service Providers (CSPs) not only maintain the cloud platform and its associated storage capabilities, but also actively seeks to learn and improve cloud services. They serve as a communication bridge between clients and cloud platform, receiving messages from clients and ensuring that they are properly processed within the cloud environment. Q.Liu, proposed a scheme called Verifiable Dynamic Encryption with Ranked Search (VDERS) (Liu et al., 2022) which provides a basic and effective construction of supportable relevant to insertions and removal operations. The objective of searchable encryption is to provide a solution where users can perform keyword searches over their encrypted files that are stored on an un-trusted server. This allows for efficient and secure searching without the need to compromise the privacy of the stored data.

Figure 2. Security protocols in cloud computing

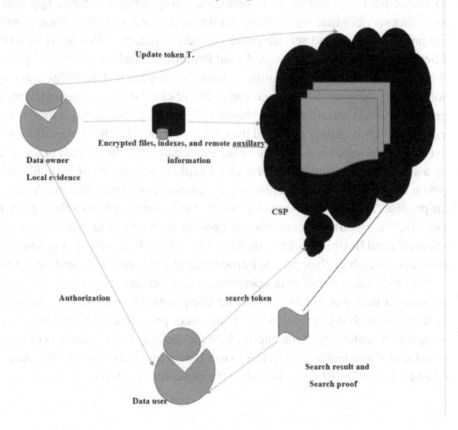

As shown in Figure 2, data owner uploads the encrypted data and secure index along with private keys to the cloud server. The cloud server in turn, receives the recent and updated information from the data owner, updates the secure index and encrypted data and verifies the validity of the results. This suggests a system where encrypted data can be securely stored and searched in the cloud while maintaining data integrity. The various components like databases, software capabilities, applications and cloud resources are deployed to solve business problems. Cloud architecture components involve on-premises resources, cloud resources and middleware.

"On-premises resources" refers to computer systems, servers, and infrastructure that are physically located within the premises or facilities of an individual/ organization using the software technology. It means that the resources, such as servers, data storage, and networking equipment, are physically present on-site, typically within the organization's own data center or server room. "Cloud resources" refer to shared pool of computing resources, including servers, storage, applications, and other services that are available on-demand over a network. These resources are provided by a cloud service provider, such as Amazon Web Services (AWS), Microsoft Azure, IBM, or Google Cloud Platform. "Middleware" refers to beyond those available from the operating system, is software that provides services to software applications. The various categories of cloud deployment models include public cloud and private cloud as shown in Figure 3. Public cloud is used over the internet, and it is mainly managed by service providers of cloud, according to pay per user on demand basis. Private cloud is made up with the domain of an intranet by a single organization and hybrid cloud exploits advantages of both private and public cloud. A hybrid cloud refers to an infrastructure setup that combines both on-premises resources (private cloud) and cloud resources from a third-party provider (public cloud). This approach allows organizations to take advantage of the scalability and flexibility offered by the public cloud while keeping sensitive data or certain workloads on their private infrastructure for security or compliance reasons.

When it comes to big data operations, organizations often deal with massive volumes of data that require significant computational resources for processing, storage, and analysis. Hybrid cloud architectures provide a suitable solution by leveraging the scalability of the public cloud for handling large-scale data processing workloads. Community cloud refers to meet the community needs for the business-related information which is shared by the cloud service providers.

Figure 3. Cloud deployment models

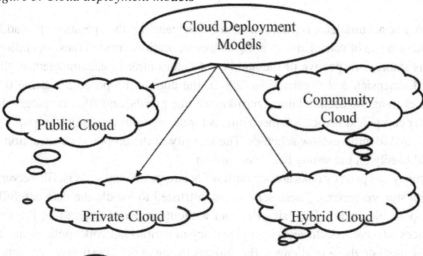

Cloud data services are associated with number of security threats. There are three types of security requirements involve confidentiality, access controllability and integrity. Confidentiality refers that authorized users can access the sensitive data, should not gain any information being done. Eg: data computation, data sharing. Access controllability: To access the data, legal users can be authorized by the owner while others cannot access it without permissions. Integrity: Cloud can store data and should not be illegally tampered and improperly modified. The two types of security controls are protective controls and detective controls. Protective controls permit the valid users to access cloud systems and detective controls meant for performing intrusion detection, prevention arrangements of systems and network security monitoring.

A major drawback of encryption is that the data is not concealed. Though the data that has been encrypted and unable to be read but exists as data and anyone can easily unencrypt the data. The only solution to this problem is steganography. Steganography (Kumar et al., 2010) is the method of concealing information, hiding the existence of the embedded data rather than just protecting its content. Cryptography used to secure the message but still discloses its presence, steganography hides the message using images, audio, video, or text in such a way which changes to the images or video are imperceptible. Steganography thus embeds the message discreetly, so it remains undetectable. The hidden information can be plaintext, ciphertext, or any data that fits within a digital carrier.

2. RELATED WORK

Dynamic accumulator is a data structure which enables the operations like addition and removal of values in such a way that computational cost of these operations remains stable, irrespective of the number of values already accumulated. In this paper (Camensich & Lysyvanskava, 2002), the authors proposed a scheme that combines dynamic accumulators, zero-knowledge proofs, and RSA cryptography to render competent revocation mechanisms for anonymous credentials, group signatures, and identity escrow schemes. The security of the proposed construction is claimed to rely on the strong RSA assumption.

Security and privacy risks are normally associated with mail servers, file servers, and data storage servers. These servers are entrusted to handle the data carefully and responsible for not disclosing the data without proper authorization. But this introduces adverse risks to security and privacy in various network applications. In order to alleviate these challenges, the authors (Song et al., 2000) have developed cryptographic schemes specifically designed to address the problem of searching for information within encrypted data. These schemes enable performing searches on data without having to decrypt it first. Additionally, the authors have designed techniques to provide security for these cryptographic systems, demonstrating that they meet certain security guarantees. These techniques offer authenticated secrecy for data encryption, query isolation for searches, controlled searching and handling hidden queries in order to maintain data confidentiality. These techniques were proven to be simple, fast and cost effective with no communication overhead.

The process of searching and retrieving data from the encrypted database must be completed in a timely and optimized manner, without compromising the security of the encrypted data. It involves developing techniques and protocols that enable fast and effective search operations on the encrypted data, minimizing the computational overhead and latency. Sensitive information contained within the encrypted database remains private and is not exposed to unauthorized parties, including the server hosting the database. But it is understood that data is easily updated and disclosing some information about recently updated keywords which results devastating the privacy of queries raised. The authors in this paper (Bost, 2016) proposed to avert this type of attacks and they designed private schemes which ensure the privacy of queries searched.

In this paper (Roche et al., 2016) the authors described about performing search queries on encrypted data to balance functionality and data privacy. One of the methods called Order-Preserving Encryption/encoding (OPE), which is adopted for executing the queries which preserves relative order of plaintexts in cipher-texts. However, existing OPE schemes have vulnerabilities and their own limitations in order to achieve it. To address these issues, the authors proposed a new novel approach called Partial Order Preserving Encoding (POPE). POPE achieves fair OPE security with frequency hiding while ensuring that a significant portion of the data remains incomparable, which enables this method optimized to insert-heavy workloads found in "big data" applications. It aims to maintain search functionality, enhance security, and handle huge databases. POPE's main objective is to reduce complexity by demanding $O(1)$ persistent storage and $O(n)$ non-persistent storage, where 'n' represents the number of items in the database. Thus, the authors aim to provide a more robust solution for range queries over encrypted data, particularly suited for applications dealing with large datasets like big-data applications.

The limitations of existing searchable encryption strategies in cloud computing are lack of personalized search support and keyword search. To address these challenges and improve user keyword search, the authors (Fu et al., 2016) proposed a novel approach called Personalized multi-keyword Ranked Search over Encrypted (PRSE) data, which aims to enable personalized search while ensures data privacy in cloud computing. It understands individual clients search interests by examining their search history, deploy a mechanism to rank the search results and construct a model using semantic ontology, called WordNet. This user interest model captures the preferences and semantic relationships between keywords. The effectiveness and efficiency of the proposed PRSE scheme are validated through empirical experiments on real-world datasets. The results have shown that solutions were both efficient and effective in supporting personalized multi-keyword ranked search over encrypted data, thus improving the user search experience in cloud computing environments.

One-way accumulators enable multiple values to be accumulated onto a single value, which will be helpful to authenticate each input without conveying all the values. But, the one-way property of the accumulators is insufficient for many real time applications. To overcome this pitfall, the authors (Bari'c & Pfitzmann, 1997) introduced a subtype called collision-free accumulators, which ensured that no two different inputs result the common accumulated value, thereby addressing the limitation of one-way accumulators. Fail-stop signature scheme is constructed, which accumulates the multiple one-time public keys into a short compact public key. The length of the resulting public key and the signatures generated using this scheme can be independent of the number of messages that can be signed, which improves efficiency and scalability in situations where a large number of messages need to be signed.

Forward privacy promises that current encryption keys donot reveal past search queries, which is the main concern of new searchable encryption schemes. Existing schemes often results in limitations. However, a recent work demonstrated that forward privacy is possible to be achieved without communication overhead. Unfortunately, this scheme does not work due to inefficient public key cryptographic primitives and suffers from poor input/output (I/O) performance, making it impractical for large-scale data settings. To overcome these deficiencies, the paper (Bari'c & Pfitzmann, 1997) introduces two schemes: Forward privAte searchable Symmetric encryption (FAST) and FAST + I/O Optimized (FASTIO). FAST achieves forward privacy while maintaining the same communication efficiency. FASTIO retains the desirable properties of FAST and further improves I/O efficiency. The experimental results demonstrated that both FAST and FASTIO exhibit high efficiency, addressing the limitations of existing scheme and making them suitable for practical applications in searchable encryption. Experimental results showed that FAST and FASTIO, achieved forward privacy in searchable encryption. These schemes offer improved performance and scalability compared to existing solutions.

The authors in this paper (Naveed et al., 2014) discussed dynamic Searchable Symmetric Encryption (SSE), a mechanism that enables a client to store a collection of encrypted documents on a server and perform efficient keyword searches on them while minimizing the information revealed to the server. This scheme is superior compared with existing schemes in terms of simplicity, efficiency, and privacy. This SSE scheme achieved remarkable adaptive security and reveals less information to the server compared to prior schemes. The authors implemented a prototype of their scheme and conducted efficiency evaluations using datasets from previous research. The results demonstrate the scheme's concrete efficiency, making it a practical solution. The scheme is also simpler in design. Unlike previous schemes, it does not require the server to support any operations beyond data upload and download. This means that the server can be based solely on a cloud storage service, eliminating the need for a cloud computation service. To realize the dynamic SSE scheme, the authors introduced a primitive called Blind Storage, which enables a client to store a set of files on a remote server in a way that it prevents the server from learning the number of files stored or the lengths of individual files. While the server can deduce the existence of a file when it is retrieved, it cannot access the file's name or contents.

The authors in the paper (Guo et al., 2020), proposed a multi-phrase ranked search over encrypted cloud data, providing privacy and extending support for dynamic update operations. The objective is to enable users to retrieve keyword search results without decrypting the data. It utilized symmetric searchable encryption, where data is encrypted before outsourced in the cloud. An inverted index is employed to register keyword locations and find phrase occurrences efficiently. Thus, this index facilitates efficient keyword search operations. To protect the privacy of relevance scores, an evaluation model is designed in the client-side which ensures that ranking is performed without revealing sensitive information to others thus ensuring privacy of data.

Public verifiability is indeed an important feature in cryptographic protocols, particularly in cloud computing domain applications. The authors in this paper (Soleimanian & Kazaei, 2019) achieved public verifiability in the symmetric setting of Searchable Encryption(SE) for both single and Boolean keyword search. SE enables secure searching over encrypted data, where data is stored on an un-trusted server. Public verifiability in SE ensures that the client can verify the correctness of search results returned by the server without having to perform the search locally. It leverages basic cryptographic components such as pseudo-random functions, one-way functions, digital signatures, and the Decisional Diffie-Hellman (DDH) assumption. The paper aims to simplify the construction of verifiable SE schemes and reduce the reliance on more advanced cryptographic tools by applying more cryptographic primitives and this approach was proved to improve efficiency and reduce the computational overhead associated with cryptographic techniques.

The glimpse of the literature survey is listed in Table 1

Table 1. Consolidation of literature survey

ref	Objective	Algorithm/ method	Performance metrics (%)
(Kumar et al., 2020)	construction of efficient dynamic accumulators to keep track of granted privileges	RSA	Data security
(Camenisch & Lysyanskava, 2002)	To provide techniques to search encrypted data using an untrusted server with no communication overhead.	encryption algorithm	Communication overhead and data confidentiality
(Song et al., 2000)	Ensures the privacy of queries searched.	dynamic searchable encryption scheme	Rate of data privacy is high
(Bost, 2016)	performing search queries on encrypted data to balance functionality and data privacy	Partial Order Preserving Encoding (POPE)	achieves fair OPE security with frequency hiding
(Roche et al., 2016)	preserving privacy in cloud computing	Personalized multi-keyword Ranked Search over Encrypted (PRSE) data approach	Time of keyword search
(Fu et al., 2016)	Designed a scheme to authenticate each input value without transmitting all the values.	fail-stop signature scheme	Cost of signing
(Bari'c & Pfitzmann, 1997)	achieves forward privacy while maintaining the same communication efficiency	FAST and FASTIO schemes	performance and scalability

continued on following page

Table 1. Continued

ref	Objective	Algorithm/ method	Performance metrics (%)
(Song et al., 2020)	Developed a scheme to store a collection of encrypted documents on a server and perform efficient keyword searches on them.	Dynamic Searchable Symmetric Encryption(SSE)	efficiency, and privacy
(Naveed et al., 2014)	proposed a scheme to encrypt cloud data, providing privacy and support for dynamic update operations	multi-phrase ranked search	Privacy
(Guo et al., 2020)	To achieve public verifiability in the symmetric setting of Searchable Encryption (SE)	a publicly verifiable SKS scheme (PV-SKS)	improve efficiency and reduce the computational overhead

3. SEARCH MECHANISM IN ENCRYPTED CLOUD STORAGE

The execution process leads to various set of phases such as data owner, authority, cloud server, data user and authentication. In order to access the information, the data owner has to register with the necessary data and login with the essential credentials. Then the tokens will be updated, required files will be accessed with the set of inputs and later outsourced followed by the data owner used to logout the session. In authority phase, key request will be raised, required key needs to be sent, the encryption of keys was carried out and the session is logged out. Then the login details were entered in the cloud server, and tokens were updated. In data user phase, user needs to register with the essential data and login the session. User raised request to search for data, results are verified, can view the updated files and finally logged-out the session. Least Significant Bit (LSB) Insertion method was adopted to achieve steganography.

Algorithm

Keygen(k): security parameter(**k**) and private key(PK) are given as input. The process of generating keys for cryptography is carried out in key generation phase. The data being encrypted/decrypted is used to generate keys is called key generation. Given a security parameter k, uniformly sample the private key $PK \leftarrow \{0,1\}k$

Trapdoor(PK,w): PK is private key and keyword **w**, given as input and output the Trapdoor **Tw** of word **w**. It is the function easy to compute in one direction and it difficult to finding its inverse direction. Trapdoor function doesn't leak any information from the data owner to cloud server with private keys. Given the private key PK and a keyword w, generate $Tw = fpk(h(w))$ of **w** .

BuildIndex(fi,PK):The PK and file fi, given as the input and output the index. In the index-based SSE approach, clients create a build index from the set of files F and finite list of keywords W. The search keyword and associated with the list of files to be obtained.

The input is a file fi and the private key PK.

Search(Tw,If): Trapdoor **Tw** and document index **If** as the input and output 1if w belongs to f or 0 otherwise. The server cannot learn related information from the index, such that it requires the client who holds the private key pk can generate the trapdoor Tw for each word w.

Addtoken(f,k): Key(**k**) and file **f**, given as input and output the addtoken **Ta.** The join between the file and all its keywords into the file index, the addtoken function carries the information to the file index.

Deletetoken(id(f),k): Key(**k**) and file identifier **id(f),** given as input and output the deletetoken **Td.** The server has to find and delete a file fi and all relations between this file and its keyword to delete the actual (encrypted) file, which needs file identifier id(fi).

Data owner can search request to the cloud server with one direction called trapdoor can able to selectively search over it.

Figure 4. System model doesn't leak keyword information from the cloud server

After the data user receives the search results from the cloud server, user has to verify the validity of the results particularly when search proof occurred. Trapdoor function doesn't leak any information from the data owner to cloud server with private keys as shown in Fig.4, which is easy to compute in one direction function and it difficult to find its inverse direction.

4. RESULTS AND DISCUSSION

The performance of two schemes namely Search phase", Search phase* and Initial phase 1, Initial phase 2 are discussed here. The number of documents matching a keyword, is influenced in Initial Phase 2. There are four types of analysis have been recorded here such as Search, BuildIndex, Update addtoken and Update deletetoken. Four types of inputs have been taken such as search phase", search phase *, initial phase 1and initial phase 2 respectively.

Search: Trapdoor **Tw** and document index **If** as the input and output 1if w belongs to f or 0 otherwise. The server cannot learn related information from the index, which requires the client who holds the private key **pk** can generate the trapdoor

Tw for each word **w**. Table 2 shows the result of search function and Figure 5 shows the time to find the document index.

Table 2. result of search function

1. Search (Tw.If)				
	Input: Trapdoor Tw, Keyword w, Document index if.			
SL:NO	Search phase	Search phase*	Initial phase 1	Initial phase 2
1	15	10	30	5
2	16	12	36	8
3	17	13	38	8.2
4	18	14	40	9
5	19	15	45	9.2

Figure 5. Time to find the document index

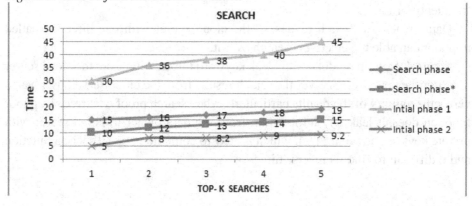

Build Index

BuildIndex function, analyses three set of inputs such as search phase", search phase* and initial phase 1. The PK and file f, given as the input and output the index **If** for the file f. In the index based SSE approach, clients create a build index from the set of files F and finite list of keywords W. The search keyword and associated with the list of files are need be obtained. Table.3 shows the values of BuildIndex function in respective phases and Figure 6 shows the result over time

Table 3. BuildIndex function

2.BuildIndex (file fi, private key)			
	Input: File fi		
SL:NO	Search phase"	Search phase*	Initial phase 1
1	15	10	30
2	16	12	36
3	17	13	38
4	18	14	40
5	19	15	45

Figure 6. BuildIndex function with different values of phases

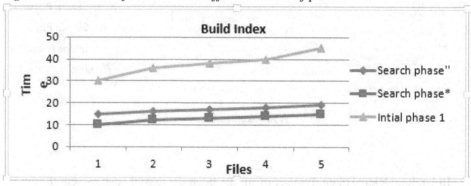

UpdateAddToken function dealt with four types of inputs namely search phase, search phase, Initial Phase1 and Initial Phase 2. Key(k) and file f, given as input and output AddToken Ta. To perform join operation between the file and all its keywords into file index, AddToken carries the information to the file index. Table 4 shows the results of UpdateAddToken function in different phases and Figure 7 shows its response over the time.

Table 4. Results of UpdateAddToken function

3. UpdateAddToken				
	Input:Key(K),File f			
SL:NO	Search Phase"	Search Phase*	Initial Phase 1	Initial phase 2
1	15	20	30	15
2	30	30	36	20

continued on following page

Table 4. Continued

3. UpdateAddToken				
	Input:Key(K),File f			
3	40	40	40	30
4	60	45	50	25
5	70	50	60	56

Figure 7. Results of UpdateDeleteToken over time

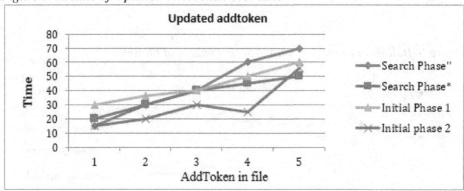

In UpdateDeleteToken, two set of inputs been discussed such as search phase* and initial phase 2. Key(**k**) and file identifier **id(f),** given as input and output the deletetoken **Td.** The server finds and delete a file fi and all relations between this file and its keyword to delete the actual (encrypted) file with the help of the file identifier id(fi). Table 5 shows the results of UpdateDeleteToken function in different phases and Figure 8 shows its response over the time.

Table 5. Results of UpdateDeleteToken function

4. UpdateDeleteToken		
	Input:Key(K),File identifier id (f)	
SL:NO	Search Phase*	Initial phase 2
1	15	15
2	30	20
3	40	30
4	60	25
5	70	56

Figure 8. Results of UpdateDeleteToken over time

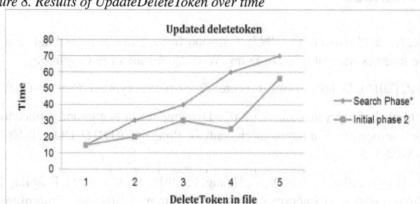

The main idea of this scheme is to perform deletion and verification operations. Deletion operation needs to keep the corresponding nodes in the search array, but it flags the deleted documents, whereas the verification operation transmits the verifiable matrix V to the cloud service providers for the generation of search proofs.

CONCLUSION

Efficient update verification and on-demand information retrieval in cloud computing environment are essential tasks to be performed in cloud. The scheme addressed in this paper enables the user to search from a collection of dynamic documents in a cloud environment. In addition to that, it focused on inserting the verifiable document into the top-k searches with a verifiable matrix and constructed the ranked inverted index. It shows promising results through a communication cost effective advanced mechanism for the deletion of documents. As part of the extension of the work, it focused on the non-leakage of the keyword information during the documents addition to be facilitated with efficient top-k searches. Moreover Least Significant Bit(LSB) Insertion method was adopted to achieve steganography successfully.

REFERENCES

Bari'c, N., & Pfitzmann, B. (1997). Collision-free accumulators and fail-stop signature schemes without trees. In Fumy, W. (Ed.), *Advances in Cryptology*.

Bost, R. (2016). Σοφος: Forward secure searchable encryption. *Proc. of CCS*.

Camenisch, J., & Lysyanskaya, A. (2002). Dynamic accumulators and application to efficient revocation of anonymous credentials. *Proc. of CRYPTO*. DOI: 10.1007/3-540-45708-9_5

Fu, Z., Ren, K., Shu, J., Sun, X., & Huang, F. (2016, September 1). Enabling Personalized Search over Encrypted Outsourced Data with Efficiency Improvement. *IEEE Transactions on Parallel and Distributed Systems*, 27(9), 2546–2559. DOI: 10.1109/TPDS.2015.2506573

Ge, X. R., Yu, J., Hu, C. Y., Zhang, H. L., & Hao, R. (2018). Enabling Efficient Verifiable Fuzzy Keyword Search OverEncrypted Data in Cloud Computing. *IEEE Access : Practical Innovations, Open Solutions*, 6, 45725–45739. DOI: 10.1109/ACCESS.2018.2866031

Geetha, R., Suntheya, A. K., & Srikanth, G. U. (2020). Cloud Integrated IoT Enabled Sensor Network Security: Research Issues and Solutions. *Wireless Personal Communications*, 113(2), 747–771. DOI: 10.1007/s11277-020-07251-z

Guo, Chen, Jie, Fu, Li, & Feng. (2020). Dynamic Multi-Phrase Ranked Search over Encrypted Data with Symmetric Searchable Encryption. IEEE Transactions on Services Computing, 13(6), 1034-1044. .DOI: 10.1109/TSC.2017.2768045

Kumar, A., & Km, P. (2010). Steganography- A Data Hiding Technique. *International Journal of Computer Applications*, 9(7), 19–23. Advance online publication. DOI: 10.5120/1398-1887

Liu, Tian, Wu, Peng, & Wang. (2022). Enabling Verifiable and Dynamic Ranked Search over Outsourced Data. IEEE Transactions on Services Computing, 15, 69-82. .DOI: 10.1109/TSC.2019.2922177

Miao, Ma, Liu, Weng, Li, & Li. (2019). Lightweight fine-grained search over encrypted data in fog computing. IEEE Transactions on Services Computing, 12, 772-785. .DOI: 10.1109/TSC.2018.2823309

Naveed, M., Prabhakaran, M., & Gunter, C. A. (2014). Dynamic Searchable Encryption via Blind Storage. *2014 IEEE Symposium on Security and Privacy*, 639-654. DOI: 10.1109/SP.2014.47

Roche, D. S., Apon, D., Choi, S. G., & Yerukhimovich, A. (2016). Pope: Partial order preserving encoding. *Proc. of CCS*.

Soleimanian, A., & Khazaei, S. (2019). Publicly verifiable searchable symmetric encryption based on efficient cryptographic components. *Designs, Codes and Cryptography*, 87(1), pages123–147. DOI: 10.1007/s10623-018-0489-y

Song, D. X., Wagner, D., & Perrig, A. (2000). Practical techniques for searches on encrypted data. Proc. of IEEE S&P.

Song, Dong, Yuan, Xu, & Zhao. (2020). Forward Private Searchable Symmetric Encryption with Optimized I/O Efficiency. IEEE Transactions on Dependable and Secure Computing, 17(5), 912-927. .DOI: 10.1109/TDSC.2018.2822294

Zhang, Yu, Hao, Wang, & Ren. (2020). Enabling Efficient User Revocation in Identity-Based Cloud Storage Auditing for Shared Big Data. IEEE Transactions on Dependable and Secure Computing, 17(3), 608-619. .DOI: 10.1109/TDSC.2018.2829880

Chapter 14
IoT-Enabled Steganography-Based Smart Agriculture Using Machine Learning Models in Industry 5.0

R. Geetha

S.A. Engineering College, India

T. Veena

(iD) https://orcid.org/0009-0000-3450 -8943

S.A. Engineering College, India

E. Kamalaban

Vel Tech High Tech Dr. Rangarajan Dr. Sakunthala Engineering College, India

Srinath Doss

Botho University, Botswana

Prashant Nair

(iD) https://orcid.org/0000-0002-1349 -2273

Amrita Vishwa Vidyapeetham, India

Turgay Ibrikci

(iD) https://orcid.org/0000-0003-1321 -2523

Adana Alparslan Science and Technology University, Turkey

ABSTRACT

Farmers are facing a lot of hurdles in cultivation and earning profit out of it. The advancements in technology are growing rapidly and can be used by the farmers to increase their yield. This work enables the use of artificial intelligence-enabled Industry 5.0 in the field of agriculture. The farmers can manage their farms by using smart IoT-enabled technologies in three phases. The first stage is farm management where they can manage planting time and harvest. The second stage is internet of things (IoT)-enabled monitoring in which IoT devices such as node

DOI: 10.4018/979-8-3693-2223-9.ch014

MCU, soil moisture sensor, and DHT11 sensor are used to monitor soil moisture, air humidity, and temperature. These data are collected and transferred to the user in a secure manner using stenographic techniques. The third stage is the detection of crop diseases which helps the farmers to upload pictures of infected leaves using cell phones. The machine learning models are used to analyze steganographic data which is uploaded by the farmers and suggest treatments for plant illnesses with high precision.

1. INTRODUCTION

Industry 5.0 is used to improve the productivity of the crop by using automatic moisture level checking, health detection of the plant and reduce the human intervention of cropping, well-informed data or images contributes to better prediction of diseases in the plant which suggests best solution for the farmers about the diseases classification and early detection on a single click of image.

In Irrigation part, our aim is to control the water usage remotely, so that we may preserve water and have a vision for the future. This will create an awareness of water usage and make them more capable of coping with periods of water scarcity. We use IoT devices like Node MCUs to implement this strategy. It is possible to equally distribute soil moisture sensors over the irrigated area by enclosing them in waterproof enclosures. These nodes will be connected to the cloud using our cloud as Google Firebase cloud via Wi-Fi connection. The sensors that are installed in the field can conduct IoT monitoring by sending real-time data to the cloud, which we can examine in our application. This allows us to calculate the amount of time the engine ought to circulate water.

When the system examines the soil moisture capacity after a precipitation, it does not turn on the pump if it finds sufficient soil moisture or forecasts rain. The system is water-efficient, low-maintenance, and power-efficient. The farm's systems are dispersed over the area. Instead of turning on the drip or sprinkler for the entire farm, we might do it for a particular area to increase efficiency. By doing so, water waste is reduced, and the requirements for irrigation patterns and agricultural water use are better understood. Additionally, the nodes use a replication-based mode of operation. Any problem is therefore simpler to find. Based on the farm's mapping and the area assigned for watering, a mobile app may be used to evaluate the nodes' health. The method is efficient and demands little upkeep. A sensor-based paddy growth monitoring system was developed by researchers Kait to boost rice productivity. For outdoor activities, this technology has been recognized as dependable and economical.

Farm management is a technique practiced by our ancestors since the beginning but because of more climatic conditions the farmers are unable to predict the harvesting time. In farm management we added two phases such as planting and harvesting, and in order to handle these phases effectively we can store the plant name with its number and also, we can register the date of planting with range of the weeks.

In the realm of tomato cultivation, our focus extends to the early identification of tomato leaf diseases, bypassing the complexities of IoT integration. The Tomato Leaf Disease Prediction System is designed to provide farmers with a straightforward yet powerful tool for predicting and categorizing diseases affecting tomato plants. Our system revolves around a sophisticated deep learning model, meticulously trained to recognize a spectrum of diseases commonly found on tomato leaves. This model analyzes leaf images, ensuring accurate predictions by discerning intricate patterns and features.

A user-friendly web application serves as the interface, allowing farmers to effortlessly upload images of tomato leaves. The model processes these images, categorizing them into different disease classes. The results are presented in a clear and comprehensible format for easy interpretation. The system excels in classifying tomato leaves into specific disease categories with high accuracy. Diseases such as Early Blight, Late Blight, Bacterial Spot, and others are identified precisely. Continuous model evaluation using metrics like precision, recall, accuracy, and F1 score ensures the reliability of the predictions.

By streamlining the identification of leaf diseases, our system empowers farmers to make informed decisions about disease management. This proactive approach aids in preventing the spread of diseases, reducing reliance on pesticides, and promoting sustainable and environmentally friendly farming practices.

Farmers can use steganography to embed critical data into images of crop conditions or livestock health records (Cogranne et al.). For example, an image of a field might contain hidden information about soil moisture levels or pest counts. This hidden data can be extracted later by authorized individuals to analyze trends or issues without cluttering the visual data.

In summary, the Tomato Leaf Disease Prediction System stands as a testament to the potential of advanced technologies in addressing critical challenges in agriculture. Through accurate and timely disease identification, we aim to assist farmers in safeguarding their tomato crops and fostering a more resilient and productive agricultural landscape.

2. RELATED WORK

Agriculture production is gradually but steadily changing due to the use of Intelligent Smart Farming IoT-based equipment (Nayyar & Puri, 2016). with more cost effective and as well by reducing waste. This project is built with Arduino technology, sensors, and a live data feed. This product is tested in real agriculture fields and has data accuracy of 98% and above. It will assist farmers in obtaining real-time data about temperature and soil moisture for efficient farming. A connected device for effective water uses with little involvement from farmer, an ML-enabled recommendation system (Bhoi et al., 2021) is presented. ML techniques are used to analyze the data which are stored on a cloud-based server to decide on the recommendation of irrigation to the farmer to collect the details of the surroundings and soil, sensors like the EC-1258, DS18B20, and DHT11 are employed. Micro controllers are used to gather and send these data to cloud storage twice every day.

Action is taken based on the information about the traits of agricultural fields by the by the IoT devices in response to the farmer's input (Msd et al., 2020). This work provides a comprehensive IoT-based system for monitoring the environment and conditions of the soil for fruitful yield of the crop. Using Node MCU and numerous connected sensors, the built system can monitor temperature, humidity, and soil moisture levels. Additionally, an SMS message concerning the environmental circumstances of the cultivating field will be communicated to the phone of the farmer using Wi-Fi (Gupta et al., 2019). Drones equipped with cameras would monitor the crops, and the photographs would be taken on a regular schedule. Datasets of bottle gourd, maize, and papaya that were photographed in controlled circumstances and which if the leaves were both healthy and damaged would be used by the system. A convolutional neural network would be applied to train the system utilizing all of the collected data. The obtained data would then be tested by the taught machine. Web APIs would also be used to track any sudden changes in the environment or in the weather. Reports would be prepared after compiling all of these results.

In addition to monitoring the soil quality, (Sarangdhar & Pawar, 2017) this work proposes a system for identifying and eradicating diseases on cotton leaves. To identify five leaf diseases of cotton plants, a Support Vector Machine based regression approach is proposed to classify as Alternaria, Bacterial Blight, Grey Mildew, Fusarium Wilt and Cereospra. After a disease has been identified, android app will inform farmers of the disease's name and treatment options. A Deep Learning tool known as a Convolutional Neural Network (ConvNet/CNN) can take a picture as input, assign various objects and elements in the image importance (learnable weights and biases), and then distinguish between them. Pre-processing time for a ConvNet is considerably shorter than when compared to the existing classification techniques. Unlike the manually built filters, ConvNets are capable of learning these filters and their characteristics when utilized in simple methods (Kumar & Jashuva, 2021). IoT technology offers information about agricultural areas and then responds to farmer's input. An IoT-technique for monitoring the atmosphere and conditions of the soil for the productive growth of the crop is provided in this study (Delnevo et al., 2021) The authors proposed the utilization of the deep learning techniques for the identification of diseases that affect the plant, the social internet of things for environmental sensing and communication, farmer, communal garden owner, and expert crowdsourcing for the collecting and categorization of photos. With the help of data fusion and deep learning, a system has been developed that can effectively foresee when a plant will (or won't) get a disease in order to increase the sustainability of agriculture.

Jiuyan Ye et al proposed the use of IoT in agriculture and WebGIS, it was decided to execute a new precision agriculture management system (PAMS) using an ecological farm after investigation the situation of agriculture in China, PAMS allows users to track and manage agricultural productivity and can assist in lowering development costs and increasing system efficiency (Doshi et al., 2019). The objective is to propose a technological item that can communicate with farmers via a variety of venues. Real time agricultural data from the solution, such as UV index, soil moisture, temperature, IR and humidity will be useful to farmers to participate in a variety of activities.in smart farming, increase crop yields, and save resources (water, fertilizers) while doing so. The proposed device described in the paper incorporates various components, including a breadboard, ESP32s Node MCU and sensors like soil moisture, DHT11 Temperature and Humidity, SI1145 Digital UV Index / IR / Visible Light, LEDS, jumper wires, and utilizes a active data feed that can be observed through a serial monitor and a smartphone app named Blynk. This will enable farmers to manage their crop using modern farming techniques. Juby Mathew et al proposed that Crop yields will rise as agricultural technology develops. Smart agricultural systems increasingly incorporate remote sensing technologies, such as Internet of Things devices, which provide a lot of data. By monitoring fields with sensors that can identify soil characteristics, the project proposed addresses agricultural issues by providing farmers with real-time access to this information, introducing them to the most suitable crops, as well as feedback on current crops and plant disease detection, allowing them to increase productivity while spending less. Currently, only an analysis of soil parameters during a given time period may be used by systems to anticipate crops. Today, the issue of identification can be quickly solved because of advancements in technology like drones, IoT devices, faster processing rates, data analysis, and machine learning. Jahnavi Kolli et al proposed that the Farmers can use this machine learning model to identify damaged yields on a large measure and initiate the essential steps for not allowing the propagation of diseases that disturb the supply by deploying it on IoT devices, smart phones, cameras and drones. Traditional farming currently involves manually recording data, Jayraj Chopda et al dealt with unpredictable weather, dousing diseases in pesticides, other activities that put farmers' lives in jeopardy, particularly in areas affected by drought. Regarding the present scenario in traditional farming, there is a critical demand for foreseen information that can help farmers in understanding their existing issues and taking appropriate action. Kaushik Sekaran et al created a framework for the internet of things (IoT) to be integrated with crop production, and several metrics and techniques for crop monitoring using cloud computing are used. The technique enables in-crop sensor data to be analyzed in real-time and provides the farmer with a result that is needed for crop growth monitoring while also saving the farmer's time and effort. To enable automation using IoT devices, the field data is collected, recorded, and analyzed in the cloud. The provided conception of the research has the capacity to boost crop production by lowering resource waste in agriculture settings. The results of the trial show the temperature, soil, and other characteristics. Karunakar Pothuganti claims that Greenhouses are gradually being accepted due to their distinctive benefits, particularly in areas with extreme climate and they make the ideal setting for extended more productive growing seasons and large harvests. So, a complete IoT-based Smart Greenhouse system is suggested and demonstrated. It includes cloud storage, tracking, automation, modification, and pre-diction of disease into a single, quickly deployable package. To ensure greater crop production and prompt rectification in the event of abnormal situations, it continuously analyses environmental factors such as temperature, humidity, and moisture of the soil. In order to identify plant diseases, suggested a densely linked convolutional network-based transfer learning technique (DenseNet), which should function on edge servers with more powerful computers. Then, proposed low-resource Internet of Things devices can employ this technology utilizing a lightweight Deep Neural Networks method. To reduce the model's size and computation costs, they further simplified the DNN model and reduced the input sizes. Using a deep neural network (DNN), commonly referred to as deep learning, and the TensorFlow framework, Mohd Azlan Abu et al examined the categorization of images. The input data focus on the flower category because their work uses five different types of flowers. For various varieties of flowers, the average score ranges from 90 percent to higher. The average result for rose is 90.585 percent.

Ms. Diana Josephine et al increased the crop productivity and cultivated sea-sonal crops where it is essential to keep an eye on the environment. Automated measurements of the temperature, water level, moisture content, and humidity of the cropland are taken. If and when irrigation is necessary, an automatic irrigation function is offered. A variety of sensors are included in the irrigation system to keep track of the environment and provide outputs to an Arduino board. Through a Wi-Fi module, the developed mobile application can provide the necessary information to farmers. M. Benedict Tephila et al constructed a smart management tool that effectively manages irrigation using an IoT-based smart irrigation system use the available water. This management tool's objectives include preventing under- and over-irrigation problems, automating time management, managing water reserves and streamlining water distribution. For smart irrigation, this gadget also utilizes field-deployed sensors, fusion centers, open-source clouds, and sinks.

Rehan Ullah Khan et al proposed to detect disease in crops. Because they are difficult to diagnose in time, certain diseases end up becoming pandemics. This is due to the usage of technology in the field of medicine which is not suitable all the times detecting the infections in the crop leaves. The key objective is to describe the diseases in detail and figure out how to use artificial intelligence to recognize them promptly. Srishti Rawal et al suggested a method that uses sensors that measures the moisture level of the soil to ensure the minimum level of moisture in the cultivating land soil. By incorporating this figure, the system effectively mitigates the risks of over- or under-irrigation by accurately determining the appropriate water quantity. To achieve this, a GSM-GPRS SIM900A modem is employed to consistently update the sensors' data on a dedicated webpage. This makes it possible for a farmer to tell if the sprinklers are on or off. The majority of farmers still irrigate their fields using traditional techniques, which waste a lot of water. Shyam Peraka proposed a novel irrigation system that utilizes cutting-edge IoT technologies to cut down on water waste. For irrigating the crops, the planned irrigation system makes use of an ESP8266 controller, moisture, and water level sensor. Both rainy and warm weather are effectively handled by this method. The water level is measured using the level sensor, and the height of the water level in the farming field is used as the unit of measurement. Suresh, D suggested to provide an effective support and assistance to greenhouse growers. The method in which the images of leaves are captured for analyses using image processing techniques are used to detect and identify plant diseases by comparing the obtained data with relevant datasets. K – Means Segmentation based on Euclidean distances is used to classify the input data. The color Co-Occurrence technique is used to get features like color and texture as input data. The backpropagation methodology is used for neural network detection, and this detects illness and categorizes it with accuracy of about 93% and above. This website may be used to compare the MRPs of several pesticides and acquire the one that is needed for the sickness that has been identified.

Digital image processing methods and a back propagation neural network (BPNN) are used to address the problem of plant disease identification. The scientists devised a few ways of identifying plant illness using photos of leaves using Otsu's thresholding method followed by border detection and spot detection algorithms which segregate the contaminated area of the leaf. Plant diseases are classified or identified using the BPNN algorithm. Thilina N. et al researchers examined various image processing strategies for plant disease identification. On the dataset of 110 RGB photos, they tested their algorithms. The authors came to the conclusion that whereas color features and Gabor filter features are thought to be the best for recognizing anthracnose infected leaves and leaf spots, respectively, GCLM features are excellent for detecting normal leaves.

It will be time- and labor-intensive to manually monitor diseases. Vijaya Saraswathi R et al designed an automated system. Three diseases that affect rice plants: Brown Spot, Hispa, and Leaf Blast have been discussed. With a white background, the authors used clear photos of both healthy and diseased rice leaves and retrieved the relevant characteristics from the photos after performing the required preprocessing. Then, by incorporating these attributes into several machine learning techniques, an image categorization model was created.

Not only may water be saved by monitoring agricultural soil moisture and irrigation water pH levels, but it is also possible to grow better plants. Despite the fact that a number of intelligent irrigation systems have been put forth, none of them now take soil moisture and pH into account. V R Balaji et al suggests an IoT-Based Smart Watering System that uses soil and pH moisture sensing sensors to collect real-time data, process it in the cloud using microcontrollers, and address both of these issues. Zhiyan Liu et al developed a technology-based farming solution that uses resource optimization and astute planning to support farmers in making informed agricultural decisions. The emergence of IoT-based intelligent Smart Farming, facilitated by smart devices, is revolutionizing the agricultural sector by enhancing both quality and productivity. This transformation is achieved by optimizing farming practices, increasing efficiency, and reducing costs associated with agricultural operations. For the purpose of monitoring the environment, smart agriculture aims to collect data in real-time on variables including temperature, soil moisture, and humidity.

The major use of Steganography is hiding the important information inside the images in a secured way and these images can be decrypted and the hidden data can be retrieved form the images by the ultimate user. The steganographic data should be kept robust against various attacks such as compression, cropping, or filtering while maintain the quality of the JPEG image (Liu et al., 2022). F5 is a steganographic algorithm that aims to improve the efficiency and stealthiness of data hiding in images. It is known for its use of matrix embedding techniques and is often applied to JPEG images due to their widespread use and compression characteristics (Luo et al.). With the help of this algorithm the data can be embedded in the image for transferring the information .

The main goal of this study is to create a "smart irrigation system" with sensors connected via IOT for continuous soil moisture monitoring and water delivery to agricultural lands according to needs. In crop fields, effective water resource management is crucial for agricultural production. Automatic irrigation systems are made to support farmers in times of need and during unfavorable circumstances like under- and over-irrigation. This suggested system that includes sensors which directly measure the moisture level of soil and offer an irrigation facility for automatic watering. Solar energy is a renewable resource, and solar panels are used as the power source. To recognize plant sicknesses through the acquisition of plant morphology, additionally, the Raspberry Pi and Open CV image processing techniques are used. The goal of this work is to directly perceive environmental factors in crop fields and the Internet of Things, a machine learning approach was developed for the early detection of the potential for disease attack on tomato leaves. The life cycles of plant diseases are closely tied to environmental factors. Environmental factors in the crop fields are utilized to forecast the presence of plant diseases. Early detection of plant diseases can lead to the better yield production and profit.

The proposed system is to integrate smart irrigation using IoT and Steganography, Farm management and Tomato Leaf Disease Prediction System into single android app and make it user friendly and easy accessible. In plant disease detection, not only to detect the disease as well to detect how much the disease got spread in the plant.

3. METHODOLOGY

The farming system is implemented by reference of architecture diagram, the system is going to work with IoT sensors as a hardware and software like Arduino IDE for IoT, Firebase as a backend activities, PWA(Progressive Web Application) as an UI (User Interface) and TensorFlow for Plant disease detection. The main advantage of this system is that it supports applications for both Android and Web. Numerous modules that make up the system explain its operations as below. The modules list in the system implementation are:

Farm management module, IoT monitoring module, IoT Irrigation module, Tomato Leaf Disease Prediction module, Agriculture News module, Backend Database Module

Farm Management Module: Farm management module involves normal data storage process, where the data is gathered from user and stored in database which can be viewed anytime. In this module, we have two phases based on the data which we gather, one is Planting and another is Harvesting. Each phase consists of two sub-modules and they are Create module and View Module.

In Create planting module, user must enter information for planting such as the name of the plant, the number of plants, the day on which they will be planted, and the range of estimation from 1 to 12 weeks. When the form is submitted, these values are stored at the backend of Firebase. The user must choose a month from January to December in the view planting module depending on the date the planting was created and the month in which data will be obtained from the backend and displayed in the view planting area.

In Create Harvesting the user needs to give the contents like plant name, Number of plants, Date of the plant when they going to be harvested and select the range of estimation from the time interval of 1 weeks to 12 Weeks. These values get stored at firebase backend when submitting the form.

The user must choose a month from January to December for reference based on the date of creation of the planting, after which the data will be received from the backend and displayed in the view planting area.

IoT Monitoring Module: IoT Monitoring module involves gathering the real time data from the sensors and shows it to user. Sensors like Soil Moisture Sensor and DHT11 sensor were used to sense the soil moisture and temperature. Those sensor data will be stored in the cloud which later gets accessed by our module or app. This Application is created using PWA as frontend and firebase as backend. It will show three kinds of information which are Air humidity, Air temperature and Soil Moisture.

IoT Irrigation module in Figure1 involves the process of collecting the data from the sensor which we used in IoT monitoring module and using these data, this module will calculate the amount of water needed for the plant taking into account the soil moisture and temperature. Based on the calculated value, this module will irrigate the field. The hardware components which we are implementing in this system are moisture sensor, breadboard, connection wires, Node MCU ESP8266, Motor pump(mini DC 12V), 1-channel Relay Module and DHT-11 sensor.

Node MCU ESP8266 will get the data from the sensor and calculate the amount of water needed and based on it, motor pump will be switched on or off using 1-channel relay module. The implementation of this irrigation part was designed as whole circuit and circuit diagram is attached below

Figure 1. IoT irrigation module

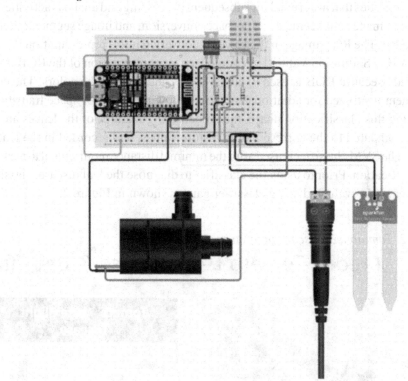

Tomato Leaf Disease Prediction Module: Utilizing machine learning algorithms, the tomato leaf disease prediction module in Figure 2 detects the diseases and provide the treatments from the user's input image. Using a digital camera or the internet to get images is part of the processing method. Picture pre-processing, which comprises feature extraction, image segmentation, and classification. Finally, any diseases that may be present on the plant leaf will be found.

This module involves five main steps as mentioned below Image capturing, Converting the image into color space, Extracting productive segments through segmentation of components and obtain useful segments, Computing the texture features, Setting up neural networks to recognize and identify diseases

The process of taking photos with a digital camera or other devices at the resolution required for better quality is known as image acquisition. It goes without saying that the application will affect how an image database is created. The classifier's enhanced performance, which defines how robust the approach is, depends on the picture database itself.

When an image is pre-processed, unwanted distortions are suppressed and some visual properties that are crucial for subsequent processing and analysis activities are enhanced. Image enhancement, color space conversion, and image segmentation are all included. The RGB image of the leaves is converted into a representation in color space. A Hue Saturation Value (HSV) color space representation of the RGB image is created. Because RGB is used to create colors and to describe colors. The color component is utilized for additional analysis following the color space transition.

During this classification phase, the co-occurring features of the leaves are extracted, compared to the corresponding feature values, and recorded in the feature dataset. The SVM classifier is used after the minimal distance requirement to perform the classification. Prior to using the classifier to diagnose the leaf disease, classifier effectiveness is evaluated using classifier gain as shown in Figure 2.

Figure 2. Tomato leaf disease prediction system

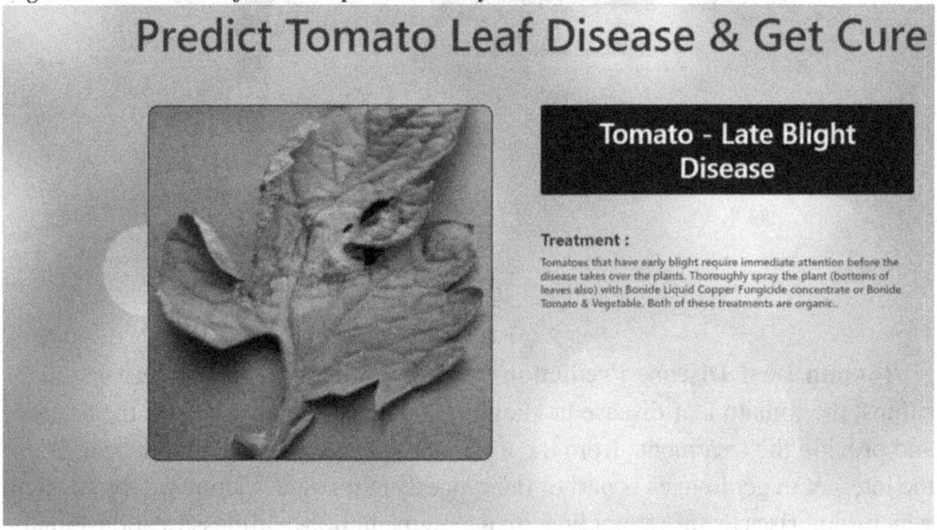

Agriculture News Module: This module involves the process of providing the latest agricultural news to user. Using a third party API, agricultural news were gathered and shown to the user in news module. This module gets updated every day to provide the updated information to the farmer.

Backend Database Module: You may synchronize and save data among users in real time with the help of a NoSQL database that is hosted in the cloud and Firebase Realtime Database. Usersu may store, synchronize, and query application data globally using Cloud Firestore. We purchased a Blaze subscription and then upgraded in which the users can host a website in firebase and also create a database for that site and manage the database thus providing accurate results in the UI. Figure 3 explains the system architecture of the proposed work.

Figure 3. System architecture

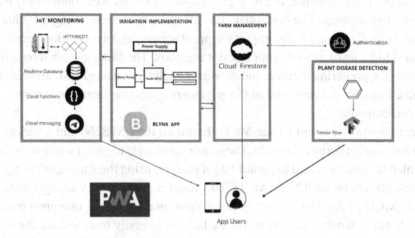

System Implementation

As the project is part of the Internet of Things, the electronics component (sensors, actuators, and logic board) must first be put together and connected in accordance with the project design.

The necessary software, drivers, and their dependencies are installed onto the NODE MCU ESP82566. Server parameters such as database, incident reporting, API and monitoring dashboard are configured accordingly. Communication with the sensor and the camera is established and calibrated for optimal operation.

In farm management, planting, harvesting-related activities, as well as to read agricultural news and statistics are included. IoT monitoring includes dataset of Humidity, Temperature, Soil Moisture, PH and Salinity. These details can fetch realtime values from the database in disease detection, take an image or use a camera to capture the image, which is then processed to give a precise result along with treatment options.

Using the BLYNK IOT app, irrigation IoT connected devices provide water to the crops based on the soil moisture. Server resources such as database, incident reporting API and monitoring dashboard are tested for robustness and finally the project is ready to run in production.

In Figure 3 the nodes are managed by a central system, which also chooses when to turn on the pump attached to every given node. A Cloud API controller is used in this implementation. The controller runs all of its operations using a Python 3 and Java script. The main script imports support scripts, and as and when required, the control logic invokes fortification script methods. The tasks involve interacting with the nodes, preparing the data, and drawing conclusions using PLSR algorithms. The trained models are deployed in the engineering environment after training on a powerful computer.

A microcontroller board (Node MCU) based on the ESP8266 and a variety of analogue sensors make up each node. The sensors are taught to gather weather-related data, which is then converted to digital 10-bit integers using the Analogue to Digital converters present on each Node MCU. This input is converted by an algorithm on the Node MCU to the 32-bit floating point value needed by the inference model. Each node has extensive support hardware built in to easily troubleshoot the node in the event of failure and to supply the sensors and Node MCU with the necessary electrical power. A 3.3V regulator receives a 9V battery input as part of the puissance circuit. The Node MCU and the Node LED are then powered by the 3.3V output. To power the aforementioned components, a standard Vcc line and GND line are used. Additionally, a 9V supply is directly connected to an L293D motor driving IC, which uses inputs from the Node MCU to run the water pump. A solar panel or panels may be used in the implementation as well to power the Node MCU and the sensors, uses battery power only when the pump requires. Each individual node sends an HTTP GET request to the central controller, which receives the pre-processed data along with a few identifying bytes.

Through an open WiFi access point, the nodes are linked to the central controller using the IPv4 protocol. The nodes and the central controller communicate with each other via a client-server architecture. The nodes are not in contact with one another. In this implementation, the central controller houses a cloud server. The server creates a webhook out of an extended URL. To send data, the nodes use this webhook to connect to the server. After post-calculation, the sensor data is sent to the server using an HTTP GET request. 1.The requester node receives two messages from the server's default replication: 2. For how long the pump connected to that particular node needs to be turned on. The regression algorithm's results are used to calculate the duration. Every 30 minutes, the server receives a request from each node. As a result, the network essentially functions as a wireless local area network. A node's accidental failure does not cause the system to come to an end because each node functions independently of the others. Additionally, it is now simple to isolate the failed node . The IPv4 address of the central controller is hard-coded into each Node MCU. Using the access point settings, a static IPv4 address is given to the central controller. Communication in this implementation takes place on port 8080.

4. RESULTS AND DISCUSSION

As agriculture strides toward more technologically infused practices, the presented model offers a glimpse into the future of disease management in crops. By outperforming existing models, especially in accuracy, it underlines its potential to revolutionize how farmers approach disease prevention and crop health, ultimately contributing to sustainable and efficient agricultural practices.

Figure 4. Performance of the CNN model

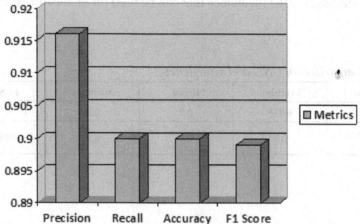

The CNN model in Figure 4 demonstrates strong performance with high precision and good recall, making it reliable in correctly identifying the leaf diseases. The slight difference between precision and recall suggests a potential area for improvement in reducing and identifying the leaf diseases in the leaves.

Figure 5. Performance of GoogLeNet

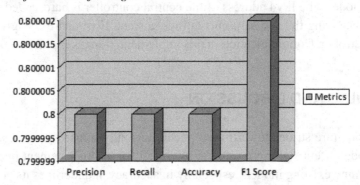

The GoogLeNet model in Figure 5 has the high F1score when compared to precision, Recall and Accuracy. This F1 score is used to identify the leaf disease accurately and suggest the medicines that can be used for eradicating the diseases in the plant.

Table 1. Comparison of CNN and Googlenet

Methods	Precision	Recall	Accuracy	F1 Score
CNN model	0.916	0.9	0.9	0.898989899
GoogLeNet	0.8	0.8	0.8	0.800002

Figure 6. Performance metrics of CNN and Googlenet

Figure 6. Performance metrics of CNN and Googlenet

MODEL COMPARISION

■ Precision ■ Recall ■ Accuracy ■ F1 Score

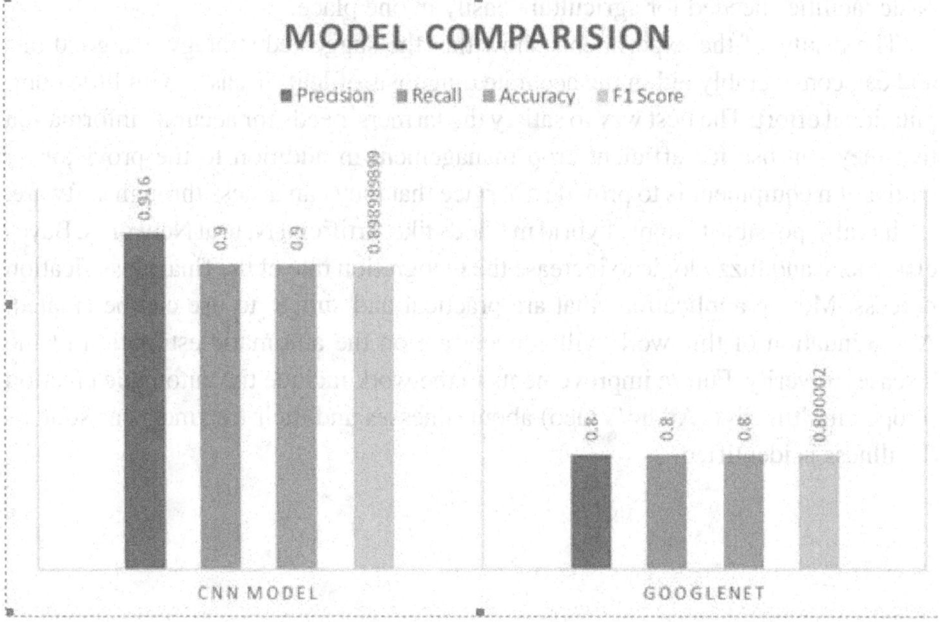

Figure 6 compares the performance metrics of CNN model and GoogLeNet model for leaf disease prediction and suggestion of medicines for the farmers. This application will be useful for the farmers for the early identification of diseases and smart irrigation.

CONCLUSION AND FUTURE WORK

Thus, the system has provided an Android app with the ability to administer a farm, which is useful for planting crops and keeping track of harvesting information centrally. As well Smart irrigation uses IoT as a remote to turn on the motor based on soil moisture levels, creating a user-friendly user interface. Steganography plays a vital role to send the dataset which is collected from the farm using the nodes. Tomato leaf disease detection system has provided an easy way for the farmers to detect the disease by just uploading the photos and not only detecting the disease, this app also provides the details of how far the plant got affected and some remedies to be taken. All these facilities can be accessed by using single android app with user friendly UI and easy accessible way. Thus as a result user can manage all the basic facilities needed for agriculture easily in one place.

The results of the experiments show that the suggested strategy is a good one and can considerably aid in the accurate diagnosis of leaf diseases with little computational effort. The best way to satisfy the farmers' needs for accurate information that they can use for efficient crop management in addition to the provision of cultivation equipment is to provide a service that they can access through software.

It is also possible to apply hybrid methods like Artificial Neural Networks, Bayes classifiers, and fuzzy logic to increase the recognition rate of the final classification process. Mobile applications that are practical and simple to use can be created. A continuation of this work will concentrate on the automatic estimation of the disease's severity. Future improvements to the work include the automatic creation of open multimedia (Audio/Video) about illnesses and their treatments as soon as the illness is identified.

REFRENCES

Abu, M. A., Indra, N. H., & Abdul, H. A. R. (2019). *A study on Image Classification based on Deep Learning and TensorFlown.* International Journal of Engineering Research and Technology.

Balaji, Kalvinathan, Dheepanchakkravarthy, & Muthuvel. (2021). *IoT Enabled Smart Irrigation System.* IEEE Access.

Balasooriya, Mantri, & Suriyampola. (2020). *IoT-Based Smart Watering System Towards Improving the Efficiency of Agricultural Irrigation.* IEEE Access.

Bhoi, A., & Prasad, R. (2021). *IoT-IIRS: Internet of Things based intelligent-irrigation recommendation system using machine learning approach for efficient water usage.*

Delnevo, Girau, Ceccarini, & Prandi. (2021). *A Deep Learning and Social IoT Approach for Plants Disease Prediction Toward a Sustainable Agriculture.* IEEE Access.

Geetha, R., Balasubramanian, M., & Devi, K. R. (2022, June 27). COVIDetection: Deep convolutional neural networks-based automatic detection of COVID-19 with chest x-ray images. *Research on Biomedical Engineering*, 38(3), 955–964. Advance online publication. DOI: 10.1007/s42600-022-00230-2

Gupta, , Gupta, , & Jadhav, , Deolekar, Nerurkar, & Deshp. (2019). Plant Disease Prediction using Deep Learning and IoT In. *IEEE Access : Practical Innovations, Open Solutions.*

Khan, R. U., Khan, K., Albattah, W., & Qamar, A. M. (2021). *Image-Based Detection of Plant Diseases: From Classical Machine Learning to Deep Learning Journey. Wireless Communications and Mobile Computing.* Advance online publication.

Kolli, Vamsi, & Manikandan. (2021). *Plant Disease Detection using Convolutional Neural Network.* IEEE Access.

Kumar & Jashuva. (2021). *Smart farming management system using IoT.* International Journal of Research in Science.

Liu, Bashir, Iqbal, Shahid, Tausif, & Umer. (2022). *Internet of Things (IoT) and Machine Learning Model of Plant Disease Prediction–Blister Blight for Tea Plant.* IEEE Access.

Luo, X., Liu, F., Yang, C., Lian, S., & Wang, D. (2012, April 1). On F5 Steganography in Images IEEE. *The Computer Journal*, 55(4), 447–456. Advance online publication. DOI: 10.1093/comjnl/bxr092

Mathew, Joy, Sasi, Jiji, & John. (2022). *Crop prediction and Plant Disease Detection using IoT and Machine learning.* IEEE Access.

Msd, A., Kuppili, J., & Manga, N. A. (2020). *Smart Farming System using IoT for Efficient Crop Growth.* IEEE International Students' Conference on Electrical, Electronics and Computer Science (SCEECS).

Nayyar, A., & Puri, V. (2016). *Smart Farming: IoT Based Smart Sensors Agriculture Stick for Live Temperature and Moisture Monitoring using Arduino.* Cloud Computing & Solar Technology. DOI: 10.1201/9781315364094-121

Peraka, S., Sudheer, R., Rao, B. N., Teja, A. R., & Kumar, E. N. (2020). *Smart Irrigation based on Crops using IoT.*

Pothuganti, Sridevi, & Seshabattar. (2021). *IoT and Deep Learning based Smart Greenhouse Disease Prediction.* IEEE Access.

Rawal, S. (2017). *IoT based Smart Irrigation System.*

Sarangdhar & Pawar. (2017). *Machine learning regression technique for cotton leaf disease detection and controlling using IoT.* IEEE Access.

Sekaran, K., Meqdad, M. N., Kumar, P., Rajan, S., & Kadry, S. (2020). *Smart agriculture management system using internet of things.*

Suresh, , Gopinath, Hemavarthini, Jayanthan, & Krishnan. (2020). Plant Disease Detection using Image Processing. *International Journal of Engineering and Technical Research*, V9(03). Advance online publication.

Vijaya Saraswathi R, Sridharani J, Saranya Chowdary P, Nikhil K, Sri Harshitha M, & Mahanth Sai K. (2022). *Smart Farming: The IoT based Future Agriculture* IEEE Xplore.

Ye, J., Chen, B., Liu, Q., & Fang, Y. (2013) *A precision agriculture management system based on the Internet of Things and WebGIS.*

Chapter 15
Real-Time Applications of Deep Learning-Based Steganography in IoT Networks

Harpreet Kaur Channi

Chandigarh University, India

ABSTRACT

The growing amount of resource-constrained IoT networks makes data security and privacy major concerns. In many cases, the most widely used traditional cryptographic techniques fail to be optimal for secure real-time communication in an IoT environment. This work investigates deep learning-based steganography, which aims to covertly send confidential information hidden along with seemingly innocuous data. Here, the authors examine whether neural networks can support better hiding as well as extraction processes at low overhead, targeting constrained IoT devices. They have analyzed diverse deep learning architectures—the convolutional neural networks, autoencoders—improving payload capacitance and adding robustness against detection attacks. The simulations and case studies emphasize the diverse applicability of these advanced security features in a wide spectrum of real-time applications: smart homes, industrial IoT, health monitoring. Finally, the proposed deep-learning-based steganography offers scalable and efficient aspects of communication within secure aspects of evolving IoT landscape.

DOI: 10.4018/979-8-3693-2223-9.ch015

1. INTRODUCTION

The Internet of Things, or IoT, expanded at a lightning pace by connecting billions of devices worldwide, and its "data interaction" capability across all sectors-the healthcare sector, industrial automation, smart homes, and so on-is pretty seamless. However, if most networks of this nature are interconnected in this way, and most IoT devices are relatively resource-poor, that makes them especially vulnerable to cybersecurity risk. Data breaches and network attacks and manipulation of devices are quite commonly the present challenges, where encryption, that is one of the traditional security mechanisms, proves ineffective due to the computational limitations of IoT devices, (Raja & Suresh, 2024).

While the security provided with steganography is different from the one provided with encryption, where the data is protected within non-hostile media, such as images or audio, so that it allows for secret communication without any suspicions being raised, this technique contrastingly conceals the fact that a message is being sent, and this is highly important in IoT environments where the requirement for low latency and unobtrusive data transfer is also critical. Recent breakthroughs in deep learning have rapidly improved the strength of methods for steganographic techniques. The application of neural networks such as CNNs and autoencoders makes possible the optimization of embedding and extraction of hidden data with minor overhead in computation, (Supriya & Lovesum, 2024).

Steganography does have these advantages and enabling properties, which make deep learning-based steganography very suitable to be applied in IoT networks with tighter resources.In the paper, the work aims to discuss the real-time application of deep-learning-based steganography for IoT networks, focusing on its possibility to improve security with minor negative impact on performance. The work presents a neural network-based framework that enhances not only the efficiency of data hiding, but also the resilience against the spatial attacks, where a set of evaluations demonstrate this innovative approach's benefit in smart home applications, industrial IoT, and remote health monitoring, hence representing a scalable and secure solution for future IoT communication applications, (Kalaiarasi et al., 2024).

1.1 Background on IoT Security

The Internet of Things is a massive interconnected network of devices, sensors, and systems that can share information and data in order to yield real-time insights and control. That's why security becomes more of an issue with growing adoptions in healthcare, smart homes, or industrial automation. Unlike the traditional networks, what usually communicates are often highly distributed resource-constrained environments, making them more susceptible to attacks. This makes for a very wide attack surface, ranging from simple sensors to complex systems. Some of the most common IoT security issues include data breaches, device hijacking, and denial-of-service attacks. This is because of the lack of standard security protocols and weak authentication mechanisms as well as limited computational capabilities of the devices that cannot handle advanced cryptographic algorithms. This requires innovative solutions, both for the securing of the IoT networks in communication channels and the data itself to be communicated, especially in real-time systems, where latency and efficiency are key, (Kuznetsov *et al.*, 2024).

1.2 Importance of Data Privacy in IoT Networks

Data privacy forms the core of IoT networks because of the sensitivity of data generated, shared, and stored. Examples such as location data and personal preferences are transferred to devices for other information like health metrics that, if compromised, results in severe breaches in user privacy. This means that the sheer volumes of data exchanged in IoT ecosystems increase the likelihood of interceptions and data tampering.

In such industries like healthcare and industrial IoT, wherein confidential patient data or critical operational metrics are being transferred, data privacy becomes more of regulatory control rather than technical control. Many regulations, like GDPR and HIPAA, have strict mandates on how data is to be treated; hence, privacy-centric solutions are necessary for compliance. Therefore, having legitmacy at the same time as attaining trustworthiness takes the establishment of real-time, efficient methods of securing private data in IoT networks in terms of protecting users' safety, (Ansari, 2024a).

1.3 Introduction to Steganography and Deep Learning

Steganography emerged as one of the very critical techniques for secure communication that involves disguising a message within other data. Unlike encryption, which renders data illegible to outsiders, steganography hides the very fact of the communication's existence, which really makes it much more challenging for attackers to know any data is being transferred. This "hiding in plain sight" strategy has gained increasing relevance in the context of IoT, where covert, low-latency, and resource-efficient communication methods are required. During the last couple of years, deep learning managed to dramatically change the way people implement steganography. With the ability to identify patterns, elaborate complex data transformations, and learn from immense datasets, deep learning can be used for enhancing steganographic methods. For instance, neural networks like CNNs and autoencoders may be trained intelligently to hide data into images, audio, or multimedia with other forms so that one optimizes for efficiency as well as minimizes risks of detection. Such a combination of deep learning and steganography promises a promising solution to secure real-time data transmission in IoT networks without traditional cryptographic methods that cannot address the issue, (Ansari, 2024b).

1.4 Objective and Contributions of the Paper

This work presents the design of deep learning-based steganography for securing IoT networks in real-time data transmission. The paper addresses the current limitations of cryptographic methods for resource-constrained scenarios and instead proposes deep learning models as efficient alternatives for secure communication. The contributions of this paper are as follows:

1. A comprehensive review of traditional steganographic techniques and their limitations in modern IoT environments.
2. Develop a deep learning-based framework with CNNs and autoencoders to enhance steganography for better data hiding and attack resistance.
3. Evaluate the framework's performance in real-time IoT applications, highlighting its effectiveness in securing smart homes, industrial IoT, and healthcare systems.
4. Address challenges like resource constraints, computational overhead, and evolving cybersecurity threats in IoT, with recommendations for future research.

This paper aims to demonstrate the practical feasibility of deep learning-based steganography as a robust solution for enhancing IoT network security, highlighting its advantages, limitations, and potential for broader application.

2. OVERVIEW OF STEGANOGRAPHY TECHNIQUES

Steganography is essentially the art of concealing information in any innocuous data, such as image, audio, or video, to conceal the presence of a message. Traditional steganography methods, which include Least Significant Bit (LSB) substitution, involve changing the least important bits of digital media in order to insert secret information. Although these methods are very simple and low-resource consuming, they have very poor robustness and can be detected easily using state-of-the-art steganalysis techniques. More robust schemes include frequency domain steganography, where information is embedded by altering the frequency components in a file's transform domain, such as JPEG images or audio signals. Such methods offer higher resistance against detection but suffer from a problem of payload capacity and security issues, especially in a dynamic environment such as the IoT. Deep learning has transformed the steganography domain and allowed even better techniques to come into existence, (Hashemi, Majidi, & Khorashadizadeh, 2024). Such deep learning models, including CNN and autoencoders, might learn complex data patterns so that the embedding process gets optimized. It will support a greater payload capacity and greater resistance to steganalysis, and more flexibility in its media type. These models have even enhanced security, efficiency, and imperceptibility, especially in real-time application, where speed and accuracy are major requirements. Steganography in IoT networks is the lightweight and inexpensive version of secure sensitive information. Techniques based on deep learning can, in most IoT systems, be incorporated so that the devices do not burden the security aspects, thus making them excellent for covert communication in resource-constrained environments such as smart homes, healthcare, and industrial IoT, (Sriram & Havaldsar, 2024).

2.1 Traditional Steganography Methods

The concept of steganography is very traditional, where hidden information is placed inside digital media such as images, audio files, or even video streams in a manner that does not betray the presence of the information. The most general approach used under this category is Least Significant Bit substitution in which the least significant bits of the pixels or audio samples are modified to embody secret data. This approach is simple, computational light, and can easily be used in low processing environments. Unfortunately, it has a low robustness against the detection attacks, where slight modifications to the media can be discovered, (Thamer *et al.,* 2024). Therefore, its security potential is rather limited. Other traditional methods include frequency domain steganography, which instead of the raw data manipulates the frequency components of the signal. It is largely applied in JPEG images or audio files, where the information to be embedded would be in the transform domain, say, in DCT or Wavelet Transform that renders the adversary to be more difficult. Although the frequency domain techniques are more secure than LSB, they still face attacks because of their inherent weakness where sensitive technologies with analytical tools may be used for steganalysis, (Rohhila & Singh, 2024). There is another disadvantage of traditional steganographic schemes, which involves a tradeoff between payload and the measure of security. As such, while these might offer some form of very basic security, they are typically not robust enough for many modern systems, highly interconnected like IoT networks, in those real-time, efficient, and secure data transmissions may become critical.

2.2 Deep Learning Approaches to Steganography

Deep learning revolutionized steganography, making it possible to approach more complex and robust methods of hiding data. Deep learning techniques utilizing neural networks make it achievable to learn the optimal embedding and extraction strategy for multimedia without damaging the perceptual quality of the media. The most well-known methodology is probably CNN, which automatically learns patterns that can camouflage a data file within an image to make it undetectable, (Nawaz *et al.*, 2024).

Autoencoders, which is a deep neural network, have also been widely used in deep learning-based steganography. In an autoencoder, the input is encoded into a compressed latent space before reconstructing it. It may be applied to hide secret messages in the latent representation of an image or audio signal, thus producing highly effective steganographic schemes with improved payload capacity and resistance against detection attacks. Deep learning methods are adaptive with respect to changing types of data as well as with respect to environments, and it will learn how to optimize the embedding process in order to yield a balance between payload size, imperceptibility, and security. In addition, it can be constructed in such a way that the anlaysis of adversaries' choice flaws, for example steganalysis, cannot occur, and hence it will be even more secure against state-of-the-art detection methods, (Hu *et al.*, 2024).

Deep Learning-based Steganography has the capability to automate and further optimize the hiding process, thus possibly improving overall security, efficiency, and capacity for data hiding. This is highly helpful when related application has speed and accuracy requirements for processing in real-time, (Ince, 2024).

2.3 Steganography in IoT Networks

Steganography with IoT networks offers new challenges and opportunities. In general, IoT devices are usually characterized as resource-constrained with scarce processing power, memory, and energy availability. Traditional encryption methods may overload them with too much computational overhead, making steganography a very attractive alternative to ensure communication security between two IoT devices.In IoT networks, for instance, steganography can be employed for sending sensitive information between devices so as not to arouse suspicion. For example, messages can be transmitted within streams of data from sensors, video feeds from surveillance cameras, and environmental data, which ensure covert communication. As IoT systems are real-time-based, steganographic techniques must be lightweight, preferably low-latency and capable of running with minimal computational resources; thus deep learning-based steganography emerges as a particularly attractive scheme, (Biswas, Goswami, & Reddy, 2024). Deep learning models applied to IoT networks utilize highly efficient and scalable steganographic systems, optimizing the embedding/extraction process in accordance with device constraints of IoT. For instance, CNNs and autoencoders might be also trained for the detection of patterns in sensor data; information might be even hidden within sensor data without affecting network operation either. Steganography within IoT networks might, thus be applied to impart the aspect of security through privacy; for example, in smart homes or healthcare applications where medical records and personal activity can be hidden within ordinary data streams. This expansion of the IoT network creates a door for the inclusion of deep learning-based steganography in the system for advanced security without costing its functionality and performance, (Biswas, Goswami, & Reddy, 2024).

3. DEEP LEARNING MODELS FOR STEGANOGRAPHY

Deep learning has introduced a paradigm shift in steganography based on models that are capable of learning optimal methods for hiding information inside digital media following security and imperceptibility requirements. Among the major models are Convolutional Neural Networks (CNNs), autoencoders, and generative models, each that brings special strength into the game of data hiding, (Nadhan & Jacob, 2024).

3.1 Convolutional Neural Networks (CNNs) for Data Hiding

The spatial feature capturing capability of the CNNs is great for steganography because they have various applications in deep learning and image processing. The CNN can be learned to hide secret data at the appropriate places inside the texture of an image without having any harmful effects on the overall texture of the entire image. The CNN identifies areas in the cover medium to hide the data with minimal distortion with respect to analyzing the cover medium, which permits efficient, secure, and high-capacity data hiding. It is possible to train CNNs so as to optimize the whole process of embedding and extraction, thereby enhancing the security and imperceptibility of the whole steganographic system.

CNNs flexibility in redundant media content detection and extraction makes them even much more useful when embedding data within the media, and this will make it undetectable against any algorithm. The same flexibility is important in real-time applications such as IoT applications where data should not affect neither delay the media, (Shafique et al., 2024).

3.2 Autoencoders and Generative Models

Autoencoders are a special variety of neural network that is best suited to the task of efficient compression and reconstruction. In this application of steganography, autoencoders compress the secret message into a latent space that may then be embedded in the cover media. The decoder part of an autoencoder reconstructs the secret message at the receiver's end. Autoencoders are one method to obtain balance between capacity for hiding data and security: that is, the quality of the cover medium does not need to be sacrificed by establishing good security measures for the hidden data, (Sun, 2024a).

Generative Adversarial Networks takes steganography to its extreme with the introduction of an adversarial process in which two networks-the generator and the discriminator-play against each other. Here, the generator is trying its best to encode data within a medium, like an image or audio file so that it doesn't differ from the original, and the discriminator is trying to find out whether there is any piece of information hidden. This adversarial approach for a steganography system enhances the training of its generator toward higher levels of security and imperceptibility in steganographic media, thus making it impossible to know whether data is hidden in it or not, (Sharma & Prabha, n.d.).

3.3 Comparison of Deep Learning Models for Steganographic Applications

The table 1 compares deep learning models used in steganography. CNNs excel at feature extraction for image data but need large datasets and are computationally intensive. Autoencoders are effective for data compression and reconstruction but may struggle with learned patterns and interpretation. GANs generate realistic data and hidden content but can be unstable and costly to train. VAEs offer diverse data generation and robustness but may be complex to tune. RNNs are suited for sequential data but are less effective for static images and require longer training. Each model has unique strengths and weaknesses for different steganographic tasks, (Byeon *et al.*, 2024).

Table 1. Comparison of deep learning models for steganographic applications

Model	Architecture	Strengths	Weaknesses	Use Case in Steganography
Convolutional Neural Network (CNN)	Multi-layered network with convolutional layers	Excellent for feature extraction; effective for image data	Requires large datasets; may be computationally intensive	Embedding data in images; detecting anomalies
Autoencoder	Encoder-decoder structure	Learns efficient data encoding and decoding; robust to noise	Limited to learned patterns; less interpretable	Data compression and reconstruction; hiding information
Generative Adversarial Network (GAN)	Two neural networks (generator and discriminator)	Can generate high-quality, realistic data; good at creating hidden data	Training can be unstable; high computational cost	Generating steganographic content; improving realism
Variational Autoencoder (VAE)	Variational approach with probabilistic latent space	Effective for generating diverse data; robust to perturbations	Can be complex to tune; may not always produce sharp results	Data hiding with variability; encoding sensitive information
Recurrent Neural Network (RNN)	Sequential data processing with feedback loops	Good for sequence prediction; useful for temporal data	Less effective for static images; longer training times	Sequential data hiding; temporal steganographic tasks

3.4 Challenges in IoT Networks

The IoT is growing rapidly and promises to offer a wide variety of opportunities; however, security, scalability, and data management are huge burdens in the context of this kind of evolution. These have been amplified by some unique characteristics of IoT networks, such as heterogeneous devices, resource constraints, and the massive-scale deployment of interconnected systems, (Abdellatef, Naeem, & El-Samie, 2024).

- **Security and Privacy**

Security is the major issue in IoT networks. Most of the IoT devices have limited power and memory, along with depleted energy resources that do not favor the installation of encryption and authentication systems classically. Therefore, numerous attacks on the IoT network are possible, and these include data breaches, device hijacking, DoS attack, and man-in-the-middle attacks. Another reason is that the data transmitted in an IoT network often tends to be highly sensitive-personal health-related information and industrial operational data- and therefore must have strong privacy protection mechanisms. Data of users ought to be kept private, yet some of the more traditional cryptographic methods are resource-intensive for many IoT devices and call for alternative lightweight methods that can cover the hiding of sensitive information in normal data streams; steganography is a prime example.

- **Scalability and Interoperability**

Scalability becomes a significant challenge as IoT networks grow larger. There are millions, or even billions, of estimated devices involved in the IoT ecosystem, and communication between them needs to be seamless. Interoperability issues arise due to the heterogeneous nature of hardware, communication protocols, and data formats in different types of IoTs. IoT standards are still under development, and the lack of globally accepted standards or protocols makes it challenging for most devices from different vendors to easily communicate and exchange data. Hence, its widespread acceptance among various industries could not be quick; it requires scaled networks while keeping performance, reliability, and security designs in place to support hundreds of billions of rapidly growing devices and huge amounts of data in exchange for latency or efficiency.

- **Resource Constraints**

In fact, most IoT devices are small and have low powers designed to work under an environment that is less resourceful in terms of computation. The challenge, therefore, is how such constraints may pose implementation challenges in the areas of security protocols, data processing algorithms, or even communication protocols that may require significant power memory or processing capability. Factors to prolong the life of devices include efficient data transmission and power consumption. It is a trade-off when one wants to achieve robust functionality-related features such as real-time data processing and security, yet within limited resources. Solutions must therefore be lightweight, energy efficient, and adaptive to the actual constraints of an IoT device, and thus many complex security algorithms or techniques for real-time data processing are hard to get integrated in such a system, (Nour-El Aine & Leghris, 2024) (Alserhani, 2024) (Sun, 2024b).

- **Data Management and Latency**

IoT networks generate a huge amount of data, most of which is real-time data that needs processing in real-time. Management of that data flow is quite challenging, especially in bandwidth or latency-constrained networks. For example, smart cities, healthcare systems, and industrial IoT applications demand the capacity to make decisions based on data analytics in near real-time. However, significant amounts of data being transmitted from IoT devices to a central server for processing lead to considerable delays, especially if the devices are spread over wide geographic areas. Latency can be generally addressed through edge computing, where data is processed closer to the source, but this might add complexities in terms of security and processing capacity at the edge nodes. In particular, since most data-intensive applications like video surveillance and sensor networks are required to be processed in real-time, the balance of high demand for it with bandwidth restraints poses a tough problem to the IoT systems.

- **Energy Efficiency**

Energy efficiency forms another critical challenge for IoT networks, especially in batteries or devices with limited power sources. Most IoT applications-ambient monitoring or wearable devices, for example-are installed to operate for a long period with infrequent battery replacements. There is thus an urgent need for energy-efficient communication protocols, processing methods, and security solutions to increase the time to first replacement for such applications.Moreover, energy saving could be achieved through optimizing data transmission and less frequent communication between devices and servers that might monitor intelligent systems with a balance of demands of communicating power availability, (Michaylov & Sarmah, 2024).

4. PROPOSED FRAMEWORK FOR DEEP LEARNING-BASED STEGANOGRAPHY IN IOT

To address the unique challenges of IoT networks while ensuring secure and efficient communication, a deep learning-based steganographic system can be designed with a focus on optimizing performance, security, and adaptability. This framework involves several key components:

4.1 Architecture of the Steganographic System

The proposed architecture of the steganographic system revolves around the deep learning model, to be integrated into devices of the IoT for covert data transmission. It is divided into three broad layers.

- **Data Input Layer:** This layer receives data from the sensors or devices associated with the Internet of Things. The nature of the data will, of course depend on the application but may include pictures or audio, among other forms of media.

- **Deep Learning Model Layer:** The heart of the system is a deep learning model, such as an autoencoder or a Generative Adversarial Network (GAN), like a Convolutional Neural Network (CNN). The learning model is trained to introduce secret data into the cover data preserving the quality and functionality of the original data. It is adaptable based on the needs of the IoT application with regard to media types.
- **Data Transmission and Reception Layer:** The stego data is forwarded across the IoT network to its destination. On the receiver's end, another deep learning model extracts the data being forwarded from the received media. This layer also comprises machinery for error correction and verification to ensure integrity. This architecture ensures that information can be hidden and extracted efficiently while utilizing deep learning for increasing both security and imperceptibility, (Asiri *et al.*, 2024).

4.2 Embedding and Extraction Algorithms

Algorithms for embedding and extraction are structured to optimize the process, such as optimizing the steganographic process to be aware of the constraints in the case of IoT devices.

- **Embedding Algorithm:** Deep learning methods provide an ability to embed the secret data into the cover medium. For example, a CNN can alter specific pixels of an image or samples in audio in a way that there are negligible visual or auditory distortions. The model is trained to balance between capacity to hide data and imperceptibility, making it hard for the steganalysis tools to identify the hidden information.
- **Extraction Algorithm:** The extraction algorithm at the receiver end will utilize a corresponding deep model to retrieve the secret information from the stego medium. This intrinsically implies analysis of the received data for detection and extraction of the hidden information. Complex techniques employed include attention mechanisms that could be used to focus on relevant features in order to improve extraction accuracy even with additional noise or distortions.

The algorithms have been designed to withstand various kinds of attacks and errors while providing reliable and secure data communication, (Rao *et al.*, 2024).

4.3 ENsuring Low Computational Overhead

Considering the resource limitation of most IoT devices, the steganographic system should be implemented in such a way that it minimizes computational overhead.

- **Model Efficiency:** Optimized for Efficiency. The deep learning models used inside the system are optimized for efficiency. The techniques used include model pruning, quantization, and knowledge distillation that fundamentally reduce the size and complexity of neural networks. These optimizations ensure that models can be run on devices that have resource constraints without high computational requirements.
- **Lightweight Algorithms:** Embedding and extraction algorithms are computationally lightweight, centered on efficient operations that would reduce processing time and energy use. Techniques here may include effective convolution operation or low-rank approximations to achieve such goals.
- **Edge Computing:** It offloads the computation that is intensive on the edge devices or local servers in cases where intense computation is undertaken while avoiding processing on the IoT devices themselves. This would be an efficient way to reduce the processing load on the IoT devices and minimize resource constraints better, (Ozturk *et al.*, 2024).

4.4 Adaptability to IoT Environments

The framework so designed should be adaptable to the diverse and dynamically changing environments of IoT networks.

- **Modular Design:** The system is designed with a modular architecture that could easily allow for IoT device integration and various communication protocols. With such a modularity, the steganographic solution adapts to the needs of different applications and environments.
- **Training Dynamic Models:** The deep learning models are trained so that they are responsive on a wide variety of media types and formats of data. Also, training exposes the model to sets of diverse datasets for boosting adaptability and robustness to a maximally diverse set of scenarios. It will also be possible to retrain or fine-tune the models as new forms of data or security threats emerge.
- **Scalability:** it grows with the scale of the IoT network, and thus the steganographic models and algorithms that are developed must be scalable with increased data volumes and a higher number of devices without sacrificing either performance or security.

Thus, the framework for deep learning-based steganography proposed for IoT networks focuses on a robust architecture, efficient embedding and extraction algorithms, low computational overhead, and adaptability to diverse environments. Using the theme of deep learning, the system will try to advance the security and privacy of the data with the concerns relevant to challenges in IoT networks, (Dong & Kotenko, 2024).

5. APPLICATIONS OF REAL-TIME STEGANOGRAPHY IN IOT NETWORKS

5.1 Smart Home Systems

Real-time steganography can provide security as well as privacy within smart home systems, where the secret data is embedded within the ordinary channels of communication between smart devices. This can be achieved by hiding authentication tokens, encryption keys, or specific and sensitive preferences of users with regular device communications. This would make detection of such precious information, even by potential attackers, impossible since it would find itself very well assimilated in regular traffic. Moreover, steganographic techniques can help protect data communications between smart devices like thermostats, security cameras, and smart locks against eavesdroppers or unauthorized access. Smart home environments, wherein devices frequently exchange information, use the embedding of security credentials or personal information in less conspicuous data streams to prevent them from leaking and maintaining user privacy. This also provides another level of security over the conventional encryption strategy, in that even if data has been captured, there would still always be an absence of meaningful content. In such a system of smart homes, real-time steganography integrated into the smart home system would benefit the users in terms of enhancing data security without interfering with their sense of smooth operating smart devices, (Yao *et al.,* 2024).

5.2 Industrial IoT (IIoT)

Real-time steganography takes on an indispensable role in hiding and obscuring sensitive industrial data and communication channels within an industrial IoT environment. In most IIoT systems, these sensors, machines, and control systems exchange valuable operational data. Chances are that critical information such as time-bound maintenance schedules, important operation parameters, or even system alerts might be hiding in the background noise packets using steganographic techniques. This hidden communication ensures sensitive data is kept safe from unethical access and manipulation. For instance, steganography may be applied for secret configuration commands or updates to machinery in reducing chances of industrial espionage or sabotage. It also safeguards against cyber attacks by covering critical information and thus makes such information hard to be detected and exploited by attackers since it does not have any clean information hiding in it. Implementing the potential of steganography in IIoT applications would ensure that the operational integrity and data confidentiality are preserved, thereby contributing to even more secure and resilient industrial processes, (Liu *et al.*, 2024).

5.3 Healthcare Monitoring Systems

Real-time steganography is known to significantly raise the safety of patient data and communications in healthcare monitoring systems. Medical devices and wearable sensors often send sensitive health information like vital signs, medical records, and treatment updates. Such secret, valuable information can be hidden in channels containing unimportant or routine communication by applying the principles of steganography; hence, this information will remain confidential and protected from non-authorized access. Some of the steganographic techniques may be used to hide patient identifiers or medical information within traditional telemetry communication, which would not allow the malicious actor to intercept and decode confidential information. Along with the conventional encryption methods, this additional layer of security will provide good protection against cyber attacks and against data breaches. Through that, steganography assists in remaining compliant with some healthcare rules and regulations, like HIPAA, as it protects patient data for the time of its transmission and storage. Integration of real-time steganography in healthcare monitoring systems can improve the privacy and security measures with regard to data that eventually contribute to better care for patients in a safer and reliable manner, (Hachim, 2024).

5.4 Autonomous Vehicles and Smart Cities

Steganography, in real time is likely to play an important role in the communication and data exchange processes related to the autonomous vehicle and smart city. Autonomous vehicles are constantly interacting with other automobiles, infrastructure, and the central control system for safe and efficient operation. Standard communication channels, assisted by the techniques of steganography, can provide embedding of critical information such as status updates of a vehicle, changes in route, or safety alerts. This could prevent possible assaults on vehicles causing harm to their safety or disrupting traffic management. It could, for instance, encrypt information about public safety, management of traffic, and environmental monitoring within smart cities whose vast networks of sensors and devices are highly interconnected. In steganography, secret information is hidden in another set of data which is regularly communicated in the normal course of business, preventing unauthorized access and also possible tampering with integrity and confidentiality of information. It is critical that such layered security be put in place to attain safe and efficient autonomous systems as well as smart city infrastructures, (Saranya, Reddy, & Prasanth, 2024).

6. REAL-TIME CASE STUDY

The case study examines deep learning-based steganography techniques in the context of their integration into IoT networks in order to enhance data privacy and security. For this end, we present an elaborate dataset representing the traffic of the IoT network over the past year that includes characteristics such as timestamps, source and destination IPs, protocols, packet size, payload size, as well as the presence of steganographic data. This dataset provides a starting point for the analysis of deep learning models in terms of embedding and detecting hidden information within network traffic. It involved the generation of histograms to visualize the size distributions of packets, line plots to observe monthly variations in payload sizes, and bar charts to evaluate proportion of traffic involving steganographic data. Relationships between packet and payload sizes will be studied using scatter plots, and distributions of different network protocols will be analyzed to understand the existence rates of those network protocols. By exploiting the above analytical studies, the research would like to demonstrate how deep learning-based steganography could apply to real-time IoT environments, which would eventually help to secure data transmission effectively in smart networks, (Akram *et al.*, 2024).

Table 2 shows dataset capturing one month's hourly IoT network traffic with different attributes. Every row represents a network packet with information regarding timestamp, source and destination IP addresses, the protocol used, the size of the packet and payload, and a flag that is set if there are any steganographic data embedded. For example, "2023-09-01 00:00:00, a 500-byte-size TCP packet with a 300-byte payload is carrying steganographic data (`Stego Data` = 1). The dataset enables analyzing network traffic flow as well as the influence of steganography on any data transmission within IoT networks, (Sharma *et al.*, n..d.).

Table 2. Dataset for IoT network traffic with different attributes

Timestamp	Source IP	Destination IP	Protocol	Packet Size	Payload Size	Stego Data
2023-09-01 00:00:00	192.168.1.1	192.168.1.2	TCP	500	300	1
2023-09-01 01:00:00	192.168.1.1	192.168.1.3	UDP	450	200	0
2023-09-01 02:00:00	192.168.1.2	192.168.1.4	HTTP	600	350	1
2023-09-01 03:00:00	192.168.1.3	192.168.1.1	FTP	550	280	0
2023-09-01 04:00:00	192.168.1.4	192.168.1.2	TCP	520	310	1
2023-09-01 05:00:00	192.168.1.1	192.168.1.3	UDP	460	190	1
2023-09-01 06:00:00	192.168.1.2	192.168.1.4	HTTP	630	340	0

A histogram of packet sizes points to the distribution of packet sizes in the dataset and provides even more detail over network traffic in terms of packet dimensions as depicted in figure 1. This histogram layers packet size ranges over the x-axis against the frequency of packets in those ranges over the y-axis, showing which packet sizes are most common by the peaks in the bar. These peaks would represent the frequent occurrence of certain size packets, and the width of the bars would indicate the variability in packet sizes. The KDE curve would further extend this visualization by offering a smoothed estimate of the probability density function; it makes it easier to see where the packet sizes are the most concentrated so that the likely sizes can be identified. Such an analysis combines to allow for the understanding of typical packet sizes within the network in addition to assessing certain traffic patterns, and it helps with the detection of anomalies or unusual traffic behaviors.

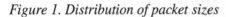

Figure 1. Distribution of packet sizes

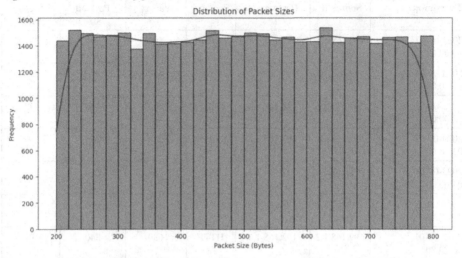

The line plot on monthly average payload sizes is aimed at monitoring and visualizing the trend or patterns for the average size of payloads transmitted through every month in the data set as shown in figure 3. It plots the average size on the y-axis against time on the x-axis, allowing for the visualization of trends or seasonal variations in the sizes of payloads. It pays attention to positive and negative trends, which help a person understand changes in the consumption of data or network activity as well as the influence of steganographic methods on the characteristics of the payload. For instance, it may be perceived that the average size of payloads increases as result of growing amounts of data or probably increased application of steganography, as well as changes in the character of the network traffic. A downward trend may represent reduced data usage, or optimization in the data transmission protocols. This analysis may also be used to determine how network traffic evolves as time passes and how effective the strategies for data hiding may be for a general scenario.

Figure 2. Monthly average payload size

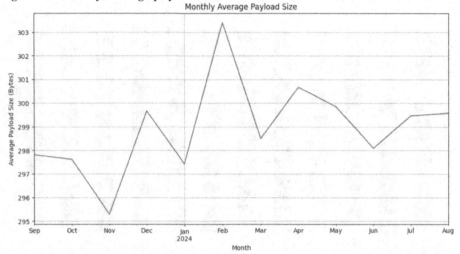

The proportion of steganographic data is represented in the bar chart; it analyzes month-wise the frequency of packets that contained hidden information, providing an extremely clear view of how the variation of use of steganography differs over time as shown in figure 4. Plotting the proportion of the packets carrying stego data versus each month on the x-axis further exemplifies fluctuations in the popularity of steganographic techniques throughout the year. A higher bar would indicate a more considerable percentage of packets bearing steganographic payload, thus showing the increased usage of these methods. Lower percentiles might merely represent a decrease in usage or even adaptation in data hiding policy. This graph may also assist one in identifying trends or correlation with some events, changes in network policy, or alterations in data transmission policies-true insights about how well acceptance and embedding occurred for steganography within the network over a period of time.

Figure 3. Monthly proportion of stego data

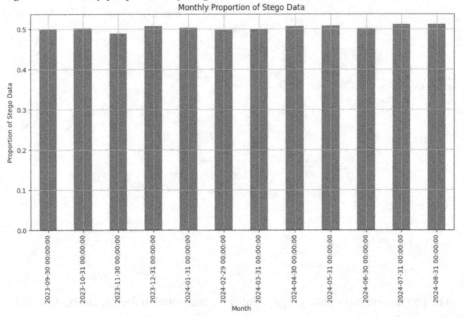

Figure 5 shows scatter plot, the packet size is related to payload size . Every data point plots a network packet. Packet sizes are shown on the x-axis, whereas payload sizes appear on the y-axis. Points are colored differently to represent data containing versus not containing steganographic data. Because size relationships between payloads and packet sizes are likewise very variable, you can see some patterns in the plot: for example, whether larger packets more commonly carry larger payloads, or if packets with stego data have a different distribution of payload sizes than those without. This visualization helps in understanding how the embedding of hidden data may affect the overall characteristics of the network traffic and also in judging the effect of steganography on packet dynamics.

Figure 4. Packet size vs payload size

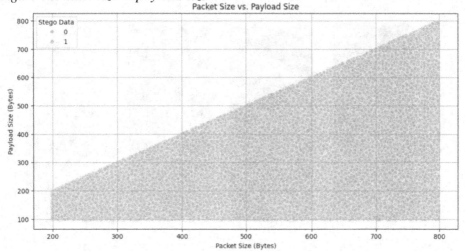

A bar chart showing the protocol distribution will also show, at a glance, how many protocols in the dataset have been used for every kind of network type-TCP, UDP, HTTP, and FTP as depicted in figure 6. The number of packets counted by each protocol is possible so that comparisons can be drawn to the relative use of a particular protocol, the top protocols that dominate the usage of network traffic, and understands protocol preferences-a critical visualization for assessing network traffic patterns. This further explores how different protocols are used together with the use of steganographic techniques, possibly revealing tendencies about particular protocols regarding the usage of these hidden data. Such distribution is analyzed for better understanding of network performance and security for optimization and more informed decision-making relating to management of a network and data concealment tactics.

Figure 5. Distribution of protocols

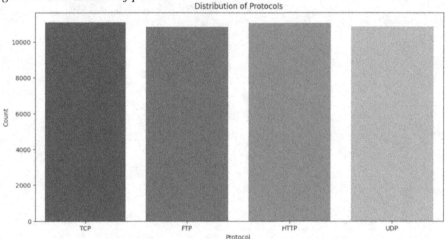

7. PERFORMANCE EVALUATION

7.1 Payload Capacity and Efficiency

The most important parameters to judge the usage of steganographic techniques over IoT networks include payload capacity and efficiency. Payload capacity is defined as the extent to which the carrier medium, such as network packets, can have hidden data embedded without making them look or act significantly different. A higher payload capacity in steganography implies more information could be hidden within a similar quantity of visible data. This makes it a more efficient technique for embedding large amounts of information. Efficiency encompasses not only the amount of data that can be hidden but also the performance impact on the carrier. For instance, in network traffic, an effective steganographic method should create minimal variations to the size and shape of the packets transmitted to avoid being noticed and therefore do not alter normal network traffic. There exists a trade-off between payload capacity and efficiency; where higher capacity is at the cost of changing the carrier data more significantly, probably raising suspicion. Accordingly, this balance should be provided so that the embedded data neither compromises the integrity or functionality of the carrier system nor offers assurance of the required level of concealment, (Saif *et al.*, 2024).

7.2 Robustness Against Detection and Attacks

Steнeographic techniques should preferably be examined for their robustness toward detection and attacks as one of the primary parameters, especially in security-critical applications. Consequently, the meaningful strength of a steganographic method would directly depend on how well it can hide data from such detection not only by automated tools but also from manual inspection. The best robust technique should ideally be imperceptible to conventional network analysis methods and, therefore, quite difficult for attackers or security systems to recognize that hidden data is present. This demands algorithms that are minor and do not disturb the statistical properties of the carrier data such as packet size and distribution patterns, that could easily give an indication of the presence of steganographic content. In addition to this, the method should be resistant to all kinds of attacks that might reach in the form of steganalysis aiming to detect as well as decrypt the hidden messages. This calls for continuous improvement and the development of new steganographic techniques capable of negating emerging detection schemes and insecurity data arising from changing threat landscapes. Therefore, a must in the forms of strong resistance techniques is required in order to safeguard the secrecy and integrity of secret information towards application in intelligent environments where confidentiality has become paramount, (Aberna & Agilandeeswari, 2024).

7.3 Real-Time Implementation and Latency Considerations

In the case of real-time application, the foremost requirements for the actual deployment of steganographic methods in IoT networks are implementation in real time and minimum latency. In the field of real-time systems, data have to be processed and transmitted with minimum delay such that the operation takes place at the right time and is reliable. Therefore, steganographic methods have to be optimized so they don't compromise on performance and latency during communications. It involves algorithmic design for embedding hidden data efficiently as well as pulling it out without major delays and heavy computing overheads. In an IoT network, which continuously involves a great number of devices communicating, steganography techniques cannot interrupt the data stream or degrade their transmission time. An efficient implementation of real-time ensures that the process of steganography integrates with existing network protocols and infrastructures being used without any disturbance to network operations. Latency also plays a vital role in applications such as autonomous vehicles or real-time health monitoring systems that require immediate data exchange. In that context, steganographic techniques should not compromise the responsiveness and functionality of those systems; otherwise, it will affect the operational effectiveness and user satisfaction. Therefore, balancing the complexity of steganographic algorithms with the need for real-time performance is a prerequisite to successful deployment in dynamic environments, (Sheikh *et al.*, 2024).

8. DISCUSSION

8.1 Advantages of Deep Learning-Based Steganography

Compared to the other traditional methods of steganography, deep learning-based steganography offers a number of important advantages. In this technique, it learns and adapts automatically to tackle all the complex patterns that occur in data. This in turn enhances efficiency and effectiveness in terms of how data can be concealed. Carrier data has subtle features that deep learning models like CNNs and autoencoders can capture to create minimal distortion for hiding information. These result in higher payload and robust concealing since more optimal embedding might be conducted as less detectable and resilient to compression or transformation attacks. Techniques based on deep learning will enhance adaptability since they can learn from various datasets and generalize better across different types of data and channels of communication. This ability can be used to train algorithms against specific detection methods so that they are strong against steganalysis. All these advantages make the technique more secure and efficient for hiding information data in environments where information confidentiality is of utmost importance, (Antora *et al.*, n.d.).

8.2 Limitations and Open Challenges

Deep learning-based steganography, despite the huge benefits it provides, has several limitations and open challenges. Limitations involved include the great computation associated with training and deploying deep models. Important resources, such as powerful GPUs and large datasets, may act as obstacles to implementation in resource-constrained environments such as IoT devices. Moreover, deep learning-based steganography techniques may also be vulnerable to adversarial attacks; that is, slight perturbations of data may expose the secret information or degrade the performance of a model. Another challenge is overfitting since models trained on specific datasets might fail to depict satisfactory performance on different datasets and environments. This further implies that interpretability of deep learning models becomes often limited to a point where understanding and trusting the decision-making process behind data concealment is a significant task. To surpass these problems, research and development that involve enhancing model efficiency, robustness, and generalization capabilities are must for deep learning-based steganographic systems, including enhancing transparency and trust, (Ponnusamy *et al.*, 2024).

8.3 Future Trends in IoT Security

The Internet of Things (IoT) will evolve further into incorporating enhancements based on more recent technological advancements and changes in threat landscapes. AI and ML are likely to be adopted to a greater extent in IoT security-they might even install more sophisticated intrusion detection systems, anomaly detection, and automated threat response. They can process large amounts of data in real-time and identify patterns and thus respond to new threats much more effectively than the traditional procedures do. Some others are concerns related to preservation of privacy, particularly in cases of advanced encryption methods as well as secure protocols for data sharing that aim at protecting sensitive information carried out over IoT networks. Another trend gaining popularity is decentralized security frameworks, including blockchain. It will ensure that data integrity and access control are much stronger. Edge computing is another trend that will enhance security through local processing so that much more of the processing occurs closer to where data originates and reduces the chances of data being lost while in transmission. Hence, with the spread of the Internet of Things to all corners and niches, it is the ability to address security concerns using such emerging technologies that will be the key determinant in safeguarding network integrity, privacy, and trust in the connected world, (Raja & Suresh, 2024).

9. CONCLUSION

The investigation on deep learning-based steganography in IoT networks brought attention to great promise for advancing data security and privacy. Findings were observed that can model CNNs and autoencoders, which can quite effectively hide any data within the network traffic yet not easily detectable in a highly efficient manner. Histogram packet sizes highlighted the distribution and variability of packet dimensions, which proved to be crucial in designing effective steganographic techniques. The plot of average payload sizes unraveled the trends and fluctuations of data transmitted and showed how steganographic practices can emerge through time. The bar chart of proportion of stego data indicated how frequently the hidden information is in the packets and usually in the prevalence of its response with the dynamics of the network. While the scatter plot of packet size against payload size examines how steganographic data impacts packet characteristics, the bar chart of protocol distribution marks the most commonly used network protocols thus illuminates how it interacts with various categories of traffic. Due to the presence of certain downsides into deep learning-based steganography, for instance, computationally heavy, vulnerable to adversarial attacks, and not interpretable. Hence, more significant future improvements are anticipated to focus on the development of technology that easily mitigates these defects and enhances its applicability in distinct areas such as smart home systems, industrial IoT, health monitoring, and autonomous vehicles. With the emergence of IoT environments, any type of technology applied has to be built with a robust and efficient steganographic technique that will maintain data integrity and confidentiality, adapt to emerging threats, and maximize the overall security in the network. Hence, these innovative techniques promise to make data more secure with the optimal protection and enhance the privacy of data over time with the advancing cyber threat landscape.

REFERENCES

Abdellatef, E., Naeem, E. A., & El-Samie, F. E. A. (2024). DeepEnc: Deep learning-based CT image encryption approach. *Multimedia Tools and Applications*, 83(4), 11147–11167. DOI: 10.1007/s11042-023-15818-8

Aberna, P., & Agilandeeswari, L. (2024). Digital image and video watermarking: Methodologies, attacks, applications, and future directions. *Multimedia Tools and Applications*, 83(2), 5531–5591. DOI: 10.1007/s11042-023-15806-y

Akram, A., Khan, I., Rashid, J., Saddique, M., Idrees, M., Ghadi, Y. Y., & Algarn, A. (2024). Enhanced Steganalysis for Color Images Using Curvelet Features and Support VectorMachine. *Computers, Materials & Continua*, 78(1), 1311–1328. DOI: 10.32604/cmc.2023.040512

Alserhani, F. M. (2024). Integrating deep learning and metaheuristics algorithms for blockchain-based reassurance data management in the detection of malicious IoT nodes. *Peer-to-Peer Networking and Applications*, 1–27. DOI: 10.1007/s12083-024-01786-9

Ansari, A. S. (2024). A Review on the Recent Trends of Image Steganography for VANET Applications. *Computers, Materials & Continua*, 78(3), 2865–2892. DOI: 10.32604/cmc.2024.045908

Antora, K. F., Alam, N. A., Al-Thani, M., Al-Subaiey, A., Rahman, A., Thomas, K. K., ... Khandakar, A. (n.d.). Aiblocknet-Novel Framework for Authenticity Validation Using Blockchain and Machine Learning for Fake Image Detection.

Biswas, S., Goswami, R. S., & Reddy, K. H. K. (2024). Advancing quantum steganography: A secure IoT communication with reversible decoding and customized encryption technique for smart cities. *Cluster Computing*, 27(7), 1–20. DOI: 10.1007/s10586-024-04429-z

Byeon, H., Shabaz, M., Surbakti, H., Keshta, I., Soni, M., & Bhatnagar, V. (2024). Deep learning and encryption algorithms based model for enhancing biometric security for artificial intelligence era. *Journal of Ambient Intelligence and Humanized Computing*, 1–14. DOI: 10.1007/s12652-024-04855-2

Dong, H., & Kotenko, I. (2024). Image-based malware analysis for enhanced IoT security in smart cities. *Internet of Things : Engineering Cyber Physical Human Systems*, 27, 101258. DOI: 10.1016/j.iot.2024.101258

Hachim, E. A. W. (2024). Cloud Data Protection Based On Crypto-Steganography Approach. *Journal La Multiapp*, 5(4), 336–345.

Hashemi, S. H. O., Majidi, M. H., & Khorashadizadeh, S. (2024). A new architecture based resnet for steganography in color images. *Multimedia Tools and Applications*, 1–20. DOI: 10.1007/s11042-024-19675-x

Hu, K., Wang, M., Ma, X., Chen, J., Wang, X., & Wang, X. (2024). Learning-based image steganography and watermarking: A survey. *Expert Systems with Applications*, 249, 123715. DOI: 10.1016/j.eswa.2024.123715

Ince, K. (2024). Exploring the potential of deep learning and machine learning techniques for randomness analysis to enhance security on IoT. *International Journal of Information Security*, 23(2), 1117–1130. DOI: 10.1007/s10207-023-00783-y

Kalaiarasi, G., Sudharani, B., Jonnalagadda, S. C., Battula, H. V., & Sanagala, B. (2024, July). A Comprehensive Survey of Image Steganography. In *2024 2nd International Conference on Sustainable Computing and Smart Systems (ICSCSS)* (pp. 1225-1230). IEEE.

Kuznetsov, A., Luhanko, N., Frontoni, E., Romeo, L., & Rosati, R. (2024). Image steganalysis using deep learning models. *Multimedia Tools and Applications*, 83(16), 48607–48630. DOI: 10.1007/s11042-023-17591-0

Liu, C., Chen, B., Shao, W., Zhang, C., Wong, K. K., & Zhang, Y. (2024). Unraveling Attacks to Machine Learning-Based IoT Systems: A Survey and the Open Libraries Behind Them. *IEEE Internet of Things Journal*, 11(11), 19232–19255. DOI: 10.1109/JIOT.2024.3377730

Michaylov, K. D., & Sarmah, D. K. (2024). Steganography and steganalysis for digital image enhanced Forensic analysis and recommendations. *Journal of Cyber Security Technology*, 1-27.

Nadhan, A. S., & Jacob, I. J. (2024). Enhancing healthcare security in the digital era: Safeguarding medical images with lightweight cryptographic techniques in IoT healthcare applications. *Biomedical Signal Processing and Control*, 88, 105511. DOI: 10.1016/j.bspc.2023.105511

Nawaz, S. A., Li, J., Bhatti, U. A., Shoukat, M. U., & Ahmad, R. M. (2024). Deep Learning Applications in Digital Image Security. *Deep Learning for Multimedia Processing Applications: Volume One: Image Security and Intelligent Systems for Multimedia Processing*, 110.

Nour-El Aine, Y., & Leghris, C. (2024, June). IoMT based Embedded Systems for healthcare: A Confidentiality and Privacy Approach throught Key Generation and Steganography. In *2024 International Conference on Circuit, Systems and Communication (ICCSC)* (pp. 1-6). IEEE.

Ozturk, B. A., Emad, H., Shafeeq, F., Shamaileh, A. A., Mohammedqasim, H., & Rane, M. E. (2024). Independent Video Steganalysis Framework Perspective of Secure Video Processing. *Journal of Electrical Systems*, 20(6s), 2541–2549. DOI: 10.52783/jes.3241

Ponnusamy, S., Antari, J., Bhaladhare, P. R., Potgantwar, A. D., & Kalyanaraman, S. (Eds.). (2024). *Enhancing Security in Public Spaces Through Generative Adversarial Networks (GANs)*. IGI Global. DOI: 10.4018/979-8-3693-3597-0

Raja, V., & Suresh, K. S. (2024). Deep Steg Block: Deep Learning-Enhanced Steganography for Secure Communication in IoT Devices Using Blockchain. *Educational Administration: Theory and Practice*, 30(4), 2958–2972.

Rao, A. S., Dalavai, L., Tata, V., Vellela, S. S., Polanki, K., Kumar, K. K., & Andra, R. (2024, February). A Secured Cloud Architecture for Storing Image Data using Steganography. In *2024 2nd International Conference on Computer, Communication and Control (IC4)* (pp. 1-6). IEEE. DOI: 10.1109/IC457434.2024.10486495

Rohhila, S., & Singh, A. K. (2024). Deep learning-based encryption for secure transmission digital images: A survey. *Computers & Electrical Engineering*, 116, 109236. DOI: 10.1016/j.compeleceng.2024.109236

Saif, S., Das, P., Biswas, S., Khan, S., Haq, M. A., & Kovtun, V. (2024). A secure data transmission framework for IoT enabled healthcare. *Heliyon*, 10(16), e36269. DOI: 10.1016/j.heliyon.2024.e36269 PMID: 39224301

Saranya, S. S., Reddy, P. L. C., & Prasanth, K. (2024, July). Digital audio steganography using LSB and RC7 algorithms for security applications. In *AIP Conference Proceedings* (Vol. 3075, No. 1). AIP Publishing. DOI: 10.1063/5.0217203

Shafique, A., Mehmood, A., Alawida, M., Elhadef, M., & Rehman, M. U. (2024). A fusion of machine learning and cryptography for fast data encryption through the encoding of high and moderate plaintext information blocks. *Multimedia Tools and Applications*, 1–27. DOI: 10.1007/s11042-024-18959-6

Sharma, D., & Prabha, C. Hybrid security of EMI using edge-based steganography and three-layered cryptography. In *Applied Data Science and Smart Systems* (pp. 278–290). CRC Press. DOI: 10.1201/9781003471059-37

Sheikh, A., Singh, K. U., Jain, A., Chauhan, J., Singh, T., & Raja, L. (2024, March). Lightweight Symmetric Key Encryption to Improve the Efficiency and Safety of the IoT. In *2024 IEEE International Conference on Contemporary Computing and Communications (InC4)* (Vol. 1, pp. 1-5). IEEE. DOI: 10.1109/InC460750.2024.10649289

Sriram, K. V., & Havaldar, R. H. (2024). Chronological Gazelle Optimization with Deep Learning-Based pixel prediction for video steganography in H. 264 video for defence applications. *Journal of Visual Communication and Image Representation*, 98, 104024. DOI: 10.1016/j.jvcir.2023.104024

Sun, T. (2024). Advancements in Communication Systems: From Image Compression Techniques to Deep Learning Applications. *Journal of Electrical Systems*, 20(10s), 1124–1132.

Sun, Y. (2024). Enhancing image steganalysis via integrated reinforcement learning and dilated convolution techniques. *Signal, Image and Video Processing*, 18(S1), 1–16. DOI: 10.1007/s11760-024-03113-4

Supriya, K. S., & Lovesum, S. P. J. (2024). Review on lightweight cryptography techniques and steganography techniques for IoT environment. *International Journal of System Assurance Engineering and Management*, 1–19. DOI: 10.1007/s13198-024-02476-8

Thamer, K. A., Ahmed, S. R., Almashhadany, M. T. M., Abdulqader, S. G., Abduladheem, W., & Algburi, S. (2024, May). Secure Data Transmission in IoT Networks using Machine Learning-based Encryption Techniques. In *Proceedings of the Cognitive Models and Artificial Intelligence Conference* (pp. 285-291). DOI: 10.1145/3660853.3660929

Yao, Q., Xu, K., Li, T., Zhou, Y., & Wang, M. (2024). A secure image evidence management framework using multi-bits watermark and blockchain in IoT environments. *Wireless Networks*, 30(6), 5157–5169. DOI: 10.1007/s11276-023-03229-4

Conclusion

The journey through the diverse chapters of this book underscores the multifaceted nature of cybersecurity and the innovative strategies being developed to counteract increasingly sophisticated cyber threats. From steganography and deep learning to machine learning applications in health information security, the contributions within this volume highlight the significant advancements and ongoing research efforts aimed at enhancing digital security.

The integration of traditional steganographic methods with modern deep learning techniques represents a significant leap forward in the field of cybersecurity. These advancements have not only improved the robustness and imperceptibility of steganographic systems but also opened new avenues for securing digital communications against unauthorized access and surveillance.

In the realm of health information security, the application of machine learning has demonstrated remarkable potential in safeguarding sensitive medical data. The insights gained from these studies can inform the development of more sophisticated intrusion detection systems and enhance compliance with stringent regulatory frameworks like HIPAA and GDPR.

The exploration of automatic speaker verification systems and the use of residual networks to mitigate replay attacks further exemplifies the depth and breadth of research in this book. These efforts are crucial in ensuring the reliability and security of biometric authentication systems, which are becoming increasingly prevalent in various sectors.

Moreover, the focus on responsible AI techniques in steganography emphasizes the need for ethical considerations in the development of secure communication methods. By promoting transparency and trust, these approaches ensure that the benefits of advanced cybersecurity techniques are realized without compromising ethical standards.

The insights presented in this book have far-reaching implications for practitioners, researchers, and policymakers in the field of cybersecurity. The practical applications of these findings can significantly enhance the security protocols of organizations, healthcare institutions, and smart agricultural systems, among others.

As cyber threats continue to evolve, the research and innovations discussed in this book will serve as a foundation for future advancements in cybersecurity. The collaborative efforts of experts from various domains underscore the importance of interdisciplinary approaches in addressing the complex challenges of the digital age.

In conclusion, this book provides a comprehensive overview of the current state of cybersecurity research and its practical applications. The contributions within these chapters offer valuable insights and innovative solutions that will undoubtedly shape the future of digital security, ensuring a safer and more secure digital environment for all.

Chiranji Lal Chowdhary

School of Computer Science Engineering and Information Systems, Vellore Institute of Technology, Vellore, India

Compilation of References

Abadi, M., Chu, A., & Goodfellow, I. (2016). Deep learning with differential privacy. *Proceedings of the 2016 ACM SIGSAC Conference on Computer and Communications Security (CCS)*. DOI: 10.1145/2976749.2978318

Abbasi, R., Martinez, P., & Ahmad, R. (2022). The digitization of agricultural industry–a systematic literature review on agriculture 4.0. *Smart Agricultural Technology*, 2, 100042. DOI: 10.1016/j.atech.2022.100042

Abd Aziz, A. Z., Sultan, M. F. M., & Zulkufli, N. L. M. (2024). Image Steganography: Comparative Analysis of their Techniques, Complexity and Enhancements. *International Journal on Perceptive and Cognitive Computing*, 10(1), 59–70. DOI: 10.31436/ijpcc.v10i1.449

Abdar, M., Samami, M., Mahmoodabad, S. D., Doan, T., Mazoure, B., Hashemifesharaki, R., Liu, L., Khosravi, A., Acharya, U., Makarenkov, V., & Nahavandi, S. (2021, August 1). Uncertainty quantification in skin cancer classification using three-way decision-based Bayesian deep learning. *Computers in Biology and Medicine*, 135, 104418. DOI: 10.1016/j.compbiomed.2021.104418 PMID: 34052016

Abdellatef, E., Naeem, E. A., & El-Samie, F. E. A. (2024). DeepEnc: Deep learning-based CT image encryption approach. *Multimedia Tools and Applications*, 83(4), 11147–11167. DOI: 10.1007/s11042-023-15818-8

Abdelwahab, A. A., & Hassaan, L. A. (2008, March). A discrete wavelet transform based technique for image data hiding. In *2008 National Radio Science Conference* (pp. 1-9). IEEE. DOI: 10.1109/NRSC.2008.4542319

Abdulazeez, S., Nawar, A. K., Lubna, E., & Jahefer, M. M. (2023). Hiding Information in Digital Images Using LSB Steganography Technique. *International Journal of Interactive Mobile Technologies*, 17(7), 167–178. DOI: 10.3991/ijim.v17i07.38737

Aberna, P., & Agilandeeswari, L. (2024). Digital image and video watermarking: Methodologies, attacks, applications, and future directions. *Multimedia Tools and Applications*, 83(2), 5531–5591. DOI: 10.1007/s11042-023-15806-y

Abiri, R., Rizan, N., Balasundram, S. K., Shahbazi, A. B., & Abdul-Hamid, H. (2023). Application of digital technologies for ensuring agricultural productivity. *Heliyon*, 9(12), e22601. DOI: 10.1016/j.heliyon.2023.e22601 PMID: 38125472

Abu, M. A., Indra, N. H., & Abdul, H. A. R. (2019). *A study on Image Classification based on Deep Learning and TensorFlown*. International Journal of Engineering Research and Technology.

Adhiyaksa, F. A., Ahmad, T., Shiddiqi, A. M., Jati Santoso, B., Studiawan, H., & Pratomo, B. A. (2022). Reversible Audio Steganography using Least Prime Factor and Audio Interpolation. *2021 International Seminar on Machine Learning, Optimization, and Data Science (ISMODE)*, 97–102. DOI: 10.1109/ISMODE53584.2022.9743066

Adla, D., Reddy, G. V., Nayak, P., & Karuna, G. (2022, December). Deep learning-based computer aided diagnosis model for skin cancer detection and classification. *Distributed and Parallel Databases*, 40(4), 717–736. DOI: 10.1007/s10619-021-07360-z

Adnan, S. M., Irtaza, A., Aziz, S., Ullah, M. O., Javed, A., & Mahmood, M. T. (2018). Fall detection through acoustic local ternary patterns. *Applied Acoustics*, 140, 296–300. DOI: 10.1016/j.apacoust.2018.06.013

Agrafiotis, I., Nurse, J. R. C., Goldsmith, M., Creese, S., & Upton, D. (2018). A taxonomy of cyber-harms: Defining the impacts of cyber-attacks and understanding how they propagate. *Journal of Cybersecurity*, 4(1), tyy006. DOI: 10.1093/cybsec/tyy006

Ahammed, M., Al Mamun, M., & Uddin, M. S. (2022, November 1). A machine learning approach for skin disease detection and classification using image segmentation. *Healthcare Analytics*, 2, 100122. DOI: 10.1016/j.health.2022.100122

Ahmad, S., Ogala, J. O., Ikpotokin, F., Arif, M., Ahmad, J., & Mehfuz, S. (2024). Enhanced CNN-DCT Steganography: Deep Learning-Based Image Steganography Over Cloud. *SN Computer Science*, 5(4), 408. DOI: 10.1007/s42979-024-02756-x

Ahmed, S. F., Alam, M. S. B., Afrin, S., Rafa, S. J., Rafa, N., & Gandomi, A. H. (2024). Insights into Internet of Medical Things (IoMT): Data fusion, security issues and potential solutions. *Information Fusion*, 102, 102060. DOI: 10.1016/j.inffus.2023.102060

Ahmed, S. S., Memon, M., Jaffari, R., & Jawaid, M. (2021). StegoBound: A Novel Image Steganography Technique Using Boundary-Based LSB Substitution. *Journal of Hunan University Natural Sciences*, 48(6).

Akram, A., Khan, I., Rashid, J., Saddique, M., Idrees, M., Ghadi, Y. Y., & Algarn, A. (2024). Enhanced Steganalysis for Color Images Using Curvelet Features and Support VectorMachine. *Computers, Materials & Continua*, 78(1), 1311–1328. DOI: 10.32604/cmc.2023.040512

Al Zakitat, M. A. S., Abdulrazzaq, M. M., Ramaha, N. T., Mukhlif, Y. A., & Ismael, O. A. (2023, September). Harnessing Advanced Techniques for Image Steganography: Sequential and Random Encoding with Deep Learning Detection. In *International Conference on Emerging Trends and Applications in Artificial Intelligence* (pp. 456-470). Cham: Springer Nature Switzerland.

Alam, T. S., Jowthi, C. B., & Pathak, A. (2024). Comparing pre-trained models for efficient leaf disease detection: A study on custom CNN. *Journal of Electrical Systems and Information Technology*, 11(1), 12. DOI: 10.1186/s43067-024-00137-1

Alanzy, M., Alomrani, R., Alqarni, B., & Almutairi, S. (2023). Image Steganography Using LSB and Hybrid Encryption Algorithms. *Applied Sciences (Basel, Switzerland)*, 13(21), 11771. DOI: 10.3390/app132111771

Aldweesh, A., Derhab, A., & Emam, A. Z. (2020). Deep learning approaches for anomaly-based intrusion detection systems: A survey, taxonomy, and open issues. *Knowledge-Based Systems*, 189, 105124. DOI: 10.1016/j.knosys.2019.105124

Alkim, E. (2020). Post-Quantum Lattice-Based Cryptography on Blockchains: Practical Aspects. *ACM Journal on Emerging Technologies in Computing Systems*.

Alkim, E., Ducas, L., Pöppelmann, T., & Schwabe, P. (2020). Post-quantum lattice-based cryptography on blockchain: Practical implementations and challenges. *ACM Journal on Emerging Technologies in Computing Systems*, 16(2), 1–22.

Alserhani, F. M. (2024). Integrating deep learning and metaheuristics algorithms for blockchain-based reassurance data management in the detection of malicious IoT nodes. *Peer-to-Peer Networking and Applications*, 1–27. DOI: 10.1007/s12083-024-01786-9

Anderson, R., Barton, C., Böhme, R., Clayton, R., Van Eeten, M. J. G., Levi, M., Moore, T., & Savage, S. (2013). Measuring the cost of cybercrime. *The Economics of Information Security and Privacy*, 265–300.

Andrew, J., Isravel, D. P., Sagayam, K. M., Bhushan, B., Sei, Y., & Eunice, J. (2023). Blockchain for healthcare systems: Architecture, security challenges, trends and future directions. *Journal of Network and Computer Applications*, 103633. Advance online publication. DOI: 10.1016/j.jnca.2023.103633

Ansari, A. S. (2024). A Review on the Recent Trends of Image Steganography for VANET Applications. *Computers, Materials & Continua*, 78(3), 2865–2892. DOI: 10.32604/cmc.2024.045908

Antora, K. F., Alam, N. A., Al-Thani, M., Al-Subaiey, A., Rahman, A., Thomas, K. K., ... Khandakar, A. (n.d.). Aiblocknet-Novel Framework for Authenticity Validation Using Blockchain and Machine Learning for Fake Image Detection.

Aravind, P. R., Nechiyil, U., & Paramparambath, N. (2020). Audio spoofing verification using deep convolutional neural networks by transfer learning. *ArXiv Preprint ArXiv:2008.03464*.

Arefolov, A., Adam, L., Brown, S., Budovskaya, Y., Chen, C., Das, D., Farhy, C., Ferguson, R., Huang, H., Kanigel, K., Lu, C., Polesskaya, O., Staton, T., Tajhya, R., Whitley, M., Wong, J.-Y., Zeng, X., & McCreary, M. (2021). Implementation of the FAIR data principles for exploratory biomarker data from clinical trials. *Data Intelligence*, 3(4), 631–662. DOI: 10.1162/dint_a_00106

Artz, D. (2001). Digital steganography: Hiding data within data. *IEEE Internet Computing*, 5(3), 75–80. DOI: 10.1109/4236.935180

Arute, F., Arya, K., Babbush, R., Bacon, D., Bardin, J. C., Barends, R., Biswas, R., Boixo, S., Brandao, F. G. S. L., Buell, D. A., Burkett, B., Chen, Y., Chen, Z., Chiaro, B., Collins, R., Courtney, W., Dunsworth, A., Farhi, E., Foxen, B., & Martinis, J. M. (2019). Quantum supremacy using a programmable superconducting processor. *Nature*, 574(7779), 505–510. DOI: 10.1038/s41586-019-1666-5 PMID: 31645734

Awasthi, D., Tiwari, A., Khare, P., & Srivastava, V. K. (2023). A comprehensive review on optimization-based image watermarking techniques for copyright protection. *Expert Systems with Applications*, 122830.

Awaysheh, F. M., Alazab, M., Gupta, M., Pena, T. F., & Cabaleiro, J. C. (2020). Next-generation big data federation access control: A reference model. *Future Generation Computer Systems*, 108, 726–741. DOI: 10.1016/j.future.2020.02.052

Azmi, R., Tibben, W., & Win, K. T. (2018). Review of cybersecurity frameworks: Context and shared concepts. *Journal of Cyber Policy*, 3(2), 258–283. DOI: 10.1080/23738871.2018.1520271

Bagga, M., & Goyal, S. (2024). Image-based detection and classification of plant diseases using deep learning: State-of-the-art review. *Urban Agriculture & Regional Food Systems*, 9(1), e20053. DOI: 10.1002/uar2.20053

Balaji, Kalvinathan, Dheepanchakkravarthy, & Muthuvel. (2021). *IoT Enabled Smart Irrigation System*. IEEE Access.

Balasooriya, Mantri, & Suriyampola. (2020). *IoT-Based Smart Watering System Towards Improving the Efficiency of Agricultural Irrigation*. IEEE Access.

Baluja, S. (2017). Hiding images in plain sight: Deep steganography. *Advances in Neural Information Processing Systems*, 30.

Bamanga, M. A., Babando, A. K., & Shehu, M. A. (2024). *Recent Advances in Steganography*. Online First.

Banerjee, S., & Singh, G. K. (2021). A new approach of ECG steganography and prediction using deep learning. *Biomedical Signal Processing and Control*, 64, 102151. DOI: 10.1016/j.bspc.2020.102151

Bansal, K., Agrawal, A., & Bansal, N. (2020). A Survey on Steganography using Least Significant bit (LSB) Embedding Approach. *International Conference on Trends in Electronics and Informatics (ICEI)*, 64-69. DOI: 10.1109/ICOEI48184.2020.9142896

Bari'c, N., & Pfitzmann, B. (1997). Collision-free accumulators and fail-stop signature schemes without trees. In Fumy, W. (Ed.), *Advances in Cryptology*.

Bassel, A., Abdulkareem, A. B., Alyasseri, Z. A., Sani, N. S., & Mohammed, H. J. (2022). Automatic Malignant and Benign Skin Cancer Classification Using a Hybrid Deep Learning Approach. *Diagnostics (Basel)*, 12(10), 2472. DOI: 10.3390/diagnostics12102472 PMID: 36292161

Baumann, R., Malik, K. M., Javed, A., Ball, A., Kujawa, B., & Malik, H. (2021). Voice spoofing detection corpus for single and multi-order audio replays. *Computer Speech & Language*, 65, 101132. DOI: 10.1016/j.csl.2020.101132

Ba, Z., Wen, Q., Cheng, P., Wang, Y., Lin, F., Lu, L., & Liu, Z. (2023). Transferring Audio Deepfake Detection Capability across Languages. *Proceedings of the ACM Web Conference 2023*, 2033–2044. DOI: 10.1145/3543507.3583222

Bebortta, S., Tripathy, S. S., Basheer, S., & Chowdhary, C. L. (2023). Deepmist: Towards deep learning assisted mist computing framework for managing healthcare big data. *IEEE Access : Practical Innovations, Open Solutions*, 11, 42485–42496. DOI: 10.1109/ACCESS.2023.3266374

Bellare, M., Boldyreva, A., Desai, A., & Pointcheval, D. (2001). Key-privacy in public-key encryption. *International Conference on the Theory and Application of Cryptology and Information Security*, 566–582.

Ben Jabra, S., & Ben Farah, M. (2024). Deep Learning-Based Watermarking Techniques Challenges: A Review of Current and Future Trends. *Circuits, Systems, and Signal Processing*, 43(7), 1–30. DOI: 10.1007/s00034-024-02651-z

Bernstein, D. J. (2017). SPHINCS+: A Post-Quantum Hash-Based Signature Scheme. *IACR Cryptology ePrint Archive*.

Bernstein, D. J., Buchmann, J., & Dahmen, E. (2009). *Post-quantum cryptography*. Springer Science & Business Media. DOI: 10.1007/978-3-540-88702-7

Bhattacharya, A., Seth, A., Malhotra, D., & Verma, N. (2022). Cloud Steganography: An Intelligent Approach to Improve Data Security in the Cloud Environment. *Proceedings of the 4th International Conference on Information Management & Machine Intelligence*, 1–5. DOI: 10.1145/3590837.3590902

Bhimavarapu, U., & Battineni, G. (2022). Skin lesion analysis for melanoma detection using the novel deep learning model fuzzy GC-SCNN. In Healthcare (Vol. 10, No. 5, p. 962). MDPI. DOI: 10.3390/healthcare10050962

Bhoi, A., & Prasad, R. (2021). *IoT-IIRS: Internet of Things based intelligent-irrigation recommendation system using machine learning approach for efficient water usage*.

Bisogni, F., & Asghari, H. (2020). More than a suspect: An investigation into the connection between data breaches, identity theft, and data breach notification laws. *Journal of Information Policy*, 10, 45–82. DOI: 10.5325/jinfopoli.10.2020.0045

Biswas, S., Goswami, R. S., & Reddy, K. H. K. (2024). Advancing quantum steganography: A secure IoT communication with reversible decoding and customized encryption technique for smart cities. *Cluster Computing*, 27(7), 1–20. DOI: 10.1007/s10586-024-04429-z

Blake, B. J. (2010). *Secret language: Codes, tricks, spies, thieves, and symbols*. OUP Oxford.

Blanco-Carmona, P., Baeza-Moreno, L., Hidalgo-Fort, E., Martín-Clemente, R., González-Carvajal, R., & Muñoz-Chavero, F. (2023). AIoT in Agriculture: Safeguarding Crops from Pest and Disease Threats. *Sensors (Basel)*, 23(24), 9733. DOI: 10.3390/s23249733 PMID: 38139579

Bocean, C. G. (2024). A Cross-Sectional Analysis of the Relationship between Digital Technology Use and Agricultural Productivity in EU Countries. *Agriculture*, 14(4), 519. DOI: 10.3390/agriculture14040519

Bohra, S., Naik, C., Batra, R., Popat, K., & Kaur, H. (2024). Advancements in Modern Steganography Techniques for Enhanced Data Security: A Comprehensive Review. *2024 11th International Conference on Computing for Sustainable Global Development (INDIACom)*, 941–944. DOI: 10.23919/INDIACom61295.2024.10498587

Boroumand, M., Chen, M., & Fridrich, J. (2018). Deep residual network for steganalysis of digital images. *IEEE Transactions on Information Forensics and Security*, 14(5), 1181–1193. DOI: 10.1109/TIFS.2018.2871749

Bost, R. (2016). Σοφος: Forward secure searchable encryption. *Proc. of CCS*.

Budiman, G., & Novamizanti, L. (2015). White space steganography on text by using lzw-huffman double compression. *International Journal of Computer Networks & Communications*, 7(2), 136A. DOI: 10.5121/ijcnc.2015.7210

Bui, T., Agarwal, S., Yu, N., & Collomosse, J. (2023). Rosteals: Robust steganography using autoencoder latent space. In *Proceedings of the IEEE/CVF Conference on Computer Vision and Pattern Recognition* (pp. 933-942). DOI: 10.1109/CVPRW59228.2023.00100

Byeon, H., Shabaz, M., Surbakti, H., Keshta, I., Soni, M., & Bhatnagar, V. (2024). Deep learning and encryption algorithms based model for enhancing biometric security for artificial intelligence era. *Journal of Ambient Intelligence and Humanized Computing*, 1–14. DOI: 10.1007/s12652-024-04855-2

Cabaj, K., Caviglione, L., Mazurczyk, W., Wendzel, S., Woodward, A., & Zander, S. (2018). The New Threats of Information Hiding: The Road Ahead. IT P, 20, 31–39.

Caballero, H., Muñoz, V., & Ramos-Corchado, M. A. (2023). A comparative study of steganography using watermarking and modifications pixels versus least significant bit. *Iranian Journal of Electrical and Computer Engineering*, 13(6), 6335–6350. DOI: 10.11591/ijece.v13i6.pp6335-6350

Cakir, M., & McHenry, M. P. (2014). International research collaborations in agriculture. In *Environmental and Agricultural Research Summaries* (Vol. 1). Nova Science Publishers.

Camenisch, J., & Lysyanskaya, A. (2002). Dynamic accumulators and application to efficient revocation of anonymous credentials. *Proc. of CRYPTO*. DOI: 10.1007/3-540-45708-9_5

Cassavia, N., Caviglione, L., Guarascio, M., Liguori, A., & Zuppelli, M. (2024). Learning autoencoder ensembles for detecting malware hidden communications in IoT ecosystems. *Journal of Intelligent Information Systems*, 62(4), 925–949. DOI: 10.1007/s10844-023-00819-8

Celik, M. U., Sharma, G., Tekalp, A. M., & Saber, E. (2005). Lossless generalized-LSB data embedding. *IEEE Transactions on Image Processing*, 14(2), 253–266. DOI: 10.1109/TIP.2004.840686 PMID: 15700530

Chai, P., & Lang, J. (2023). Behavior steganography in social networks based on AES encryption algorithm. *Third International Conference on Advanced Algorithms and Neural Networks*. DOI: 10.1117/12.3005092

Chakravarty Mohit, N. (2023). Data Augmentation and Hybrid Feature Amalgamation to detect Audio Deep Fake attacks. *Physica Scripta*. http://iopscience.iop.org/article/10.1088/1402-4896/acea05

Chakravarty, N., & Dua, M. (2022). Noise Robust ASV Spoof Detection Using Integrated Features and Time Delay Neural Network. *SN Computer Science*, 4(2), 127. DOI: 10.1007/s42979-022-01557-4 PMID: 35036930

Chakravarty, N., & Dua, M. (2023). Spoof Detection using Sequentially Integrated Image and Audio Features. *International Journal of Computing and Digital Systems*, 13(1), 1. DOI: 10.12785/ijcds/1301111

Chakravarty, N., & Dua, M. (2024a). A lightweight feature extraction technique for deepfake audio detection. *Multimedia Tools and Applications*, 83(26), 1–25. DOI: 10.1007/s11042-024-18217-9

Chakravarty, N., & Dua, M. (2024b). An improved feature extraction for Hindi language audio impersonation attack detection. *Multimedia Tools and Applications*, 83(25), 1–26. DOI: 10.1007/s11042-023-18104-9

Chandel, B., & Jain, S. (2016). Gurumukhi Text Hiding using Steganography in Video. *International Journal of Computer Applications*, 975(6), 8887. DOI: 10.5120/ijca2016909843

Chatlani, N., & Soraghan, J. (2010). *Local binary patterns for 1-D signal processing*.

Chaudhary, A., Sharma, A., & Gupta, N. (2023). A Novel Approach to Blockchain and Deep Learning in the field of Steganography. *International Journal of Intelligent Systems and Applications in Engineering*, 11(2s), 104–115.

Chaudhary, A., Sharma, A., & Gupta, N. (2023). Designing A Secured Framework for the Steganography Process Using Blockchain and Machine Learning Technology. *International Journal of Intelligent Systems and Applications in Engineering*, 11(2s), 96–103.

Chaumont, M. (2020). Deep learning in steganography and steganalysis. In *Digital media steganography* (pp. 321–349). Academic Press. DOI: 10.1016/B978-0-12-819438-6.00022-0

Cheddad, A., Condell, J., Curran, K., & Mc Kevitt, P. (2010). Digital image steganography: Survey and analysis of current methods. *Signal Processing*, 90(3), 727–752. DOI: 10.1016/j.sigpro.2009.08.010

Chen, L. (2016). Report on post-quantum cryptography. *NIST*, 2016.

Cheng, L., Liu, F., & Yao, D. (2017). Enterprise data breach: Causes, challenges, prevention, and future directions. *Wiley Interdisciplinary Reviews. Data Mining and Knowledge Discovery*, 7(5), e1211. DOI: 10.1002/widm.1211

Chen, J. A., Niu, W., Ren, B., Wang, Y., & Shen, X. (2023). Survey: Exploiting data redundancy for optimization of deep learning. *ACM Computing Surveys*, 55(10), 1–38. DOI: 10.1145/3564663

Chen, J., Chen, J., Zhang, D., Sun, Y., & Nanehkaran, Y. A. (2020). Using deep transfer learning for image-based plant disease identification. *Computers and Electronics in Agriculture*, 173, 105393. DOI: 10.1016/j.compag.2020.105393

Chen, L., Wang, R., Yan, D., & Wang, J. (2021). Learning to Generate Steganographic Cover for Audio Steganography Using GAN. *IEEE Access : Practical Innovations, Open Solutions*, 9, 88098–88107. DOI: 10.1109/ACCESS.2021.3090445

Chen, Z., Xiao, F., Guo, F., & Yan, J. (2023). Interpretable machine learning for building energy management: A state-of-the-art review. *Advances in Applied Energy*, 9, 100123. DOI: 10.1016/j.adapen.2023.100123

Choi, S., Chung, S., Lee, S., Han, S., Kang, T., Seo, J., Kwak, I.-Y., & Oh, S. (2024). TB-ResNet: Bridging the Gap from TDNN to ResNet in Automatic Speaker Verification with Temporal-Bottleneck Enhancement. *ICASSP 2024-2024 IEEE International Conference on Acoustics, Speech and Signal Processing (ICASSP)*, 10291–10295.

Chollet, F. (2021). *Deep learning with Python*. Simon and Schuster.

Choudhary, P., Singhai, J., & Yadav, J. S. (2022, November 15). Skin lesion detection based on deep neural networks. *Chemometrics and Intelligent Laboratory Systems*, 230, 104659. DOI: 10.1016/j.chemolab.2022.104659

Chowdhary, C. L., Sai, G. V., & Acharjya, D. P. (2016). Decrease in false assumption for detection using digital mammography. In Computational Intelligence in Data Mining—Volume 2: Proceedings of the International Conference on CIDM (pp. 325-333). Springer India. DOI: 10.1007/978-81-322-2731-1_30

Chowdhary, C. L., Goyal, A., & Vasnani, B. K. (2019). Experimental assessment of beam search algorithm for improvement in image caption generation. *Journal of Applied Science and Engineering*, 22(4), 691–698.

Clark, R. M., & Hakim, S. (2017). Protecting critical infrastructure at the state, provincial, and local level: issues in cyber-physical security. *Cyber-Physical Security: Protecting Critical Infrastructure at the State and Local Level*, 1–17.

Conway, M. (2017). Code wars: steganography, signals intelligence, and terrorism. In *Technology and Terrorism* (pp. 171–191). Routledge. DOI: 10.4324/9781315130712-12

Cox, I. J. (2007). Digital Watermarking and Steganography. Morgan Kaufmann google schola, 2, 893-914.

Cox, I., Miller, M., Bloom, J., & Honsinger, C. (2002). Digital watermarking. *Journal of Electronic Imaging*, 11(3), 414. DOI: 10.1117/1.1494075

Dadgostar, H., & Afsari, F. (2016). Image steganography based on interval-valued intuitionistic fuzzy edge detection and modified LSB. Journal of information security and applications, 30, 94-104.

Dalal, M., & Juneja, M. (2021). A survey on information hiding using video steganography. *Artificial Intelligence Review*, 54(8), 1–65. DOI: 10.1007/s10462-021-09968-0

Das, A., Wahi, J. S., Anand, M., & Rana, Y. (2021). Advances in neural information processing systems: Vol. 30. *Multi-image steganography using deep neural networks. arXiv preprint arXiv:2101.00350.*

De La Croix, N. J., Ahmad, T., & Han, F. (2023). Enhancing Secret Data Detection Using Convolutional Neural Networks with Fuzzy Edge Detection. *IEEE Access : Practical Innovations, Open Solutions*, 11, 131001–131016. DOI: 10.1109/ACCESS.2023.3334650

Delgado, H., Evans, N., Kinnunen, T., Lee, K. A., Liu, X., Nautsch, A., Patino, J., Sahidullah, M., Todisco, M., & Wang, X. (2021). ASVspoof 2021: Automatic speaker verification spoofing and countermeasures challenge evaluation plan. *ArXiv Preprint ArXiv:2109.00535.*

Delmi, A., Suryadi, S., & Satria, Y. (2020). Digital image steganography by using edge adaptive based chaos cryptography. In *Journal of Physics: Conference Series*. IOP Publishing. DOI: 10.1088/1742-6596/1442/1/012041

Delnevo, Girau, Ceccarini, & Prandi. (2021). *A Deep Learning and Social IoT Approach for Plants Disease Prediction Toward a Sustainable Agriculture*. IEEE Access.

Demircan, Y. Y., & Ozekes, S. (2024). A Novel LSB Steganography Technique Using Image Segmentation, JUCS -. *Journal of Universal Computer Science*, 30(3), 308–332. DOI: 10.3897/jucs.105702

Dhanaraju, M., Chenniappan, P., Ramalingam, K., Pazhanivelan, S., & Kaliaperumal, R. (2022). Smart farming: Internet of Things (IoT)-based sustainable agriculture. *Agriculture*, 12(10), 1745. DOI: 10.3390/agriculture12101745

Dhawan, S., Gupta, R., Bhuyan, H. K., Vinayakumar, R., Pani, S. K., & Rana, A. K. (2023). An efficient steganography technique based on S2OA & DESAE model. *Multimedia Tools and Applications*, 82(10), 14527–14555. DOI: 10.1007/s11042-022-13798-9

Ding, Y., Wang, Z., Qin, Z., Zhou, E., Zhu, G., Qin, Z., & Choo, K. K. R. (2023). Backdoor Attack on Deep Learning-Based Medical Image Encryption and Decryption Network. *IEEE Transactions on Information Forensics and Security*.

Djebbar, F., Ayad, B., Meraim, K. A., & Hamam, H. (2012). Comparative study of digital audio steganography techniques. *EURASIP Journal on Audio, Speech, and Music Processing*, 2012(1), 1–16. DOI: 10.1186/1687-4722-2012-25

Dong, H., & Kotenko, I. (2024). Image-based malware analysis for enhanced IoT security in smart cities. *Internet of Things : Engineering Cyber Physical Human Systems*, 27, 101258. DOI: 10.1016/j.iot.2024.101258

Dong, Z., Lai, C. S., Zhang, Z., Qi, D., Gao, M., & Duan, S. (2021). Neuromorphic extreme learning machines with bimodal memristive synapses. *Neurocomputing*, 453, 38–49. DOI: 10.1016/j.neucom.2021.04.049

Dua, M., Meena, S., & Chakravarty, N. (2023). Audio Deepfake Detection Using Data Augmented Graph Frequency Cepstral Coefficients. *2023 International Conference on System, Computation, Automation and Networking (ICSCAN)*, 1–6. DOI: 10.1109/ICSCAN58655.2023.10395679

Dua, M., Sadhu, A., Jindal, A., & Mehta, R. (2022). A hybrid noise robust model for multireplay attack detection in Automatic speaker verification systems. *Biomedical Signal Processing and Control*, 74, 103517. DOI: 10.1016/j.bspc.2022.103517

Duan, X., Guo, D., Liu, N., Li, B., Gou, M., & Qin, C. (2020). A new high capacity image steganography method combined with image elliptic curve cryptography and deep neural network. *IEEE Access : Practical Innovations, Open Solutions*, 8, 25777–25788. DOI: 10.1109/ACCESS.2020.2971528

Duan, X., Jia, K., Li, B., Guo, D., Zhang, E., & Qin, C. (2019). En Zhang and Chuan Qin, Reversible Image Steganography Scheme Based on a U-Net Structure. *IEEE Access : Practical Innovations, Open Solutions*, 7, 9314–9323. DOI: 10.1109/ACCESS.2019.2891247

Duhan, S., Gulia, P., Gill, N. S., Yahya, M., Yadav, S., Hassan, M. M., Alsberi, H., & Shukla, P. K. (2024). An analysis to investigate plant disease identification based on machine learning techniques. *Expert Systems: International Journal of Knowledge Engineering and Neural Networks*, 41(8), 13576. DOI: 10.1111/exsy.13576

Elharrouss, O., Almaadeed, N., & Al-Maadeed, S. (2020). An image steganography approach based on k-least significant bits (k-LSB). *2020 IEEE International Conference on Informatics, IoT, and Enabling Technologies (ICIoT)*, 131–135. DOI: 10.1109/ICIoT48696.2020.9089566

Eunice, J., Popescu, D. E., Chowdary, M. K., & Hemanth, J. (2022). Deep learning-based leaf disease detection in crops using images for agricultural applications. *Agronomy (Basel)*, 12(10), 2395. DOI: 10.3390/agronomy12102395

Fadel, M. M., Said, W., Hagras, E. A., & Arnous, R. (2023). A Fast and Low Distortion Image Steganography Framework Based on Nature-Inspired Optimizers. *IEEE Access : Practical Innovations, Open Solutions*, 11, 125768–125789. DOI: 10.1109/ACCESS.2023.3326709

Fadhil, A. M., Jalo, H. N., & Mohammad, O. F. (2023). Improved Security of a Deep Learning-Based Steganography System with Imperceptibility Preservation. *International journal of electrical and computer engineering systems, 14*(1), 73-81.

Fan, P., Zhang, H., & Zhao, X. (2023). Exploring Frame Difference to Enhance Robustness for Video Steganography on Social Networks. *Security and Communication Networks*, 2023, 1–11. DOI: 10.1155/2023/6295486

Farooq, N., & Selwal, A. (2023). Image steganalysis using deep learning: A systematic review and open research challenges. *Journal of Ambient Intelligence and Humanized Computing*, 14(6), 7761–7793. DOI: 10.1007/s12652-023-04591-z

Fateeva, A., & Chen, S. (2024, February 20). Study on the Complex Melanoma. *Cancers (Basel)*, 16(5), 843. DOI: 10.3390/cancers16050843 PMID: 38473205

Fei-Fei, N., Deng, J., Russakovsky, O., & Berg, A. L. (2020). ImageNet. Stanford University.

Fei-Fei, L., Deng, J., Russakovsky, O., Berg, A., & Li, K. (2020). *ImageNet*. Stanford University.

Fu, Z., Ren, K., Shu, J., Sun, X., & Huang, F. (2016, September 1). Enabling Personalized Search over Encrypted Outsourced Data with Efficiency Improvement. *IEEE Transactions on Parallel and Distributed Systems*, 27(9), 2546–2559. DOI: 10.1109/TPDS.2015.2506573

Gambhir, P., Dev, A., Bansal, P., Sharma, D. K., & Gupta, D. (2024). Residual networks for text-independent speaker identification: Unleashing the power of residual learning. *Journal of Information Security and Applications*, 80, 103665. DOI: 10.1016/j.jisa.2023.103665

Gao, Y., Yang, J., Chen, C., Pang, K., & Huang, Y. (2024, April). Enhancing Steganography of Generative Image Based on Image Retouching. In *ICASSP 2024-2024 IEEE International Conference on Acoustics, Speech and Signal Processing (ICASSP)* (pp. 4945-4949). IEEE. DOI: 10.1109/ICASSP48485.2024.10448006

Gautam, N., & Lall, B. (2020, February). Blind channel coding identification of convolutional encoder and reed-solomon encoder using neural networks. In *2020 National Conference on Communications (NCC)* (pp. 1-6). IEEE. DOI: 10.1109/NCC48643.2020.9056082

Geetha, R., Balasubramanian, M., & Devi, K. R. (2022, June 27). COVIDetection: Deep convolutional neural networks-based automatic detection of COVID-19 with chest x-ray images. *Research on Biomedical Engineering*, 38(3), 955–964. Advance online publication. DOI: 10.1007/s42600-022-00230-2

Geetha, R., Suntheya, A. K., & Srikanth, G. U. (2020). Cloud Integrated IoT Enabled Sensor Network Security: Research Issues and Solutions. *Wireless Personal Communications*, 113(2), 747–771. DOI: 10.1007/s11277-020-07251-z

Gençoğlu, M. T., & Steganography, B. (2022). in Social Networks. *Turkish Journal of Nature and Science*, 11(4), 135–141.

Ge, X. R., Yu, J., Hu, C. Y., Zhang, H. L., & Hao, R. (2018). Enabling Efficient Verifiable Fuzzy Keyword Search OverEncrypted Data in Cloud Computing. *IEEE Access : Practical Innovations, Open Solutions*, 6, 45725–45739. DOI: 10.1109/ACCESS.2018.2866031

Ghamizi, S., Cordy, M., Papadakis, M., & Le Traon, Y. (2021). Evasion attack steganography: Turning vulnerability of machine learning to adversarial attacks into a real-world application. Proceedings of the IEEE/CVF International conference on computer vision, 31-40.

Ghosh, P., Azam, S., Quadir, R., Karim, A., Shamrat, F. J., Bhowmik, S. K., Jonkman, M., Hasib, K. M., & Ahmed, K. (2022, August 8). SkinNet-16: A deep learning approach to identify benign and malignant skin lesions. *Frontiers in Oncology*, 12, 931141. DOI: 10.3389/fonc.2022.931141 PMID: 36003775

Gordon, R. (2013). Skin cancer: an overview of epidemiology and risk factors. In Seminars in oncology nursing (Vol. 29, No. 3, pp. 160-169). WB Saunders. DOI: 10.1016/j.soncn.2013.06.002

Gouda W, Sama NU, Al-Waakid G, Humayun M, & Jhanjhi NZ. (2022). Detection of skin cancer based on skin lesion images using deep learning. In Healthcare (Vol. 10, No. 7, p. 1183). MDPI.

Grachev, Y. L., & Sidorenko, V. G. (2001). Steganalysis of the methods of concealing information in graphic containers. *Method of Estimating the Size*, 39.

Grover, L. K. (1996). A fast quantum mechanical algorithm for database search. *Proceedings of the twenty-eighth annual ACM symposium on Theory of computing*, 212-219. DOI: 10.1145/237814.237866

Guo, Chen, Jie, Fu, Li, & Feng. (2020). Dynamic Multi-Phrase Ranked Search over Encrypted Data with Symmetric Searchable Encryption. IEEE Transactions on Services Computing, 13(6), 1034-1044. .DOI: 10.1109/TSC.2017.2768045

Gupta, , Gupta, , & Jadhav, , Deolekar, Nerurkar, & Deshp. (2019). Plant Disease Prediction using Deep Learning and IoT In. *IEEE Access : Practical Innovations, Open Solutions*.

Gupta, R., Tanwar, S., Tyagi, S., & Kumar, N. (2020). Machine learning models for secure data analytics: A taxonomy and threat model. *Computer Communications*, 153, 406–440. DOI: 10.1016/j.comcom.2020.02.008

Gurunath, R., Alahmadi, A. H., Samanta, D., Khan, M. Z., & Alahmadi, A. (2021). A novel approach for linguistic steganography evaluation based on artificial neural networks. IEEE Access, 9, 120869-120879. DOI: 10.1109/ACCESS.2021.3108183

Guzman, A. R. (2022). Image Steganography Using Deep Learning Techniques (Doctoral dissertation, Purdue University Graduate School).

Hachim, E. A. W. (2024). Cloud Data Protection Based On Crypto-Steganography Approach. *Journal La Multiapp*, 5(4), 336–345.

Hanelt, A., Bohnsack, R., Marz, D., & Antunes Marante, C. (2021). A systematic review of the literature on digital transformation: Insights and implications for strategy and organizational change. *Journal of Management Studies*, 58(5), 1159–1197. DOI: 10.1111/joms.12639

Hanifa, R. M., Isa, K., & Mohamad, S. (2021). A review on speaker recognition: Technology and challenges. *Computers & Electrical Engineering*, 90, 107005. DOI: 10.1016/j.compeleceng.2021.107005

Hardesty, L. (2017). *Explained: Neural Networks*. Massachusetts Institute of Technology.

Hasan, M. K., Islam, S., Sulaiman, R., Khan, S., Hashim, A. H. A., Habib, S., Islam, M., Alyahya, S., Ahmed, M. M., Kamil, S., & Hassan, M. A. (2021). Lightweight encryption technique to enhance medical image security on internet of medical things applications. *IEEE Access : Practical Innovations, Open Solutions*, 9, 47731–47742. DOI: 10.1109/ACCESS.2021.3061710

Hashemi, S. H. O., Majidi, M. H., & Khorashadizadeh, S. (2024). A new architecture based resnet for steganography in color images. *Multimedia Tools and Applications*, 1–20. DOI: 10.1007/s11042-024-19675-x

Hayes, J., & Danezis, G. (2017). Generating steganographic images via adversarial training. *Advances in Neural Information Processing Systems*, 30.

He, K., Zhang, X., Ren, S., & Sun, J. (2016a). Deep residual learning for image recognition. *Proceedings of the IEEE Conference on Computer Vision and Pattern Recognition*, 770–778.

He, K., Zhang, X., Ren, S., & Sun, J. (2016b). Identity mappings in deep residual networks. *Computer Vision–ECCV 2016: 14th European Conference, Amsterdam, The Netherlands, October 11–14, 2016. Proceedings*, 14(Part IV), 630–645.

Hernández-Nava, C. A., Rincón-García, E. A., Lara-Velázquez, P., de-Los-Cobos-Silva, S. G., Gutiérrez-Andrade, M. A., & Mora-Gutiérrez, R. A. (2023). Voice spoofing detection using a neural networks assembly considering spectrograms and mel frequency cepstral coefficients. *PeerJ. Computer Science*, 9, e1740. DOI: 10.7717/peerj-cs.1740 PMID: 38192463

Herodotus, S., Robert, B., & Purvis, A. (2007). The landmark Herodotus: the histories.

Herodotus, S., Robert, B., & Purvis, A. (2007). *The landmark Herodotus: the histories*. No Title.

Himthani V, Dhaka VS, Kaur M, Rani G, Oza M, & Lee HN (2022). Comparative performance assessment of deep learning based image steganography techniques. Scientific Reports, 12(1), 16895.

Himthani, Dhaka, Kaur, Rani, Oza, & Lee. (2022). Comparative performance assessment of deep learning-based image steganography techniques. Scientific Reports, No. 16895.

Himthani, V., Dhaka, V. S., Kaur, M., Rani, G., Oza, M., & Lee, H. N. (2022). Comparative performance assessment of deep learning based image steganography techniques. *Scientific Reports*, 12(1), 16895. DOI: 10.1038/s41598-022-17362-1 PMID: 36207314

Huang, X., Acero, A., Hon, H.-W., & Reddy, R. (2001). *Spoken language processing: A guide to theory, algorithm, and system development*. Prentice hall PTR.

Huang, C. T., Weng, C. Y., & Shongwe, N. S. (2023). Capacity-Raising Reversible Data Hiding Using Empirical Plus–Minus One in Dual Images. *Mathematics*, 11(8), 1764. DOI: 10.3390/math11081764

Huang, H., Yao, X. A., Krisp, J. M., & Jiang, B. (2021). Analytics of location-based big data for smart cities: Opportunities, challenges, and future directions. *Computers, Environment and Urban Systems*, 90, 101712. DOI: 10.1016/j.compenvurbsys.2021.101712

Hu, D., Wang, L., Jiang, W., Zheng, S., & Li, B. (2018). A novel image steganography method via deep convolutional generative adversarial networks. *IEEE Access : Practical Innovations, Open Solutions*, 6, 38303–38314. DOI: 10.1109/ACCESS.2018.2852771

Hu, K., Wang, M., Ma, X., Chen, J., Wang, X., & Wang, X. (2024). Learning-based image steganography and watermarking: A survey. *Expert Systems with Applications*, 249, 123715. DOI: 10.1016/j.eswa.2024.123715

Hussain, I., Zeng, J., Qin, X., & Tan, S. (2020). A survey on deep convolutional neural networks for image steganography and steganalysis. *KSII Transactions on Internet and Information Systems*, 14(3), 1228–1248.

Illi, E., Qaraqe, M., Althunibat, S., Alhasanat, A., Alsafasfeh, M., de Ree, M., & Al-Kuwari, S. (2023). Physical Layer Security for Authentication, Confidentiality, and Malicious Node Detection: A Paradigm Shift in Securing IoT Networks. *IEEE Communications Surveys and Tutorials*. Advance online publication. DOI: 10.1109/COMST.2023.3327327

Ince, K. (2024). Exploring the potential of deep learning and machine learning techniques for randomness analysis to enhance security on IoT. *International Journal of Information Security*, 23(2), 1117–1130. DOI: 10.1007/s10207-023-00783-y

Irtaza, A., Adnan, S. M., Aziz, S., Javed, A., Ullah, M. O., & Mahmood, M. T. (2017). A framework for fall detection of elderly people by analyzing environmental sounds through acoustic local ternary patterns. *2017 Ieee International Conference on Systems, Man, and Cybernetics (Smc)*, 1558–1563. DOI: 10.1109/SMC.2017.8122836

Isinkaye, F. O., Olusanya, M. O., & Singh, P. K. (2024). Deep learning and content-based filtering techniques for improving plant disease identification and treatment recommendations: A comprehensive review. *Heliyon*, 10(9), e29583. DOI: 10.1016/j.heliyon.2024.e29583 PMID: 38737274

Iurgenson, N., Wang, X., Kong, L., Sun, X., Legin, A., Wang, P., Wan, H., & Kirsanov, D. (2024). Feasibility study of multisensor systems for the assessment of water pollution index induced by heavy metal contamination. *Microchemical Journal*, 197, 109762. DOI: 10.1016/j.microc.2023.109762

Jahromi, Z. T., Hasheminejad, S. M. H., & Shojaedini, S. V. (2024). Deep learning semantic image synthesis: A novel method for unlimited capacity, high noise resistance coverless video steganography. *Multimedia Tools and Applications*, 83(6), 17047–17065. DOI: 10.1007/s11042-023-16278-w

Jamil, T. (1999). Steganography: The art of hiding information in plain sight. *IEEE Potentials*, 18(1), 10–12. DOI: 10.1109/45.747237

Jammoul, H., Rube, M., Sebeloue, M., Sadli, I., Dejous, C., Perrine, C., Pousset, Y., & Tamarin, O. (2023). Investigating Water Contamination with LoRa-Enabled Surface Acoustic Wave Sensors. *2023 7th International Symposium on Instrumentation Systems, Circuits and Transducers (INSCIT)*, 1–5. DOI: 10.1109/INSCIT59673.2023.10258483

Javed, R., Rahim, M. S., Saba, T., & Rehman, A. (2020, December). A comparative study of features selection for skin lesion detection from dermoscopic images. *Network Modeling and Analysis in Health Informatics and Bioinformatics*, 9(1), 4. DOI: 10.1007/s13721-019-0209-1

Jean Camp, L., & Wolfram, C. (2004). Pricing security: A market in vulnerabilities. In *Economics of information security* (pp. 17–34). Springer. DOI: 10.1007/1-4020-8090-5_2

Ji, G., Tian, L., Zhao, J., Yue, Y., Wang, Z., & Yang, X. (2018). Error analysis and correction of spatialization of crop yield in China–Different variables scales, partitioning schemes and error correction methods. *Computers and Electronics in Agriculture*, 148, 272–279. DOI: 10.1016/j.compag.2018.03.031

Joshi, S., & Dua, M. (2022). LSTM-GTCC based Approach for Audio Spoof Detection. *2022 International Conference on Machine Learning, Big Data, Cloud and Parallel Computing (COM-IT-CON)*, 1, 656–661. DOI: 10.1109/COM-IT-CON54601.2022.9850820

Kadhim, I. J., Premaratne, P., Vial, P. J., & Halloran, B. (2019). Comprehensive survey of image steganography: Techniques, Evaluations, and trends in future research. *Neurocomputing*, 335, 299–326. DOI: 10.1016/j.neucom.2018.06.075

Kahn, D. (1996). The history of steganography. *International Workshop on Information Hiding*, 1–5.

Kalaiarasi, G., Sudharani, B., Jonnalagadda, S. C., Battula, H. V., & Sanagala, B. (2024, July). A Comprehensive Survey of Image Steganography. In *2024 2nd International Conference on Sustainable Computing and Smart Systems (ICSCSS)* (pp. 1225-1230). IEEE.

Kale, G., Joshi, A., Shukla, I., & Bhosale, A. (2024). A Video Steganography Approach with Randomization Algorithm Using Image and Audio Steganography. *2024 International Conference on Emerging Smart Computing and Informatics (ESCI)*, 1–5. DOI: 10.1109/ESCI59607.2024.10497225

Kamau, G. M. (2014). *An enhanced least significant bit steganographic method for information hiding*.

Kannadhasan, S., & Nagarajan, R. (2021). Secure Framework Data Security Using Cryptography and Steganography in Internet of Things. In *Multidisciplinary Approach to Modern Digital Steganography* (pp. 258–278). IGI Global.

Kasasbeh, D. S., Al-Ja'afreh, B. M., Anbar, M., Hasbullah, I. H., & Al Khasawneh, M. (2024). Secure map-based crypto-stego technique based on mac address. *Bulletin of Electrical Engineering and Informatics*, 13(3), 1788–1801. DOI: 10.11591/eei.v13i3.7140

Kaur, M., Kumar, V., & Singh, D. (2020). *An efficient image steganography method using multiobjective differential evolution.* Digital Media Steganography. DOI: 10.1016/B978-0-12-819438-6.00012-8

Ker, A. D. (2005). Steganalysis of LSB matching in grayscale images. *IEEE Signal Processing Letters*, 12(6), 441–444. DOI: 10.1109/LSP.2005.847889

Khalid, N., Qayyum, A., Bilal, M., Al-Fuqaha, A., & Qadir, J. (2023). Privacy-preserving artificial intelligence in healthcare: Techniques and applications. *Computers in Biology and Medicine*, 158, 106848. DOI: 10.1016/j.compbiomed.2023.106848 PMID: 37044052

Khandelwal, J., & Sharma, V. K. (2023, July). Reversible Image Steganography Using Deep Learning Method: A Review. In *International Conference on Human-Centric Smart Computing* (pp. 625-635). Singapore: Springer Nature Singapore.

Khan, M. A., Akram, T., Zhang, Y. D., & Sharif, M. (2021, March 1). Attributes based skin lesion detection and recognition: A mask RCNN and transfer learning-based deep learning framework. *Pattern Recognition Letters*, 143, 58–66. DOI: 10.1016/j.patrec.2020.12.015

Khan, R. U., Khan, K., Albattah, W., & Qamar, A. M. (2021). *Image-Based Detection of Plant Diseases: From Classical Machine Learning to Deep Learning Journey. Wireless Communications and Mobile Computing.* Advance online publication.

Kheddar, H., Hemis, M., Himeur, Y., Megías, D., & Amira, A. (2023). Deep learning for diverse data types steganalysis: A review. *arXiv preprint arXiv:2308.04522*.

Kheddar, H., Hemis, M., Himeur, Y., Megías, D., & Amira, A. (2024). Deep learning for steganalysis of diverse data types: A review of methods, taxonomy, challenges and future directions. *Neurocomputing*, 581, 127528. DOI: 10.1016/j.neucom.2024.127528

Kholdinasab, N., & Amirmazlaghani, M. (2023). An adversarial learning based image steganography with security improvement against neural network steganalysis. *Computers & Electrical Engineering*, 108, 108725. DOI: 10.1016/j.compeleceng.2023.108725

Kiel, J. M. (2022). Data privacy and security in the US: HIPAA, hitech and beyond. In *Nursing Informatics: A Health Informatics, Interprofessional and Global Perspective* (pp. 427–435). Springer International Publishing. DOI: 10.1007/978-3-030-91237-6_28

Kingma, D. P., & Ba, J. (2014). Adam: A method for stochastic optimization. *arXiv preprint arXiv:1412.6980*.

Kinnunen, T., Sahidullah, M., Delgado, H., Todisco, M., Evans, N., Yamagishi, J., & Lee, K. A. (2017). *The ASVspoof 2017 challenge: Assessing the limits of replay spoofing attack detection.*

Kolli, Vamsi, & Manikandan. (2021). *Plant Disease Detection using Convolutional Neural Network.* IEEE Access.

Krizhevsky, A., Hinton, G. E., & Nair, V. (2009). *CIFAR-10 dataset.* University of Toronto.

Kumar & Jashuva. (2021). *Smart farming management system using IoT.* International Journal of Research in Science.

Kumar, L., Singh, K. U., Sharma, B. K., Singhal, M., Singh, T., & Raja, L. (2024). Deep Learning and Crow Search to Detect Skin Cancer in Dermoscopic Images. In 2024 IEEE International Conference on Contemporary Computing and Communications (InC4) (Vol. 1, pp. 1-7). IEEE. DOI: 10.1109/InC460750.2024.10649363

Kumar, A., & Km, P. (2010). Steganography- A Data Hiding Technique. *International Journal of Computer Applications*, 9(7), 19–23. Advance online publication. DOI: 10.5120/1398-1887

Kumar, A., Rani, R., & Singh, S. (2023). A survey of recent advances in image steganography. *Security and Privacy*, 6(3), e281. DOI: 10.1002/spy2.281

Kumar, A., Rani, R., & Singh, S. (2023). Encoder-Decoder Architecture for Image Steganography using Skip Connections. *Procedia Computer Science*, 218, 1122–1131. DOI: 10.1016/j.procs.2023.01.091

Kumar, V. (2023). Digital Enablers. In *The Economic Value of Digital Disruption: A Holistic Assessment for CXOs* (pp. 1–110). Springer Nature Singapore. DOI: 10.1007/978-981-19-8148-7_1

Kumar, V., Choudhary, A., & Vardhan, H. (2022). Image-to-Image Steganography Using Encoder-Decoder Network. *International Journal of Social Ecology and Sustainable Development*, 13(1), 1–12.

Kumar, V., Rao, P., & Choudhary, A. (2020). Image steganography analysis based on deep learning. *Review of Computer Engineering Studies*, 7(1), 1–5. DOI: 10.18280/rces.070101

Kumar, V., & Sharma, S. (2024). Steganography-based facial re-enactment using generative adversarial networks. *Multimedia Tools and Applications*, 83(3), 7609–7630. DOI: 10.1007/s11042-023-15946-1

Kumar, V., Sharma, S., Kumar, C., & Sahu, A. K. (2023). Latest trends in deep learning techniques for image steganography. *International Journal of Digital Crime and Forensics*, 15(1), 1–14. DOI: 10.4018/IJDCF.318666

Kunhoth, J., Subramanian, N., Al-Maadeed, S., & Bouridane, A. (2023). Video steganography: Recent advances and challenges. *Multimedia Tools and Applications*, 82(27), 41943–41985. DOI: 10.1007/s11042-023-14844-w

Kuznetsov, A., Luhanko, N., Frontoni, E., Romeo, L., & Rosati, R. (2023). Image steganalysis using deep learning models. *Multimedia Tools and Applications*, 1–24.

Kuznetsov, O., Frontoni, E., & Chernov, K. (2024). Beyond traditional steganography: Enhancing security and performance with spread spectrum image steganography. *Applied Intelligence*, 54(7), 5253–5277. DOI: 10.1007/s10489-024-05415-z

Le, Y., & Yang, X. (2015). Tiny imagenet visual recognition challenge. *CS 231N*, 7(7), 3.

Lehto, M., Neittaanmäki, P., Pöyhönen, J., & Hummelholm, A. (2022). Cyber Security in Healthcare Systems. In *Cyber Security: Critical Infrastructure Protection* (pp. 183–215). Springer International Publishing. DOI: 10.1007/978-3-030-91293-2_8

Lin, T. Y. (2014). Microsoft COCO: Common Objects in Context. *European Conference on Computer Vision*.

Liu, Bashir, Iqbal, Shahid, Tausif, & Umer. (2022). *Internet of Things (IoT) and Machine Learning Model of Plant Disease Prediction–Blister Blight for Tea Plant.* IEEE Access.

Liu, Tian, Wu, Peng, & Wang. (2022). Enabling Verifiable and Dynamic Ranked Search over Outsourced Data. IEEE Transactions on Services Computing, 15, 69-82. .DOI: 10.1109/TSC.2019.2922177

Liu, C., Chen, B., Shao, W., Zhang, C., Wong, K. K., & Zhang, Y. (2024). Unraveling Attacks to Machine Learning-Based IoT Systems: A Survey and the Open Libraries Behind Them. *IEEE Internet of Things Journal*, 11(11), 19232–19255. DOI: 10.1109/JIOT.2024.3377730

Liu, H., & Lang, B. (2019). Machine learning and deep learning methods for intrusion detection systems: A survey. *Applied Sciences (Basel, Switzerland)*, 9(20), 4396. DOI: 10.3390/app9204396

Liu, J., Ke, Y., Zhang, Z., Lei, Y., Li, J., Zhang, M., & Yang, X. (2020). Recent advances of image steganography with generative adversarial networks. *IEEE Access : Practical Innovations, Open Solutions*, 8, 60575–60597. DOI: 10.1109/ACCESS.2020.2983175

Liu, J., & Wang, X. (2021). Plant diseases and pests detection based on deep learning: A review. *Plant Methods*, 17(1), 1–18. DOI: 10.1186/s13007-021-00722-9 PMID: 33627131

Liu, L., Liu, X., Wang, D., & Yang, G. (2024). Enhancing image steganography security via universal adversarial perturbations. *Multimedia Tools and Applications*, 1–13. DOI: 10.1007/s11042-024-19122-x

Li, W., Wang, H., Chen, Y., Abdullahi, S. M., & Luo, J. (2023). Constructing immunized stego-image for secure steganography via artificial immune system. *IEEE Transactions on Multimedia*, 25, 8320–8333. DOI: 10.1109/TMM.2023.3234812

Li, Y., Wu, J., & Cao, Z. (2023, December). Childhood sunburn and risk of melanoma and non-melanoma skin cancer: A Mendelian randomization study. *Environmental Science and Pollution Research International*, 30(58), 122011–122023. DOI: 10.1007/s11356-023-30535-3 PMID: 37962759

Lou, D. C., Wu, N. I., Wang, C. M., Lin, Z. H., & Tsai, C. S. (2010). A novel adaptive steganography based on local complexity and human vision sensitivity. *Journal of Systems and Software/the Journal of Systems and Software, 83*(7), 1236–1248.

Luo, J., He, P., Liu, J., Wang, H., Wu, C., & Zhou, S. (2023). Reversible adversarial steganography for security enhancement. *Journal of Visual Communication and Image Representation*, 97, 103935. DOI: 10.1016/j.jvcir.2023.103935

Luo, X., Liu, F., Yang, C., Lian, S., & Wang, D. (2012, April 1). On F5 Steganography in Images IEEE. *The Computer Journal*, 55(4), 447–456. Advance online publication. DOI: 10.1093/comjnl/bxr092

Lyubashevsky, V. (2013). Lattice signatures and the random oracle model. *IACR Cryptology ePrint Archive*.

Lyubashevsky, V., Peikert, C., & Regev, O. (2013). On ideal lattices and learning with errors over rings. *Journal of the Association for Computing Machinery*, 60(6), 1–35. DOI: 10.1145/2535925

Ma, B., Li, K., Xu, J., Wang, C., Li, J., & Zhang, L. (2023). Enhancing the security of image steganography via multiple adversarial networks and channel attention modules. *Digital Signal Processing*, 141, 104121. DOI: 10.1016/j.dsp.2023.104121

Macrakis, K. (2014). *Prisoners, Lovers, & Spies: The Story of Invisible Ink from Herodotus to Al-Qaeda*. Yale University Press. DOI: 10.2307/j.ctt5vkzst

Maiti, A., Laha, S., Upadhaya, R., Biswas, S., Choudhary, V., Kar, B., . . . Sen, J. (2024). Boosting Digital Safeguards: Blending Cryptography and Steganography. *arXiv preprint arXiv:2404.05985*.

Maitra, A., & Damle, M. (2024, March). Revolutionizing Plant Health Management with Technological Digital Transformation to Enhance Disease Control & Fortifying Plant Resilience. In 2024 3rd International Conference for Innovation in Technology (INOCON) (pp. 1-8). IEEE. DOI: 10.1109/INOCON60754.2024.10511728

Malik, K., Javed, A., Malik, H., & Irtaza, A. (2020). A Light-Weight Replay Detection Framework For Voice Controlled IoT Devices. *IEEE Journal of Selected Topics in Signal Processing, PP*. DOI: 10.1109/JSTSP.2020.2999828

Malik, K. M., Malik, H., & Baumann, R. (2019). Towards vulnerability analysis of voice-driven interfaces and countermeasures for replay attacks. *2019 IEEE Conference on Multimedia Information Processing and Retrieval (MIPR)*, 523–528. DOI: 10.1109/MIPR.2019.00106

Mandal, P. C., Mukherjee, I., Paul, G., & Chatterji, B. N. (2022). Digital image steganography: A literature survey. *Information Sciences*, 609, 1451–1488. Advance online publication. DOI: 10.1016/j.ins.2022.07.120

Martín, A., Hernández, A., Alazab, M., Jung, J., & Camacho, D. (2023). Evolving Generative Adversarial Networks to improve image steganography. *Expert Systems with Applications*, 222, 119841. DOI: 10.1016/j.eswa.2023.119841

Mathew, Joy, Sasi, Jiji, & John. (2022). *Crop prediction and Plant Disease Detection using IoT and Machine learning*. IEEE Access.

Mawgoud, A. A., Taha, M. H. N., Abu-Talleb, A., & Kotb, A. (2022). A deep learning based steganography integration framework for ad-hoc cloud computing data security augmentation using the V-BOINC system. *Journal of Cloud Computing (Heidelberg, Germany)*, 11(1), 97. DOI: 10.1186/s13677-022-00339-w PMID: 36569183

Mawla, N. A., & Khafaji, H. K. (2023). Enhancing Data Security: A Cutting-Edge Approach Utilizing Protein Chains in Cryptography and Steganography. *Computers*, 12(8), 166. DOI: 10.3390/computers12080166

Mazurczyk, W., Wendzel, S., Zander, S., Houmansadr, A., & Szczypiorski, K. (2016). *Information hiding in communication networks: fundamentals, mechanisms, applications, and countermeasures*. John Wiley & Sons.

Melman, A., & Evsutin, O. (2023). Comparative study of metaheuristic optimization algorithms for image steganography based on discrete Fourier transform domain. *Applied Soft Computing*, 132, 109847. DOI: 10.1016/j.asoc.2022.109847

Meng, Y., & Li, J. Image Steganography of convolutional neural network based on neural architecture search, *Research square*, 2022 DOI: 10.21203/rs.3.rs-2245407/v1

Miao, Ma, Liu, Weng, Li, & Li. (2019). Lightweight fine-grained search over encrypted data in fog computing. IEEE Transactions on Services Computing, 12, 772-785. .DOI: 10.1109/TSC.2018.2823309

Michael, K., Kobran, S., Abbas, R., & Hamdoun, S. (2019). Privacy, data rights and cybersecurity: Technology for good in the achievement of sustainable development goals. *2019 IEEE International Symposium on Technology and Society (ISTAS)*, 1–13. DOI: 10.1109/ISTAS48451.2019.8937956

Michaylov, K. D., & Sarmah, D. K. (2024). Steganography and steganalysis for digital image enhanced Forensic analysis and recommendations. *Journal of Cyber Security Technology*, 1-27.

Mikhail, D. Y., Hawezi, R. S., & Kareem, S. W. (2023). An Ensemble Transfer Learning Model for Detecting Stego Images. *Applied Sciences (Basel, Switzerland)*, 13(12), 7021. DOI: 10.3390/app13127021

Mishra, P., & Ahuja, R. (2022). A Novel Image Watermarking Method Against Crop Attack Using Two-Step Sudoku Puzzle. *ECS Transactions*, 107(1), 8351–8360. DOI: 10.1149/10701.8351ecst

Mittal, S., Kaur, P., & Ramkumar, K. R. (2021). Achieving Privacy and Security Using QR-Code through Homomorphic Encryption and Steganography. *2021 9th International Conference on Reliability, Infocom Technologies and Optimization (Trends and Future Directions)(ICRITO)*, 1–6.

Mittal, A., & Dua, M. (2021). Static–dynamic features and hybrid deep learning models based spoof detection system for ASV. *Complex & Intelligent Systems*, 1–14.

Mondal, A. (2018). An Approach to Ensure the Secrecy of Scene Images (Doctoral dissertation, Khulna University of Engineering & Technology (KUET), Khulna, Bangladesh).

Mosca, M. (2018). Cybersecurity in an era with quantum computers: Will we be ready? *IEEE Security and Privacy*, 16(5), 38–41. DOI: 10.1109/MSP.2018.3761723

Moura, J. C. Z. da S. (2022). *Smart techniques and tools to detect Steganography-a viable practice to Security Office Department.*

Mo, X., Tan, S., Tang, W., Li, B., & Huang, J. (2023). ReLOAD: Using reinforcement learning to optimize asymmetric distortion for additive steganography. *IEEE Transactions on Information Forensics and Security*, 18, 1524–1538. DOI: 10.1109/TIFS.2023.3244094

Msd, A., Kuppili, J., & Manga, N. A. (2020). *Smart Farming System using IoT for Efficient Crop Growth*. IEEE International Students' Conference on Electrical, Electronics and Computer Science (SCEECS).

Muhammad, T., Munir, M. T., Munir, M. Z., & Zafar, M. W. (2022). Integrative Cybersecurity: Merging Zero Trust, Layered Defense, and Global Standards for a Resilient Digital Future. *International Journal Of Computer Science And Technology*, 6(4), 99–135.

Mukherjee, S., Mukhopadhyay, S., & Sarkar, S. (2024). IoTSLE: Securing IoT systems in low-light environments through finite automata, deep learning and DNA computing based image steganographic model. *Internet of Things : Engineering Cyber Physical Human Systems*, 101358, 101358. Advance online publication. DOI: 10.1016/j.iot.2024.101358

Murugan, A., Nair, S. A., Preethi, A. A., & Kumar, K. S. (2021, March 1). Diagnosis of skin cancer using machine learning techniques. *Microprocessors and Microsystems*, 81, 103727. DOI: 10.1016/j.micpro.2020.103727

Nadhan, A. S., & Jacob, I. J. (2024). Enhancing healthcare security in the digital era: Safeguarding medical images with lightweight cryptographic techniques in IoT healthcare applications. *Biomedical Signal Processing and Control*, 88, 105511. DOI: 10.1016/j.bspc.2023.105511

Nahar, M., Kamal, A. H. M., & Hossain, G. (2023). Protecting health data in the cloud through steganography: A table-driven, blind method using neural networks and bit-shuffling algorithm. *Journal of Network and Computer Applications*, 217, 103689. DOI: 10.1016/j.jnca.2023.103689

Namasudra, S. (2022). A secure cryptosystem using DNA cryptography and DNA steganography for the cloud-based IoT infrastructure. *Computers & Electrical Engineering*, 104, 108426. DOI: 10.1016/j.compeleceng.2022.108426

Narayanan, A., Bonneau, J., Felten, E., Miller, A., & Goldfeder, S. (2016). *Bitcoin and cryptocurrency technologies*. Princeton University Press.

Nashat & Mamdouh. (2019). An efficient steganographic technique for hiding data. Journal of the Egyptian Mathematical Society, 57.

Naveed, M., Prabhakaran, M., & Gunter, C. A. (2014). Dynamic Searchable Encryption via Blind Storage. *2014 IEEE Symposium on Security and Privacy*, 639-654. DOI: 10.1109/SP.2014.47

Nawaz, S. A., Li, J., Bhatti, U. A., Shoukat, M. U., & Ahmad, R. M. (2024). Deep Learning Applications in Digital Image Security. *Deep Learning for Multimedia Processing Applications: Volume One: Image Security and Intelligent Systems for Multimedia Processing*, 110.

Nayyar, A., & Puri, V. (2016). *Smart Farming: IoT Based Smart Sensors Agriculture Stick for Live Temperature and Moisture Monitoring using Arduino*. Cloud Computing & Solar Technology. DOI: 10.1201/9781315364094-121

Neelakandan, S., Beulah, J. R., Prathiba, L., Murthy, G. L. N., Irudaya Raj, E. F., & Arulkumar, N. (2022). Blockchain with deep learning-enabled secure healthcare data transmission and diagnostic model. *International Journal of Modeling, Simulation, and Scientific Computing*, 13(04), 2241006. DOI: 10.1142/S1793962322410069

Nematollahi, M. A., Vorakulpipat, C., & Rosales, H. G. (2017). *Digital watermarking*. Springer Singapore. DOI: 10.1007/978-981-10-2095-7

Ngugi, H. N., Ezugwu, A. E., Akinyelu, A. A., & Abualigah, L. (2024). Revolutionizing crop disease detection with computational deep learning: A comprehensive review. *Environmental Monitoring and Assessment*, 196(3), 302. DOI: 10.1007/s10661-024-12454-z PMID: 38401024

Nguyen, V. D., Bui, N. D., & Do, H. K. (2022, October 4). Skin lesion classification on imbalanced data using deep learning with soft attention. *Sensors (Basel)*, 22(19), 7530. DOI: 10.3390/s22197530 PMID: 36236628

Nour-El Aine, Y., & Leghris, C. (2024, June). IoMT based Embedded Systems for healthcare: A Confidentiality and Privacy Approach throught Key Generation and Steganography. In *2024 International Conference on Circuit, Systems and Communication (ICCSC)* (pp. 1-6). IEEE.

Nunna, K. C., & Marapareddy, R. (2020). Secure data transfer through internet using cryptography and image steganography. *2020 SoutheastCon, 2*, 1–5.

O'Toole, J. M. (1991). Herodotus and the Written Record. *Archivaria*.

Ogiela, M. R., & Koptyra, K. (2015). False and multi-secret steganography in digital images. *Soft Computing*, 19(11), 3331–3339. DOI: 10.1007/s00500-015-1728-z

Ognjanovski, G. (2019). Everything you need to know about neural networks and backpropagation—machine learning easy and fun. Towards Data Science.back-propagation-machine-learning-made-easy-e5285bc2be3a

Ognjanovski, G. (2019). Everything you need to know about neural networks and backpropagation—machine learning easy and fun. *Towards Data Science*.back-propagation-machine-learning-made-easy-e5285bc2be3a.

Oprea, A., & Vassilev, A. (2023). Adversarial machine learning: A taxonomy and terminology of attacks and mitigations. *NIST Artificial Intelligence*, 100-2, E2023. DOI: 10.6028/NIST.AI.100-2e2023.ipd

Orchi, H., Sadik, M., & Khaldoun, M. (2021). On using artificial intelligence and the internet of things for crop disease detection: A contemporary survey. *Agriculture*, 12(1), 9. DOI: 10.3390/agriculture12010009

Ottakath, N., Al-Ali, A., Al-Maadeed, S., Elharrouss, O., & Mohamed, A. (2023). Enhanced computer vision applications with blockchain: A review of applications and opportunities. *Journal of King Saud University. Computer and Information Sciences*, 35(10), 101801. DOI: 10.1016/j.jksuci.2023.101801

Ouhami, M., Hafiane, A., Es-Saady, Y., El Hajji, M., & Canals, R. (2021). Computer vision, IoT and data fusion for crop disease detection using machine learning: A survey and ongoing research. *Remote Sensing (Basel)*, 13(13), 2486. DOI: 10.3390/rs13132486

Owen, S., Fojtik, R., Braga, B., & Raghunathan, K. (2023). *Interoperability and User Experience. Digital Health: A Transformative Approach.*

Ozturk, B. A., Emad, H., Shafeeq, F., Shamaileh, A. A., Mohammedqasim, H., & Rane, M. E. (2024). Independent Video Steganalysis Framework Perspective of Secure Video Processing. *Journal of Electrical Systems*, 20(6s), 2541–2549. DOI: 10.52783/jes.3241

Padinjappurathu Gopalan, S., Chowdhary, C. L., Iwendi, C., Farid, M. A., & Rama-samy, L. K. (2022). An efficient and privacy-preserving scheme for disease predic-tion in modern healthcare systems. *Sensors (Basel)*, 22(15), 5574. DOI: 10.3390/s22155574 PMID: 35898077

Pandey, B. K., Pandey, D., Nassa, V. K., George, S., Aremu, B., Dadeech, P., & Gupta, A. (2022, July). Effective and secure transmission of health information using advanced morphological component analysis and image hiding. In *Artificial Intelligence on Medical Data: Proceedings of International Symposium*, ISCMM 2021 (pp. 223-230). Singapore: Springer Nature Singapore. https://doi.org/DOI: 10.1007/978-981-19-0151-5_19

Pandey, B. K., Pandey, D., Alkhafaji, M. A., Güneşer, M. T., & Şeker, C. (2023). A reliable transmission and extraction of textual information using keyless encryption, steganography, and deep algorithm with cuckoo optimization. In *Micro-Electronics and Telecommunication Engineering: Proceedings of 6th ICMETE 2022* (pp. 629–636). Springer Nature Singapore. DOI: 10.1007/978-981-19-9512-5_57

Parekh, R., Patel, N., Gupta, R., Jadav, N. K., Tanwar, S., Alharbi, A., Tolba, A., Neagu, B.-C., & Raboaca, M. S. (2023). Gefl: Gradient encryption-aided privacy preserved federated learning for autonomous vehicles. *IEEE Access : Practical Innovations, Open Solutions*, 11, 1825–1839. DOI: 10.1109/ACCESS.2023.3233983

Parra, L., Sendra, S., Lloret, J., & Bosch, I. (2015). Development of a Conductivity Sensor for Monitoring Groundwater Resources to Optimize Water Management in Smart City Environments. *Sensors (Basel)*, 15(9), 20990–21015. DOI: 10.3390/s150920990 PMID: 26343653

Pathak, H., Igathinathane, C., Howatt, K., & Zhang, Z. (2023). Machine learning and handcrafted image processing methods for classifying common weeds in corn field. *Smart Agricultural Technology*, 5, 100249. DOI: 10.1016/j.atech.2023.100249

Patil, H. V., & Sonaje, V. P. (2024). A Study of The Performance of Various Media for Information Security Via LSB Steganography Method for Text Messaging. *Journal of Electrical Systems*, 20(9).

Patwari, B., Nandi, U., & Ghosal, S. K. (2023). Image steganography based on difference of Gaussians edge detection. *Multimedia Tools and Applications*, 82(28), 43759–43779. DOI: 10.1007/s11042-023-15360-7

Peng, Y., Fu, C., Zheng, Y., Tian, Y., Cao, G., & Chen, J. (2024). Medical steganography: Enhanced security and image quality, and new SQ assessment. *Signal Processing*, 223, 109546. DOI: 10.1016/j.sigpro.2024.109546

Peng, Y., Fu, G., Yu, Q., Luo, Y., Hu, J., & Duan, C. (2024). Enhancing the anti-steganalysis ability of steganography via adversarial examples. *Multimedia Tools and Applications*, 83(2), 6227–6247. DOI: 10.1007/s11042-023-15306-z

Peraka, S., Sudheer, R., Rao, B. N., Teja, A. R., & Kumar, E. N. (2020). *Smart Irrigation based on Crops using IoT.*

Płachta, M., Krzemień, M., Szczypiorski, K., & Janicki, A. (2022). Detection of image steganography using deep learning and ensemble classifiers. *Electronics (Basel)*, 11(10), 1565. DOI: 10.3390/electronics11101565

Plant, W., & Schaefer, G. (2011). Visualisation and browsing of image databases. In *Multimedia Analysis, Processing and Communications* (pp. 3–57). Springer. DOI: 10.1007/978-3-642-19551-8_1

Ponnusamy, S., Antari, J., Bhaladhare, P. R., Potgantwar, A. D., & Kalyanaraman, S. (Eds.). (2024). *Enhancing Security in Public Spaces Through Generative Adversarial Networks (GANs).* IGI Global. DOI: 10.4018/979-8-3693-3597-0

Pothuganti, Sridevi, & Seshabattar. (2021). *IoT and Deep Learning based Smart Greenhouse Disease Prediction.* IEEE Access.

Pournaghi, S. M., Bayat, M., & Farjami, Y. (2020). MedSBA: A novel and secure scheme to share medical data based on blockchain technology and attribute-based encryption. *Journal of Ambient Intelligence and Humanized Computing*, 11(11), 4613–4641. DOI: 10.1007/s12652-020-01710-y

Prabhu, R., Archana, P., Anusooya, S., & Anuradha, P. (2023). Improved Steganography for IoT Network Node Data Security Promoting Secure Data Transmission using Generative Adversarial Networks. *The Scientific Temper*, 14(03), 938–943. DOI: 10.58414/SCIENTIFICTEMPER.2023.14.3.58

Preston, R. (2022). Stifling Innovation: How Global Data Protection Regulation Trends Inhibit the Growth of Healthcare Research and Start-Ups. *Emory Int'l L. Rev*, 37, 135.

Puchalski, D., Caviglione, L., Kozik, R., Marzecki, A., Krawczyk, S., & Choraś, M. (2020). Stegomalware Detection through Structural Analysis of Media Files. *Proceedings of the 15th International Conference on Availability, Reliability and Security, ARES'20.* DOI: 10.1145/3407023.3409187

Qayyum, A., Qadir, J., Bilal, M., & Al-Fuqaha, A. (2020). Secure and robust machine learning for healthcare: A survey. *IEEE Reviews in Biomedical Engineering*, 14, 156–180. DOI: 10.1109/RBME.2020.3013489 PMID: 32746371

Radha, K., Bansal, M., & Pachori, R. B. (2024). Speech and speaker recognition using raw waveform modeling for adult and children's speech: A comprehensive review. *Engineering Applications of Artificial Intelligence*, 131, 107661. DOI: 10.1016/j.engappai.2023.107661

Rahman, Uddin, Hussain, Ahmed, Khan, Zakarya, Rahman, & Haleem. (2023). A Huffman code LSB based image steganography technique using multi-level encryption and achromatic component of an image. Scientific Reports, No. 14183.

Rahman, S., Uddin, J., Zakarya, M., Hussain, H., Khan, A. A., Ahmed, A., & Haleem, M. (2023). *A Comprehensive Study of Digital Image Steganographic Techniques* (Vol. 11). IEEE Access.

Rahman, S., Uddin, J., Zakarya, M., Hussain, H., Khan, A. A., Ahmed, A., & Haleem, M. (2023). A comprehensive study of digital image steganographic techniques. *IEEE Access: Practical Innovations, Open Solutions*, 11, 6770–6791. DOI: 10.1109/ACCESS.2023.3237393

Rajaram, G., Dash, S., Arslan, F., Venu, D., Ahmed, M. A., & Lydia, E. L. (2023). Polynomial cryptographic optical steganography substitution model for the telehealth system with multimedia data. *Optical and Quantum Electronics*, 55(9), 819. DOI: 10.1007/s11082-023-05084-1

Raja, V., & Suresh, K. S. (2024). Deep Steg Block: Deep Learning-Enhanced Steganography for Secure Communication in IoT Devices Using Blockchain. *Educational Administration: Theory and Practice*, 30(4), 2958–2972.

Raj, U. A. S., & Maheswaran, C. P. (2023). Secure File Sharing System Using Image Steganography and Cryptography Techniques. *2023 International Conference on Inventive Computation Technologies (ICICT)*, 1113–1116. DOI: 10.1109/ICICT57646.2023.10134163

Raman, C. J. (2024). An Accurate Plant Disease Detection Technique Using Machine Learning. EAI Endorsed Transactions on Internet of Things, 10.

Ramkumar, G., Bhuvaneswari, P., Radhika, R., Saranya, S., Vijayalakshmi, S., Karpagam, M., & Wilfred, F. (2022, September 20). Implementation of machine learning mechanism for recognising prostate cancer through a photoacoustic signal. *Contrast Media & Molecular Imaging*, 2022(1), 2022. DOI: 10.1155/2022/6862083 PMID: 36262985

Ramtekkar, P. K., Pandey, A., & Pawar, M. K. (2023, December). Accurate detection of brain tumors using optimized feature selection based on deep learning techniques. *Multimedia Tools and Applications*, 82(29), 44623–44653. DOI: 10.1007/s11042-023-15239-7 PMID: 37362641

Rao, A. S., Dalavai, L., Tata, V., Vellela, S. S., Polanki, K., Kumar, K. K., & Andra, R. (2024). A Secured Cloud Architecture for Storing Image Data using Steganography. *2024 2nd International Conference on Computer, Communication and Control (IC4)*, 1–6. DOI: 10.1109/IC457434.2024.10486495

Rathidevi, M., Yaminipriya, R., & Sudha, S. V. (2017). Trends of cryptography stepping from ancient to modern. *2017 International Conference on Innovations in Green Energy and Healthcare Technologies (IGEHT)*, 1–9. DOI: 10.1109/IGE-HT.2017.8094107

Rathi, R., & Acharjya, D. P. (2018). A rule based classification for vegetable production using rough set and genetic algorithm. *International Journal of Fuzzy System Applications*, 7(1), 74–100. DOI: 10.4018/IJFSA.2018010106

Rawal, S. (2017). *IoT based Smart Irrigation System*.

Ren, K., Zheng, T., Qin, Z., & Liu, X. (2020). Adversarial attacks and defenses in deep learning. *Engineering (Beijing)*, 6(3), 346–360. DOI: 10.1016/j.eng.2019.12.012

Reyers, P. M. (2023). *A comparative analysis of audio steganography methods and tools* (Bachelor's thesis, University of Twente).

Roche, D. S., Apon, D., Choi, S. G., & Yerukhimovich, A. (2016). Pope: Partial order preserving encoding. *Proc. of CCS*.

Rohhila, S., & Singh, A. K. (2024). Deep learning-based encryption for secure transmission digital images: A survey. *Computers & Electrical Engineering*, 116, 109236. DOI: 10.1016/j.compeleceng.2024.109236

Rout, H., & Mishra, B. K. (2014). Pros and cons of cryptography, steganography and perturbation techniques. *IOSR Journal of Electronics and Communication Engineering*, 76, 81.

Rustad, S., Andono, P. N., & Shidik, G. F. (2023). Digital image steganography survey and investigation (goal, assessment, method, development, and dataset). *Signal Processing*, 206, 108908. DOI: 10.1016/j.sigpro.2022.108908

Rustad, S., Setiadi, D. R. I. M., Syukur, A., & Andono, P. N. (2022). Inverted LSB image steganography using adaptive pattern to improve imperceptibility. *Journal of King Saud University. Computer and Information Sciences*, 34(6), 3559–3568. DOI: 10.1016/j.jksuci.2020.12.017

Sahu, A. K., & Gutub, A. (2022). Improving grayscale steganography to protect personal information disclosure within hotel services. *Multimedia Tools and Applications*, 81(21), 30663–30683. DOI: 10.1007/s11042-022-13015-7

Saidakhmedovich, G. S., Uralovich, M. D., Saidakhmedovich, G. S., & Tishabayevna, R. M. (2024). Application of Digital Technologies for Ensuring Agricultural Productivity. *British Journal of Global Ecology and Sustainable Development*, 25, 6–20.

Saif, S., Das, P., Biswas, S., Khan, S., Haq, M. A., & Kovtun, V. (2024). A secure data transmission framework for IoT enabled healthcare. *Heliyon*, 10(16), e36269. DOI: 10.1016/j.heliyon.2024.e36269 PMID: 39224301

Sakshi, S., Verma, S., Chaturvedi, P., & Yadav, S. A. (2022). Least Significant Bit Steganography for Text and Image hiding. *2022 3rd International Conference on Intelligent Engineering and Management (ICIEM)*, 415–421. DOI: 10.1109/ICIEM54221.2022.9853052

Salim, S. K., Msallam, M. M., & Olewi, H. I. (2023). Hide text in an image using Blowfish algorithm and development of least significant bit technique. *Indonesian Journal of Electrical Engineering and Computer Science*, 29(1), 339–347. DOI: 10.11591/ijeecs.v29.i1.pp339-347

Sarangdhar & Pawar. (2017). *Machine learning regression technique for cotton leaf disease detection and controlling using IoT*. IEEE Access.

Saranya, S. S., Reddy, P. L. C., & Prasanth, K. (2024, July). Digital audio steganography using LSB and RC7 algorithms for security applications. In *AIP Conference Proceedings* (Vol. 3075, No. 1). AIP Publishing. DOI: 10.1063/5.0217203

Sarkar, A., & Samanta, S. (2023). A Radical Image Steganography Method Predicated on Intensity and Edge Detection. In *Novel Research and Development Approaches in Heterogeneous Systems and Algorithms* (pp. 173–190). IGI Global. DOI: 10.4018/978-1-6684-7524-9.ch010

Satrio, T. A., Prabowo, W. A., & Yuniati, T. (2022). Hiding Document Format Files Using Video Steganography Techniques With Least Significant Bit Method. *2022 IEEE International Conference on Communication, Networks and Satellite (COMNETSAT)*, 399–406. DOI: 10.1109/COMNETSAT56033.2022.9994367

Sekaran, K., Meqdad, M. N., Kumar, P., Rajan, S., & Kadry, S. (2020). *Smart agriculture management system using internet of things*.

Sethy, P. K., Behera, S. K., & Kannan, N. (2022, October). Categorization of common pigmented skin lesions (CPSL) using multi-deep features and support vector machine. *Journal of Digital Imaging*, 35(5), 1207–1216. DOI: 10.1007/s10278-022-00632-9 PMID: 35524077

Shadmand, F., Medvedev, I., & Gonçalves, N. (2021). CodeFace: A Deep Learning Printer-Proof Steganography for Face Portraits. *IEEE Access : Practical Innovations, Open Solutions*, 9, 167282–167291. DOI: 10.1109/ACCESS.2021.3132581

Shafique, A., Mehmood, A., Alawida, M., Elhadef, M., & Rehman, M. U. (2024). A fusion of machine learning and cryptography for fast data encryption through the encoding of high and moderate plaintext information blocks. *Multimedia Tools and Applications*, 1–27. DOI: 10.1007/s11042-024-18959-6

Shahi, T. B., Xu, C. Y., Neupane, A., & Guo, W. (2022). Machine learning methods for precision agriculture with UAV imagery: A review. *Electronic Research Archive*, 30(12), 4277–4317. DOI: 10.3934/era.2022218

Sharma, D., & Kawatra, R. (2022). Security Techniques Implementation on Big Data Using Steganography and Cryptography. In *ICT Analysis and Applications: Proceedings of ICT4SD 2022* (pp. 279–302). Springer.

Sharma, D., & Prabha, C. Hybrid security of EMI using edge-based steganography and three-layered cryptography. In *Applied Data Science and Smart Systems* (pp. 278–290). CRC Press. DOI: 10.1201/9781003471059-37

Sharma, G., & Garg, U. (2024). Unveiling vulnerabilities: Evading YOLOv5 object detection through adversarial perturbations and steganography. *Multimedia Tools and Applications*, 83(30), 1–20. DOI: 10.1007/s11042-024-18563-8

Sheikh, A., Singh, K. U., Jain, A., Chauhan, J., Singh, T., & Raja, L. (2024, March). Lightweight Symmetric Key Encryption to Improve the Efficiency and Safety of the IoT. In *2024 IEEE International Conference on Contemporary Computing and Communications (InC4)* (Vol. 1, pp. 1-5). IEEE. DOI: 10.1109/InC460750.2024.10649289

Shi, H., Dong, J., Wang, W., Qian, Y., & Zhang, X. (2018). SSGAN: Secure steganography based on generative adversarial networks. In *Advances in Multimedia Information Processing–PCM 2017:18th Pacific-Rim Conference on Multimedia, Harbin, China, September 28-29, 2017, Revised Selected Papers, Part I 18* (pp. 534-544). Springer International Publishing.

Shoaib, M., Shah, B., Ei-Sappagh, S., Ali, A., Ullah, A., Alenezi, F., Gechev, T., Hussain, T., & Ali, F. (2023). Corrigendum: An advanced deep learning models-based plant disease detection: a review of recent research. *Frontiers in Plant Science*, 14, 1282443. DOI: 10.3389/fpls.2023.1282443 PMID: 37841599

Shopova, E. G., & Vaklieva-Bancheva, N. G. (2006). BASIC—A genetic algorithm for engineering problems solution. *Computers & Chemical Engineering*, 30(8), 1293–1309. DOI: 10.1016/j.compchemeng.2006.03.003

Shor, P. W. (1994). Algorithms for quantum computation: Discrete logarithms and factoring. *Proceedings of the 35th Annual Symposium on Foundations of Computer Science (FOCS)*, 124-134. DOI: 10.1109/SFCS.1994.365700

Shuaib, M., Alam, S., Alam, M. S., & Nasir, M. S. (2021). Compliance with HIPAA and GDPR in blockchain-based electronic health record. *Materials Today: Proceedings*. Advance online publication. DOI: 10.1016/j.matpr.2021.03.059

Shynu, P. G., Shayan, H. M., & Chowdhary, C. L. (2020, February). A fuzzy based data perturbation technique for privacy preserved data mining. In 2020 International Conference on Emerging Trends in Information Technology and Engineering (ic-ETITE) (pp. 1-4). IEEE. DOI: 10.1109/ic-ETITE47903.2020.244

Singh Yadav, A. K., Xiang, Z., Bhagtani, K., Bestagini, P., Tubaro, S., & Delp, E. J. (2024). Compression Robust Synthetic Speech Detection Using Patched Spectrogram Transformer. *ArXiv E-Prints*, arXiv-2402.

Singh, N., Bhardwaj, J., & Raghav, G. (2017). Network Steganography and its Techniques: A Survey. *International Journal of Computer Applications*, 174(2), 8–14. DOI: 10.5120/ijca2017915319

Singh, R. K., Gorantla, R., Allada, S. G., & Narra, P. (2022, October 31). SkiNet: A deep learning framework for skin lesion diagnosis with uncertainty estimation and explainability. *PLoS One*, 17(10), e0276836. DOI: 10.1371/journal.pone.0276836 PMID: 36315487

Smith, L. D. (1955). *Cryptography: The science of secret writing*. Courier Corporation.

Soleimanian, A., & Khazaei, S. (2019). Publicly verifiable searchable symmetric encryption based on efficient cryptographic components. *Designs, Codes and Cryptography*, 87(1), pages123–147. DOI: 10.1007/s10623-018-0489-y

Song, D. X., Wagner, D., & Perrig, A. (2000). Practical techniques for searches on encrypted data. Proc. of IEEE S&P.

Song, Dong, Yuan, Xu, & Zhao. (2020). Forward Private Searchable Symmetric Encryption with Optimized I/O Efficiency. IEEE Transactions on Dependable and Secure Computing, 17(5), 912-927. .DOI: 10.1109/TDSC.2018.2822294

Song, B., Wei, P., Wu, S., Lin, Y., & Zhou, W. (2024). A survey on Deep-Learning-based image steganography. *Expert Systems with Applications*, 254, 124390. DOI: 10.1016/j.eswa.2024.124390

Sreedevi, A. G., Harshitha, T. N., Sugumaran, V., & Shankar, P. (2022). Application of cognitive computing in healthcare, cybersecurity, big data and IoT: A literature review. *Information Processing & Management*, 59(2), 102888. DOI: 10.1016/j. ipm.2022.102888

Sriram, K. V., & Havaldar, R. H. (2024). Chronological Gazelle Optimization with Deep Learning-Based pixel prediction for video steganography in H. 264 video for defence applications. *Journal of Visual Communication and Image Representation*, 98, 104024. DOI: 10.1016/j.jvcir.2023.104024

Subramanian, N., Cheheb, I., Elharrouss, O., Al-Maadeed, S., & Bouridane, A. (2021). End-to-end image steganography using deep convolutional autoencoders. *IEEE Access : Practical Innovations, Open Solutions*, 9, 135585–135593. DOI: 10.1109/ACCESS.2021.3113953

Subramanian, N., Elharrouss, O., Al-Maadeed, S., Bouridane, A., & Steganography, I. (2021). A Review of the Recent Advances. *IEEE Access : Practical Innovations, Open Solutions*, 9, 23409–23423. DOI: 10.1109/ACCESS.2021.3053998

Sukumar, A., Subramaniyaswamy, V., Ravi, L., Vijayakumar, V., & Indragandhi, V. (2021). Robust image steganography approach based on RIWT-Laplacian pyramid and histogram shifting using deep learning. *Multimedia Systems*, 27(4), 651–666. DOI: 10.1007/s00530-020-00665-6

Sultan, B., & ArifWani, M. (2023). A new framework for analyzing color models with generative adversarial networks for improved steganography. *Multimedia Tools and Applications*, 82(13), 19577–19590. DOI: 10.1007/s11042-023-14348-7

Sun, T. (2024). Advancements in Communication Systems: From Image Compression Techniques to Deep Learning Applications. *Journal of Electrical Systems*, 20(10s), 1124–1132.

Sun, Y. (2024). Enhancing image steganalysis via integrated reinforcement learning and dilated convolution techniques. *Signal, Image and Video Processing*, 18(S1), 1–16. DOI: 10.1007/s11760-024-03113-4

Sun, Y., Lo, F. P.-W., & Lo, B. (2019). Security and privacy for the internet of medical things enabled healthcare systems: A survey. *IEEE Access : Practical Innovations, Open Solutions*, 7, 183339–183355. DOI: 10.1109/ACCESS.2019.2960617

Supriya, K. S., & Lovesum, S. P. J. (2024). Review on lightweight cryptography techniques and steganography techniques for IoT environment. *International Journal of System Assurance Engineering and Management*, 1–19. DOI: 10.1007/s13198-024-02476-8

Suresh, , Gopinath, Hemavarthini, Jayanthan, & Krishnan. (2020). Plant Disease Detection using Image Processing. *International Journal of Engineering and Technical Research*, V9(03). Advance online publication.

Swain, G. (2018). Digital image steganography using eight-directional PVD against RS analysis and PDH analysis. *Advances in Multimedia*, 2018, 2018. DOI: 10.1155/2018/4847098

Tak, H., Patino, J., Nautsch, A., Evans, N., & Todisco, M. (2020). Spoofing attack detection using the non-linear fusion of sub-band classifiers. *ArXiv Preprint ArXiv:2005.10393*. DOI: 10.21437/Interspeech.2020-1844

Tak, H., Patino, J., Todisco, M., Nautsch, A., Evans, N., & Larcher, A. (2021). End-to-end anti-spoofing with rawnet2. *ICASSP 2021-2021 IEEE International Conference on Acoustics, Speech and Signal Processing (ICASSP)*, 6369–6373.

Tan, X., & Tan, L. (2023). Research on the Underlying Principles and Deep Learning Algorithms based on Image Style Conversion Techniques. *Transactions on Computer Science and Intelligent Systems Research*, 1, 58–63. DOI: 10.62051/2z2ngm94

Tan, X., & Triggs, B. (2010). Enhanced local texture feature sets for face recognition under difficult lighting conditions. *IEEE Transactions on Image Processing*, 19(6), 1635–1650. DOI: 10.1109/TIP.2010.2042645 PMID: 20172829

Tekouabou, S. C. K., Diop, E. B., Azmi, R., Jaligot, R., & Chenal, J. (2022). Reviewing the application of machine learning methods to model urban form indicators in planning decision support systems: Potential, issues and challenges. *Journal of King Saud University. Computer and Information Sciences*, 34(8), 5943–5967. DOI: 10.1016/j.jksuci.2021.08.007

Thamer, K. A., Ahmed, S. R., Almashhadany, M. T. M., Abdulqader, S. G., Abduladheem, W., & Algburi, S. (2024, May). Secure Data Transmission in IoT Networks using Machine Learning-based Encryption Techniques. In *Proceedings of the Cognitive Models and Artificial Intelligence Conference* (pp. 285-291). DOI: 10.1145/3660853.3660929

Thanh-Tung, H., Tran, T., & Venkatesh, S. (2019). *Improving generalization and stability of generative adversarial networks*. arXiv preprint arXiv:1902.03984.

Thanki, R., & Borra, S. (2018). A color image steganography in hybrid FRT–DWT domain. Journal of Information Security and Applications, 40, 92-102.

Thapa, C., & Camtepe, S. (2021). Precision health data: Requirements, challenges and existing techniques for data security and privacy. *Computers in Biology and Medicine*, 129, 104130. DOI: 10.1016/j.compbiomed.2020.104130 PMID: 33271399

Todisco, M., Delgado, H., & Evans, N. W. D. (2016). A New Feature for Automatic Speaker Verification Anti-Spoofing: Constant Q Cepstral Coefficients. *Odyssey*, 2016, 283–290. DOI: 10.21437/Odyssey.2016-41

Tsividis, P. A., Loula, J., Burga, J., Foss, N., Campero, A., Pouncy, T., ... Tenenbaum, J. B. (2021). *Human-level reinforcement learning through theory-based modeling, exploration, and planning*. arXiv preprint arXiv:2107.12544.

Tsouros, D. C., Bibi, S., & Sarigiannidis, P. G. (2019). A review on UAV-based applications for precision agriculture. *Information (Basel)*, 10(11), 349. DOI: 10.3390/info10110349

Vaccari, I., Orani, V., Paglialonga, A., Cambiaso, E., & Mongelli, M. (2021). A generative adversarial network (gan) technique for internet of medical things data. *Sensors (Basel)*, 21(11), 3726. DOI: 10.3390/s21113726 PMID: 34071944

Vamsi Thalatam, M. N., Lanka, P., & Kumar, J. N. V. R. S. (2023). An IoT Based Smart Water Contamination Monitoring System. *2023 International Conference on Intelligent Systems for Communication, IoT and Security (ICISCoIS)*, 387–391. DOI: 10.1109/ICISCoIS56541.2023.10100559

Varghese, B., & Buyya, R. (2018). Next generation cloud computing: New trends and research directions. *Future Generation Computer Systems*, 79, 849–861. DOI: 10.1016/j.future.2017.09.020

Vayadande, K., Bhosle, A. A., Pawar, R. G., Joshi, D. J., Bailke, P. A., & Lohade, O. (2024, April 12). Innovative approaches for skin disease identification in machine learning: A comprehensive study. *Oral Oncology Reports*, 10, 100365. DOI: 10.1016/j.oor.2024.100365

Venkata Krishna, G. P. C., & Vivekananda Reddy, D. (2024). Machine learning-enhanced hybrid cryptography and image steganography algorithm for securing cloud data. *Journal of Intelligent & Fuzzy Systems*, (Preprint), 1-11.

Vijaya Saraswathi R, Sridharani J, Saranya Chowdary P, Nikhil K, Sri Harshitha M, & Mahanth Sai K. (2022). *Smart Farming: The IoT based Future Agriculture* IEEE Xplore.

Vitale, A., Donati, E., Germann, R., & Magno, M. (2022). Neuromorphic edge computing for biomedical applications: Gesture classification using emg signals. *IEEE Sensors Journal*, 22(20), 19490–19499. DOI: 10.1109/JSEN.2022.3194678

Wang, X., & Yamagishi, J. (2021). A comparative study on recent neural spoofing countermeasures for synthetic speech detection. *ArXiv Preprint ArXiv:2103.11326*. DOI: 10.21437/Interspeech.2021-702

Wang, X., Yamagishi, J., Todisco, M., Delgado, H., Nautsch, A., Evans, N., Sahidullah, M., Vestman, V., Kinnunen, T., Lee, K. A., Juvela, L., Alku, P., Peng, Y.-H., Hwang, H.-T., Tsao, Y., Wang, H.-M., Le Maguer, S., Becker, M., Henderson, F., & Ling, Z.-H. (2020). ASVspoof 2019: A large-scale public database of synthesized, converted and replayed speech. *Computer Speech & Language*, 64, 101114. DOI: 10.1016/j.csl.2020.101114

Wang, Z., Byrnes, O., Wang, H., Sun, R., Ma, C., Chen, H., Wu, Q., & Xue, M. (2021). *Data Hiding with Deep Learning: A Survey Unifying Digital Watermarking and Steganography*. Arxiv.

Wani & Sultan. (2023). Deep learning based image steganography: A review. *Wiley Interdisciplinary Reviews. Data Mining and Knowledge Discovery*, 13(3).

Wani, M. A., & Sultan, B. (2023). Deep learning based image steganography: A review. *Wiley Interdisciplinary Reviews. Data Mining and Knowledge Discovery*, 13(3), e1481. DOI: 10.1002/widm.1481

Wardhani, R. W., Putranto, D. S. C., Ji, J., & Kim, H. (2024). Towards Hybrid Classical Deep Learning-Quantum Methods for Steganalysis. *IEEE Access : Practical Innovations, Open Solutions*, 12, 45238–45252. DOI: 10.1109/ACCESS.2024.3381615

Wu, H., Liu, S., Meng, H., & Lee, H. (2020). Defense against adversarial attacks on spoofing countermeasures of ASV. *ICASSP 2020-2020 IEEE International Conference on Acoustics, Speech and Signal Processing (ICASSP)*, 6564–6568.

Wu, P., Yang, Y., & Li, X. (2018). StegNet: Mega Image Steganography Capacity with Deep Convolutional Network. *Future Internet*, 10(6), 54. DOI: 10.3390/fi10060054

Wu, Z., Evans, N., Kinnunen, T., Yamagishi, J., Alegre, F., & Li, H. (2015). Spoofing and countermeasures for speaker verification: A survey. *Speech Communication*, 66, 130–153. DOI: 10.1016/j.specom.2014.10.005

Wu, Z., Kinnunen, T., Evans, N., Yamagishi, J., Hanilçi, C., Sahidullah, M., & Sizov, A. (2015). ASVspoof 2015: the first automatic speaker verification spoofing and countermeasures challenge. *Sixteenth Annual Conference of the International Speech Communication Association*. DOI: 10.21437/Interspeech.2015-462

Xu, X., Sun, Y., Tang, G., Chen, S., & Zhao, J. (2017). Deep learning on spatial rich model for steganalysis. In *Digital Forensics and Watermarking:15th International Workshop, IWDW 2016,Beijing, China,September 17-19, 2016, Revised Selected Papers 15* (pp. 564-577). Springer International Publishing. DOI: 10.1007/978-3-319-53465-7_42

Yamashita, R., Nishio, M., Do, R. K. G., & Togashi, K. (2018). Convolutional neural networks: An overview and application in radiology. *Insights Into Imaging*, 9(4), 611–629. DOI: 10.1007/s13244-018-0639-9 PMID: 29934920

Yao, L., & Miller, J. (2015). Tiny imagenet classification with convolutional neural networks. *CS 231N, 2*(5), 8.

Yao, Q., Xu, K., Li, T., Zhou, Y., & Wang, M. (2024). A secure image evidence management framework using multi-bits watermark and blockchain in IoT environments. *Wireless Networks*, 30(6), 5157–5169. DOI: 10.1007/s11276-023-03229-4

Yao, Y., Wang, J., Chang, Q., Ren, Y., & Meng, W. (2024). High invisibility image steganography with wavelet transform and generative adversarial network. *Expert Systems with Applications*, 249, 123540. DOI: 10.1016/j.eswa.2024.123540

Yassein, M. B., Aljawarneh, S., Qawasmeh, E., Mardini, W., & Khamayseh, Y. (2017). Comprehensive study of symmetric key and asymmetric key encryption algorithms. *2017 International Conference on Engineering and Technology (ICET)*, 1–7. DOI: 10.1109/ICEngTechnol.2017.8308215

Ye, J., Chen, B., Liu, Q., & Fang, Y. (2013) *A precision agriculture management system based on the Internet of Things and WebGIS.*

Yuan, C., Wang, H., He, P., Luo, J., & Li, B. (2022). GAN-based image steganography for enhancing security via adversarial attack and pixel-wise deep fusion. *Multimedia Tools and Applications*, 81(5), 6681–6701. DOI: 10.1007/s11042-021-11778-z

Zakaria, A. A., Hussain, M., Wahab, A. W. A., Idris, M. Y. I., Abdullah, N. A., & Jung, K. H. (2018). High-capacity image steganography with minimum modified bits based on data mapping and LSB substitution. *Applied Sciences (Basel, Switzerland)*, 8(11), 2199. DOI: 10.3390/app8112199

Zeng, L., Yang, N., Li, X., Chen, A., Jing, H., & Zhang, J. (2023). Advanced Image Steganography Using a U-Net-Based Architecture with Multi-Scale Fusion and Perceptual Loss. *Electronics (Basel)*, 12(18), 3808. DOI: 10.3390/electronics12183808

Zha, H., Zhang, W., Yu, N., & Fan, Z. (2023). Enhancing image steganography via adversarial optimization of the stego distribution. *Signal Processing*, 212, 109155. DOI: 10.1016/j.sigpro.2023.109155

Zhang, C., Lin, C., Benz, P., Chen, K., Zhang, W., & Kweon, I. S. (2021). A brief survey on deep learning based data hiding. *arXiv preprint arXiv:2103.01607.*

Zhang, Yu, Hao, Wang, & Ren. (2020). Enabling Efficient User Revocation in Identity-Based Cloud Storage Auditing for Shared Big Data. IEEE Transactions on Dependable and Secure Computing, 17(3), 608-619. .DOI: 10.1109/TDSC.2018.2829880

Zhang, J., Chen, K., Li, W., Zhang, W., & Yu, N. (2023). Steganography with Generated Images: Leveraging Volatility to Enhance Security. *IEEE Transactions on Dependable and Secure Computing*.

Zhang, J., Zhao, X., & He, X. (2023). Robust JPEG steganography based on the robustness classifier. *EURASIP Journal on Information Security*, 2023(1), 11. DOI: 10.1186/s13635-023-00148-x

Zhang, N., Cai, Y. X., Wang, Y. Y., Tian, Y. T., Wang, X. L., & Badami, B. (2020, January 1). Skin cancer diagnosis based on optimized convolutional neural network. *Artificial Intelligence in Medicine*, 102, 101756. DOI: 10.1016/j.artmed.2019.101756 PMID: 31980095

Zhang, X., Zhang, X., Zou, X., Liu, H., & Sun, M. (2022). Towards Generating Adversarial Examples on Combined Systems of Automatic Speaker Verification and Spoofing Countermeasure. *Security and Communication Networks*, 2666534, 1–12. Advance online publication. DOI: 10.1155/2022/2666534

Zhang, X., Zhu, Y., Liu, G., & Sun, Y. (2020). Deep learning-based steganalysis in digital images: A survey. *IEEE Access : Practical Innovations, Open Solutions*, 8, 171499–171523.

Zhang, Y., Ren, J., Liu, J., Xu, C., Guo, H., & Liu, Y. (2017). A Survey on Emerging Computing Paradigms for Big Data. *Chinese Journal of Electronics*, 26(1), 1–12. DOI: 10.1049/cje.2016.11.016

Zhang, Z., Cao, Y., Jahanshahi, H., & Mou, J. (2023). Chaotic color multi-image compression-encryption/ LSB data type steganography scheme for NFT transaction security. *Journal of King Saud University. Computer and Information Sciences*, 35(10), 101839. DOI: 10.1016/j.jksuci.2023.101839

Zheng, S., Lu, J., Zhao, H., Zhu, X., Luo, Z., Wang, Y., & Zhang, L. (2021). Rethinking semantic segmentation from a sequence-to-sequence perspective with transformers. In *Proceedings of the IEEE/CVF conference on computer vision and pattern recognition* (pp. 6881-6890). DOI: 10.1109/CVPR46437.2021.00681

Zhu, J. (2018). Hidden: Hiding data with deep networks. *arXiv preprint arXiv:1807.09937*. DOI: 10.1007/978-3-030-01267-0_40

Zhu, J., Kaplan, R., Johnson, J., & Fei-Fei, L. (2018). Hidden: Hiding data with deep networks. In *Proceedings of the European conference on computer vision (ECCV)* (pp. 657-672).

Zoccali, C., Mark, P. B., Sarafidis, P., Agarwal, R., Adamczak, M., Bueno de Oliveira, R., Massy, Z. A., Kotanko, P., Ferro, C. J., Wanner, C., Burnier, M., Vanholder, R., Mallamaci, F., & Wiecek, A. (2023). Diagnosis of cardiovascular disease in patients with chronic kidney disease. *Nature Reviews. Nephrology*, 19(11), 1–14. DOI: 10.1038/s41581-023-00747-4 PMID: 37612381

Zouak, A., Busawon, K., & Li, X. (2024). Video Steganography System Based on Optical Flow for Object Detection. *2024 14th International Symposium on Communication Systems, Networks and Digital Signal Processing (CSNDSP)*, 598–602. DOI: 10.1109/CSNDSP60683.2024.10636505

Zou, Y., Zhang, G., & Liu, L. (2019). Research on image steganography analysis based on deep learning. *Journal of Visual Communication and Image Representation*, 60, 266–275. DOI: 10.1016/j.jvcir.2019.02.034

About the Contributors

Vijay Kumar is Associate Professor and HoD in Information Technology Department, Dr B R Ambedkar NIT Jalandhar, Punjab. He received his Ph.D. degree from NIT Kuruksherta. Previously, he received M.Tech. and B.Tech. degrees from GJUS&T, Hisar and Kurukshetra University Kurukshetra, respectively. He has more than 3 years of teaching and research experience at NIT Hamirpur. Prior, he had 12 years of teaching experience in various reputed institutes like Manipal University Jaipur and Thapar University Patiala. He completed 2 DST SERB and 1 CSIR-sponsored research projects. He has published more than 180 research papers in International Journals/Conferences. He has many book chapters in international repute publishers. He has supervised many Ph.D. and M.Tech. thesis on Metaheuristics, Image Mining, and Data Clustering. He is the reviewer of several reputed SCI journals. He is member of ACM, CSI, International Association of Engineers, International Association of Computer Science and Information Technology, Singapore. His current research area is Soft Computing, Data Mining, Deep Learning, Steganography, and Pattern Recognition.

Chiranji Lal Chowdhary is a Professor in the SCORE at VIT University, where he has been since 2010. He received a B.E. (CSE) from MBM Engineering College (currently named MBM University) at Jodhpur, and M. Tech. (CSE) from the M.S. Ramaiah Institute of Technology in Bangalore. He received his PhD in Information Technology and Engineering from the VIT University Vellore. From 2006 to 2010 he worked at MSRIT in Bangalore, eventually as a Lecturer. His research interests span both computer vision and image processing. Much of his work has been on images, mainly through the application of image processing, computer vision, pattern recognition, machine learning, biometric systems, deep learning, soft computing, and computational intelligence. Professor Chowdhary is editor/co-editor of 8 books and is the author of over forty articles on computer science. He filed four patents deriving from his research. Austrian Science Fund (FWF), Vienna, Austria identified him as International Reviewer forlong-term funding projects at Austria. He also has an ongoing sponsored project from British council through SPARC as Co-PI.

Sandeep Singh Sengar is a Lecturer in Computer Science at Cardiff Metropolitan University, United Kingdom. He also holds the position of Cluster Leader for Computer Vision/Image Processing at this place. Before joining this position, he worked as a Postdoctoral Research Fellow at the Machine Learning Section of the Computer Science Department, at the University of Copenhagen, Denmark (a ranked #1 university in Denmark). He completed his Ph.D. degree in Computer Vision at the Department of Computer Science and Engineering from the Indian Institute of Technology (ISM), Dhanbad, India, and an M. Tech. degree from Motilal Nehru National Institute of Technology, Allahabad, India. He is also a Fellow of HEA, a Senior Member of IEEE, and a Professional Member of ACM. Dr. Sengar's broader research interests include Machine/Deep Learning, Computer Vision, Image/Video Processing, and its applications. He has published several research articles in reputable international journals and conferences. He is an Editorial Board Member, Guest Editor, and Reviewer at reputed International Journals. He is a reviewer of research grants at EPSRC and Cardiff Met.

* * *

Pawankumar B. is a software engineering student based in Vellore, India. His work focuses on cloud computing, artificial intelligence, and DevOps practices.

Nidhi Chakravarty finished her MTech in Computer Engineering at the Centre for Development of Advanced Computing in Noida. She is currently pursuing a Ph.D. in Automatic Speaker Verification at the National Institute of Technology in Kurukshetra.

Mohit Dua received Ph.D. in the area of Automatic Speech Recognition from National Institute of Technology, Kurukshetra, India in 2018. He is presently working as Assistant Professor in Department of Computer Engineering at NIT Kurukshetra, India. He has more than 17 years of Teaching and Research experience. He is a member of Institute of Electrical and Electronics Engineers (IEEE), and life member of Computer Society of India (CSI) and Indian Society for Technical Education (ISTE). His research interests include Speech processing, Chaos based Cryptography, Information Security, Theory of Formal languages, Statistical modelling and Natural Language Processing. He has published approximately 60 research papers including abroad paper presentations including USA, Canada, Australia, Singapore, Mauritius and Dubai.

Rita Komalasari is a lecturer at YARSI University. Her current work is focused on Machine Learning in Health Information Security: Unraveling Patterns, Concealing Secrets, and Mitigating Vulnerabilities.

Angulakshmi M. is currently working as an Associate professor in School of Computer science engineering and Information systems Engineering, Vellore Institute of Technology, Vellore, India. She earned her Ph.D. in Information Technology from VIT, in the year 2018. Her research interests include Image processing, machine learning and Deep learning She published around 25 international papers for the past five years. She is a life member of Indian science congress.

Deepa Mani is currently working as an Associate Professor(Sr) in School of Information Technology and Engineering, Vellore Institute of Technology, Vellore, India. She earned her Ph.D. in Information Technology from VIT, in the year 2018. Her research interests include computer networks, Cloud Computing. She published around 25 international papers for the past five years. She is a life member of Indian science congress.

Visvanathan P. completed his M.E. [CSE] from Tagore Engineering college. He is working as an Assistant professor at GTEC, vellore, Her research area includes Soft computing, Data mining, Deep Learning, Image processing.

Hemlata Parmar is an accomplished scholar and educator with a strong background in computer science and a remarkable research portfolio. She earned her Ph.D. in Computer Science Engineering from Kalinga University in 2021. Prior to her Ph.D., she completed her M.Tech. in Computer Science Engineering at MDU in 2016 and her B.Tech. in Information Technology from the same institution in 2014. Dr. Hemlata's research contributions are extensive, and she has made significant contributions to the field of computer science. Her publications in various renowned journals and conferences showcase her expertise in areas such as encryption algorithms, cryptography, artificial intelligence, blockchain, and cyber security. Her research has been recognized for its innovation and practical applications. Apart from her research endeavors, Dr. Hemlata is also an enthusiastic educator. She has delivered lectures and participated in various academic programs and workshops, demonstrating her commitment to knowledge dissemination and pedagogical excellence. Her dedication to both research and education underscores her passion for advancing the field of computer science and contributing to its practical applications. Furthermore, Dr. Hemlata has shown her inventiveness through the filing of multiple patents related to AI, blockchain, and medical services. Her commitment to innovation and technology-driven solutions is evident in her patent applications. Dr. Hemlata has delivered guest lectures and participated in various academic programs and workshops, including topics like Artificial Intelligence in Media and Lean Startup & Minimum Viable Product/Business. Dr. Hemlata is an active researcher with several patent applications related to AI, blockchain, and medical services. Her inventions demonstrate a commitment to technology-driven solutions. In addition to her academic and research achievements, Dr. Hemlata has actively engaged in various national and international conferences, seminars, and workshops, further expanding her academic network and contributing to the academic community. Dr. Hemlata's multifaceted contributions to the fields of computer science, research, education, and innovation make her a prominent figure in the academic and technological landscape. Her continued pursuit of excellence and dedication to advancing knowledge are noteworthy attributes that define her career.

Rajeshkumar S. completed a B.E. in Computer Science Engineering at Annai Mira College of Engineering and Technology, Vellore - 632517, in 2022. He is currently conducting research (Direct PhD) at Vellore Institute of Technology, Vellore.

Index

Printed in the United States
by Baker & Taylor Publisher Services